Women's and Gender History

General Editor
June Purvis
Professor of Women's and Gender History, University of Portsmouth

Published
Lynn Abrams and Elizabeth Harvey (editors)
Gender relations in German history: power, agency and experience from the sixteenth to the twentieth century

Shani D'Cruze
Crimes of outrage: sex, violence and working women in Victorian England

Carol Dyhouse
No distinction of sex? Women in British universities, 1870-1939

Bridget Hill
Women, work and sexual politics in eighteenth-century England

Linda Mahood
Policing gender, class and family: Britain, 1850-1940

Jane McDermid and Anna Hillyar (editors)
Midwives of the revolution: female Bolsheviks and women workers in 1917

June Purvis (editor)
Women's history: Britain, 1850-1940

Wendy Webster
Imagining home: gender, "race" and national identity, 1945-64

Barbara Winslow
Sylvia Pankhurst: sexual politics and political activism

Forthcoming titles include:
Elizabeth Crawford
The Women's Suffrage movement: a reference guide 1866-1928

Elizabeth Edwards
Women in teacher training colleges: a culture of femininity, 1900-1960

Louise Jackson
Child sexual abuse and the law in Victorian England

Gender and crime in modern Europe

Margaret L. Arnot and Cornelie Usborne
Roehampton Institute London

Routledge
Taylor & Francis Group

LONDON AND NEW YORK

First published in 1999 by UCL Press

Reprinted 2003 by Routledge
11 New Fetter Lane
London, EC4P 4EE

Routledge is an imprint of the Taylor & Francis Group

© Margaret L. Arnot, Cornelie Usborne and contributors 1999

Typeset in Hong Kong by Graphicraft Ltd
Printed and bound by Antony Rowe Ltd, Eastbourne

British Library Cataloguing in Publication Data
A CIP record for this book is available from the British Library.

Library of Congress Cataloging-in-Publication data are available

ISBNs:
1-85728-745-2 HB
1-85728-746-0 PB

Contents

CONTENTS

₃₅

Foreword

Clive Emsley

In March 1850 an assize judge in Yorkshire directed the jury to acquit three men charged with the manslaughter of Mary Duggan. While Duggan's body had been found exposed and much bruised, the judge explained that she was "a woman of abandoned character" who, drunk, had gone of her own volition into a field with the three accused. She was not a child in need of protection, he insisted; she had brought her death upon herself. Some 40 years later, on the other side of Europe, the author Maxim Gorky was beaten senseless by a group of Russian peasants. He had taken the part of a woman who, stripped naked in front of a baying crowd, was being horsewhipped by her husband for alleged adultery. These two appalling stories are resonant with the themes of this book - crime and gender.

Communities, institutions, states - all create rules for their members; they also create sanctions for those who breach the rules. Within the context of the state many of the rules are characterized as laws, and breaches of laws are commonly labelled as crimes. The ways in which the rules and laws are structured, and the ways in which they are interpreted and enforced, provides a valuable route into understanding the mores and values of particular societies. The recognition of this is now a commonplace, at least in academic circles, yet it is only in the last 20 years or so that social historians have turned their attention to the study of crime and criminal justice. The initial research in this area was driven by such major themes as the general shift from a rural to an urban world and the growth of industrial capitalism; how far did the move from a rural to an urban environment generate a shift from interpersonal crime to property crime? How far was property crime a response to new definitions of property linked with the development of capitalism and to new relations at the workplace? More recently a feminist perspective has fostered new questions for research. It is not simply that historians and criminologists have begun to explore the role of women in criminal activity (as both victims and perpetrators) and the experience of women enmeshed in the various elements of the criminal justice system, but, more importantly, there is a recognition that gender is central to economic, political and social relations, and as such it contributes to the ways in which communities, institutions and states formulate their regulations and their laws as well as to the ways in which these regulations and laws are interpreted and enforced.

There are a variety of reasons why the period covered by this volume, from the late eighteenth to the mid-twentieth centuries, is significant for the history of crime. The period witnessed a cluster of new legal codes, several of which were inspired by that of Napoleon with its formal imposition of inequality between the sexes. There was the development of professional, bureaucratic police systems; and there was also the expansion of other professions, members of which, notably different kinds of medical men, were increasingly called upon to deploy their expertise in the struggle against different forms of crime. Finally the two centuries also saw the growth of the science of criminology.

The new police were charged with enforcing the state's laws; and, with states becoming increasingly jealous of their authority, the policeman was also charged with ensuring an end to the vestiges of other forms of justice, such as the blood feud, the duel, or the folkloric justice which commonly came in the unruly form of *charivari* or "rough music" – elements of which were present in the violent punishment with which Gorky sought to interfere. Exploring the clashes that occasionally occurred between state functionaries, such as policemen and magistrates, and those who sought justice through means other than the state's legal sanctions can reveal much about popular attitudes towards gender roles and popular conceptions of masculinity and femininity. State legislators increasingly saw themselves as progressive, not simply in seeking to stamp out the "primitive" practices of popular punishment and feuding. They claimed also to be passing laws to iron out abuses and to protect the weak and vulnerable; but, of course, the concept of protecting the weak could mean the state sanctioning and underpinning by law the dominant position of the male as head of a family. Moreover, the interpretation and enforcement of laws depended on functionaries such as policemen and magistrates who, for most of the period here, were all male, and who commonly shared the prejudices of patriarchy. Thus it is not so surprising to find the judge in Yorkshire dismissing the case against those accused of causing Mary Duggan's death since, in his view, she had denied her gender role by being an "abandoned" woman. Victorian Britain also had leading experts in the nascent study of gynaecology who doubted the existence of incest, queried the extent of rape, and feared that the principal result of an increase in the age of consent would be to put respectable gentlemen in danger of false accusations. Yet it is all too easy to posit gender perceptions and behaviour in black and white terms. The situations, as is invariably the case in historical analysis, are infinitely more complex. While some judges and some gynaecologists in Victorian Britain made, to modern eyes, outrageous statements about women victims and offenders, all male juries confounded the letter of the law by showing increasing relùctance to find young women guilty on charges of infanticide.

The new science of criminology had two principal strands: the charting of patterns and practices in criminal behaviour and the criminal justice system, and the attempt to explain the ways in which offenders could be differentiated from non-offenders. Throughout the nineteenth and twentieth centuries a majority of the offenders brought before the courts in Europe and the United States were male. This prompted the assumption that crime was essentially a male activity, and a young male activity at that. For Cesare Lombroso, the Italian doctor commonly seen as the founding father of positivist criminology, the majority of male criminals were born as such and their phrenology and physiognomy revealed the criminal as a primitive within an advanced society. When, more than a decade after *L'uomo delinquente* (1876), Lombroso collaborated with Gugielmo Ferrero on *La donna delinquente* (1893), they stressed that women were biologically disposed to conformity. For Lombroso, the majority of women offenders were law breakers rather than "criminals" and the few that were actually "criminal" were "doubly monstrous" since, not only were they atavistic, but they also acted completely contrary to what he considered as the natural behaviour of women.

Recently radical criminologists writing from a feminist perspective have characterized preceding generations of their discipline as practising "malestream" criminology. Yet they acknowledge that there is little point in searching for huge numbers of hidden female offenders in an attempt to prove that women were the same as men. The historical evidence suggests that female offending was simply different: across Europe those accused of infanticide were usually women; soliciting for prostitution was, predominantly, a female offence; and, in Victorian England, the only summary offence for which women were consistently convicted in higher numbers than men was the unlawful pledging of goods at a pawnbroker's. Historical explorations of such offences commonly underline the vulnerability of women, especially young women, in the labour markets of the nineteenth and early twentieth centuries. The instances of infanticide, of abortion and attempts at it, also commonly point to a desire to maintain a good character and the appearance of female purity and chastity that was given such high esteem in the societies discussed in this volume.

But if some female offences appear to have been linked closely with women's economic position or a society's perceptions of femininity, might there not be parallels with at least some of the offences committed predominantly by males? If, for example, the male sphere was supposed to be the public sphere, and if aggression and acquisitiveness were seen as desirable attributes of public man, is it not conceivable that this may have fed in various ways into patterns of behaviour which were not always desirable within society? There are no easy answers to such questions, and no easy ways to approach them, but the juxtaposition of crime and gender in the essays that follow offer important new perspectives on understanding our past and our present and make the collection truly pathbreaking in its aims and scope.

Acknowledgements

We cannot even begin to thank the many librarians and archivists in repositories across the world who have assisted the authors of this book, although for Chapter 1 various librarians have been particularly helpful, especially those at the British Library and Roehampton Institute London library. As this book began life as an international conference held at Roehampton Institute London in 1995, our first debt lies with those who made the conference possible in the first place. Both the British Academy and Roehampton Institute London Research Office together supplied sufficient funds to help with many airfares and some administrative costs and we thank them greatly for this support. Thanks, too, to the Women's History Seminar at the Institute of Historical Research for feedback on some of our ideas for Chapter 1.

Although Stephen Frank and Ann-Louise Shapiro were not able to attend the conference, on our invitation they agreed to contribute essays to the volume in order to enrich its geographic coverage, and we thank them for coming on board this collective enterprise. "Gender and crime in Britain and Europe, early modern and modern" was made a very special event indeed by the particular mix of individual scholars who attended. Many who spoke at the conference have not been able to appear in this volume, for all sorts of reasons, and others provided excellent commentaries to the papers that made the conference a lively event with lots of thinking-in-process occurring: Lynne Amidon, John Archer, Richard Bessel, Lucy Bland, James Cockburn, Cathy Crawford, Andy Davis, Shani D'Cruze, Trevor Dean, Peter Edwards, Florike Egmond, Clive Emsley, Richard Evans, Joanna Geyer-Kordesch, Sue Grace, Elizabeth Harvey, Olwen Hufton, Martin Ingram, Richard Ireland, Mark Jenner, Eric Johnson, Philippa Levine, Anthony McElligott, Angus McLaren, Thomás Mantecón, Gwenda Morgan, Ursula Nienhaus, Lisa Pine, Lyndal Roper, Susan Rose, Mark Roseman, Eve Rosenhaft, Alison Rowlands, Ulinka Rublack, Peter Rushton, Nick Stargardt, Deborah Thorn, David Tidswell, Martin Wiener, and probably some others whose names haven't survived in the printed records of the conference, because they agreed at the last minute to offer on-the-spot commentaries. We would like to thank these people, including anyone whose names have been left out, the authors of this book, and everyone who came to hear what we all had to say for making our conference sufficiently memorable and significant to inspire the publication of this collection of essays.

But this is not simply a volume of printed conference papers. All the essays have been carefully reworked and developed, and we thank the contributors for their patience with our editorial demands. And our final thanks go to the changing editorial staff at UCL Press.

Notes on contributors

Lynn Abrams lectures in modern European history at the University of Glasgow. She has published widely on marriage and divorce in nineteenth-century Germany and edited, with Elizabeth Harvey, *Gender relations in German history* (1996). She has recently completed a book on the history of child welfare in modern Scotland.

Margaret L. Arnot lectures in modern history - including women's, gender and crime history - at Roehampton Institute London. She has published articles on different aspects of gender and crime and is currently completing a book on infanticide and child abuse in nineteenth-century England.

Willem de Blécourt is Associate Fellow in the History Department at Warwick University and Honorary Research Fellow at the Huizinga Institute of Cultural History, Amsterdam. He is the author of numerous publications in Dutch, English and German on witchcraft, irregular healing and popular culture. He has just completed a monograph in Dutch on irregular women healers in the Netherlands, 1850-1930, forthcoming in 1999.

Gabriele Czarnowski is a political scientist completing her *Habilitation* at the Free University Berlin on the theme she addresses in this book. Her publications include *Das Kontrollierte Paar: Ehe- und Sexualpolitik im Nationalsozialismus* (1991) and a number of articles on abortion and the politics of sexuality in modern German history.

Stephen P. Frank is Associate Professor of History at the University of California, Los Angeles. He has jointly edited *The world of the Russian peasant: post-emancipation society and culture* (1990) and *Cultures in flux: lower-class values, practices and resistance in late Imperial Russia* (1994). His most recent work is forthcoming as *Crime, cultural conflict and justice in rural Russia, 1856-1914* (1999).

Ute Frevert is Professor of Modern History at the University of Bielefeld, having previously held chairs at the Free University in Berlin and the University of Constance. Her major research areas include the social history of medicine and medical policy, women's and gender history, the history of military institutions and general conscription. Two of her books have been translated into English: *Women in German history* (1989) and *Men of honour: a social and cultural history of the duel* (1995).

Barry Godfrey lectures in criminology at Keele University, specializing in the history of crime. He completed his PhD on nineteenth-century workplace appropriation at the University of Leicester in 1997 and has published a number of articles. He is now working on the history of violence in four English towns in the 1880-1930 period.

Louise Ainsley Jackson is a history lecturer in the School of Cultural Studies, Leeds Metropolitan University, UK. She is the author of a number of articles and a forthcoming book on child sexual abuse and the law in Victorian England.

Peter King is Professor of Social History at Nene University College Northampton. He has published more than a dozen articles on crime, law and society, including a recent study of "Female offenders, work and lifecycle change". He was joint editor of *Chronicling poverty: the voices and strategies of the English poor, 1640-1840* (1997) and is currently completing a book on law and society in England 1740-1820.

Valeria Pizzini-Gambetta has finished a doctorate in contemporary Italian history at the University of Turin. She has done research on the South of Italy during the Fascist regime, and on the Mafia. She is now writing a book on the Sicilian Mafia and women.

Ann-Louise Shapiro is Professor of History at Wesleyan University, Middletown, CT, and Associate Editor of *History and Theory*. She is the author of *Housing the poor of Paris, 1850-1902* (1985), *Breaking the codes: female criminality in fin-de-siècle Paris* (1996) and has edited *Feminists revision history* (1994).

Heather Shore completed her University of London doctoral thesis in 1996 and is now the Finley Research Fellow at Darwin College Cambridge. She has published an article in the collection on poverty edited by Peter King (see above) and has others forthcoming. She is currently completing a monograph on youth and crime in early nineteenth-century London, and researching London crime in the period 1725-45.

Bertrand Taithe read history at the Sorbonne and Manchester University where he completed his thesis on the Contagious Diseases Acts. A senior lecturer at the university of Huddersfield, he has published *The Essential Mayhew* and *Meanings of War, Sense of Defeat*, a number of articles on the history of venereal disease, the body and warfare and co-edited three books *Prophecy, War, Propaganda* for Sutton Publishing. A new monograph *The Struggle for the Third Republic: Citizenship and Wars* is forthcoming with UCL Press.

Cornelie Usborne lectures in European and women's history at Roehampton Institute London. She is the author of *The politics of the body in Weimar Germany: women's reproductive rights and duties* (1992) and of numerous articles in women's history and the social history of medicine in both English and German. She is currently writing a monograph on cultures of abortion in Weimar and Nazi Germany.

Chapter 1

ৠ

Why gender and crime? Aspects of an international debate[1]

Margaret L. Arnot and Cornelie Usborne

As recently as 1985 one historian of crime bemoaned the fact that women's roles in connection with crime in past societies had received very little scholarly attention and he offered two tentative explanations for this: first, because women have traditionally been perceived as "exceptionally law-abiding"; and secondly, citing the criminologist Doris Klein, because of "the preponderance of male theorists in the field".[2] This dearth of interest was despite the publication at the turn of the century of a number of prominent studies of female criminality by male authors. But these were, to use Klein's words, "classist, racist and sexist", based, as they were, on prejudiced notions of female physiological and psychological peculiarities; they hardly qualifed as role models.[3] Certainly, many major studies of the 1970s investigating patterns of crime and punishment in modern Europe paid scant attention to women[4] although there were some important exceptions: for England, John Beattie published his germinal article on the criminality of women in eighteenth-century England in 1975 and certain specific "crimes" of central interest to women's and gender history attracted attention from scholars from a wide range of sub-disciplines within history.[5] Yet it was even possible as late as 1985 for a general crime history book to omit a clear entry for "women" from the index,[6] although by this time most historians of crime gave women at least this level of recognition.[7]

One major reason for the relative neglect of women was that the major questions being posed by this work were not the right ones to "find" much material significant to women's lives and gender relations more broadly. In Britain, major growth in the history of crime at this time comprised one element in the development of social history. Historians usually came from the left, and an examination of "social crime" was central to their agenda of writing "History from Below". Criminals such as rioters, smugglers, poachers and rebels in industry could be seen in political terms as dissidents in a social system where law was the cement that held the hierarchy together.[8] By the

1980s the major trend was towards quantitative approaches.[9] While British historians utilized the detailed records of that nation's criminal justice records first, European scholars soon followed. Most of the records referred to related only to the activities of the highest courts in any nation, where the most serious, indictable felonies were tried. The vastly greater number of petty offences – where women probably featured significantly – were very often lost to the historian.[10] Furthermore, in interrogating court records, historians very often followed the logic of the surviving sources. As Australian historian Judith Allen has explained, crime history monographs tended to mirror the patterns of crime prosecuted and indicted: the priorities that police and magistrates employed in the past in selecting offenders for prosecution and trial tended to give shape to the crime histories.[11] Two historians of Italy have eloquently explained a fundamental challenge for crime historians that such a critique presents:

> Although historians so often masquerade as participants in the judicial process, they cannot passively accept the schema of roles and results assigned by the dominating ideology of the criminal justice system. Instead they must seek to discover opportunities in a disturbing moment of the past to identify other ideologies, values, and lives often masked or obliterated by the hegemonic vision of criminal records. Thus, even as he [sic] snitches on the dead, the historian's fundamental obligation is to respect them in their own terms rather than in those of the judicial record that brings their experiences to view.[12]

Though crime historians clearly set out to develop critical perspectives on crime and criminal justice systems,[13] following the logic of the sources sometimes suggested the underlying and continuing influence of positivist definitions of crime. B. L. Ingraham, a historian of political crime, has usefully explained the implications: "Implicit in this approach is the confinement of one's analysis of 'crime' and legal behaviour with respect to 'crimes' to those categories of behaviour officially defined as 'criminal'."[14] Even while so carefully discussing definitional problems, Ingraham was himself caught out by androcentric myopia. He included in his list of acts deemed either "treason" or "political offenses" in western Europe from ancient times until the beginning of the nineteenth century certain "sexual crimes, including rape of, or adultery committed with or by, the monarch's wife or close female relatives and intermarriage between persons of the political in-group and the political out-group."[15] These fitted into a broader category he defined as "challenges to political authority and legitimacy: those which concern the safety and security of rulers and the legitimizing principles on which their right to rule and their authority depends."[16] This carried enormous potential for an analysis of political crime that integrated an understanding of the central place of sex and gender in the broad social contract of modern western societies,[17] but after constructing these definitions the book was written assuming more conventional definitions of the "political" that wrote sex and gender out of consideration.

We would agree with Allen's assessment that such approaches resulted in the neglect of crimes and associated activities which may have been extremely insignificant in the overall criminal statistics gleaned from macro-studies of whole criminal justice systems – or indeed, absent from the record because the practices were "secret"[18] – but which were of great significance in the construction of gender relations, and indeed, of wider European culture and politics. This is not, however, to say that quantitative history is of no use to women's history.[19] Indeed, the deconstruction and critical interrogation of the "terms . . . of the judicial record" is a crucial part of the project of under-standing the historical relationships between gender norms and institutional processes.[20]

Leaving women out, and focusing studies on questions that do not reveal essential elements of the operation of gender in society is one level of criti-cism that can be made of some work in criminal justice history. But feminist historians have also pleaded that if female criminality is studied, it should be done with careful reference to the social, economic and political contexts of women's lives, and with feminist perspectives.[21] Nevertheless, by the mid-1980s, a valuable and interesting historiography in the social history of crime and criminal justice was developing. These developments benefited greatly from feminist theory[22] and the new research in women's history. Both stimu-lated new theoretical and methodological approaches, the latter by question-ing some of the basic concerns of historical thought like "periodization, the categories of social analysis, and theories of social change".[23] It was the cross-fertilization between the new social history of crime and women's history that proved so beneficial to both subjects. Women's historians began with questions that had not been addressed head-on by criminal justice historians. They wanted to understand the nature of gender relations and gendered power structures in the past and used the study of particular aspects of crime to provide powerful insights into these broad questions. The resulting feminist history of crime has focused most frequently on questions about sexuality, reproduction, marriage and family relations, and historians have sought out records associated very often with illicit practices that have been erratically and unevenly policed, even sometimes tacitly condoned.[24] These were the sorts of offences that might not appear particularly "significant" to earlier criminal justice historians (although some sexual offences in particular were discussed by crime historians: prosti-tution could not be ignored because of its ubiquity, nor rape, because of the severity with which it was met in the past).[25]

Whatever the main focus of studies by women's historians – women's role as perpetrators, their place on the receiving end of crime, the legal procedures and punishments that faced them, the discourse about particular crimes or gendered criminality itself – these histories always recognized the importance of social history contexts, sometimes to the point that the very concepts of "crime" and "criminality" began to dissolve. From her Australian perspective, Judith Allen has argued for the complete rejection of these categories.[26] In Regina Schulte's work on infanticide in rural Bavaria in the nineteenth century, infanticide as a "crime" disappeared almost completely, as she unravelled the complex social explanations for why some infanticidal women were exposed to the authorities, while others were not.[27] Judith Walkowitz clarified that before the Contagious Diseases Acts were passed in England in the 1860s, working-class women could pass in and out of prostitution as economic circumstances demanded, while still being accepted as part of their working-class communities: "criminality" is of little use as a concept in such contexts.[28] Yet such radical deconstruction can add immeasurably to our understandings of European criminal justice systems and has done a great deal to fill the void in the crime historiography. Work in women's history has also inspired some criminal justice historians to begin to address issues about women from a more nuanced perspective, and whole monographs have begun to appear from such historians about issues of central concern to women's history.[29]

Many who have contributed to the pioneering, compensatory stage of women's history have more recently invested their energy to open up a wider field of study and re-interpret all social relations of the past from a feminist perspective. After women's history laid the groundwork for a new methodology and theory and offered new insights into the role of women as historical actors, some scholars broadened their attention from the role of women to include gender as a whole. Their interest has been to investigate how societies were shaped by the relations of power between women and men, and the historical construction of masculinity has become as important as femininity for understanding the past.[30] But it remains the case that while criminal justice history has developed strongly as a distinctive sub-discipline of social history and while there is a proliferation of specific studies on aspects of gender relations, there is considerably less work that brings these areas together. And what integrative work there is tends to focus on "women" and crime rather than on the conceptual category "gender". Feminist crime historians who centred their account on women only were aware of the advantages of the conceptual category of gender but often felt they had to provide access to criminal women or female crime victims first before gendered structures could be examined.[31] Garthine Walker and Jenny Kermode, for example, argued for gender history on the gounds that this would limit the "extent to which 'women's' history can be considered in isolation from women's relation to men" and would discourage "the treatment of women as an homogeneous group with a common interest, viewpoint and experience. But it also . . . forces the historian's attention to focus more critically upon the relative power of women and men."[32] Nevertheless, they decided to concentrate on women rather than gender to explore the common constraints and processes women shared and to emphasize "female agency in the face of a legal system institutionally biased towards men".[33] The importance of gender was also recognized by one of the foremost scholars in the field of the history of crime, Clive Emsley, the author of the foreword to this book. His most recent edition of *Crime and society in England 1750-1900* (1996) now has a chapter on "Crime and Gender", a welcome corrective, although a gender analysis integrated more thoroughly throughout the book would have been even more satisfactory. But within this special chapter, too, references to masculinity are only fleeting, and Emsley's focus remains "women" rather than "gender". Most work in other European countries on an integrated gender analysis of the history of crime is at a similarly rudimentary stage. What work there is that more successfully integrates a gender perspective is scattered:[34] we hope this book provides the field with added focus.

We opted for a book on "gender" and crime rather than on "women" and crime because we believe that the concept of femininity cannot be understood without also addressing the concept of masculinity and that women's experience cannot be reconstructed except in the context of a complex set of relations and processes which includes both women and men. Yet while choosing "gender" for our title, we do not want to suggest that "women" should be forgotten or elided: the project of gender history must continue to include the search for the hidden experiences of women, but the historicity of masculinity is fundamental too. The new and significant insights that can be achieved through focusing on both men and women rather than on women alone can be found throughout this book. But the sorts of insights stressed by Walker and Kermode remain as important for "gender" history as they are for "women's" history. "Gender" is a vital analytical tool for understanding masculinity and the historical construction of traditional male institutions and male experiences. Historians have until recently rather neglected this aspect simply because men traditionally had less reason to question their "gendered status", a privilege of those in a dominant position to take that position for granted and to think of the social hierarchy as natural.[35] In addressing men and masculinity as well as women and femininity, this book hopes to illuminate the ways that societies have been shaped by the relations of power between women and men. By examining in depth crimes alleged to have been committed by - or perpetrated against - women or men, or both sexes, and by refusing to use gender as a synonym for women, but rather as a category of analysis, our edited collection moves in the direction anticipated by but not accomplished by studies that focus primarily on women. We have also aimed to contribute to the social history of crime, that is, to situate criminal deeds and their perceptions into relevant contemporary economic, political and social contexts.

This book arises from an international conference we organized at Roehampton Institute London in 1995, which was much wider in scope than this book as far as both period and topics were concerned. In producing an edited collection of some of the papers, we wanted to explore the relationship of gender and crime within a comparative European framework and faced the difficult task of deciding how to limit the book in order to give it some coherence. We decided to examine different ways in which criminality was gendered, together with aspects of the gendered judicial process - and, where possible, the wider historical significance of these phenomena: a great many papers delivered at the conference fitted into this focus. But as a consequence we do not address in any detail a number of relevant topics, the most obvious being the histories of punishment and policing.[36] For reasons of coherence we also decided to include in this volume papers about the modern period only (late eighteenth- to mid-twentieth-century Europe) in order to facilitate comparison if that became possible.

While this book offers an international approach to the study of gender and crime in as much as our contributions range across some six European countries, only a minority of papers contain a genuinely comparative angle, concentrating instead on an in-depth national or local study of their given problem. At the same time, the authors of this volume address the broad theme of "gender and crime" from many different perspectives; many different questions are asked and different theoretical approaches pursued. One of the themes is the construction of gender norms as they are reflected and reinforced by legal institutional practices: prosecution patterns and judicial processes, from dialogue in court rooms to conviction and sentencing patterns, are discussed. Our authors focus on victims and perpetrators of different age-groups, from children suffering abuse, juvenile offenders to adult men and women. Constructions of femininity are explored by analysing women at various key points in their life cycles, ranging from early sexual experience, through abortion, childbirth to divorce and crises of poverty and of power and emotion leading to crimes of violence. Constructions and representations of masculinity are examined in diverse ways: through examination of the "invention" of the juvenile offender and the cross-examination of child witnesses in court; and by analysing the participation of adult men in the Sicilian Mafia, in duels in Germany and in prostitution in France and Britain.

Even within the limited framework we chose for *Gender and crime in modern Europe*, this very richness makes broad transnational comparisons challenging. The purpose of this chapter is to draw out some of the comparisons that can be made. In particular, we have unravelled many embedded and implicit links on theoretical issues of interest to both crime historians and gender historians. More self-consciously comparative work is required to deepen international perspectives, particularly where the details of different types of "crime" are concerned. We simply hope to have further explored the field and opened more areas for investigation. When we organized the conference we settled on a few major questions for which we hoped to find some answers. In this chapter these are organized into two broad and somewhat overlapping sections: first, how does gender as an analytical category help us to understand crime? And secondly, how does the study of crime contribute to our understanding of gender relations, thereby illuminating the recent past more broadly?

How does the concept of gender help in the understanding of crime?

In this section we discuss some of the growing criminal justice historiography that explores gender issues, and demonstrate how the papers in *Gender and crime in modern Europe* contribute to the debate. It is now generally accepted that in the past European legal systems treated women and men differently, and that women and men were also likely to use the law in different ways. Gender differences have been found at many levels, including the existence of strongly gendered crimes (such as prostitution and duelling), prosecution, trial procedures, conviction and punishment. It is also axiomatic that until very recently European criminal justice systems were controlled either entirely or almost entirely by men, and that most – if not all – remain male dominated. What is less clear is whether this overwhelming male power always privileged men and disadvantaged women: some recent work suggests its effects could sometimes be contradictory. The following discussion will indicate how focusing in depth upon the crucial variable of gender in a particular problem in criminal justice history can provide a critical lens of great value. The construction of what is considered wrongdoing (or "deviance") in any society, and the ways in which that is dealt with are of fundamental importance to the social fabric. Therefore, if gender has been an important variable (which it clearly has been and remains), understanding of both "crime" and society as a whole will be impoverished if it is left out of consideration.

Quantitative approaches

Within the quantitative approach to crime history, historians have asked questions about the incidence and nature of female criminality as opposed to male. Were women less "criminal" than men? How have the relative gendered prosecution and conviction rates changed over time? Women have been consistently under-represented in crime statistics and have therefore been traditionally regarded as more law-abiding than men. Yet one significant finding made by historians has been that at different times and places in the past the historical record reveals higher numbers of women being involved in the criminal justice process than is the case today. The first contrast drawn was discovered by John Beattie in 1975. He found a marked urban/rural difference in women's criminality in eighteenth-century England: women's crime was very much more extensive in the large urban area of South London than in the market towns and rural parishes of Surrey and Sussex.[37] More recently, Malcolm Feeley's conclusion from a range of data collected by British and Dutch historians is that women "were once two and one-half to four times more likely to be involved in serious crime than they were at the end of the nineteenth century and have been throughout the twentieth."[38] While he has tried to make sense of long-range data covering the period from the seventeenth century onwards, some other historians have certainly confirmed his findings for shorter periods.[39]

Explanations for such variations have themselves varied considerably. Social and cultural contexts specific to time and place are emphasized by some;[40] factors internal to the criminal justice system, especially the shift of significant amounts of recorded crime from higher level jurisdictions to lower jurisdictions

7

which are not always covered in official criminal statistics are also mentioned.[41] Some historians have formulated both short-term and long-term explanations in the context of theories of patriarchy and male dominance. For example, Eric Johnson has argued that women's increased economic activity and public visibility had comparatively little impact on their criminal behaviour while their chances of becoming a victim of crime, especially of homicide, were increasing faster than men's in Imperial Germany in the late nineteenth century. The continuity of German women's low crime levels during the period of accelerated industrialization led Johnson to conclude that German women remained "law-abiding citizen[s]" who "accepted a traditional role" in society. On the other hand, he concluded that women's new activities in the public realm posed a threat to the established order and caused more men to react violently "to arrest this threat to their former dominance."[42] Thus the gender differential in crime statistics tended to re-affirm the traditional images of femininity as obedient and passive, and masculinity as aggressive and deviant. More recently, Malcolm Feeley has asserted an extremely sweeping explanation for the long-term reduction in women's criminality that he says is demonstrated by the criminal statistics: he argues that the trend can be explained by long-term major shifts in the structure of patriarchy.[43] The hoary problem of the extent to which criminal statistics can be deemed to represent "real" crime lies at the base of much of the current disagreement between scholars, though this often remains implicit.

So what does this volume contribute to the quantification debates? Stephen Frank's careful study of crime statistics in Imperial Russia between 1834 and 1913 suggests that more comparative work on long- and shorter-term trends in levels of women's recorded crime needs to be completed, because his conclusions for Russia provide a different perspective on changing crime rates from some recent work. While Frank himself suggests that his study provides "evidence of a similar, albeit less dramatic, decline in women's proportional representation" in crime statistics[44] to that found in other jurisdictions, within his period there was a significant increase in women's proportion of felony prosecutions between the 1870s and 1890s that goes against the grain of the trend, and needs further comparative explanation. At the same time, once lower court records are examined, Frank found a higher proportion of women than in the circuit courts, and an actual increase in the proportion of women convicted at this level, at the same time as the general trend for women's proportion of felony prosecutions was decreasing. What decrease there was in the proportion of female felony prosecutions he explains by a combination of decriminalization of religious offences and fornication, and a shift in jurisdiction over a large amount of property crime to lower courts. The lower the historian moves down the jurisdictional ladder, the larger was the proportion of women. His research suggests another reason for a new comparative assessment. While there have been recent suggestions that both crime as a whole, and women's crime in particular, were decreasing across the nineteenth century, in Russia Frank has found that both per capita crime as a whole, and women's per capita crime specifically, increased, and within this rise the growth rate for female crime exceeded that for male crime. This paradox is explained by the fact that at the beginning of his period there were vastly more men in the convict population than women, so that numerical growth in female crime looks more impressive statistically. But the increase becomes more significant when the nature of the crimes women were committing is considered: the felonies committed by women that were increasing fastest were not traditional "female" crimes, but rather those that proved harmful to state revenues (such as smuggling and bootlegging), resistance to authorities and various forms of disorder.

The overall picture Frank presents is vastly at odds with the way in which female criminality was constructed from the statistics by contemporary commentators. They used crime statistics to argue that gender itself determined the nature and parameters of criminality while also explaining why women apparently perpetrated fewer crimes than men and a narrower range of offences. As a result in Imperial Russia, as in the rest of Europe, crime was considered to constitute largely a male domain, and female crime was considered in essentialist terms. But, Frank argues, "the definition of crime as a male domain placed women's criminal activity at the periphery while denying it either a history or a dynamic".[45] By challenging conventional interpretations of the Russian statistics, Frank shows women's crime to be far from static - proportions, per capita rates and offences prosecuted varied significantly across both time and space. Furthermore, complex interaction of various social, economic, legal and jurisdictional matters constructed female criminality in this period: it was not something essentially "feminine" as contemporaries suggested, nor were popular perceptions of female crime as largely insignificant compared to male crime correct.

Like Frank, Barry Godfrey succeeds in throwing doubt on the common assumption that women were more law-abiding than men and proposes some reasons for the inadequacy of the criminal statistics for revealing the "true" level of women's workplace appropriation in West Yorkshire 1840-1880. By a number of shrewd questions about women's lives and work relations he has managed to re-insert women into the story when they had been absent from the judicial data. He argues that female appropriators were not included in criminal files for two related reasons. First, although use of the formal legal convention of *feme covert*, which reduced women's responsibility before the law, was becoming uneven and unclear by the mid-nineteenth century, Godfrey suggests that its underlying assumption may have functioned to dissuade aggrieved factory owners from prosecuting.[46] And secondly, informal methods of workplace discipline took the place of formal prosecution.

The relevance of Valeria Pizzini-Gambetta's work on the Mafia for this discussion remains implicit. Women, she argues, were excluded from the Mafia and as a consequence they did not commit mafia-related crimes: they would therefore not appear in Italian criminal statistics for such crimes. Yet other scholars of the Mafia have lamented the effective continuing existence of an

Italian version of *femes covert* associated with organized crime, criticizing the fact that "the judiciary should assume them to be not responsible, and therefore inferior".[47] In Shore's study of juvenile crimes she asks related questions: why did the number of boys entering the criminal justice system increase more markedly than the number of girls? Were girls more likely to be treated more informally than boys, this treatment based upon judges' views about appropriate treatment of boys and girls? She indicates that judicial discretion may have been exercised in different ways that depended upon the sex of the offender, an important insight for our understanding of the criminal justice system, and a practice which affected whether or not a particular transgression entered the criminal statistics.

Less attention has been paid to analysing in detail the extent to which court decisions at conviction and sentencing stages have been affected by the gender of the defendant. Here, Peter King's work in this volume provides an important contribution. He analyses property crimes tried at assize level in a number of English courts in selected years between the 1780s and 1820s. Both the aggregated data and that for individual property offences indicate a consistent national pattern of conviction and sentencing that was remarkably gendered – and that pattern ensured greater lenience to women. Women were more likely to avoid public trial completely, their prosecutors failing to turn up, or the grand jury dismissing the prosecution case. Once cases came before petite juries, men were consistently convicted more frequently than women. Juries also returned "partial verdicts" for women more frequently than for men; that is, they were found guilty of an offence less serious than that charged. Once it came to sentencing, the pattern continued: men consistently received harsher sentences than women. King suggests that an examination of secondary literature indicates that such lenience could also be found at both quarter sessions and summary levels, and that broad continuity can be discerned from the early modern period to the present.

But underneath the apparent continuity, King argues, there was in fact very great change in the ways in which the criminal justice system reflected and constructed notions of femininity. The modern tendency to treat more harshly women who do not fit stereotypes of "normal" or "respectable" femininity may not have operated so powerfully in his period, or indeed, at all. At the same time, *feme covert* affected judicial outcomes in his period whereas the convention no longer operates. Just what happened in the transition period needs more analysis. Changes in various social, economic and cultural factors need also to be put into the balance, especially the effects on the sympathies of juries of many things: women's marginalized employment status; their maternal status; notions of women as more docile and less threatening than men; and changing perceptions of women's appropriate spheres of activity. Furthermore, a wide range of variables such as ethnicity and age have not been adequately researched, and may have affected trial outcomes for women in combination with their gender in different ways in the past than they do today. So King is not yet in a position to explain the trend, but he raises many crucial questions;

historians need to undertake more qualitative research in combination with statistical analyses in order to begin answering them.

Another area of explanation that has received considerably less attention from scholars is the relationship between criminal statistics and the construction of masculinity in the nineteenth century. Martin Wiener's paper delivered at our conference was groundbreaking in this respect.[48] In it he argued that the "vanishing female", particularly in the nineteenth century, was at least in part an artifact of the increasing visibility and prominence of the male criminal. Alongside the growth of private, informal modes of social control of women that have been argued contributed to this decline of women coming before the criminal justice system[49] went the growth of public and formal modes of social control of men. Disproportionately male behaviour (particularly involving violence) was increasingly proscribed by law in the course of the nineteenth century as new constructions of middle-class masculinity placed increasing pressure upon men to be upright, religious and family-oriented.

What remains to be achieved in this field is an integrated analysis of both long-term and short-term variation in the relative proportions of women and men coming before criminal justice systems and their relative treatment by the courts that takes into account both "macro" explanations that presume at least some degree of "fit" between statistics and "real" crime, and "micro" explanations that consider more detailed social and cultural factors, as well as fundamentally important changes within the criminal justice system itself that can lead to statistical variation.[50] And at the same time, such work needs to carefully unpack the relationships of both changing femininities and masculinities to the criminal record. We hope someone out there takes up the challenge!

Microhistory, discourse analysis and cultural approaches to crime

Recently many social historians of crime have become more sceptical as to the analytical force and reliability of statistics and have instead opted to work qualitatively combining analytical and hermeneutic approaches to the topic, often making extensive use of historical anthropology, microhistory and/or discourse analysis, approaches that are very closely related and can be intertwined.[51] The development of such approaches has added nuance and complexity to our understanding of the cultural meanings of crime. While this has occurred within criminal justice history independent from feminist perspectives,[52] the complex theoretical perspectives of some feminist writers have added further impetus to the cultural/microhistory approach.[53] It can also be seen that an emphasis upon textual and discourse analysis has something in common with much earlier approaches to the history of crime.[54]

In this volume, we offer the reader plenty of analysis of discourses to supplement this area of research. Heather Shore's investigation of the public discourse on juvenile delinquency in early nineteenth-century England finds that the adult masculinity and femininity ascribed to juvenile delinquents and their "molls" was closely related to the construction of childhood at that time. Childhood was increasingly being seen as a special time of innocence, so constructing juvenile criminals in this way helped to distance these children from the children of the middle-class philanthropists and social reformers who were discussing juvenile crime: the children who committed crime were not really "children", so were not commensurate with their own children. But the female juvenile criminal was almost entirely absent from the discourse, which Shore argues had less to do with girls' more docile nature and much more to do with the prejudiced way the data was collected. The committee interviewed hundreds of boys in Middlesex prisons and houses of correction but not girls, presumably because girls were considered by nature not prone to delinquency. However, by asking questions herself about the missing female actors Shore has been able to re-insert them into the picture and establish how gendered the construction of juvenile crime was at this time. Boy juveniles who mostly indulged in theft were portrayed as somewhat heroic and their offences linked to their biological make-up: they were perceived as bold and physically aggressive whereas girls were perceived as victims of their own dangerous sexuality, as prostitutes or flash-girls, that is, as sexual predators. Louise Jackson's article on children's evidence in child sexual abuse cases in London 1870–1914 suggests how a similar gendered delinquency model affected courtroom proceedings in this later period. She has very creatively "combined a close reading of courtroom narratives with techniques of textual analysis to work towards an understanding of the wider social and cultural 'knowledges' which influenced courtroom decisions and the treatment of witnesses."[55]

While women to a certain extent have been written out of general crime statistics, and therefore also often out of the history of crime, men are often missing from both the statistics as well as the discourse about the classic women's crime, prostitution. Bertrand Taithe compares the discourses about prostitution in nineteenth-century France and Britain and finds that in both societies male customers were "the vacuous centre" of both moral and scientific discourse. They were vacuous because there was a silence about men in the dominant pronouncements, yet central because "it was their masculinity and their sexual identity which were threatened and threatening".[56] Taithe reveals the importance of masculinity for understanding the history of prostitution through a rich layering of stories. The dominant trope seems at first to be melodrama: this sentimental rhetoric was used by British repealers to shift attention away from concern about the nature of syphilis, back to the nature of prostitution and its effects on prostitutes' lives. Contemporary melodrama constructed the customer as villain and this moral imperative of male sexual continence was reinforced by the French medical discourse favouring regulation that emphasized heredity through male sexuality. Yet Taithe's story does not have a simple melodramatic resolution: women were not redeemed from their "fallen" state, nor did the rhetoric lead to controls on men in practice: women alone continued as the targets of policing which became more draconian in both France and Britain. The attempt to construct a more continent masculinity must provide part of the explanation for the increasing pressure on women working in prostitution.

Pizzini-Gambetta also takes silence and absence as the central point of departure in her analysis. She finds that the very absence of women from Mafia membership, and the rule of silence prohibiting conversations about women between male *mafiosi*, contributed to the power of women's symbolic function within male Mafia culture - which had profound practical significance for the women connected with *mafiosi*. Criminal statistics have little relevance for Shapiro for, as she points out, the burgeoning concern about female criminality in *fin de siècle* France occurred in spite of, not because of, criminal statistics: in fact, recorded female crime was declining in this period. Her main concern is to explore the meaning of the attention paid to criminal women, and by so doing she reveals the ways in which this figure came to powerfully evoke wider contemporary concerns. During the course of her analysis she pays particular attention to narratives of women's criminality: those of the female criminals as recorded in court records; those told about the court cases as a whole; and literary narratives, to name a few. Lynn Abrams, too, is particularly interested in the stories told by women in courtroom settings, and how they mirrored and reproduced conventional constructions of masculinity and femininity. But not all our contributors who concern themselves with discourse dismiss entirely the validity of statistical analysis. Stephen Frank is interested in the ways in which criminal statistics were used discursively to sustain belief that criminal women were deviant socially, culturally, morally, psychologically and biologically, thereby bolstering culturally constructed stereotypes of femininity. Criminal statistics in this way became an important element in criminological discourse.

Power

All of the above papers that focus on discourse in one way or another recognize the contribution that discourses made to the shaping of crime and the criminal justice system; or, in other words, they recognize the historical power of discourses. Exactly how such discursive power is unravelled may vary, and views on how power is best analysed vary too, but all the contributors to the book share the assumption that understanding the complexities of the operation of power in society is critical for understanding how crime is defined, how it is dealt with, and what it means within any society at any time. Early social history of crime focusing on "social crime", particularly in eighteenth-century Britain, contained the assumption that state power was rather monolithic, and functioned in an increasingly repressive way to redefine what had been regarded as traditional "rights" - such as collecting wood, gleaning and the like - into crimes: ". . . the ideology of the ruling oligarchy, which places a supreme value upon property, finds its visible and material embodiment above all in the ideology and practice of the law".[57] An assumption that the power of social control regarding crime lay as good as exclusively

13

within the judicial system is also frequently associated with a positivist definition of crime.

But more recently challenging and complex understandings of power have developed, influenced in particular by the work of Michel Foucault. Foucault rejected the relevance for modern European history of the "juridical" notion of power based upon sovereign authority inherent in the work discussed in the previous paragraph. Instead, he argued that in western societies from the Enlightenment onwards it was replaced by a more subtle disciplining of bodies through institutions and discourses. And here power was dispersed, decentred, complex and shifting – indeed, it was everywhere, everybody shared in it and took part in constant re-negotiations. Part of those re-negotiations were the resistances to it, especially to the "major dominations" or "hegemonic effects" that the operation of power produced.[58] For the study of crime, this has important implications, for it directs attention to a myriad of informal ways of dispensing "justice", to various forms of administrative control, rather than simply to the formal judicial system.[59] Although crime historians do not necessarily formally recognize the theoretical influence of Foucault (and of course, some do), some of the best criminal justice history now provides rich understanding of informal justice systems. And at the same time Foucault's complex view of power in modern society has inspired huge volumes of work on a wide range of disciplinary apparatuses, ranging from psychiatric institutions to the welfare state, which tend to blur the sense that there can be any clearly defined "criminal justice system" – such as one comprised of police, courts and prisons – that can be the limited focus of scholarship.[60]

Gender historians have added significantly in many ways to our increasingly sophisticated understandings of power and its effects. Much debate has ensued around the usefulness, or otherwise, of Foucault's theories.[61] One of the reasons for feminists' engaging so much with Foucault is that he expressed many key ideas that women's historians and feminist theorists were already developing, particularly concerning the ways in which the body and sexuality were historically and socially constructed. Major elements of women's lives were already leading early second-wave feminists to criticize centralized, class-based understandings of power as too limited for analysing gender.[62] But feminist critiques of Foucault have also pointed to lacunae in his theory that have relevance for the development of criminal justice history as a whole. In particular, it is important to recognize the continuing importance of juridical power and coercive powers within complex systems of power relations. The continuing existence of sexual violence against women, for example, makes this essential.[63] And the impact of some crimes can only be understood in relation to the challenge that they pose to juridical (state) power. Treason is the most obvious example, but there are others. In this volume, Ute Frevert has shown the way in which the duel posed a powerful double challenge to juridical power: it opposed the state's function to guarantee physical protection to its subjects; and it opposed the rule of law designed to settle conflicts between subjects in a peaceful, legally controlled way. The practise of this form of autonomous self-regulation in the nineteenth century was in direct opposition to the increasing power of the modern state and the increasing importance of the rule of law in the definition of the modern state - which made juridical power one key element in the complex play of power that constructed duelling in modern Germany.

Sometimes influenced by French theory and sometimes independently from it, but always building from early second-wave feminist work, Anglo-American and some European feminists have developed sophisticated analyses of the interaction between gender and other vectors of power in society, such as class, race/ethnicity, age/generation, religion and sexual preference. In Denise Riley's words, the very term "'women' is historically, discursively constructed, and always relative to other categories which themselves change".[64] Such insights have led to an extraordinarily diverse range of work that is impossible to review here. Suffice it to say that attention has been directed towards "difference": the problem for analysis is not simply "patriarchy" and power differentials between a homogeneous group called "men" and another called "women". Rather, relationships among women (and, of course, among men, and between women and men) are constructed by differences, of class, race and so on. The authors in this book in their various ways cast light on at least some of these dynamics.

Returning to crime, how do the essays in this book further contribute to these debates about power, and how do they, by so doing, enrich our understanding of crime and the criminal justice system? Louise Jackson has undertaken a deep analysis of the ways in which children were cross-examined in quarter sessions courtrooms as witnesses in cases alleging child sexual abuse. Although what goes on in the courtroom may end up in very obvious displays of state power that fundamentally affect people's lives, her work emphasizes that it is not simply in the courtroom proceedings where power lies. At least some of the power that resulted in a particular conviction could well lie in the clearly gendered discourse that existed outside the courtroom and impacted upon its proceedings.

The cross-examinations she analysed both constructed and reinforced gendered notions of childhood innocence. More particularly, she has argued that the "gendered delinquency model" was used to discredit child witnesses. Boy witnesses were challenged as thieves or blackmailers; girl witnesses were cross-examined to establish their sexual innocence or precocity. Because nearly all assailants were male, it was particularly important not to sexualize the male child, as this would threaten prevalent views that healthy, normal male sexuality was always heterosexual - yet another discourse feeding into courtroom practices. Evidence of either kind of delinquency was used to discredit the prosecution case. But there was also an interplay of power between the witnesses speaking up for the innocent and wronged child victim and the adult man accused of indecent assault who portrayed the same child as deceitful and corrupt. Such contrasts were connected with a wider romantic discourse about the innocence of childhood and the corruption made possible in different ways by both working-class and middle-class environments. Sexual abuse always led to corruption, so the court was left with the delicate problem of establishing whether the child was "innocent" before this "corruption", something which was done within the context of wider discourses about childhood innocence.

But Jackson also sees an oppositional discourse as influencing the court proceedings in such cases. While court practices problematized the veracity of children's witness statements, the social purity and feminist movements of the later nineteenth century placed great emphasis upon the importance of the word of the child when allegations of child sexual abuse were made: the child had to be heard, and respected as telling the truth. This attitude was reflected in the work of the National Society for the Prevention of Cruelty to Children, which in the later nineteenth century became the chief prosecuting agency in cases of child sexual abuse, and which campaigned to improve conditions for child witnesses in courtrooms.

It wasn't only discourses outside the courtroom that affected what was said inside the courtroom. Jackson's work provides a poignant example of the power of police agencies to influence both debates about gender and court practices related to gender. One police surgeon was employed by Birmingham city constabulary to examine all children who complained of indecent assault in that city. His construction of these girl complainants as "little minxes" was reflected in cross-examination practices in the courtroom, but, more importantly, his views prevented most accusations of child sexual abuse in Birmingham getting to court in the first place.

A very different approach is taken by Barry Godfrey. His study suggests the ways in which judicial power was only the very "final" form of power providing sanctions for what he calls "workplace appropriation" - and already, Jackson's work has shown how that judicial power was dependent upon the power of discourses and practices extraneous to the courtroom itself. Godfrey argues that because the relationship between the male overlooker and the female worker tended to mirror patriarchal father/daughter and husband/wife relations, much disciplining of women for workplace transgressions (quite possibly including petty pilfering) occurred in this primary workplace relationship. As the male overlooker was considered responsible for the actions of the women workers under his supervision, any lapses on their part would be considered by his bosses to be an indication of his failings, so the overlooker took whatever steps he considered necessary, and made no further complaint about the women's actions.

Godfrey also suggests that women's low rates of prosecution were partly the result of women's family ties. The family served not so much as a site of discipline as a network of relationships that affected women's actions. He suggests that in some cases poverty and the need to provide for children may have encouraged women to pilfer at work; but on the other hand, the dire threat of separation from family that would occur if convicted may have acted as a deterrent to women's workplace appropriation. Furthermore, as already outlined in the section on statistics, women's low crime profile was related to the power of a discourse of women's lesser responsibility that was intrinsic to the legal convention of *feme covert*. Thus a complex range of power relations explain the low rates of female factory appropriation revealed by criminal statistics.

And what of the inter-relations between different categories such as race, class, religion, generation and profession with the category gender? And what are some of the contributions to crime history that unpicking these relationships can make? Interrogating sources for crime history from the perspective of gender can then stimulate questioning and research on a multitude of variables affecting outcomes in the criminal justice system. Peter King's enquiry about gender in this volume has resulted in his calling for work to be done on the interrelationship between these different categories in determining judicial outcomes.

In dealing with abortion Gaby Czarnowski necessarily discusses a crime that is associated on the one hand with an age-specific group of women, mostly young women of reproductive age, but on the other hand with lay abortionists, who were often older women. Even more important, Czarnowski links abortion not only with gender and age, but also in Nazi Germany crucially also with race and eugenics. In Hitler's Third Reich reproductive rights, especially the right to terminate an unwanted pregnancy, depended more than ever before or since on medical, eugenic and "racial" classifications. Nazi abortion policies represented an unremitting subversion of the prohibition on abortion by urging or coercing abortion for "hereditarily diseased" women and those of "alien races" while simultaneously restricting, prosecuting and increasing the penalties for abortion for women of the preferred "race" with "valuable" or "flawless hereditary material". Terminations of pregnancy on racial hygienic grounds were legalized if the woman was also compulsorily sterilized. Although terminations of pregnancy on medical grounds were also legalized for the first time, this did not mean a concession for women eager to control their fertility. The new law was accompanied by such restrictive bureaucratic measures that as a result the number of abortions performed on grounds of health declined dramatically between the Weimar Republic and the end of the Nazi regime. And in 1941 abortionists deemed "habitual offenders" could be sentenced to death; at least 25 women abortionists were indeed executed. According to Czarnowski, National Socialism dissolved the traditional association between abortion, criminality and the female gender. Whether abortion was outlawed and punished or permitted – even coerced – decisions were always taken utterly without regard for the women involved. Eugenic abortions, like sterilizations, were always carried out against women's will: abortion ceased to be a predominantly female crime and became instead a crime of the state against women. Thus, this examination of race and gender has resulted in the definition of crime being turned on its head.

There were other social divisions that powerfully interacted with gender to shape the construction of gender norms and crime. Willem de Blécourt's essay on the prosecution of irregular midwives in the Netherlands demonstrates the overriding influence of class, age and professional identity in dividing registered and irregular midwives. This new, younger breed of trained, licensed midwives did not display gender solidarity against their male superiors, but rather identified with the professional status that their training and association with the medical profession gave them. Registered midwives together with doctors became the main persecutors of unlicensed midwives. The criminalization of irregular midwifery did not lead simply to the exercise of a controlling juridical power. In fact, the medical profession remained the driving force behind prosecutions. Public prosecutors, police and judges were drawn into events by regional inspectors of public health, to whom complaints of unlicensed practise had to be addressed. Most of these complaints came from official midwives and doctors. Yet the younger professional women appeared to many potential clients, particularly those in the countryside, as rather masculine and brusque (even if they were submissive towards their masters, the doctors) while illicit midwives conformed to the ideal of femininity in that they seemed patient, motherly and soft in their touch. This goes some way to explain why many of these women seemed to prefer the unlicensed services of women of the neighbourhood for the delivery of their children even if official midwives were available. Individual women's choices based upon strongly gendered perceptions interacted with women's need for attendance at births and the local medical economy to limit the power of both medical profession and law.

Both Shore and Jackson have, as we have seen, problematized age by concentrating on juveniles before the law and not only shown how jurisdiction changed according to specific age-groups (even if these were often uncertain, contradictory and changing) but also how the integrity of all young people was often the target of attack in law courts. In her examination of children's evidence in child sexual abuse cases, Jackson has argued that delinquency was a stage associated with puberty, seen to commence earlier for girls than for boys. Girls as young as nine were questioned on their sexual precocity, whereas no boy under thirteen in her sample of cases was implied by the approach of the court to be a blackmailer or thief. But once the boy victims reached the age of between 14 and 16, all the defendants were either discharged or acquitted: the boys had all been constructed by the court as juvenile delinquent, thus undermining the prosecution case. But class is also important for both their arguments. In Shore's analysis of juvenile crime the desire of the middle-class commentators to distance the child criminals from their own children – to construct them as fundamentally different – contributed to the ways in which the delinquent children were seen in terms of adult masculinity and femininity. Jackson, too, found that it was impossible for a middle-class child to be seen as a delinquent. In her work, age and class operated together with gender in the evaluation of the delinquency or otherwise of the child victims of alleged sexual assault in late nineteenth-century England. A stimulating and perhaps controversial argument about class can be found in Ute Frevert's paper on duelling in nineteenth-century Germany but as its most important element concerns the symbolic relation between gender and class, it is developed later in this chapter where we discuss gender as symbol.

For Stephen Frank, discursive paternalistic and moral concerns affected the types of offences for which women were prosecuted and convicted. This operated together with many other variables - in particular, class and occupation, including the rural/urban distinction and women's changing economic role, age, gender, state interests and shifting legal and jurisdictional definitions - to determine patterns of prosecution in Imperial Russia. None of these factors was "primary"; rather, all need to be taken into account in reaching an explanation for the unique scenario he is seeking to explain. Perhaps this is what unites all the perspectives in this book: a rejection of mono-causal explanation based upon models of power which prioritize one vector over another, and a determination to unravel the complexities of individual historical moments.

Crime as social construct

The central project of sociology, to unravel the "social construction of reality",[65] is shared by the sub-discipline of criminology.[66] In the preceding pages it has already become clear that in many complex and diverse ways criminal justice history, too, is exploring how "crime" and "criminality" have been historically constructed - and that in important ways the historical and sociological projects have intermeshed. However, we are not sure whether there would be consensus amongst our authors about the definition of an ethical dimension of "essential" wrongdoing. Although not explicit, there is a thread that can be discerned in our book that does assume that some crimes (particularly certain crimes of violence) are wrong in themselves, and we would not side-step making this claim. Mafia sub-culture defined as acceptable appalling acts of violence that society as a whole condemned: murder in most western societies in most circumstances today is considered a fundamental violation of a very basic human right to life.[67] In Nazi Germany the state, not a secret criminal organization, became the power condoning acts of criminal violence. Nazi population policy rather than any concept of fundamental human rights became the principle by which abortion (and, of course, murder on a massive scale - although that is not addressed in our volume) became either sanctioned or defined as criminal. Furthermore, our inclusion of a paper on divorce and marital violence in a book about "crime", although it was not construed as "crime" in nineteenth-century Germany, is based upon the assumption that in feminist analysis spouse abuse was and is a "crime" in itself. These comments rest on the notion that there are certain basic human rights - to life and to bodily integrity, for example - upon which civil society and the rule of law should be based; and that if they are transgressed, fundamental abuses of human rights (which may or may not be defined as "crimes" in that society) have occurred. Of course, we recognize the very historicity of such a

19

definition, but stress the importance of such definitions for contemporary politics. But this is not a book about ethics or political philosophy, and we have left the problematic relationship between any ethically defined wrongdoing and the socially constructed character of "crime" and "criminality" for others to debate. In the remainder of this section we would like to outline a few more ways in which the studies here show crime to be historically and socially constructed.

Historical studies in different contexts on topics such as child care, infanticide and abortion have shown that there could be major disjunctures between official penal prescription and popular perceptions and practices.[68] In *Gender and crime in modern Europe* this dichotomy emerges in different ways. Women in the Dutch countryside never thought they did any wrong by calling on irregular midwives to help them in childbirth and, for that matter, magistrates as well as public prosecutors seemed to share their perceptions since they were clearly reluctant to prosecute or punish. As de Blécourt demonstrates, the misdemeanour to attend a woman lying-in without an official midwifery registration was an "invention" of the medical profession who campaigned for hegemony in the medical market. They were supported in this by official midwives protecting their newly found official status. But the criminalization of irregular midwifery was also an example of gender hierarchy at a time when doctors were nearly all male and midwives female. Though doctors themselves were not interested in attending births themselves because it was a lengthy procedure with low financial rewards, they sought to regulate it and relegate it as a lesser skilled area requiring their supervision. Once they had achieved this, they then sought to outlaw irregular midwifery as a professional crime. But, because their motives were economic and professional status, a system of double standards prevailed: irregular midwives were tolerated if no regular help was available but prosecuted if they competed with existing regular midwives.

Similarly, in Germany duelling had been a crime not just since 1871 with the introduction of the new Reich penal code but in various earlier penal codes of different German states. Yet wide sections of the German middle and upper classes thought of this act not only as inevitable but also as honourable and reflecting well on the noble character of both parties. The pro-duel stance was shared by many high-ranking civil servants who were expected to show total loyalty to the state and its laws; and even many lawyers defended the practice. Duelling thus had a highly ambiguous role in society: on the one hand it was proscribed and punishable as a crime, on the other it was openly condoned, even applauded and in practice men indicted for it could often expect some degree of mitigation by the sovereign. This showed a conflict of interest between the legislature on the one hand, eager to impose its influence over its citizens and deal with offences by official legal procedure, and the military traditions and rules upheld by the aristocracy who traditionally had dominated the military and the civil service – and which were still being condoned to some extent by the sovereign.

Pizzini-Gambetta, too, is at pains to reveal the dichotomy between official policy in which the Mafia represented a criminal behaviour in Sicilian culture and what it represented for *mafiosi* themselves. For them Cosa Nostra was an organization made up of individual units or "families" which were hierarchically structured and strictly regulated by cultural norms, such as honour, friendship and reciprocity and the special quality of *omertà*, the ability to keep silent. The dichotomy between official policy and legal codes on the one hand and social practice on the other is also very apparent in the case of abortion in Germany. During the end of the Weimar Republic when up to a million abortions were estimated to have been procured but only a tiny proportion ever detected and prosecuted, official sanctions were widely believed to have failed and a powerful campaign sought to adapt the law to current practices by liberalizing it.[69] During Nazi Germany, however, the dichotomy between state policy and popular perceptions reached its nadir: as Czarnowski shows in her chapter, the National Socialist regime regulated abortion entirely according to its putative effects on the genetic and racial make-up of the nation: the network of "underground" illegal abortions at first continued and illustrated that termination of unwanted pregnancy was still widely practised and condoned but when women had so-called desirable genetic health, it was increasingly and systematically attacked by the state authorities. By contrast, non-Aryan women or those considered racially and eugenically inferior, whatever their circumstances or their wishes, were encouraged and even forced to undergo abortions.

Rural and urban differences can also be found in the way transgressions of various kinds were constructed and experienced. De Blécourt finds the rejection of the notion that unlicensed midwifery was "criminal" to be a particularly rural phenomenon in the Netherlands. Frank locates a differentiation between the structure of rural and urban court jurisdictions in Imperial Russia as a major determinant in the construction of urban women as more "criminal" than rural women, as well as the characterization of rural crime as fundamentally violent and brutal when it did occur. Lynn Abrams suggests that victims of wife-abuse in nineteenth-century Germany could experience very different fates depending on where they lived. In rural communities right up to the end of the century, "rough music", family support and general community surveillance protected women within families. Individual cases of abuse that have entered court records indicate that beaten rural women were readily provided with protection and support: wife abuse was a "crime" which the local community would not tolerate, and informal systems of policing and protection came into play when it occurred. On the other hand, in the same period in Hamburg, neighbourly intervention was considerably more half-hearted, yet it was only at the end of the century that the police began to be used for regulation of such domestic affairs. Urban women experienced a hiatus in support: somewhere, somehow, domestic violence became less of a "crime" in urban areas, perhaps because of the increasing importance of the notion of the family as a "private" domain.

At the same time, Abrams's discussion of legislative change of divorce laws in a number of countries highlights the ways in which people's options and experiences when the victims of particular "crimes" can be fundamentally affected by legislation. Similarly, Louise Jackson's examination of the sexual abuse of children reminds us that a whole new tranche of "crimes" was constructed each time the age of consent was raised in England in the nineteenth century, then again in 1908 when incest was criminalized for the first time. Yet the construction of sexual crimes in the nineteenth century did not relentlessly proceed in the direction of greater regulation and definition: Stephen Frank's paper on Russia suggests that one of the reasons for the reduction in the numbers of women coming before the courts was that "fornication" was decriminalized in 1903.

How does the study of crime contribute to understanding of gender relations, thereby illuminating the recent past more broadly?

The value of criminal records for history is often not only that they can tell us much about a specific crime but also that they can give precious insights into private relations usually hidden from history because they are deemed too intimate to be openly discussed. In this volume, papers dealing with abortion, marital violence, the dramas enacted between women and men as sexual partners, and adults sexually abusing children provide examples of this sort. We recognize that the question of "voice" in criminal records is a vexed one because words are mediated through (male) court officials who transcribe testimony and what people say is strongly structured by questions coming from the court. Yet careful attention to subtext and unwitting testimony contained in court narratives can significantly further our understanding of gendered perceptions of specific intimate experiences. At the same time, the records enable the historian to examine the construction of gender norms as they are reflected and reinforced by the institutional practices of one of the key structures in all western societies: the criminal justice system. In a recent study, Regina Schulte has demonstrated how this can work. Sharing the view of E. P. Thompson and many others that studying the atypical enables the discovery of unspoken social norms, she illuminated a whole world of village culture by closely listening to defendants, plaintiffs, witnesses and those who sat in judgement and by unravelling what she called the "manifest layer" and the "latent layer" of the depositions consulted. We agree with Schulte that through judicial records we "hear the protagonists speak, but the peculiar nature of their language refers back to its context, its historical and cultural location, and gives this a voice, too" and hope that the reader finds some of this quality in places throughout this volume.[70] In what follows we draw out some of the contributions that these papers make to a selection of key theoretical concerns in women's and gender history that have not already been discussed in the previous section.

Public and private

The very possibility of reading court records to analyse intimate dimensions of human experience speaks powerfully of the judicial process as one that mediated "public" and "private". British historian Leonore Davidoff has developed nuanced analyses of the historical interrelation between these "spheres" and argued cogently for the importance of deconstructing these categories.[71] Within criminal justice historiography, Kermode and Walker have pointed out correctly that it is inadequate to discuss women's experiences in terms of the "simple paradigm" of public and private spheres: women can be found "moving easily from one to the other, indeed exploiting the paradoxes between the two";[72] and Judith Allen has discussed the ways in which the "secrets" associated with sexuality and gender relations were brought into public discourse in the criminal justice system.[73] *Gender and crime in modern Europe* contributes to such discussions in a number of ways.

One of Shapiro's central aims is to contribute to the deconstruction of the uncritical use of the public/private divide through her examination of women's criminality. The term "domestic treason" rhetorically joined intimate and political life in *fin de siècle* France; spouse murder, and women's crime more generally, condensed the significance of the connection between private and public spheres for contemporaries into highly symbolic form, demonstrating the mobility of gender issues between personal and political realms. Women's domestic crimes brought intimate relations onto the public stage and into public discourse, both generating and reflecting political concerns about issues such as responsibility for paternity, depopulation, the reform of marriage laws, women's economic role, and feminist claims for increased female autonomy. This constant traversing of the public/private boundary contributed to the way in which women's criminality was used to represent all the ills of modern urban society.

Lynn Abrams has found some similar connections between domestic discord and public discourse by examining the issue of wife-abuse and divorce. In Great Britain and the USA in particular, she found a link between the private challenges made by women to their abusive husbands and the public discourse condemning marital brutality that, in England at least, contributed directly to the 1878 Matrimonial Causes Act, enabling magistrates in the lowest courts to grant separation orders to abused wives. While feminists in Germany did not take up this issue, the boundary between private acts and public exposure was still crossed by the female victims of domestic violence who sought redress in the courts. Furthermore, the issue of marital relations had already been placed on the public agenda by late eighteenth-century Prussian legislators who saw divorce as necessary to enable unhappy spouses to remarry and procreate, thus supporting Frederick the Great's population policy.

Although Godfrey has not explicitly used these categories, his work has implications for this discussion. He argues that because the relationship in nineteenth-century textile factories between male overlookers and female workers tended to mirror patriarchal father/daughter and husband/wife relations, much disciplining of women for workplace transgressions occurred in this primary workplace relationship, without any complaint about the women's actions going any further. In a sense, although in a factory, this relationship remained "semi-privatized", yet its effect upon formal prosecution could be seen as a very "public" implication of what would by many have been considered the "private" disciplining of women workers by their male overlookers. And again, Jackson does not explicitly discuss these categories yet her work shows that the process of telling about sexual abuse breaks down the notion that sexual relations are "private": all the victims and their adult supporters in her paper have transgressed this divide in a way powerfully undermining the silence upon which this version of patriarchal sexual power depends. Furthermore, "private" acts of sexual intimacy between adults and children were constructed into a public discourse about child prostitution and gendered juvenile delinquency that was inscribed even more firmly into discourse by its reiteration through cross-examinations in the public judicial process. In a similar way, Taithe's work demonstrates how the very "private" contract to exchange sex for money was brought into the centre of the political domain by systems of state regulation and a complex discourse about prostitution.

Gender as symbol

One extremely important way in which gender mediates "public" and "private" is through its symbolic meanings within any particular society, but the significance of such symbolization runs deeper still. In one of her most valuable contributions to feminist theory, Joan Scott explained how gender is not only a "constitutive element of social relationships based on perceived differences between the sexes", but is also "a primary way of signifying relationships of power".[74] She suggested a number of ways in which gender has functioned in symbolic ways in society, and other scholars have similarly addressed this issue. Our book makes a number of contributions to this understanding.

Gender has been particularly powerful historically in the ways in which it has provided a symbol for class identity and difference.[75] One way this worked was through different versions of masculinity becoming powerful markers of class difference. The code of honour associated with the system of duelling among upper- and middle-class German men in the nineteenth century rested on the total exclusion of both women and working-class men.[76] Working-class male efforts to defend their "honour" were simply dismissed as brawls. When "ladies" duelled, as did occasionally happen – such as in 1864 when two women duelled with canes, then attacked each other with punches – they were mocked and ridiculed. Women's duels may have been seen as doubly threatening, which accounts for the derision in which they were held: by demasculinizing middle- and upper-class men, thus undermining the gender system, "lady" duellists also fundamentally undermined a powerful marker of class status. This may be one explanation for the complicity shown by most women of these classes with the values of male courage and honour that were demonstrated through duelling. Women's role was absolutely crucial to this class-based system of restoring male honour and establishing masculinity. They were the primary motive for duelling, and so crucial was women's approval and admiration that most duelling conflict arose in social situations in which women were prominent, such as balls and other places where masculinity was on display and under scrutiny. Perhaps most women of more substantial social position admired and celebrated duellists because the form of masculinity reinforced by duelling provided a very significant part of the definition of their own class position, as most of women's class status was achieved through their association with men of a particular class.[77] This powerful symbolic function of masculinity could obscure for women the very real ways in which their own personal interests were disadvantaged by the practice of duelling. They were excluded from personally holding the desirable quality "honour"; they were excluded from attending duels themselves; and a woman's dignity or reputation could never be restored by a duel. If a woman's own behaviour had caused a duel, her honour was lost forever. She could even be found guilty if a death or injury had been incurred; in fact a woman's guilt and dishonour would then be doubled. Furthermore, a wife who had offended her husband was invariably forced out of both her own and parental home and family.

Valeria Pizzini-Gambetta's work on gender norms in the Mafia in the post-Second World War period highlights the most dramatic implications for women of their cultural reification into symbols. Focusing in a different way upon dominantly or exclusively male crimes from Frevert's approach, Pizzini-Gambetta has built on subtle work that explores the symbolic power of women in Sicilian culture to analyse how that symbolic power functioned within a tight male organization, and between different criminal organizations. The fundamental defining characteristic of Mafia members was that they were "men of honour". Relations with women functioned in a symbolic way as a key aspect in defining whether or not a man was a "man of honour". Absence of women from formal Mafia membership and a rule of silence preventing talk about women strengthened their symbolic function. The subtle interaction of male and female at both symbolic and material levels provides the key to understanding. Pizzini explains that one of the practical rules concerning women was that members of Cosa Nostra avoid killing women. Indeed, in order to give themselves a good press, the Mafia made special efforts to protect women.

Another rule contributed to the impression that the Mafia had great respect for women: involvement in the protection of prostitution was forbidden to *mafiosi* because, they said, women were not commodities. However, women were used in different symbolic ways according to the audience. Although Mafia members may have said they objected to the commodification of women through prostitution, through their own symbolic objectification of women they turned them into commodities in far more brutal ways. Steady marriage and proper behaviour towards women were clear ways in which men proved their trustworthiness and reputation to other men: they were not values in and of themselves. The rule against killing women was supposed to apply to female relatives of Mafia members, and in the very public Mafia gang wars of the post-Second World War period, Mafia members have almost universally scrupulously avoided killing women on purpose. But as Pizzini-Gambetta explains:

> More convincing evidence about this rule, however, is the way it was breached. Mafia members, in fact, killed women, both relatives of theirs and not, and did so to an extent we will never be able to assess . . . These executions could not easily be recognized as Mafia murders. Very conveniently, a robbery was staged, or a shoot-out among drug dealers.[78]

Such murders were carried out to protect the reputation of Mafia members within the organization; the women were murdered because they were symbols of male honour in relations between men. Perhaps they had been unfaithful, which told against the Mafia husband; perhaps the *mafiosi* had breached another rule against informing women relatives of Mafia activities, and because of her knowledge she had to be killed to protect the *mafiosi's* reputation for trustworthiness. Far from protecting women, the place of women as symbols at the centre of the Mafia culture of male honour made them extremely vulnerable.[79]

"Woman" being used as a symbol in relations between men and gender symbolizing class were not the only ways that gender functioned in symbolic ways in relation to crime. Stephen Frank for Russia and Ann-Louise Shapiro for *fin de siècle* Paris argue that the contemporary discussion of apparently typically female crimes reflected contemporary anxieties about women's changing roles rather than the reality of women's lives and gender relations at the time, and that this moral panic, in turn, symbolized wider anxieties about both Russian and French society in a period of rapid social and demographic change. Both use the example of female spouse murder during the latter years of the nineteenth century. Contemporaries in Russia and France were horrified to discover that women had become more sexually active and destructive; spouse murderesses were both fascinating and frightening. Not only did their crimes run counter to women's perceived nature but also to the basic principles of the patriarchal order. Women who killed their husbands fundamentally challenged male authority at home and in public. Together with women who pursued their seducers and demanded retribution through paternity suits they became in the public eye "unnatural" women because they had so obviously inverted the gender system. The nurturing wife sustaining life through providing food was transformed into a murderess draining the very life entrusted to her. In the face of such treacherous wives husbands became the innocent prey to a perverted womanhood. As the adulterous, scheming, highly sexed women who publicly shamed their husbands, spouse murderesses not only undermined notions of femininity but also of masculinity: men who were normally expected to be ruled by sexual passions and to be the unfaithful ones were now often portrayed as faithful, dutiful, passive sufferers, possibly impotent, the victims of female passion and adultery.

Although such women had a high public profile, spouse murder in both Russia and France was numerically insignificant. Why then were contemporaries so fascinated by this crime? Both Frank and Shapiro suggest that we should regard spouse murderesses as scapegoats onto whom the wider fears of social ills had been transferred. As Shapiro put it, spouse murder became "a code that condensed anxieties about the nature of modern life . . . a newly unstable gender hierarchy and . . . cultural anarchy".[80] In both France and Russia this occurred at a time of radical social change. In Russia the migration from country to town and from agriculture to industry had increased women's visibility but also their demands for more rights at a time when there was little chance to escape from an unhappy marriage. In France the discourse happened at a time when gender harmony had been disturbed through a number of social reforms, especially the new divorce law of 1884 and a vociferous women's movement demanding more rights for married women. At the same time the country's virility seemed to be under attack from within by increasingly low fertility, and from without by a stronger neighbour, Germany. Women were increasingly seen as a threat to home and nation and men were seen to be losing many traditional prerogatives that defined their superior status. Better than any other public image, spouse murderesses signified to anxious contemporaries that the world had turned upside-down.

Constructing femininity and masculinity

The value of beginning with "crime" in order to understand what was "considered normative behaviour"[81] has already emerged in this discussion. For example, the outcry over the cases of spouse murderesses reveals what was perceived as deviant and by implication what was considered the traditional ideal of femininity: virtuous, passive, nurturant. Laws were aimed and did indeed also help to reinforce established notions of femininity and masculinity. As Frank's chapter shows, contemporary criminologists, judges and other commentators in Russia accused criminal women of crossing many boundaries that defined the "normal" woman. They also used crime statistics to support, refine and perpetuate culturally constructed gender stereotypes. Notions of femininity that might well have been at odds with some new roles for women in a rapidly changing society were thus reinforced. Participation by the criminal justice system in the construction of gender can be found by examining a wide range of questions, as the work in this volume and the previous discussion shows. However, examining crimes related to sexuality, reproduction, marriage and family relations can provide particularly powerful lenses through which the construction of masculinity and femininity can be understood.

Lynn Abrams explores the important links between divorce laws, male violence and female powerlessness in nineteenth-century Hamburg. She offers an important critique of the apparently liberal nature of German divorce law at this time. She does this by exploring beneath the liberal surface of the law, asking what the benefits to people were in practice, and whether the benefits were gendered. Contrary to France, Russia and Britain, nineteenth-century German states offered men and women of all classes the rare opportunity for divorce and legal separation. Particularly since marital cruelty was acknowledged as a legitimate ground for divorce or at least separation the German divorce law has been praised by historians as widely benefiting women, especially lower-class women. Abrams, however, is more critical. To start with, in the late nineteenth century access to divorce for German women became increasingly restricted – for example, marital violence was no longer recognized as a ground for divorce – just when most western European countries liberalized access. But more importantly, even before the laws had been tightened, the situation was worse for women than would first appear. In fact, divorce was made possible as a kind of safety valve for the institution of marriage which afforded German women no basic rights *vis-à-vis* their husbands. Wife-abuse was regarded as a crime against the marriage institution, rather than a criminal offence. Thus abused wives obtained no protection from the criminal law; their only recourse was to petition for divorce or legal separation, which generally left them unprovided for. This system was justified on the assumption that it was the husband's duty to protect his wife in return for her obedience to him. But as Anna Clark has pointed out, in reality this philosophy was little else than a patriarchal ploy: it justified the total subordination of wives to their husbands and thereby perpetuated and reinforced patriarchy.[82] Thus, Abrams argues, under the German system divorce was not a woman's privilege, rather it was the price nineteenth-century society was prepared to pay to maintain sexual inequality and to preserve patriarchal marriage, thereby strengthening the conventional construction of masculinity and femininity.

Crimes that were almost exclusively masculine can also provide very useful access to understanding the historical construction of masculinity and femininity. Ute Frevert demonstrates how duelling was crucial for the construction of middle- and upper-class masculinity. She argues that an integral constituent of the bourgeois sense of masculinity in the post-1848 revolutionary liberal states was the notion that men should possess the freedom of action without being curbed by either man, woman or the state. Thus, the state might outlaw duelling and prescribe official penalties but once a gentleman's honour was at stake it could only be defended by duelling. Every duellist was automatically a man of honour, even if death occurred and vice versa; a man who refused to duel was not honourable, since he revealed a lack of courage that made him an object of disdain and contempt. The logic of duelling was based on the potential death resulting from it and this in turn was linked to a widespread admiration for weapons and the bearers of arms during the nineteenth century when universal conscription had been introduced. As we have already seen, this served to mark the boundaries between upper- and middle-class men on the one hand, and the lower classes, who were excluded, on the other. At the same time, duelling helped to construct femininity, to highlight the difference between men and women and to illuminate gender relations. Difference was emphasized by women's exclusion from duelling and from holding "honour" of the male variety (women achieved "honour" in very different ways, associated with sexual probity). Female dependence and powerlessness were constructed through the way in which duels were frequently fought as a result of relations between women and men. Yet even if defence of female honour seemed to be the deeper reason for a duel, men always only fought for their own honour. In general, a woman never regained her honour through a duel, and there was no way in which she could regain it for herself.[83]

At the same time as reinforcing already established models of gender characteristics, new definitions could be forged partly through the criminal justice system and discourse about criminality. Martin Wiener's current research on spouse murder and masculinity in nineteenth-century Britain is exploring the possibility that new bourgeois notions of respectable, domestic masculinity were strengthened by increased use of legal sanctions against male violence. In this volume, Bertrand Taithe's study of prostitution in nineteenth-century France and Britain suggests that in complex and differing ways prostitution in both countries became increasingly associated with a debauched and perverted male sexuality, rather than being an option available within definitions of healthy and acceptable masculinity. Taithe argues that as commercial sex "had long channelled masculine desires and sexual urges, but through the anti-regulationst or regulationist scaremongering campaigns it became the unacceptable expression of what was essentially wrong with unrestrained masculine sexuality",[84] the control of men must be added to the victimization of women outlined in well established feminist accounts[85] as an aim and effect of the regulation of prostitution in both France and Britain during the 1870s and 1880s.

Women's agency

The legal system not only reinforced gender roles but it also provided avenues for undermining them. Contrary to traditional perceptions of a feminine norm, women were often far from passive when it came to fighting for their rights. They would often use the law as a means of empowerment even when the law subordinated individual rights to the interests of the state. By manipulating a patriarchal law, alternative models of gender relations could be established that differed significantly from established norms. Frank discusses a rise in female crimes resisting authorities in Imperial Russia, as well as explaining the use made of the law by peasant wives to gain separation from abusive husbands, indicating a considerable knowledge of law and legal change and a willingness to use the law in their own interests. Abrams shows that in nineteenth-century Germany 60 per cent of all divorce cases and 84 per cent of all separation suits were initiated by women, indicating that they were far from what the law had designated for them: helpless property of their husbands. Interestingly, Abrams contends, it was not feminists who campaigned against domestic violence (they seem to have found this too controversial and might have felt it was a class rather than a gender issue) but ordinary women who as wives fought against inadequate husbands in the courts and brought about legal change. Abrams suggests that women learnt how to manipulate the law as it stood, seeking legal separation for cruelty in jurisdictions where this was not sufficient grounds for divorce, then filing for full divorce some years later on the grounds of desertion. They worked with the world as they found it in other ways. In particular, in their narratives of domestic discord women filing for separation or divorce ensured that they represented themselves as demure and obedient wives according to social expectations, while manipulating ideal representations of masculinity to show their husbands as violent transgressors of the norm. Although their actions in challenging abusive spouses were clearly out of step with the patriarchal social structure, their language before the court was usually sufficiently accommodating for them to gain the redress they sought.

From "the shady areas of semi-crime, semi-unrest, semi-vice" evoked by Taithe emerge snapshots of women acting with determination to advance their own interests, within the limits set by the moral and police regulation of sexuality and prostitution in nineteenth-century Paris and London.[86] The common-law wife of Mayhew's "Clerk in the City" moved in with her clerk in London to lead a lower middle-class life that provided her with an escape route from promiscuous prostitution, even if she were still "an unfortunate woman" because there was no formal marriage contract. In Paris, women working as registered prostitutes both exploited the loopholes in the legislation and used the framework of regulation to complain about corrupt policemen, vicious clients and corrupt or incompetent doctors so, Taithe concludes, that they "could act within regulation almost as much as they were acted upon".[87]

Shapiro shows how in turn-of-the-century Paris ordinary women at times challenged the existing gender order, particularly when domestic issues, such as marital relationships, were at the centre of public debate. Her work demonstrates the dramatically different ways in which women could exercise their agency. A female spouse poisoner could fundamentally challenge male authority at home. In the courtroom, she could revise the formulaic widely circulated story of female perversity associated with spouse poisoners by attempting to explain the actual emotional and material circumstances that had led to her act, although in the end her efforts could be defeated by the judicial system, or by her own final complicity with the dominant script, through her own suicide.

More constructively, perhaps, feminists could appropriate the courageous and powerful elements in the image of the criminal woman for their own purposes, and rewrite the griefs that could cause a woman to murder into political grievances demanding redress. Shapiro argues that feminists in *fin de siècle* France did just this. Other authors, too, have found women acting in political capacities in response to crime and its representations. In late nineteenth-century Germany the woman president of the General German Women's Association described the male honour being defended in duels as purely egotistical, and degrading to women who were turned into objects by the practice of duelling which was a powerful sign of patriarchy. Although each group had its own arguments, the feminists joined with workers, the Social Democratic Party, left liberal and Catholic circles to form a powerful anti-duelling lobby.

In rural regions of the Netherlands unlicensed midwives continued to take responsibility for helping parturient women in need, despite their actions being formally constructed as "crimes". They placed their own interpretation on lenient treatment and marginal fines imposed by the courts, construing this as approval rather than prohibition. And many of their clients demonstrated their preference for the unlicensed midwives by continuing to call on their services. This provides one example of the limited ability of "public patriarchy" - here, the intervention of male medical control through state criminal sanctions - to control and take over woman-centred birthing culture in the Netherlands, where woman-centred obstetrics and home births remain significant. Illegal midwives, answering to popular demand, may well have contributed to this. Godfrey has demonstrated the interrelation of power and women's bodies in a different way. Even while women were controlled within factories by careful systems of overseeing and inspection, and were restricted in their movements by employment in generally more sedentary jobs than men, they still found a way to pilfer goods: hiding their booty on their bodies - a form of resistance (and agency) structured by the particular ways in which power operated in the factories.

Considering a different issue, is it possible to read between the lines of late nineteenth-century English representations of conniving mothers coaching their children to make false claims of sexual abuse - to find concerned and even courageous mothers supporting and believing their children's stories in difficult circumstances? Such a reading of some of the evidence discussed by Jackson would be consistent with the extent to which other work by the same author has suggested that there was considerable abhorrence for child sexual abuse within working-class London neighbourhoods at this time that expressed itself in very practical ways: mothers believing children's stories and investigating suspicious circumstances; and mothers, fathers and neighbours confronting suspected abusers and initiating proceedings leading to prosecution - but the agency of the abused children, if they had any at all, remains elusive.[88]

The more powerful the (juridical) power being exercised and the more closed and coercive the system in which it operated, the more difficult it is for the historian to retrieve the agency of those caught within it. There is little about women's agency in Pizzini-Gambetta's work on the Sicilian Mafia: oral history (not employed by the author) might well provide the only possible source to explore the subjectivity of Mafia women, yet given the considerable changes in Mafia culture recently with the introduction of major anti-Mafia laws and activities in Italy, together with all the complexities of human memory and retrospective narrative, Mafia women's subjectivity in the past is difficult to determine. Another scholar of Sicilian organized crime has found evidence of women's active criminal involvement, although most of this has been in very recent years that post-date Pizzini-Gambetta's focus.[89] An even more poignant example: where was a woman's agency as she lay prone, unconscious, her body invaded by a Nazi doctor removing both her child *in utero*, and her fertility, without her consent? In the face of such appalling abuse of human rights one can search for many positive and noble human virtues: courage, heroism, determination, faith; but very often, their expression will be lost forever to the historian, for it is the stark exercise of coercive, abusive power that has left its mark in the historical record, and all we can hear between the lines are cries of grief. While the search for agency and human strength remains important, such cries should be acknowledged: sometimes, whether within a Nazi death camp or hospital, within a closed and corrupt criminal organization, or within a severely abusive family, an individual can find no space for human agency or dignity; selfhood is annihilated and the individual dies.[90]

Despite the need for such caution, it is mostly people acting within the limits imposed by circumstances who populate the pages of this volume. And rather than imposing more structure on the words of our authors through further interpretations, we hand over the remaining pages to them, and further analysis to future readers.

Notes

1. While we limit the discussion mostly to modern Europe, including Britain, in places where it has seemed particularly relevant we have referred also to early modern texts, and to contributions from North American and Australian historians.
2. E. A. Johnson, "Women as victims and criminals: female homicide and criminality in Imperial Germany, 1873-1914", *Criminal Justice History* 6, 1985, pp. 151-75, quoting D. Klein, "The etiology of female crime: a review of the literature", in *The female offender*, L. Crites (ed.) (Lexington, Mass.: D. C. Heath, 1976), p. 5. See also Johnson, "Crime and the industrial revolution: the German case", *Criminal Justice History* 12, 1991, pp. 19-27; and *Urbanization and crime: Germany 1871-1914* (New York: Cambridge University Press, 1995); Johnson & R. E. Bergstrom, "The female victim: women and homicide in Imperial Germany", in *German women in the nineteenth century: a social history*, J. C. Fout (ed.) (New York: Holmes and Meier, 1984), pp. 345-67.
3. For example, C. Lombroso & W. Ferrero, *The female offender* (New York, 1895) and O. Pollack, *The criminality of women* (New York: A. S. Barnes, 1961); see also G. Buschan, *Geschlecht und Verbrechen* (Berlin/Leipzig, 1903) and P. Näcke, *Verbrechen und Wahnsinn beim Weibe* (Vienna, 1894).
4. For example: D. Blasius, *Kriminalität und Alltag: zur Konfliktgeschichte des Alltagslebens im 19. Jahrhundert* (Göttingen, 1978); D. Hay et al. (eds), *Albion's fatal tree: crime and society in eighteenth-century England* (London: Allen Lane, 1975); H. Zehr, *Crime and the development of modern society: patterns of criminality in nineteenth-century Germany and France* (London: Croom Helm, 1976); V. E. McHale & E. A. Johnson, "Urbanization, industrialization and crime in Imperial Germany: parts I and II", *Social Science History* 1, 1976/7, pp. 45-78, pp. 210-47.
5. J. M. Beattie, "The criminality of women in eighteenth-century England", *Journal of Social History* 8, 1975, pp. 80-116; (more recently, he has also contributed

"Crime and inequality in eighteenth-century London" in *Crime and inequality*, J. Hagan & R. D. Peterson (eds) (Stanford: Stanford University Press, 1995), pp. 116-39. Infanticide and prostitution were probably the areas that attracted most attention. A few examples from the vast historiography on infanticide: G. K. Behlmer, "Deadly motherhood: infanticide and medical opinion in mid-Victorian England", *Journal of Historical Medicine and Allied Sciences* **34**, 1979, pp. 403-27; R. W. Malcolmson, "Infanticide in the eighteenth century", in *Crime in England, 1550-1800*, J. S. Cockburn (ed.) (London: Methuen, 1977), pp. 187-209; L. De Mause, *The history of childhood* (London: Souvenir, 1976); R. Roth, "Juges et médicine face à l'infanticide à Genève au XIXe siècle", *Gesnerus* **34**, 1977, pp. 113-28; R. Smith, *Trial by medicine: insanity and responsibility in Victorian trials* (Edinburgh: Edinburgh University Press, 1981); D. Vallaud, "Le crime d'infanticide et l'indulgence des cours d'assises en France au XIXème siècle", *Social Science Information* **21**, 1982, pp. 475-99; K. Wrightson, "Infanticide in European history", *Criminal Justice History* **3**, 1982, pp. 1-20. And some earlier work on prostitution: E. Bristow, *Vice and vigilance: purity movements in Britain since 1700* (Dublin: Gill & Macmillan, 1977); R. J. Evans, "Prostitution, state and society in Imperial Germany", *Past and Present* **70**, 1976, pp. 106-29; W. Sanger, *The history of prostitution* (New York: 1859); G. R. Scott, *A history of prostitution from antiquity to the present day* (London: Werner Laurie, 1936); R. D. Storch, "Police control of street prostitution in Victorian London: a study in the contexts of police action", in *Police and society*, D. H. Bayley (ed.) (Beverly Hills: Sage, 1977), pp. 49-71; R. Symanski, *The immoral landscape: female prostitution in Western societies* (Toronto: Butterworths, 1981); E. Trudgill, *Madonnas and magdalens: the origins and development of Victorian sexual attitudes* (London: Heinemann, 1976).

6. G. Rudé, *Criminal and victim: crime and society in early nineteenth-century England* (Oxford: Clarendon, 1985). D. Philips, *Crime and authority in Victorian England: the Black Country 1835-1860* (London: Croom Helm, 1977) is noteworthy amongst the very earliest monographs for containing an index entry for "women".

7. Published soon after Rudé, J. M. Beattie, *Crime and the courts in England 1660-1800* (Oxford: Clarendon, 1986) contained discussion of women as both offenders and victims of crime, and dealt with many aspects of the ways in which women were treated by the courts. On the other hand, as recently as 1996, a textbook on crime and punishment could still contain only token recognition of women rather than an integrated gender analysis: J. Briggs, C. Harrison, A. McInnes, D. Vincent, *Crime and punishment in England: an introductory history* (London: UCL Press, 1996).

8. D. Hay et al. (eds), *Albion's fatal tree: crime and society in eighteenth-century England* (London: Allen Lane, 1975) is probably the best known example of such work. Others include: D. Blasius, *Kriminalität und Alltag*; E. J. Hobsbawm & G. Rudé, *Captain Swing* (London: Lawrence & Wishart, 1969); Rudé, *Criminal and victim*; E. P. Thompson, *Whigs and hunters: the origin of the Black Act* (London: Allen Lane, 1975). More recently, J. Rule and R. Wells in *Crime, protest and popular politics in southern England, 1740-1850* (London: Hambledon, 1997) recognized the "silences" in this approach regarding gender and ethnicity; nevertheless, they had "no reluctance in continuing to write within the tradition" (p. ix). Another recent and original reading in this general school is more successful at integrating

some understanding of the social conditions of women's lives: P. Linebaugh, *The London hanged: crime and civil society in the eighteenth century* (Harmondsworth: Penguin, 1991). The even earlier "Whiggish" approach to crime history pursued in the monumental work of L. Radzinowicz, *A history of English criminal law and its administration from 1750* [5 vols] (London: Stevens & Sons, 1948-1986) only occasionally cast light on matters relevant to women's lives and gender more broadly.

9. An approach pioneered by the likes of J. M. Beattie, "The pattern of crime in England 1660-1800", *Past and Present* **62**, February 1974, pp. 47-95; V. A. C. Gatrell, "The decline of theft and violence in Victorian and Edwardian England", in *Crime and the law: the social history of crime in Western Europe since 1500*, V. A. C. Gatrell, B. Lenman, G. Parker (eds) (London: Europa, 1980), pp. 238-370.

10. Some notable exceptions are: R. B. Shoemaker, *Prosecution and punishment: petty crime and the law in London and rural Middlesex, c. 1660-1725* (Cambridge: Cambridge University Press, 1991) which examined both formal and informal methods of prosecuting misdemeanours, and included gender amongst the various factors that influenced access to the law; A. Farge's nuanced *Fragile lives: violence, power and solidarity in eighteenth-century Paris* (Cambridge, Mass.: Harvard University Press, 1993) made extensive use of police and criminal sources down to summary level; G. Behlmer, "Summary justice and working-class marriage in England, 1870-1940", *Law and History Review* **12**, 1994, pp. 229-75; J. Davis, "A poor man's system of justice: the London police courts in the second half of the nineteenth century", *Historical Journal* **24**, 1984; I. Bauer, "Deviantes Verhalten von Frauen: Selbstbeschränkung und gesellschaftliche Sanktionierung", *Zeitgeschichte* **16**, 1989, pp. 438-47; I. Bauer, "Diebinnen und Betrügerinnen in Wien um die Jahrhundertwende: Zur Sozialgeschichte der Frauenkriminalität", *Jahrbuch des Vereins für Geschichte der Stadt Wien* **44/45**, 1989, pp. 187-227. All this research suggests a range of ways in which women used summary justice to seek redress for wrongs they had suffered, from the early modern period right into the twentieth century, and Stephen Frank's essay in this book points to this too in Russia.

   For earlier centuries, and the very first decades of the period covered by this book, church court records can also prove valuable: A. Clark, "Whores and gossips: sexual reputation in London 1770-1825", in *Current issues in women's history*, Arina Angerman et al. (eds) (London: Routledge, 1989), pp. 231-48; L. Gowing, *Domestic dangers: women, words and sex in early modern London* (Oxford: Clarendon Press, 1996). For discussion of sexual slander in modern secular US jurisdictions, see A. J. King, "Constructing gender: sexual slander in nineteenth-century America", *Law and History Review* **13**, 1995, pp. 63-110.

11. J. Allen, *Sex and secrets: crimes involving Australian women since 1880* (Melbourne & Oxford: Oxford University Press, 1990), p. 8.

12. E. Muir & G. Ruggiero, *History from crime* (Baltimore: Johns Hopkins University Press, 1994), p. viii.

13. For example, by questioning the assumption that "real" levels of crime were revealed by criminal statistics: V. A. C. Gatrell & T. B. Hadden, "Nineteenth-century criminal statistics and their interpretation", in *Nineteenth-century society: essays in the use of quantitative methods for the study of social data* (Cambridge: Cambridge University Press, 1972), pp. 336-96; D. Philips, *Crime and authority*, ch. 2. These were two early interventions. Scholars continue to discuss this funda-

mental point. For some recent interventions, see E. A. Johnson & E. H. Monkkonen (eds), *The civilization of crime: violence in town and country since the Middle Ages* (Urbana: University of Illinois Press, 1996) and J. M. Beattie, "Crime and inequality". And of course socialist redefinition of a "crime" as social dissent was challenging the definition of "crime".

14. B. L. Ingraham, *Political crime in Europe: a comparative study of France, Germany and England* (Berkeley: University of California Press, 1979), p. 6.
15. *Ibid.*, p. 20.
16. *Ibid.*, p. 21.
17. C. Pateman, *The sexual contract* (Cambridge: Polity, 1988).
18. Allen's point in her title *Sex and secrets*.
19. For example, J. M. Beattie, "Women's criminality in the eighteenth century"; P. C. Hoffer & N. E. H. Hull, *Murdering mothers: infanticide in England and New England 1558-1803* (New York: New York University Press, 1984).
20. See later discussion of the essays by Stephen Frank and Peter King in this volume.
21. Allen, *Sex and secrets*; Klein, "Etiology", p. 8, cited in Johnson, "Women as victims", p. 152; Bauer, "Diebinnen und Betrügerinnen", p. 189ff. Many earlier contributions to the social history of crime contained thoughtful though brief references to women within their social contexts: for example, Gatrell, Lenman, Parker (eds), *Crime and the law*; D. Jones, *Crime, protest, community and police in nineteenth-century Britain* (London: Routledge & Kegan Paul, 1982); D. Philips, *Crime and authority* - the latter a good example of a history which included women but would have benefited from a feminist analysis.
22. For example, C. Smart, *Women, crime and criminology: a feminist critique* (London: Routledge & Kegan Paul, 1977) and with J. Brophy (ed.), *Women in law: explorations in law, family and sexuality* (London: Routledge & Kegan Paul, 1985).
23. J. Kelly, "The social relation of the sexes: methodological implications of women's history", *Signs: Journal of Women in Culture and Society* 1, 1976, pp. 809-23.
24. For the modern period, see, for example: Allen, *Sex and secrets*; L. Abrams, "Companionship and conflict: the negotiation of marriage relations in the nineteenth century", in *Gender relations in German history: power, agency and experience from the sixteenth to the twentieth century*, L. Abrams & E. Harvey (eds) (London: UCL Press, 1996); M. L. Arnot, "Infant death, child care and the state: the baby-farming scandal and the first infant life protection legislation of 1872", *Continuity and Change* 9, 1994, pp. 271-311; C. Backhouse, *Petticoats and prejudice: women and law in nineteenth-century Canada* (Toronto: Women's Press, 1991); Bauer, "Deviantes Verhalten von Frauen"; Bauer, "Diebinnen und Betrügerinnen"; G. Bock, *Zwangssterilisation im Nationalsozialismus: Studien zur Rassenpolitik und Frauenpolitik* (Opladen: Westdeutscher Verlag, 1986); B. Brookes, *Abortion in England 1900-1967* (London: Croom Helm, 1988); A. Clark, *Women's silence, men's violence: sexual assault in England 1770-1845* (London: Pandora, 1987); G. Czarnowski, "Frauen als Mütter der 'Rasse': Abtreibungsverfolgung und Zwangseingriff im Nationalsozialismus", in *Unter anderen Umständen. Zur Geschichte der Abtreibung*, Deutsches Hygienemuseum (Berlin: Argon, 1993), pp. 58-72; S. D'Cruze, *Crimes of outrage: sex, violence and Victorian working women* (London: UCL Press, 1998); K. Daniels (ed.) *So much hard work: women and prostitution in Australian history* (Sydney: Allen & Unwin, 1985); M. E. Doggett,

Marriage, wife-beating and the law in Victorian England (Columbia, South Carolina: University of South Carolina Press, 1993); L. Gordon, *Heroes of their own lives: the politics and history of family violence: Boston, 1880-1960* (New York: Viking, 1988); J. Guillais, *La chair de l'autre: le crime passionel au XIXe siècle* (Paris: 1986); Ruth Harris, *Murders and madness: medicine, law, and society in the fin de siècle* (Oxford: Clarendon Press, 1989); A. J. Hammerton, *Cruelty and companionship: conflict in nineteenth-century married life* (London: Routledge, 1992); J. Harsin, *Policing prostitution in nineteenth-century Paris* (Princeton: Princeton University Press, 1985); M. Hartman, *Victorian murderesses: a true history of thirteen respectable French and English women accused of unspeakable crimes* (London: Robson, 1977); M. W. Hill, *Their sisters' keepers: prostitution in New York City, 1830-1870* (Berkeley: University of California Press, 1993); A. McLaren, *A prescription for murder: the Victorian serial killings of Dr Thomas Neill Cream* (Chicago: University of Chicago Press, 1993); L. Mahood, *The magdalenes: prostitution in the nineteenth century* (London: Routledge, 1990); L. J. Reagan, *When abortion was a crime: women, medicine, and law in the United States, 1867-1973* (Berkeley: University of California Press, 1997); R. Rosen, *The lost sisterhood: prostitution in America, 1900-1918* (Baltimore: Johns Hopkins University Press, 1982); A. Ryter, "Abtreibung in Basel zu Beginn des Jahrhunderts", in *Die ungeschriebene Geschichte: historische Frauenforschung: Dokumentation 5. Historikerinnentreffen*, Wiener Historikerinnen (eds.) (Himberg n. Vienna: Wiener Frauenverlag, 1984); R. Schulte, *Sperrbezirke: Tugendhaftigkeit und Prostitution in der bürgerlichen Welt* (Frankfurt a.M.: Syndikat, 1979); R. Schulte, *The village in court: arson, infanticide, and poaching in the court records of Upper Bavaria* (Cambridge: Cambridge University Press, 1994); A-L. Shapiro, *Breaking the codes: female criminality in fin-de-siècle Paris* (Stanford, Calif.: Stanford University Press, 1996); C. Smart (ed.), *Regulating womanhood: historical essays on marriage, motherhood and sexuality* (London: Routledge, 1992); A.-M. Sohn, "The golden age of male adultery: the Third Republic", *Journal of Social History* 28, 1995, pp. 469-90; C. Usborne, "Female voices in male courtrooms: abortion trials in Weimar Germany", in *Coping with sickness: medicine, law and human rights*, J. Woodward & R. Jütte (eds) (Sheffield: European Association for the History of Medicine and Health Publications, forthcoming); J. R. Walkowitz, *City of dreadful delight: narratives of sexual danger in late-Victorian London* (London: Virago, 1992); J. R. Walkowitz, *Prostitution and Victorian society: women, class and the state* (Cambridge: Cambridge University Press, 1980).

For the early modern period: F. E. Dolan, *Dangerous familiars: representations of domestic crime in England, 1550-1700* (Ithaca, N.Y.: Cornell University Press, 1994); J. Kermode & G. Walker (eds), *Women, crime and the courts in early modern England* (London: UCL Press, 1994); A. Rowlands, " 'In great secrecy': the crime of infanticide in Rothenburg ob der Tauber, 1501-1618", *German History* 15, 1997, pp. 179-99; U. Rublack, "The public body: policing abortion in early modern Germany", in *Gender relations in German history*, Abrams & Harvey (eds); and among the wealth of recent literature on witchcraft, for example, W. de Blécourt, "The making of the female witch: reflections on witchcraft and gender in the early modern period" (*Gender and History*, forthcoming); M. Hester, *Lewd women and wicked witches: a study of the dynamics of male domination* (London: Routledge, 1992); L. Roper, *Oedipus and the devil: witchcraft, sexuality, and religion in early modern Europe* (London: Routledge, 1994).

25. Nor witchcraft for the early modern period, for the very fascination of its difference from the modern: scholars have approached it from a variety of perspectives. See also earlier references to infanticide in note 5.

26. J. Allen, *Sex and secrets*, p. 253.

27. R. Schulte, "Infanticide in rural Bavaria in the nineteenth century", in *Interest and emotion: essays on the study of family and kinship*, H. Medick & D. W. Sabean (eds) (Cambridge: Cambridge University Press, 1984), pp. 77-102.

28. J. Walkowitz, *Prostitution and Victorian society*.

29. C. A. Conley, *The unwritten law: criminal justice in Victorian Kent* (Oxford: Oxford University Press, 1991) is a comprehensive study of the subject in the title, integrating gender into the overall framework. Although the analysis leaves something to be desired, at least F. McLynn's *Crime and punishment in eighteenth-century England* (Oxford: Oxford University Press, 1989) contains two chapters on women. Many recent collections of essays contain reasonable coverage of issues relevant to women, though not integrated gender perspectives: for example, L. A. Knafla & S. W. S. Binnie (eds), *Law, society and the state: essays in modern legal history* (Toronto: University of Toronto Press, 1995). For more specific studies, see J. Keown, *Abortion, doctors and the law: some aspects of the legal regulation of abortion in England from 1803 to 1982* (Cambridge: Cambridge University Press, 1988); P. King, "Female offenders, work and lifecycle change in late eighteenth-century London", *Continuity and Change* 11, 1996, pp. 61-90; M. Jackson, *Newborn child murder: women, illegitimacy and the courts in eighteenth-century England* (Manchester: Manchester University Press, 1996); L. Zedner, *Women, crime and custody in Victorian England* (Oxford: Oxford University Press, 1991). Similar influence can be found in early modern material, for example, M. R. Boes, "Women and the penal system in Frankfurt am Main, 1562-1696", *Criminal Justice History* 13, 1992, pp. 61-74.

30. For example, Abrams & Harvey, *Gender relations in German history*; G. Bock & P. Thane (eds), *Maternity and gender policies: women and the rise of the European welfare states 1880s-1950s* (London: Routledge, 1996); L. Davidoff & C. Hall, *Family fortunes: men and women of the English middle class, 1780-1850* (London: Hutchinson, 1987); A. Clark, *The struggle for the breeches: gender and the making of the British working class* (London: Rivers Oram Press, 1995).

31. Zedner's *Women, crime and custody* is a model account of the criminality and punishment of women. Zedner herself admitted that masculinity as much as femininity needs to be taken into account before the patterns of sexual difference can be understood and her examination of women and femininity is an important step in that direction. See also G. Walker & J. Kermode, *Women, crime and the courts*.

32. Kermode & Walker, *Women, crime and the courts*, pp. 20-21.

33. *Ibid.*, p. 21.

34. P. J. Byrne, *Criminal law and the colonial subject: New South Wales, 1810-1830* (Cambridge: Cambridge University Press, 1993); P. C. Cohen, "Unregulated youth: masculinity and murder in the 1830s city", *Radical History Review* 52, Winter 1992, pp. 33-52; Conley, *The unwritten law*; R. Harris, *Murders and madness*; J. Damousie, *Depraved and disorderly: female convicts, sexuality and gender in colonial Australia* (Cambridge: Cambridge University Press, 1997); U. Frevert, *Men of honour: the social and cultural history of the duel* (Oxford: Polity, 1995); E. Harvie, *Youth and the welfare state in Weimar Germany* (Oxford: Oxford

University Press, 1993) who attempted to bring a gendered perspective to bear on the history of Weimar social and welfare policies towards youth, including legal sanctions and informal and formal methods of control and coercion; R. Schulte, *The village in court*; R. Shoemaker, *Gender in English Society 1650-1850* (London: Longman, 1998), last chapter. For the early modern period, see especially the work of Lyndal Roper. There are some useful interventions in the criminological literature: R. E. Dobash, R. P. Dobash, L. Noaks (eds), *Gender and crime* (Cardiff: University of Wales Press, 1995); J. W. Messerschmidt, *Masculinities and crime: critique and reconceptualization of theory* (Lanham, Maryland: Rowman & Littlefield, 1993); T. Newburn & E. A. Stanko (eds), *Just boys doing business? Men, masculinities and crime* (London: Routledge, 1994); S. Walklate, *Gender and crime: an introduction* (London: Prentice Hall, 1995).

35. Cf. Editorial Collective, "Why gender and history?", *Gender & History* 1, 1989, pp. 1-2. Some key masculinity historiography: Davidoff & Hall, *Family fortunes*; T. Kühne (ed.), *Männergeschichte-Geschlechtergeschichte: Männlichkeit im Wandel der Moderne* (Frankfurt a.M.: Campus, 1996); J. A. Mangan & J. Walvin (eds), *Manliness and morality: middle-class masculinity in Britain and America 1800-1940* (Manchester: Manchester University Press, 1987); M. Roper & J. Tosh, (eds), *Manful assertions: masculinities in Britain since 1800* (London: Routledge, 1991); K. Theweleit, *Male fantasies*, vol. 1: *Women, floods, bodies, history*; vol. 2: *Male bodies: psychoanalysing the white terror* (Cambridge: Polity Press, 1987 (vol. 1); 1989 (vol. 2)); A.-C. Trepp, *Sanfte Männlichkeit und selbstständige Weiblichkeit: Frauen und Männer im Hamburger Bürgertum zwischen 1770 und 1840* (Göttingen: Vandenhoeck & Ruprecht, 1996); G. Vögler & K. von Welck (eds), *Männerbande, Männerbünde: zur Rolle des Mannes im Kulturvergleich*, [2 vols] (Cologne: Rautenstrauth-Joest Museum, 1990).

   For the early modern period, see for example: L. Roper "Blood and codpieces: masculinity in the early modern German town" and "Stealing manhood; capitalism and magic in early modern Germany", both in *Oedipus and the devil: witchcraft, sexuality and religion in early modern Europe*, L. Roper (London: Routledge, 1994), pp. 107-24, 125-44.

36. Some of the central work in both areas contains gendered perspectives, and some less so. On punishment, see for example: R. P. Dobash, R. E. Dobash, S. Gutteridge, *The imprisonment of women* (Oxford: Blackwell, 1986); F. Egmond, "Gender aspects of public punishment; a European pattern", paper presented at the international conference on "Gender and crime in Britain and Europe, early modern and modern", Roehampton Institute London, 1995; R. J. Evans, *Rituals of retribution: capital punishment in Germany, 1600-1987* (Oxford: Oxford University Press, 1996); V. A. C. Gatrell, *The hanging tree: execution and the English people 1770-1868* (Oxford: Oxford University Press, 1994); L. Mahood, *Policing gender, class and family: Britain 1850-1940* (London: UCL Press, 1995); N. Morris & D. J. Rothman (eds), *The Oxford history of the prison: the practice of punishment in Western society* (New York & Oxford: Oxford University Press, 1995); C. Naish, *Death comes to the maiden: sex and execution 1431-1933* (London: Routledge, 1991); L. Zedner, *Women, crime and custody*.

   And on policing: R. Bessel, "The people's police and gender: male police and female society in eastern Germany: 1945-1950", paper presented at conference "Gender and crime in Britain and Europe, early modern and modern", Roehampton Institute London, 1995, to appear in *Polizeieinsatz im kalten Krieg: Reform und*

Alltag der 'Sicherheitskräfte' in West- und Ostdeutschland, G. Fürmetz, H. Reinke, K. Weinhauer (eds) (forthcoming); C. Emsley, *The English police: a political and social history*, 2nd edn (London: Longman, 1996); M. Finnane (ed.), *Policing in Australia: historical perspectives* (Kensington, NSW: New South Wales University Press, 1987); D. Hay & F. Snyder (eds), *Policing and prosecution in Britain 1750-1850* (Oxford: Clarendon, 1989); G. E. Myers, *A municipal mother: Portland's Lola Greene Baldwin, America's first policewoman* (Corvallis: Oregan State University Press, 1995); U. Nienhaus, "Difference versus equality: female police in Nazi Germany", paper presented at conference "Gender and crime in Britain and Europe, early modern and modern", Roehampton Institute London, 1995; D. Taylor, *The new police in nineteenth-century England: crime, conflict and control* (Manchester: Manchester University Press, 1997).

37. Beattie, "The criminality of women", p. 80.
38. M. Feeley, "The decline of women in the criminal process: a comparative history", *Criminal Justice History* **15**, 1994, pp. 235-74. See also Feeley & D. L. Little, "The vanishing female: the decline of women in the criminal process, 1687-1912", *Law and Society Review* **25**, 1991, pp. 719-57.
39. For findings of significant decreases in women's participation in the criminal justice process from the mid-nineteenth to early twentieth centuries in England and Germany respectively, see: Zedner, *Women, crime and custody*; Johnson, "Women as victims and criminals".
40. For example, Beattie, "The criminality of women"; Zedner, *Women, crime and custody*.
41. Feeley & Little, "The vanishing female"; cf. Stephen Frank's essay in this volume.
42. Johnson, "Women as victims and criminals", p. 171.
43. Feeley, "The decline of women".
44. S. Frank, "Women and crime in Imperial Russia, 1834-1913: representing realities", this volume, p. 95.
45. S. Frank, "Women and crime in Imperial Russia", p. 95.
46. *Feme covert* was an assumption in English common law that stipulated that a married woman was "covered" by her husband. It had many well-known implications in civil law - for example, all the restrictions on married women's property rights. In criminal law, when a woman committed an offence with her husband, she could argue that she was acting under her husband's instructions in order to gain aquittal. This did not apply in cases of major felony, such as murder.
47. R. Siebert, *Secrets of life and death: women and the Mafia* (London: Verso, 1996), p. 8.
48. Unfortunately, committed elsewhere, and now published as "The Victorian criminalization of men", in *Men and violence: gender, honor and rituals in modern Europe and America*, P. Spierenburg (ed.) (Columbus: Ohio State University Press, 1998), pp. 197-212.
49. Feeley & Little, "The vanishing female" - and an example can be found in Godfrey, this volume.
50. John Beattie has recently argued for an approach to criminal statistics that takes such a "dual" view: Beattie, "Crime and inequality".
51. C. Ginzburg, "Microhistory: two or three things I know about it", *Critical Inquiry* **20**, 1993, pp. 10-34; G. Levi, "On microhistory", in *New perspectives on historical writing*, P. Burke (ed.) (Cambridge: Polity, 1991), pp. 93-113; E. Muir, "Introduction: observing trifles", in *Microhistory and the lost peoples of Europe: selections from*

Quaderni Storici, E. Muir & G. Ruggiero (eds) (Baltimore: Johns Hopkins University Press, 1991), pp. vii–xxviii; T. Kuehn, "Reading microhistory: the example of *Giovanni and Lusanna*", *Journal of Modern History* **61**, 1989, pp. 512–34; for an interesting methodological exploration of the scope and limits of microhistory, see F. Egmond & P. Mason, *The mammoth and the mouse: microhistory and morphology* (Baltimore: Johns Hopkins University Press, 1997). Nothing better exemplifies this historiographic shift than the work of V. A. C. Gatrell. Compare his earlier quantitative pieces - e.g. Gatrell & Hadden, "Nineteenth-century criminal statistics and their interpretation" and Gatrell, "The decline of theft and violence" - with his recent *The hanging tree*, which displays adroit hermeneutic skills and is rich with thick description. Historians of early modern Italy have been particularly influential in the development of crime microhistory, influenced strongly by Carlo Ginzburg, especially his *The cheese and the worms: the cosmos of a sixteenth-century miller* (London: Routledge & Kegan Paul, 1980); the journal *Quaderni Storici* has published much of the work. This approach was first taken up more widely by early modern scholars; for example, J. C. Brown, *Immodest acts: the life of a lesbian nun in Renaissance Italy* (New York & Oxford: Oxford University Press, 1986); R. Darnton, *The great cat massacre and other episodes in French cultural history* (London: Allen Lane, 1984); N. Z. Davis, *The return of Martin Guerre* (Cambridge, Mass.: Harvard University Press, 1983). Microhistory and anthropological approaches continue to flourish in early-modern history and have dominated in recent German scholarship, possibly because of the strong origins of criminal justice history in earlier witchcraft studies in that country: A. Blauert & G. Schwerhoff, "Crime and history - The German workshop 'Historische Kriminalitätsforschung in der Vormoderne' 'Early modern crime and criminal justice history' ", *Crime, Histoire & Sociétés/Crime, History & Societies* **2**, 1998, pp. 137–40. Muir & Ruggiero (eds), *History from crime* (Baltimore: Johns Hopkins University Press, 1994) includes microhistories from both early-modern and modern Italian history. Regina Schulte was a pioneer in modern scholarship influenced by anthropological approaches: "Infanticide in rural Bavaria"; Schulte, *The village in court*; and R. Evans has recently published a key modern microhistorical crime study: *Tales from the German underworld: crime and punishment in the nineteenth century* (New Haven: Yale University Press, 1998). See also: P. Guarnieri, *A case of child murder: law and science in nineteenth-century Tuscany* (Cambridge: Polity Press, 1993); Gatrell, *The hanging tree*; B. Reay, *Microhistories: demography, society and culture in rural England, 1800–1930* (Cambridge: Cambridge University Press, 1996).

52. E.g. Gatrell, *The hanging tree*.
53. E.g. Schulte, *The village in court*; Walkowitz, *City of dreadful delight*.
54. J. J. Tobias, *Crime and industrial society in the nineteenth century* (London: Batsford, 1967), argued that "criminal statistics have little to tell us about crime and criminals in the nineteenth century" (p. 21), choosing to base his study on textual sources.
55. L. Jackson, *Child sexual abuse and the law: London 1870–1914* (PhD thesis, Roehampton Institute London, 1997), p. 46. Both Shore and Jackson in this volume build on some key historiography on gendered juvenile delinquency, for example L. Mahood & B. Littlewood, "The 'vicious girl' and the 'street-corner boy': sexuality and the gendered delinquent in the Scottish child-saving movement 1850–1940", *Journal of the History of Sexuality* **4**, 1994, pp. 549–78.

56. B. Taithe, "Consuming desires: prostitutes and customers at the margins of crime and perversion in nineteenth-century France and Britain", this volume, p. 153.

57. Hay et al. (eds), *Albion's fatal tree*, p. 13.

58. M. Foucault, *An introduction*, vol. 1 of *The history of sexuality* (Harmondsworth: Penguin, 1981), p. 94. See the overall arguments in this book and his *Discipline and punish: the birth of the prison* (Harmondsworth: Penguin, 1977) for the major development of his thesis about power.

59. Foucault talked about examining "power at its extremities": M. Foucault, "Two lectures", in *Power knowledge: selected interviews and other writings, 1972-1977*, M. Morris & P. Patton (eds) (Sydney: Feral Publications, 1979), p. 96.

60. The range of work here is simply too vast to cite even a representative sample, so here are just a few examples: the collection edited by S. Cohen & A. Scull, *Social control and the state* (London: Martin Robertson, 1983) contained essays on everything from theory to criminal justice systems, punishment, psychiatry and reformatories; see also S. Cohen, *Visions of social control* (Cambridge: Polity, 1985); J. Donzelot, *The policing of families: welfare versus the state* (New York: Pantheon, 1979); Harvie, *Youth and the welfare state*; Mahood, *Policing gender, class and family*. An example of the porous boundaries now marking out the territory of "crime and criminal justice history": the new journal *Crime, Histoire & Sociétés / Crime, History & Societies* - the organ of the International Association for the History of Crime and Criminal Justice - chose in its second issue to include an article about the family and community as sources of social control in an eighteenth-century French town: "Les chemins du contrôle social entre famille et communauté: le cas de Saint-Victor-de-la-Coste en Bas-Languedoc, au XVIIIe siècle", *Crime, Histoire & Sociétés* 2, 1997, pp. 29-50. See also L. A. Knafla & S. W. S. Binnie (eds), *Law, society and the state: essays in modern legal history* (Toronto: University of Toronto Press, 1995).

61. For example, V. Bell, *Interrogating incest: feminism, Foucault and the law* (London: Routledge, 1993); J. Butler, *Gender trouble: feminism and the subversion of identity* (London: Routledge, 1990); I Diamond & L. Quinby (eds), *Feminism and Foucault: reflections on resistance* (Boston: Northeastern University Press, 1988); C. Ramazoglu, *Up against Foucault: explorations of some tensions between Foucault and feminism* (London: Routledge, 1993); J. Sawicki, *Disciplining Foucault: feminism, power, and the body* (London: Routledge, 1991); C. Weedon, *Feminist practice and poststructuralist theory* (Oxford: Basil Blackwell, 1987). Cf. C. Jones & R. Porter (eds), *Reassessing Foucault: power, medicine and the body* (London: Routledge, 1996).

62. For example, three of the very earliest theoretical interventions: S. Firestone, *The dialectic of sex: the case for feminist revolution* (New York: Morrow, 1970); K. Millett, *Sexual politics* (New York: Doubleday, 1970); J. Mitchell, *Woman's estate* (Harmondsworth: Penguin, 1971).

63. See, for example, Bell, *Interrogating incest*.

64. D. Riley, *"Am I that name?" Feminism and the category of "women" in history* (London: Macmillan, 1988), pp. 1-2.

65. P. L. Berger & T. Luckman, *The social construction of reality: a treatise in the sociology of knowledge* (London: Allen Lane, 1967).

66. See D. Downes & P. Rock, *Understanding deviance: a guide to the sociology of crime and rule breaking*, 2nd revised edn (Oxford: Clarendon, 1995) for a useful outline of different theoretical perspectives in this field.

67. The obvious exceptions are the purposeful killing of enemy soldiers in conditions of war and the continued use of the death penalty in some states in the United States, although in both cases both principles and definitions have been hotly disputed (the legitimacy of the use of state violence as a penal sanction; the definition of "conditions of war", for example, in Northern Ireland; the distinction between "enemy soldier" and "civilian" in a geurilla war, and so on).

68. Arnot, "Infant death"; Schulte, "Infanticide in rural Bavaria"; Usborne, "Female voices in male courtrooms"; Usborne, "Abortion for sale! the competition between quacks and doctors in Weimar Germany", in *Illness and healing alternatives in Western Europe*, M. Gijswijt-Hofstra, H. Marland, H. de Waardt (eds) (London: Routledge, 1997), pp. 183-204.

69. C. Usborne, *The politics of the body in Weimar Germany: women's reproductive rights and duties* (London: Macmillan, 1992), ch. 4.

70. R. Schulte, *The village in court*, p. 11.

71. Her work as a whole takes this deconstruction as its central project, but see especially Davidoff & Hall, *Family fortunes*; Davidoff, "Regarding some 'old husbands' tales': public and private in feminist history", in her *Worlds between: historical perspectives on gender and class* (Cambridge: Polity, 1995), pp. 227-76.

72. Kermode & Walker, *Women, crime and the courts*, p. 8.

73. Allen, *Sex and secrets*.

74. J. W. Scott, "Gender: a useful category of historical analysis", *American Historical Review* 91, 1986, pp. 1053-75, pp. 1067, 1069 now reprinted in Scott, *Gender and the politics of history* (New York: Columbia University Press, 1989).

75. Scott in *ibid.* highlighted this relation, and since then in the British context, Davidoff & Hall, *Family fortunes* and A. Clark, *The struggle for the breeches* have demonstrated ways in which this has worked for middle-class and working-class formation and identity respectively.

76. Ute Frevert's identification of the nineteenth-century German duel as bourgeois is controversial. Some other scholars see it as an aristocratic survival: V. G. Kiernan, *The duel in European history: honour and reign of the aristocracy* (Oxford: Oxford University Press, 1988). K. McAleer argues that it was entirely antithetical to liberal bourgeois values: *Dueling: the cult of honor in fin-de-siècle Germany* (Princeton: Princeton University Press, 1994). For early nineteenth-century England, A. E. Simpson argues that the revived popularity of duelling can be explained by upwardly mobile middle-class gentlemen adopting aristocratic values in a society where the aristocracy still held very significant power and influence: "Dandelions in the field of honor: dueling, the middle classes, and the law in nineteenth-century England", *Criminal Justice History* 9, 1988, pp. 99-155.

77. Ute Frevert has not explicitly made this point, but it is implied by the material presented in her chapter.

78. Valeria Pizzini-Gambetta, "Gender norms in the Sicilian Mafia, 1945-86", this volume, p. 269.

79. Other historians of the Mafia concur with Pizzini's conclusions about the murder of women: J. Follain, *A dishonoured society* (London: Little, Brown & Co., 1995); R. Siebert, *Secrets of life and death: women and the Mafia* (London: Verso, 1996), especially pp. 136-42.

80. Ann-Louise Shapiro, "'Stories more terrifying than the truth itself': narratives of female criminality in *fin de siècle* Paris", this volume, p. 204.

81. Zedner, *Women, crime and custody*, p. 2.

82. A. Clark, "Humanity or justice? Wifebeating and the law in the eighteenth and nineteenth centuries", in *Regulating womanhood*, C. Smart (ed.), pp. 187-206, p. 191.

83. Some scholars share at least part of Frevert's interest in the gender dynamics of duelling - for example, J. Kelly, *"That damn'd thing called honour": duelling in Ireland 1570-1860* (Cork: Cork University Press, 1995); McAleer, *Dueling* - yet others have analysed it purely through the lens of class: Kiernan, *The duel*; A. E. Simpson, "Dandelions in the field of honor".

84. Taithe, this volume, p. 152.

85. E.g. Harsin, *Policing prostitution*; Walkowitz, *Prostitution in Victorian society*.

86. B. Taithe, "Consuming desires: prostitutes and 'customers' at the margins of crime and perversion in France and Britain *c*. 1836-85", this volume, p. 155.

87. *Ibid*, p. 156.

88. L. Jackson, *Child sexual abuse and the law*.

89. C. Lonrigg, *Mafia women* (London: Chatto & Windus, 1997). One of the problems with this book is that the author slips between discussion of different criminal organizations of Italian origin, and even crosses the Atlantic, whereas Pizzini, quite rightly, is rigorous in her focus on the Sicilian Mafia only (as distinct from the Neopolitan Camorra, for example) - for drawing distinctions *between* the organizations was one of the key functions of rules and initiation rituals. So it isn't sufficiently clear whether Lonrigg's conclusions about women's involvement in Italian organized crime are entirely reliable for the Sicilian Mafia *per se*.

90. R. Siebert, too, in *Secrets of life and death: women and the Mafia* (London: Verso, 1996) has compared the terrorism of the Nazi regime with the "all-embracing system of surveillance, terror and blackmail" established by the Mafia (p. 3). On the other hand, she strongly denounces the complicity of Mafia women and the impunity which has protected them until recently, without fully exploring the possibility that many of these women may have been psychologically annihilated by the regime of terror within which they lived, making ascription of responsibility an extremely difficult issue - as it is, for example, when discussing the German civilian population living in the vicinity of Nazi extermination facilities during the Holocaust.

Chapter 2

ᴣᏚ

Gender, crime and justice in late eighteenth- and early nineteenth-century England[1]

Peter King

Current work on gender, crime and justice in eighteenth- and nineteenth-century England includes remarkably little research on the impact of gender at two of the fulcrum points of the criminal justice system – the verdicts and sentences passed by the major courts. The general texts on crime and punishment in this period give no clear indication about whether these decisions were affected by the sex of the accused, and even the recent books written by Conley and Zedner, which foreground gender issues, offer only occasional insights into the core question this paper is concerned with – to what extent did gender affect trial outcomes?[2] Although his much quoted article on "The criminality of women in eighteenth-century England" did not cover these issues, John Beattie's pathbreaking monograph *Crime and the courts in England 1660–1800* does, however, provide a number of significant, if scattered, insights based on the Surrey evidence.[3] The first section of this study follows Beattie's work in concentrating primarily on property crime and on the major courts, but it uses a much larger sample of over 11,000 cases and focuses on a different and shorter period by using selected years between the 1780s and the 1820s. The core data was collected directly from the records of the Old Bailey, which covered London and Middlesex, and from those of the Home Circuit, which covered Essex, Surrey, Sussex, Kent and Hertfordshire.[4] This was then supplemented by evidence from Lancashire and the Northern Assizes Circuit, the only jurisdictions which supplied the early nineteenth-century Parliamentary committees with separate data on male and female offenders.[5] The second section of this chapter then briefly uses work on other crimes and other courts to assess the typicality of these results, before moving on to use early modern and twentieth-century research as a means of exploring elements of continuity and change in the relationship between judicial outcomes and gender. Finally, the paper discusses the potential relevance of the explanatory frameworks developed by modern criminologists and then briefly explores a number of factors that need to be more deeply researched before any attempt can be made to explain the highly gendered nature of trial outcomes visible in the period 1780-1830.

Gender and trial outcomes in major property crime cases

Both the courts chosen for detailed study here were near the apex of the criminal justice system. The county assizes and their rough equivalents in London and Middlesex, the Old Bailey sessions, had jurisdiction over all capital offences. They also heard a very considerable proportion of non-capital property crimes. The precise division of responsibility for grand and petty larceny cases (hereafter referred to as simple larceny) between the quarter sessions and the assizes courts differed between counties[6] and these differences are reflected in the proportion of simple larceny cases among the Old Bailey and Assizes accused, seen in Table 2.1. In the late eighteenth and early nineteenth centuries an average of around two-fifths of those tried on the Home Circuit were indicted for simple, non-capital larcenies, whilst the equivalent figure at the Old Bailey was three fifths.[7] However, although the information available from these two sources is not identical, and was created at slightly different

Table 2.1 Gender and types of property crime indictment. Old Bailey and Home Circuit, 1780s-1820s

Type of crime	Old Bailey		Home Circuit	
	Male %	Female %	Male %	Female %
Simple theft	63.3	64.2	41.3	37.0
Private stealing	12.3	19.5	1.9	13.1
Stealing from dwelling house	3.4	3.4	3.7	6.9
Sheep and cow stealing	0.4	0.1	5.6	0.9
Horse stealing	0.8	0.0	6.6	0.0
Burglary / housebreaking	5.7	1.0	21.7	17.7
Robbery	6.3	4.6	11.6	7.5
Receiving	1.9	3.1	2.4	6.9
Coining / uttering	1.2	1.5	1.3	4.9
Fraud / Indirect appropriation	4.6	2.7	4.0	5.3
Total	99.9	100.1	100.1	100.2
Sample size	5096	1515	3988	452

Sources:

a Old Bailey: PRO HO26/1-2 and 26/26-28. Sample years October 1791 - September 1793: October 1820 - September 1822. Crimes not involving direct or indirect appropriation are excluded. Data collected for Old Bailey London and Middlesex prisoners only.

b Home Circuit. PRO Assi 31/13-15 (Summer assizes 1782 to Summer 1787); Assi 31/18-19 (Summer 1799 - Lent 1801); Assi 31/23-24 (1820-1); Assi 31/25 (1827).

stages in the trial process, they are broadly comparable since each was the major criminal court in its region.[8]

The Old Bailey data on verdicts (see Table 2.2) indicates clearly that female property offenders awaiting trial in London had much better prospects than their male counterparts. The majority of men (61 per cent) were convicted. The majority of women were not. Only 44 per cent of the female accused were found guilty. Women were nearly twice as likely to avoid public trial completely, either because their victims failed to turn up and prosecute them or because the grand jurors brought "not found" verdicts, thus dismissing the prosecution case before it could be presented in open court. Women also attracted a considerably higher percentage of not guilty verdicts. The combined effects of these two processes meant that males accused of property crime in late eighteeth- and early nineteenth-century London were 40 per cent more likely than their female equivalents to be convicted.

Once convicted, male offenders were also subjected to a harsher range of punishments than females (see Table 2.3). Eight per cent of women were fined and immediately released compared to five per cent of males. Whipping had long been used predominantly against men and after 1820 the law no longer permitted the whipping of women.[9] Imprisonment (which seldom lasted more than a year) was the most popular sentence for women, while transportation (which would usually be for seven to fourteen years) was the court's most frequent sentencing strategy for male offenders. Eight per cent of women were sentenced to death compared to 13 per cent of men but in reality the death penalty itself was reserved almost exclusively for men. Only one female property offender actually reached the gallows in the years sampled here (i.e. 0.15 per cent). Eighty-nine males met that fate (2.85 per cent). Amongst those sentenced to imprisonment women got only a marginally better deal than men, but nearly half spent six months or less in gaol and only a fifth were incarcerated for more than a year. Transportation may have been considered a better option by some younger prisoners – a number of contemporaries certainly feared that it was.[10] However, since most of those sentenced to transportation spent many months in gaol or on the hulks awaiting shipment, a sentence of transportation usually involved a longer period of incarceration than one of imprisonment – as well as separation from family and friends and the prospect of being subjected to the variety of often harsh regimes being developed in Australia.[11] Transportation would rarely have been a better option than imprisonment from the convict's point of view and those in charge of sentencing clearly saw the former as a heavier sanction.

The impact of gender on sentencing policies can be overemphasized. Many women were subjected to tough penalties. Nearly two-fifths of female convicts were either sentenced directly to transportation or given that punishment after being reprieved from a death sentence. The early nineteenth-century ban on the whipping of women did mean that, while many men were sentenced to whipping and imprisonment, women did not have to suffer this double penalty. However, although the Old Bailey increasingly used fines instead of

Table 2.2 Old Bailey property offenders. Verdicts analysed by gender, 1791–1822

Outcome	All property offenders		Simple larceny		Private stealing		Robbery	
	Male %	Female %	Male %	Female %	Male %	Female %	Male %	Female %
Failed to reach court / Died in gaol	1.9	1.0	1.2	0.7	0.0	0.0	8.8	5.8
Discharged – no prosecution or "Not Found"	12.9	25.1	13.3	23.4	16.1	41.0	16.6	14.5
Not guilty	23.9	30.2	21.7	28.8	20.5	28.5	36.9	49.3
Guilty	61.0	43.7	63.8	47.1	63.0	30.5	37.8	30.4
Verdict unknown	0.2	0.0	0.1	0.0	0.5	0.0	0.0	0.0
Total %	99.9	100.0	100.1	100.0	100.1	100.0	100.1	100.0
Sample size	5096	1515	3225	972	629	295	320	69

Source: see Table 2.1(a)

Table 2.3 Old Bailey property offenders. Sentences analysed by gender, 1791–1822

Sentence	All property offenders		Simple larceny		Private stealing		Robbery	
	Male %	Female %	Male %	Female %	Male %	Female %	Male %	Female %
Fined	5.4	8.3	7.5	11.1	2.3	3.3	0.0	0.0
Whipped (publicly or privately)	6.2	1.1	8.5	0.9	4.3	2.2	0.0	0.0
Imprisoned	32.3	50.0	41.0	60.1	18.8	43.3	4.1	4.8
Transported	42.5	32.6	40.5	26.0	71.9	47.8	12.4	33.3
Sentence to death and reprieved	10.4	7.9	2.2	2.0	1.5	3.3	57.0	57.1
Hanged	2.9	0.2	0.3	0.0	0.5	0.0	26.5	4.8
Punishment unknown	0.3	0.0	0.2	0.0	0.8	0.0	0.0	0.0
Total	100.0	100.1	100.2	100.1	100.1	99.9	100.0	100.0
Sample size	3127	662	2054	458	399	90	121	21

Source: see Table 2.1(a)

whipping for female offenders, some female convicts who would have been whipped and released in the eighteenth century almost certainly suffered imprisonment instead, once the whipping of women became unlawful in 1820. Thus the impact of changes in both legal frameworks and sentencing attitudes was often complex and contradictory, but significant gender-based differences in sentencing policy are clearly observable. By the 1820s almost all female property offenders were avoiding the direct physical punishments of whipping and hanging, whilst finding it relatively easy to attract sentences such as fining or imprisonment, which were usually regarded as much less intrusive and punitive than transportation. Amongst property offenders at least, the great intrusion, death, was reserved almost entirely for men in late eighteenth- and early nineteenth-century London.

Since the first two columns in Tables 2.2 and 2.3 all relate to a very broad category of offences, i.e. all types of property theft, from stealing a loaf of bread to highly lucrative robberies accompanied with violence, it remains possible that women received more lenient treatment from the courts because they less frequently committed the most serious offences. As Table 2.1 indicates, the proportions of both male and female offenders being indicted for simple larceny were very similar, but women were considerably under-represented among offences such as house-breaking, horse stealing and robbery, which attracted the heaviest sentences. It is therefore necessary to look at verdict and sentencing patterns for a number of individual offences. Once we control for type of offence do women still get noticeably more lenient treatment from the courts? The data on simple larceny alone in Tables 2.2 and 2.3 suggests that they do.[12]

The pattern of verdicts is very similar to that found for all property offenders. Women were much more likely to avoid public trial and more likely to be found not guilty if they were tried by a petty jury in open court. While 64 per cent of male larcenists were convicted, only 47 per cent of females indicted for simple larceny suffered the same fate. Sentencing patterns showed parallel similarities. Males were as likely to be transported as to be imprisoned.[13] Only a quarter of females were transported while three-fifths were imprisoned. Did women also receive more favourable treatment when they were accused of capital crimes? Since the only categories of capital crime in which more than 60 female offenders were involved were privately stealing (from the shop or person) and highway robbery, these were the two selected for detailed scrutiny.

In London women accused of shoplifting or of picking pockets[14] received remarkably lenient treatment compared to men (Tables 2.2 and 2.3). They were two-and-a-half times more likely to be discharged before public trial and a third more likely to attract a "Not guilty" verdict if they reached that stage. Sixty-three per cent of males accused of private stealing were found guilty. Thirty-one per cent of females suffered the same fate. Sentencing policies were slightly less polarized but the pattern was equally clear. While men were three times more likely to be transported than to be either imprisoned or fined, women's chances were roughly equal. In robbery cases (Tables 2.2 and 2.3) gendered differences were much smaller at the verdict stage. The relatively

49

small number of women indicted for robbery (69) were only slightly less likely than the men to avoid public trial. The main differences in robbery cases came in sentencing and pardoning policy. Thirty-eight per cent of women but only 17 per cent of men were sentenced to either transportation or imprisonment – presumably because the jury had brought in a partial verdict. Fifty-seven per cent of both men and women were sentenced to death but then reprieved. Twenty-seven per cent of males (32 individuals) went to the gallows for robbery in the four years sampled. One woman (4.8 per cent) found herself unable to avoid the fatal tree.

Were trial outcomes equally gendered on the Home Circuit 1782–1827? Tables 2.4 and 2.5 suggest that the pattern was remarkably similar. Since the Home Circuit agenda books did not systematically record cases discharged before public trial, female offenders' capacity to obtain much more lenient treatment at this stage – seen clearly in the Old Bailey evidence (Table 2.2) – cannot be analysed outside London but the Home Circuit pattern of "Guilty / Not guilty" verdicts for all property offenders (Table 2.4) is very similar to that found at the Old Bailey (Table 2.2). Female property offenders were 40 per cent more likely than their male equivalents to attract a "Not guilty" verdict. The Home Circuit data also indicates that they were more than 50 per cent more likely to attract a partial verdict (in which the jury downgraded the charge and then convicted on a lesser one)[15] rather than a full conviction. The Home Circuit judges used fining and whipping much less frequently than their Old Bailey counterparts.[16] They also used the death sentence more often than the London court – presumably because a much higher percentage of those indicted before them were accused of major capital crimes (Table 2.1). Despite these factors gender made a very similar impact on sentencing policies at both the Home Circuit assizes and the Old Bailey (Tables 2.5 and 2.3). More than three-fifths of Home Circuit female property offenders were imprisoned, and only a fifth were sentenced to death. A third of males were imprisoned and two-fifths sentenced to death. As at the Old Bailey, capitally convicted women found it very much easier to get a reprieve. Seven female property offenders reached the gallows in the 10 years sampled (2.6 per cent of the female convicted), compared to 317 males (11.6 per cent).

The similarities are equally marked when the Home Circuit data is analysed for specific categories of crime (Tables 2.4 and 2.5). At both the Old Bailey and on the Home Circuit females accused of simple larceny gained about a third more acquittals than the males. Sentencing policies in Home Circuit simple larceny cases (Table 2.5) once again favoured imprisonment more for women than for men and reserved transportation mainly for the latter. In robbery cases the assizes pattern was even more polarized than that found at the Old Bailey. Females received nearly twice as many acquittals as males and were four times more likely to attract a partial verdict. The combined effect of these two processes was that only 18 per cent of women were found guilty as charged compared to 59 per cent of men (Table 2.4). Jurors appear to have been trying to avoid convicting women on the full charge knowing that highway robbery

Table 2.4 Home Circuit. All property offenders. Verdicts analysed by gender, 1782–1827

Outcome	All property offenders		Simple larceny		Housebreaking		Robbery		Private stealing		Stealing in dwelling house	
	Male %	Female %	Male %	Female %	Male %	Female %	Male %	Female %	Male %	Female %	Male %	Female %
Not guilty	27.7	38.9	28.0	37.1	19.8	30.0	32.6	61.8	32.0	37.3	24.5	29.0
Guilty	57.2	44.3	62.9	58.0	48.0	28.8	58.8	17.7	40.0	39.0	38.1	29.0
Partial verdict	9.3	14.4	3.3	4.2	25.9	31.3	5.2	20.6	24.0	23.7	33.3	41.9
Unknown / Failed to reach trial	5.8	2.4	5.8	0.6	6.3	10.0	3.5	0.0	4.0	0.0	4.1	0.0
Total	100.0	100.0	100.0	99.9	100.0	100.1	100.1	100.1	100.0	100.0	100.0	99.9
Sample size	3988	452	1645	167	864	80	463	34	75	59	147	31

Source: Table 2.1(b)

Table 2.5 Home Circuit, all property offenders. Sentences analysed by gender, 1782–1827

Sentence	All property offenders		Simple larceny		Housebreaking		Robbery		Private stealing		Stealing in dwelling house	
	Male %	Female %	Male %	Female %	Male %	Female %	Male %	Female %	Male %	Female %	Male %	Female %
Fined	1.4	1.1	2.9	2.9	0.2	0.0	0.0	0.0	0.0	0.0	0.0	0.0
Whipped (publicly or privately)	1.2	3.4	2.5	7.7	0.5	0.0	0.0	0.0	2.0	2.6	0.0	0.0
Imprisoned	33.9	61.9	63.5	81.7	13.5	35.4	5.3	46.2	57.1	50.0	24.8	45.5
Transported	19.8	12.8	26.3	6.7	16.7	16.7	6.3	7.7	28.6	18.4	25.7	18.2
Sentence to death and reprieved	29.1	17.7	0.9	1.0	48.9	43.8	47.2	23.1	8.2	26.3	45.7	36.4
Hanged	11.6	2.6	0.4	0.0	18.4	4.2	38.6	23.1	4.1	2.6	3.8	0.0
Punishment unknown	3.0	0.4	3.6	0.0	1.8	0.0	2.6	0.0	0.0	0.0	0.0	0.0
Total	100.0	99.9	100.1	100.0	100.0	100.1	100.0	100.1	100.0	99.9	100.0	100.1
Sample size	2726	265	1128	104	651	48	303	13	49	38	105	22

Source: Table 2.1(b)

Table 2.6 County Palatine of Lancaster. Conviction and execution rates for capital crimes analysed by gender, 1798-1818

Offence	% of commitals leading to conviction		% of convicted that were hanged		Sample sizes (commitals)	
	Male %	Female %	Male %	Female %	Male No.	Female No.
Shooting, etc.						
intent to murder	34	–	20	–	29	0
Murder	12	2	100	100	86	44
Rape	33	–	25	–	12	0
Sodomy	35	–	100	–	17	0
Arson	43	0	83	–	14	1
Burglary and theft						
in dwelling house	64	39	19	7	248	36
Horse, cow and						
sheep stealing	74	0	5	–	108	1
Highway robbery	60	45	38	0	135	11
Private stealing						
from person/shop	23	30	0	0	13	23
Croft breaking	72	0	15	0	36	2
Coining and uttering	88	90	0	0	8	10
Forgery	47	47	58	14	189	30
Miscellaneous offences	94	100	18	0	18	5
All types of capital						
crime	54.5	33.7	29.9	7.3	913	163

Source: P.P. (1819), 8, pp. 228-35

attracted fewer pardons than any other form of theft. Because of this, three of the 13 female robbers found guilty (23 per cent) were actually hanged. In the same years 117 males (39 per cent) went to the gallows. The Home Circuit data on housebreaking and stealing in the dwelling house follows similar lines, and only the relatively small number indicted for privately stealing do not show highly gendered sentencing patterns.[17] Overall, therefore, the pattern is clear. At the Old Bailey and at the Home Circuit assizes women were less likely to be convicted and more likely to be given a range of sanctions which both judges and juries considered to be more lenient.

Was this pattern also found in other parts of England? The limited data available on Lancashire and on the Northern Circuit assizes[18] suggests that it was. In Lancashire between 1798 and 1818, 54.5 per cent of the male accused committed for capital crimes were described as convicted, compared to 33.7 per cent of women (see Table 2.6). Thirty per cent of capitally convicted men went to the gallows in Lancashire. Seven per cent of women went with them. This pattern is particularly marked amongst those accused of highway robbery, housebreaking and stealing from the dwelling house, while in forgery

Table 2.7 Northern Circuit assizes: verdicts and punishments analysed by gender, 1804 only

(a) Verdicts	Male %	Female %
Discharge, no prosecutor or "Not Found"	18	29
Not guilty	26	21
Guilty of capital charge	44	36
Partial verdict	12	14
Total	100	100
Sample size	34	14

(b) Punishment given to capitally convicted convicts

Punishment	Male %	Female %
Imprisonment	20	40
Transportation	60	60
Hanging	20	0
Total	100	100
Sample size	15	5

Source: *P.P.* (1819), 8, pp. 260–2

cases male and female conviction rates were very similar, but men were four times as likely to be hanged if they were capitally convicted. Unfortunately the Northern Circuit returns (which covered Yorkshire, the City of York, Newcastle, Northumberland, Cumberland and Westmorland) were only compiled for one year, 1804. They do, however, include information on the proportion of male and female offenders discharged before public trial and they confirm that women were much more likely than men to get positive decisions at this stage (see Table 2.7). Men were about 25 per cent more likely to be found guilty as charged, and amongst those who were capitally convicted women once again avoided hanging while men did not. There can be very little doubt, therefore, that the relatively favourable treatment given to women in London and the South East was not a regional but a national phenomenon.[19]

Continuity and change in the impact of gender

Technical problems, such as the inadequacy and catch-all quality of some offence definitions, mean that the findings in Tables 2.1–2.7 need to be interpreted with care.[20] Moreover, it would require a separate chapter to review in detail the myriad ways in which the criminal justice system was changing between the 1780s and the 1820s and the impact of those changes on the verdicts and sentencing policies experienced by women and men.[21] A pre-liminary comparison of the pre-1793 period and the 1820s suggests that the tightening-up of aspects of the criminal justice system between these periods (seen, for example, in the decline of acquittal levels for both male and female accused)[22] may have affected females slightly more than males.[23] However, there was no fundamental change in the overall pattern of trial outcomes. Through-out the period from the 1780s to the 1820s, in every area investigated and for almost every type of property crime indicted in the major courts, female offenders had a considerably greater chance of obtaining more lenient treat-ment than their male counterparts.

Since these findings on the relative leniency experienced by women were confined to property crimes, to the major courts and to a relatively brief period, it is necessary to use the limited research available on other crimes, other courts, and other periods to explore the typicality of these findings and their broader implications for the study of gender and justice. This will be done by asking three questions. First, was the pattern of leniency summarized in Tables 2.1-2.7 confined primarily to property crime? Very few of the felonies tried at either the assizes or the Old Bailey were non-property offences and those that were were often sex specific. Only a man could be indicted for rape or sodomy, while almost all those accused of infanticide were women.[24] Virtually the only frequently used categories of non-property felony indictment were murder and infanticide. Even here, however, women represented only a tiny proportion of the accused. Nine per cent of those accused of murder in Sur-rey 1660-1800 were female. At the Old Bailey 1791-93, 31 of the 33 offenders indicted for murder were men. Neither of the two women accused were convicted, whereas twelve of the men (39 per cent) were found guilty. John Beattie's Surrey homicide evidence suggests a similar pattern: 75 per cent of the female accused were either discharged by the grand jury or acquitted by the trial jury, compared to half of the male accused.[25] The Lancashire data in Table 2.6 is problematic both because murder and infanticide were not differ-entiated in the parliamentary returns and because the proportion of murderers found guilty is extremely low, suggesting that a conviction was only recorded when neither an acquittal nor a partial verdict of manslaughter was returned.[26] Nevertheless the Old Bailey and Surrey patterns are clearly confirmed by the fact that in Lancashire females accused of murder were six times less likely to be convicted and hanged than their male counterparts.

In theory the law by no means favoured women. If a wife was convicted of murdering her husband, for example, her action was defined as petty treason and until 1790 she was sentenced to death by burning. When a husband mur-dered his wife he was simply hanged. Equally, until 1803, in infanticide cases involving unmarried mothers the normal legal presumption of innocence was reversed if an attempt was made to conceal the birth.[27] However, in practice the limited evidence available suggests that violent female offenders received relatively lenient treatment in the eighteenth century. In Surrey between 1720 and 1802 only 1 of the 35 women indicted for infanticide was found guilty and sentenced to death, while in Staffordshire the figures were 0 out of 39.[28] Although no firm conclusions can be drawn until further comparative work has been done on the types of murder indictments brought against men and women and the relative strength of the evidence against them,[29] the aggregated data currently available for Surrey, London and Lancashire suggests that women accused of murder clearly had a better chance of obtaining a lenient verdict than their male counterparts. The pattern is therefore fairly similar to that found in major court property crime cases.

Unfortunately, even less information is currently available to answer the second key question: was the more lenient treatment given to female offenders confined only to the major courts, to the assizes and to the Old Bailey? The stakes were very high in the courts which provide the data for Tables 2.1-2.7. Public trial and full conviction meant an automatic sentence of death in many cases. Even though the judges often reprieved the vast majority of those they sentenced to death, the jurors who sat on the grand and petty juries could not predict, or even directly affect, those decisions. To be sure of preventing a female (or a male) offender from being hanged they had to find a favourable verdict themselves. At the lower jury trial court – the quarter sessions – the stakes were not nearly as high. The justices in these courts had no power to hang offenders and the range of sentences they handed out was much less severe. Did this reduce the jurors' inclinations to acquit or find partial verdicts in cases involving females? The limited research available suggests that it may have done to some extent. At Surrey quarter sessions 1660-1800, 62 per cent of the females accused of non-capital property crimes were found guilty as charged compared to 66 per cent of males. The difference in cases involving long-established capital property crimes (where hanging was a very real possibility) was vastly greater, the figures being 22 and 51 per cent respectively. The verdicts of Essex jurors followed a similar pattern: relatively little difference between male and female acquittal and partial verdict rates in petty larceny cases (which were mainly tried at quarter sessions) but much larger differences in favour of females in capital property crime cases such as burglary and highway robbery.[30]

The possibility that the quarter sessions courts were less inclined to favour women than the assizes or the Old Bailey remains open to question, however. Shoemaker's study of early eighteenth-century London misdemeanour cases indicates both that grand jurors were more sympathetic to female defendants and that, on average, women received lower fines than men. Recent work on assault prosecutions at the Essex quarter sessions 1748-1821 suggests that female offenders were treated considerably more leniently. Thirty-two per cent of females were acquitted compared to 17 per cent of males.[31] Since the vast majority of assault cases were dealt with informally at the petty sessions level, it is interesting to note that Barry Godfrey's preliminary work on the late nineteenth-century Exeter summary courts suggests a similar pattern of relative leniency towards females in assault cases.[32] Unfortunately, however, while summary court records survive in relatively large quantities for the late nineteenth century those of earlier periods do not. Since these courts only dealt with relatively minor forms of illegal appropriation (wood stealing, poaching, false reeling of yarn, etc.) and had only limited sentencing powers, this might not be seen as a major problem given that our primary aim here is to assess the gendered nature of trial outcomes in property crime cases. However, in other ways it makes a full history of gender and justice in this period very difficult to write. The summary courts dealt with a variety of ill-defined but important categories of lawbreaking which were used to discipline women. They regularly punished nightwalkers, bastard bearers, lewd women, idle and disorderly persons, and keepers of disorderly houses, for example. They were also the main formal judicial forum in which disputes relating to marital violence were settled. At the very least, therefore, an awareness that we know very little about the policies pursued towards men and women in these lower courts should warn us against overgeneralizing from the assizes and Old Bailey evidence. However, that data, and the more fragmentary quarter sessions evidence currently available, remains extremely suggestive given the consistency of findings across several regions and across many categories of both property crime and violent crime. It is therefore necessary to explore a third question. Was the more lenient treatment accorded to women in the major courts confined to the period from the 1780s to the 1820s?

It is difficult to answer this question. Methods of recording sentences, of trying offenders and of categorizing offences change over time as do legal frameworks, policing policies and sentencing alternatives. Moreover the official statistics collected in the nineteenth century did not usually record the verdicts and sentences given to men and women separately. However, the later twentieth century statistics do and these, along with the very limited data collected by early modern historians, can be used to make a preliminary survey of continuity and change in the treatment of female and male offenders.

Existing published work on crime and justice in the two centuries before 1780 contains relatively little systematic data on the gendered nature of trial outcomes. The main sources for the pre-1680 period are the brief tabulations in Cynthia Herrup's work on Sussex 1592-1640 and in Jim Sharpe's work on Essex 1620-80.[33] Since women could not plead benefit of clergy at all before the early 1620s, and were not granted completely equal access to this legal means of avoiding capital punishment until 1691, female property offenders stealing goods worth over a shilling were severely disadvantaged by the law in the seventeenth century in ways that were no longer the case between 1780 and 1830.[34] However, when the decisions actually made by the courts are analysed elements of continuity do emerge. In Sussex before 1640 men and women experienced much the same conviction rates in non-capital (i.e. petty larceny) cases, but once again in cases involving more serious crimes a highly gendered pattern emerges. Men were 75 per cent more likely to be convicted of capital thefts and two-thirds more likely to be convicted of murder. They were also nearly 50 per cent more likely to be convicted of grand larceny – an offence which the growth of benefit of clergy had effectively reduced to a

Table 2.8 Essex assizes and quarter sessions, all property offenders and housebreakers only, 1620–80. Verdicts analysed by gender

Outcome	All property offenders		Housebreakers	
	Male %	Female %	Male %	Female %
Not found	21.1	24.6	11.6	10.1
Not guilty	28.5	33.8	27.5	39.4
Guilty	50.4	41.5	60.9	50.5
Total	100	99.9	100	100
Sample size	1953	337	440	99

Source: J. Sharpe, *Crime in seventeenth-century England: a county study* (1983), pp. 95; 100. Excluding those categorized as "no details", "other", or "at large".

non-capital charge for men but not for women. Moreover, although the overall hanging rates for men and women indicate only a slight favouring of the latter, when individual offences are analysed the differences in both the categories of property crime Herrup uses are stark. Sixty-six per cent of the men convicted of capital thefts were hanged, compared to 20 per cent of the women. For grand larceny the percentages were 12 and 7 per cent respectively.[35]

Sharpe's early study of Essex 1620–80 does not include any sustained discussion of the impact of gender on trial outcomes, but it does contain data on all property offenders and on housebreakers which can be reworked to provide further insights (see Tables 2.8 and 2.9). This data brings together both quarter sessions and assizes accused.[36] Thus, if our earlier assumption that the quarter sessions courts produced less polarized patterns is correct, gender differences should be less stark. They are, but they are also still apparent - both in the figures on all property offenders and in the evidence for housebreakers alone. The proportion of men found guilty was around 20 per cent higher in both data sets, while the proportion of women sentenced to hang was consistently lower. Garthine Walker's thesis on early modern Cheshire also suggests that sentencing was weighted against men in both housebreaking and burglary cases, and that, after branding was introduced for women in the 1620s, no woman was hanged for housebreaking while the majority of men continued to go to the gallows.[37]

The various tables containing gendered data which can be found in John Beattie's book on the Surrey courts 1660–1800 suggest similar continuities. Fourteen per cent of male property offenders had their indictments dismissed by the grand jury compared to 18 per cent of females.[38] Petty jurors showed the same tendencies, acquitting 38 per cent of females but only 33 per cent of males as well as using partial verdicts much more liberally in cases involving women. While only a quarter of the women sentenced to death 1660–1800 went to the gallows, 43 per cent of the men made the same journey.[39]

Table 2.9 Essex assizes and quarter sessions, all property offenders and housebreaking only, 1620-80. Sentences analysed by gender

Sentence	All property offenders		Housebreaking	
	Male %	Female %	Male %	Female %
Whipped	40.0	68.6	9.7	22.0
Read a clerk, branded	49.3	27.9	37.3	30.0
Hanged	10.6	3.6	53.0	48.0
Total	99.9	100.1	100	100
Sample size	984	140	268	50

Source: Sharpe, *Crime*, pp. 95, 109. Excluding those categorized as "no details", "other", or "at large".

The apparent continuity of relatively lenient trial outcomes in cases involving females accused of major property crimes from the late sixteenth century to the early nineteenth clearly requires further investigation. It is very possible, for example, that this period witnessed a substantial rise in more lenient sentencing policies towards women. Walker's work certainly suggests that the introduction of branding for women in the 1620s was an important watershed in property crime cases, and that before that decade sentencing policies can by no means be assumed to have favoured women.[40] Nor can it be assumed, until further research has been published, that females found guilty of murder or infanticide in the seventeenth century necessarily received as favourable treatment as they seem to have done by the end of the eighteenth.[41] Given that women were the main recipients of the extremely heavy sentencing policies pursued towards those convicted of witchcraft in the sixteenth and seventeenth centuries, and that they were no longer subjected to such prosecutions or penalties in later centuries,[42] it would clearly be dangerous to overemphasize the theme of continuity. However, in property crime cases at least, a brief review of the extensive late twentieth-century research on pre-trial processes, verdicts and sentences does raise the possibility that the pattern of relative leniency towards women seen between 1780 and 1830 may well have survived, albeit in changing forms and with many short-term variations and exceptions, from the early modern period to the 1980s and 1990s.

In the late 1970s and early 1980s about 70 per cent of the girls but only 45 per cent of the boys dealt with by the police for indictable offences were let off with a caution. In 1985 the equivalent figures for indictable and summary offenders of all ages were 27 per cent of women cautioned compared to 20 per cent of men.[43] Modern verdict patterns are more difficult to study than eighteenth-century ones because plea bargaining and guilty pleas are now so common. However, it is interesting to find *The Times* reporting in March 1997 that a recent study had shown that "women accused of serious crimes are far

Table 2.10 England and Wales: sentences for indictable offences analysed by gender, 17–20-year-olds and offenders aged 21 or over, 1983

Outcome	17–20-year-olds		21 years and over	
	Male %	Female %	Male %	Female %
Conditional discharge	8	21	9	21
Probation	9	21	6	17
Fine	45	46	47	46
Community service order	15	4	7	2
Imprisonment / youth custody	21	7	31	12
Other	1	3	1	1
Total	99	102	101	99
Sample size	115,600	14,800	216,100	40,500

Source: A. K. Bottomley & K. Pease, *Crime and punishment: interpreting the data* (Milton Keynes, 1986), p. 88.

more likely to walk free from court than men . . . and in some areas of Britain they are twice as likely to be acquitted".[44] The yearly Criminal Statistics for England and Wales issued by the Home Office make it possible to analyse sentencing policies for all indictable offences by gender and the figures for 1983 found in Table 2.10 are not untypical.[45] Care must be taken in interpreting these figures. Sentencing options were not identical. There were no detention centres for females, for example, and community service orders seem to have been perceived by both the courts and the probation officers making recommendations to them as primarily a male sentencing option.[46] However, the overall pattern seems remarkably similar to that found for property crime cases between 1780 and 1830. Whatever their age women were more than twice as likely to be conditionally discharged or put on probation, equally likely to be fined, but two or three times less likely to be given the severest punishment – imprisonment. If they were given a custodial sentence, women were also much more likely both to be given suspended sentences and to suffer shorter terms in prison.[47]

Thus a surface reading of the data available from the late sixteenth to the late twentieth century appears to draw the reader in the direction of continuity as a key theme in the study of the impact of gender on judicial outcomes.[48] However, even a brief review of the forces that lay beneath the apparent continuation across more than 400 years of more lenient prosecution, verdict and sentencing policies towards women brings forth some rather different perspectives. Patterns of trial outcomes may appear relatively static, but did the reasons that lay beneath those patterns change fundamentally in the period being briefly surveyed here?

Explaining gendered patterns of judicial decision-making

To examine the possibilities of change, of discontinuity, it is necessary to look beneath the statistics on trial outcomes and explore some of the potential ways in which we might try to explain them. This is a complex subject which can only briefly be touched on here. It is also an extremely difficult one. Eighteenth- and early nineteenth-century observers and criminal justice administrators have left virtually no record of their reasons for favouring women. Indeed, there are few indications that contemporaries were aware that the patterns of leniency towards women seen in Tables 2.2–2.7 were a feature of their criminal justice system. It was clear to most contemporaries that very few women were hanged, particularly for property crimes. However, apart from an occasional aside by an assize judge who, in leaving a condemned woman to hang, made reference to the fact that her crime was too great to allow the normal immunity of women from hanging to apply in this case,[49] contemporaries rarely referred to this issue in public. It may yet be possible to find documents and contexts in which the reasons for these gendered patterns of trial outcomes are discussed, but they are proving difficult to uncover. Modern criminologists by contrast have produced a considerable amount of research on this issue, partly by observing and interviewing the criminal justice practitioners themselves. Some of the explanatory frameworks created by this work will be very briefly reviewed here in order to test their applicability to the evidence available for late eighteenth- and early nineteenth-century England.[50]

Although recent criminological research in this area has followed a number of complex and interwoven themes,[51] much of the work relevant to this study has revolved either implicitly or explicitly around one key question: were women treated differently because they were women or because, as a group, they were more likely to exhibit other attributes (such as fewer previous convictions) which induced those involved in deciding trial outcomes to look on them more favourably? The findings of most recent research have overwhelmingly emphasized the latter explanation. Work on cautioning, for example, has suggested that women are not more frequently cautioned because they are women, but because of the nature of their offences or because the police see them as less troublesome.[52] Equally Farrington and Morris's recent work on the Cambridge courts concluded that, while women appeared to get more lenient treatment, once allowance was made for the fact that women committed less serious offences and were less likely to have previous convictions, "the sex of the defendant did not have any direct influence on the severity of the sentence".[53] Other studies, which have attempted more sophisticated levels of analysis by making allowance for factors such as race, age and socio-economic status as well as crime, previous convictions, general demeanour, etc., have led to further diminutions in the perceived importance of the sex of the accused as a key influence on judicial decision-making.[54] Some specific circumstances in which female offenders may be more harshly treated have been uncovered – the most central finding being that female offenders who do not conform to notions of respectable female behaviour (especially sexual behaviour) are more likely to receive heavier punishment.[55] However, the over-all trend of much recent criminological work seems to have reached the point, to quote Anne Edwards' recent overview, where it is almost "the expectation that continued and careful investigation will eliminate the influence of sex/gender altogether as an independent variable with statistical significance".[56] This raises an important question for the historical work presented here – could the same have been true in the late eighteenth and early nineteenth centuries or in the early modern period? Are there hidden variables unrelated to the gender of the accused which explain the apparently lenient treatment given to women seen in Tables 2.2-2.7?

Unfortunately the data historians have to work with in the late eighteenth and early nineteenth century is much less complete than that available to modern criminologists. Accurate information on socio-economic status or even on occupations is particularly hard to come by,[57] and in the era before the arrival of professional police forces information on previous convictions is also highly fragmentary. It must also be remembered that the legal categories used in Tables 2.1-2.5, such as simple larceny, housebreaking and private stealing, encompass a wide range of crimes, and that within these categories women may have tended to commit crimes which were less lucrative, less violent, or less likely to be labelled as serious. However, where information on potential hidden variables does exist it tends, on balance, to favour discontinuity rather than continuity. Although the seriousness of the offence can only be very crudely controlled for by studying broad sets of legal categories such as private steal-ing, it remains significant that when this is done (Tables 2.2-2.5) almost every type of female offender can be seen to receive much more lenient treatment. The fragmentary evidence available about the number of previous convictions males and females brought to the early nineteenth-century courts also provides no grounds for believing that this was the hidden variable behind the relatively lenient treatment received by females. While less than 61 per cent of male transportees to Australia were recorded as having previous convictions, the equivalent figure for females was 65 per cent.[58] Moreover, when national data was first collected in 1857, 40 per cent of women admitted to local prisons had had previous commitments compared to 26 per cent of men.[59] It seems highly unlikely, therefore, that if Farrington and Morris's work on 1980s Cam-bridge could be repeated for early nineteenth-century England, their conclusions would be the same. Controlling for type of offence and previous convictions would almost certainly not eliminate the patterns of relative leniency towards female offenders seen in Tables 2.2-2.7.

Although information is difficult to come by, it also seems unlikely that con-trolling for age or race would have that effect. Indeed, since offenders in their early and mid-teens undoubtedly attracted more lenient verdicts and sentences and since, in London at least, a higher proportion of male than of female accused fell into that age group,[60] controlling for age might well have the effect of increasing the gendered differentials in trial outcomes. Race is only an issue in a tiny proportion of cases in the late eighteenth and early nineteenth centuries. Even in London Norma Myers' research on "the black presence" at the Old Bailey 1780-1830 has revealed that only about four people of African descent per year were indicted (i.e. 0.2 per cent). Only 10 per cent of this small group were female and the verdicts and sentences received by accused blacks were very similar to those given to all offenders.[61] Until research on a large sample of cases involving groups such as Irish-born offenders is completed the broader impact of ethnicity on male or female trial outcomes is difficult to evaluate,[62] but race alone was clearly not a central factor in this period. Thus many of the hidden variables modern criminologists have used to explain away the apparently lenient treatment given to women by the courts do not hold the same explanatory power for the historian of late eighteenth- and early nineteenth-century England.

While many of the other concepts and interpretative frameworks developed by modern criminologists may well be useful starting points for historians attempting to explain the patterns found in Tables 2.2-2.7, it cannot be assumed automatically that those frameworks will hold water when applied to the years between 1780 and 1830. A recurring theme in recent criminological work, for example, is that female defendants who are not considered to be "normal", "conventional" or "respectable" women (i.e. female defendants whose lifestyles violate conventional notions of women's proper roles) are more likely to receive harsher treatment within the criminal justice system.[63] However, some of the limited evidence available suggests that considerable caution needs to be used in applying such assumptions to the half century before the "bloody code" was repealed in the 1830s. A detailed reconstruction of the backgrounds of all the female property offenders whose trials were reported in the Old Bailey Sessions Papers in 1792 indicates that a considerable proportion of them were prostitutes who had stolen their client's property before or after they offered their sexual services.[64] Surprisingly, however, these women were not more harshly treated by the courts. They achieved the same or slightly higher acquittal rates and similar sentencing outcomes as all other female accused.[65] Equally, while some modern criminologists have argued that violent female offenders are treated more harshly than female thieves, because they are effectively being punished for a breach of role expectations as much as for breaking the criminal law, this was not usually the case in the later eighteenth and early nineteenth centuries. Although attitudes to violence were gradually changing, the great majority of women accused of assault between 1770 and 1820 were fined rather than imprisoned, whereas even in minor property crime cases very few women were fined, and imprisonment, transportation or whipping was the norm.[66] The same was true for males accused of assault, but females achieved considerably higher acquittal rates than their male counterparts in both assault and murder cases. They also received much more lenient treatment from judges and jurors alike when they committed the main form of property crime which involved violence - highway robbery (See Tables 2.2-2.5). In these contexts Zedner's conclusion for the Victorian years that "the seriousness of female crimes was measured primarily in terms of women's failure to live up to the requirements of the feminine ideal"[67] is difficult to apply to earlier periods. Neither sexual propriety nor non-violent behaviour were absolute preconditions for achieving better trial outcomes for the women who appeared before the courts between 1780 and 1830.

A number of the other structures of explanation found in late twentieth-century criminological work might conceivably provide helpful starting points in analysing the favourable treatment given to female offenders. For example, if most women were seen as "troubled" and in need of "treatment" or "protection", while most men were perceived as "troublesome"[68] and in need of "deterrence" and punishment; or equally if male crime were construed as decisive planned action while women's crimes were construed primarily as understandable, almost involuntary, responses to social, economic or psychological problems, a gendered pattern of trial outcomes would almost certainly have resulted. Not all of these notions would automatically have produced greater leniency towards women. Protectionism, for example, is a two-edged sword particularly where the policing of young women's sexuality is concerned. However, in routine property crime cases these underlying attitudes and patterns of action would almost certainly have resulted in trial outcomes that would have been generally favourable to women.[69] Unfortunately the extent to which these, and other, late twentieth-century attitudes and modes of action were paralleled in the late eighteenth and early nineteenth centuries remains difficult to gauge since few contemporaries or criminal justice practitioners wrote letters, diaries or pamphlets that recorded their motives or actions. Research on the eighteenth and nineteenth centuries therefore has to begin less ambitiously by investigating a group of potential influences that are more susceptible to analysis, although it is important to keep these potentially useful modern explanatory frameworks in mind.

Perhaps the most obvious potential influence was the legal principle of *feme covert* by which a woman committing an offence with her husband could gain an acquittal on the grounds that she was acting under her husband's orders (i.e. that she was coerced by him against her will). Although the majority of female offenders were single in the eighteenth century, this strange outgrowth of the logic of patriarchy undoubtedly saved a considerable number of wives from prosecution or conviction for theft.[70] However, the proportion of wives (and non-wives) who were successful in claiming immunity by using this principle remains unclear, and it is possible that its usefulness may have declined to some extent in the early nineteenth century.[71] Whatever its direct impact, *feme covert* almost certainly expressed and reinforced a broader set of discursive formations that often portrayed women as weaker, as less culpable, or as more easily led astray – attitudes which could have resulted in more lenient trial outcomes for a wide range of female offenders.

Alternatively, more material considerations may have played the most important role in these decisions. Pleas of poverty, unemployment and economic vulnerability made by women may have received a more sympathetic hearing in the courts because women were highly marginalized in the employment market during this period, forced into lower-paid and less secure types of work.[72] Judges and jurors may therefore have been more willing to treat economic hardship as a real mitigating factor in cases involving females, particularly if they were mothers. Imprisoning or transporting women with young children to support not only punished the children as well as the offender, but also produced a costly and often permanent breakdown in family life that increased the burden on the rates, and the eighteenth-century courts, like their twentieth-century counterparts, may have been particularly reluctant to remove women perceived to be "good mothers" from their families and children.[73] Equally pragmatically, but in a different way, female offenders may simply have been perceived as less of a threat. Women formed a relatively small and declining proportion of property offenders in the late eighteenth and early nineteenth centuries. They also tended to be concentrated in types of crime such as petty larceny and shoplifting which were not felt to be particularly threatening or dangerous. They posed, to quote John Beattie, "a less serious threat to lives, property and order."[74]

Pregnant women had long been able to "plead their belly" and avoid the gallows (not just temporarily in most cases),[75] but a range of less specific but equally powerful taboos about the punishments that could legitimately be inflicted on women may also have been developing in the later eighteenth and early nineteenth centuries. This period witnessed an increased sensitivity towards, and questioning of, the use of judicial violence[76] and the resulting movement away from physical and public punishments seems to have manifested itself particularly early and particularly strongly in relation to women. The 1790s witnessed the abolition of burning women at the stake. The 1810s saw the ending of the public whipping of women. After 1820 women could no longer be whipped at all, while men remained vulnerable to such punishment well into the second half of the nineteenth century.[77] Allied to this there also seems to have been a growing reluctance to send women to the gallows unless an extreme affront to patriarchy (such as the poisoning of a husband or master) had been committed.[78] Female offenders were still being hanged occasionally in the early decades of the nineteenth century but as arguments about the reform of the capital statutes gathered momentum wrongly judged or overharshly punished women were increasingly used by the anti-hanging lobby to add emotional resonance to their campaign. From the 1780s, Vic Gattrell has argued, "women's physical punishment became a delicate matter. Anxiety about executing women, about burning their bodies . . . or about whipping them . . . now tended to be activated by the sense that even at their worst women were creatures to be pitied and protected from themselves, and perhaps revered".[79] However, the precise relationship between these developments and the emergence of middle-class ideals about womanhood, such as the idealized vision of "the angel in the house", still remains to be elucidated. Although Zedner had begun to explore the implications of those changes for attitudes to female offenders, further work is clearly needed to establish in what ways, if any, the growth of ideas about separate spheres had an effect on judicial decision-makers.[80]

At this early stage of research, therefore, any attempt to explain the patterns of judicial leniency towards women found in the late eighteenth and early nineteenth centuries inevitably remains extremely tentative. However, two preliminary conclusions can perhaps be advanced on the basis of the work presented here. First, it is necessary to reappraise Zedner's observation that:

> Although male criminals were also seen as sinners, women who offended provoked a quite different response, not least an extraordinary sense of moral outrage. The moralising approach to crime that predominated in the early nineteenth century clearly distinguished, therefore, according to sex. While the male offender was merely immoral, his female counterpart was likely to be seen as utterly depraved irrespective of any actual, objective difference between them.[81]

Although she goes on to point out that "just how far such attitudes affected judgements made about women actually on trial . . . remains unknown" the implication of these remarks is that female offenders were likely to provoke a particularly outraged, and therefore presumably harsher, response from the courts. The fact that Tables 2.2–2.7 imply strongly that the opposite was the case suggests that further exploration of the relationship between broader gendered attitudes and gendered patterns of judicial decision-making is required. In particular Zedner's implicit assumption that in the period up to the mid-nineteenth-century female offenders were in double jeopardy because "women's crimes not only broke the criminal law but were viewed as acts of deviance from the 'norm' of femininity" certainly requires further refinement in the light of the more lenient verdict and sentencing policies women received in the major courts between 1780 and 1830.[82]

Secondly, the more lenient treatment given to female offenders in this period cannot, it seems, be explained simply by reference to the independent variables which twentieth-century criminologists have found to be so important. As more evidence becomes available some of these variables may well turn out to be relevant. The women accused of crimes in the major courts of England between 1780 and 1830 may, on average, have had shorter criminal records, better character references or have been perceived for other reasons as less "hardened" offenders. More important, however, the men who made all the key decisions in the criminal justice system in this period[83] almost certainly perceived female offenders very differently, and as a result felt that a different range of verdict and sentencing options was appropriate when the accused was a woman. The deeper patterns of thinking that lay beneath these perceptions and assumptions are difficult to unravel, but it is clearly inadequate to appeal simply to notions of "an often instinctive chivalry" as historians such as Elton have done.[84] Paternalism, protectionism, practicality and prejudice, not to mention growing perceptions of the differences between public and private spheres, may all have had a role to play. However, what seems clear is that somewhere within the complex contradictions of patriarchy, the interaction of various forces meant that female offenders accused of crimes in the major courts of late eighteenth- and early nineteenth-century England frequently succeeded in obtaining much more lenient treatment than their male counterparts.

Notes

1. The author would like to thank Garthine Walker, Deirdre Palk, Bob Shoemaker, Loraine Gelsthorpe, Barry Godfrey, and all those who offered comments on this paper when it was given at Nene College, at the Cambridge Early Modern Seminar and at the Institute of Historical Research. I would also like to thank Joan Noel and Cris Gostlow for their assistance in data collection and processing. The work for this article was funded by the ESRC as part of its Crime and Social Order initiative (L210252020).

2. C. Emsley, *Crime and society in England 1750-1900*, 2nd edn (London: Longman, 1996) does have a separate chapter on gender. J. Briggs et al., *Crime and punishment in England: an introductory history* (London: UCL Press, 1996) contains virtually no discussion. There is also remarkably little on gender and justice in D. Philips, *Crime and authority in Victorian England: the Black Country 1835-1860* (London: Croom Helm, 1977); D. Jones, *Crime, protest, community and police in nineteenth-century Britain* (London: Routledge, 1982); D. Jones, *Crime in nineteenth-century Wales* (Cardiff, University of Wales Press, 1992); V. Gatrell, "Crime, authority and the policeman state", in *The Cambridge social history of Britain 1750-1950*, F. M. L. Thompson (ed.) (Cambridge: Cambridge University Press, 1990); G. Rudé, *Criminal and victim: crime and society in early nineteenth-century England* (Oxford: Oxford University Press, 1985); and L. Radzinowicz & R. Hood, *A history of English criminal law and its administration from 1750*, [5 vols] (London: Stevens 1948-1986). The exceptions are C. Conley, *The unwritten law: criminal justice in Victorian Kent* (Oxford: Oxford University Press, 1991); and L. Zedner, *Women, crime and custody in Victorian England* (Oxford: Clarendon, 1991).

3. J. Beattie, *Crime and the courts in England 1660-1800* (Oxford: Clarendon, 1986); J. Beattie, "The criminality of women in eighteenth-century England", *Journal of Social History* 8, 1975, pp. 80-116.

4. HO 26/1-2 and 26/26-28, Public Record Office (henceforth PRO) - London and Middlesex data for October 1791 - September 1793 and October 1820 - September 1822, i.e. 4 full court years; Old Bailey cases only were inputted from these records. Assi 31/13-15 (Summer assizes 1782 to 1787 inclusive), Assi 31/18-19 (Summer 1799 - Lent 1801), Assi 31/23-24 (1820-21), Assi 31/25 (1827), PRO.

5. *Parliamentary Papers (PP)* 1819, 8, pp. 228-35; 260-62.

6. In Surrey and Sussex just under a third of simple larceny cases were heard at the assizes. Beattie, *Crime*, p. 284; in Essex, where the quarter sessions did not decide to take on grand larceny cases until the 1780s, 56 per cent of property crime cases 1790-99 were heard at the assizes, 35 per cent at quarter sessions, 9 per cent in the five borough courts. P. King, *Crime, law and society in Essex 1740-1820* (PhD thesis, Cambridge University, 1984), p. 33.

7. The Old Bailey registers do not usually indicate which cases involved "petty" rather than "grand" larceny.

8. The Old Bailey (or Newgate) registers appear to have been based on a list made up before the trial process (grand or petty jury) began. The Home Circuit agenda books were created, it seems, after the grand jury deliberations but before the petty jury public trial. The Old Bailey records therefore include the subgroup of offenders who were confined for property crime but were never actually tried in public, either because their prosecutor failed to turn up, or because the grand jury brought in a "not found" verdict.

9. The public whipping of women was abolished in 1817, private whipping in 1820. Radzinowicz, *A history*, vol. 1, p. 578. Whipping was already used less frequently for female than for male property offenders by the 1780s - Beattie, *Crime*, pp. 611-13.

10. Radzinowicz & Hood, *A history*, vol. 1, pp. 31-2; vol. 5, pp. 474-6.

11. R. Hughes, *The fatal shore: a history of the transportation of convicts to Australia 1787-1868* (London: Collins, 1987); Zedner, *Women, crime and custody*, pp. 174-5.

12. Unfortunately the records used here do not describe the stolen goods consistently enough to enable the "simple larceny" category to be broken down in this way. Other court records such as indictments may make it possible to control for type of goods stolen but the amount of work involved would be huge and the resulting sample sizes would be very small.

13. The fact that 2 per cent of male and female "simple larceny" accused were sentenced to death alerts the historian to the fact that offence definitions are not always detailed enough in the Old Bailey registers. A capital sentence could not have been passed if these larcenies had not been accompanied by behaviour such as pickpocketing which could turn a simple theft into a capital charge. In this 2 per cent of cases at least offence definition was clearly not complete.

14. Shoplifting and pickpocketing - the legal terms for which were "privately stealing from a shop" and "privately stealing from the person" - were, by definition, secret acts that involved no violence. They were therefore generally regarded as less serious and the statutes that made them capital offences were virtually the only substantial and widely used parts of the "bloody code" that were repealed, or extensively revised, in the first 20 years of the nineteenth century. Radzinowicz, *A history*, vol. 1, pp. 554, 580, 636-7. Picking pockets and stealing goods valued over a shilling was made non-capital in 1808. Most acts of shoplifting were made non-capital in 1820 when the threshold was raised from five shillings to 15 pounds. All were non-capital by 1823. Although these two forms of "private" stealing were put together here in order to create sample sizes large enough for gender comparisons to be made, it must be remembered in interpreting these figures that they were not necessarily similar types of offence apart from the "private" nature of the act involved.

15. Beattie, *Crime*, p. 424 on partial verdicts and their use.

16. Fining alone was rare in property crime cases in the eighteenth century. Between 1 and 2 per cent of property offenders, whether male or female, Home circuit or Old Bailey, were simply fined in the 1780s and 1790s. However, in London, but not on the assizes circuit, it had been adopted as a significant option by 1820 - especially for females and for the young.

17. The exceptional finding that sentencing policies did not favour females in private stealing cases on the Home Circuit may be related to the tiny proportion of male Home Circuit Offenders accused of private stealing (1.9 per cent compared to 13.1 per cent of females). This was not repeated at the Old Bailey where the percentages were 12.3 and 19.5 respectively (see Table 2.1). It is possible that the few males accused of this crime on the Home Circuit were particularly likely candidates for leniency, or that gender ratios amongst shoplifters and pickpockets were different on the Home Circuit. The repealing of the capital statutes relating to these offences may also have had an effect and further research on this is clearly required.

18. *PP*, 1819, 8, pp. 228-35, 260-62.

19. Since the Lancashire data is drawn almost exclusively from a wartime period it also confirms that the patterns found in Tables 2.1-2.7 were not confined to peacetime periods alone. The London and Home Circuit samples were drawn largely from peacetime years because they were originally chosen in order to analyse the changing age structure of offenders in two similar periods. Since wartime recruitment severely depressed the numbers of juveniles and young adults reaching the courts, this was thought to be best achieved by sampling mainly before and after the period of the French Wars 1793-1815.

20. More work needs to be done, for example, on variations between counties and time periods in the proportions of non-capital offenders tried outside the assizes or the Old Bailey.

21. D. Philips, "A new engine of power and authority: the institutionalisation of law-enforcement in England 1780-1830", in *Crime and the law: the social history of crime in Western Europe since 1500*, V. A. C. Gatrell, B. Lenham, G. Parker (eds) (London: Europa, 1980), pp. 155-89. The proportion of indicted offenders who were female also fell in this period: M. Feeley & D. Little, "The vanishing female: the decline of women in the criminal process, 1687-1912", *Law and Society Review* 25, 1991, pp. 719-57.

22. National figures first appeared in *PP*, 1819, 8, pp. 126-7. The proportion of indicted offenders acquitted fell from 23.7 per cent in 1805 to 19.3 per cent in 1818.

23. To summarize briefly: at the Old Bailey in 1791-3 slightly under a third of women avoided public trial, slightly over a third were acquitted and 31 per cent were found guilty. By 1820-22 the equivalent proportions were a fifth avoiding trial, a quarter acquitted and 53 per cent found guilty. Men also suffered adverse changes but they were not quite as great. The proportion of males found guilty rose from 50 to 68 per cent. At the Home Circuit assizes the proportion of men found guilty rose 9 per cent while the proportion of females rose 18 per cent. Gendered differences in sentencing policies altered comparatively little, although sentencing policies in general changed in diverse ways as hanging and whipping declined, imprisonment grew to be more central and transportation re-emerged after the 1780s crisis. Imprisonment remained the most popular sentence handed out to women throughout the period from the 1780s to the 1820s in both jurisdictions.

24. Beattie, *Crime*, pp. 6, 74-139; Conley, *The unwritten law*, pp. 81-95, 187-8.

25. Beattie, *Crime*, p. 97; HO 26/1-2, PRO - same sample periods as Tables 1-8.

26. The Old Bailey documents make it difficult to trace partial verdicts of manslaughter directly, but if sentencing is used as a guide, the figures come out as very similar to those recorded in Lancashire. Three of the 31 males accused of murder were sentenced to death (9.7 per cent), none of the females were. In London all those

fully convicted and therefore sentenced to death were hanged - an identical pattern to that found in Lancashire.

27. This provision was repealed in 1803 by Lord Ellenborough's Act (42 Geo. III, C. 58) after which infanticide was tried in the same way as other murders except that in infanticide cases a jury could bring in a lesser verdict of "concealment of birth" which carried a maximum penalty of two years' imprisonment.

28. Radzinowicz, *A history*, vol. 1, pp. 209-13; this was changed in 1803. L. Rose, *Massacre of the innocents: infanticide in Great Britain 1800-1939* (London: Routledge, 1986), pp. 70-87; M. Jackson, *New-born child murder: women, illegitimacy and the courts in eighteenth-century England* (Manchester: Manchester University Press, 1996), pp. 168-77; Beattie, *Crime*, p. 130; R. Malcolmson, "Infanticide in the eighteenth century" in *Crime in England 1550-1800*, J. Cockburn (ed.) (London: Methuen, 1977), pp. 196-7.

29. See the brief discussion of wilful murder in Beattie, *Crime*, p. 97, and his warnings about comparability, p. 437. Women accused of poisoning their husbands or masters (a crime which was sometimes portrayed as a potential threat to patriarchy) may also have found it particularly difficult to obtain merciful verdicts from the middle-aged, propertied, male jurors of this period.

30. Beattie, *Crime*, p. 437; P. King, *Crime, law and society*, p. 308.

31. R. Shoemaker, *Prosecution and punishment: petty crime and the law in London and rural Middlesex c. 1660-1725* (Cambridge: Cambridge University Press, 1991), pp. 149-59; P. King, "Punishing assault: the transformation of attitudes in the English courts", *Journal of Interdisciplinary History* 27, 1996, pp. 43-55, especially p. 55. It should be noted that the gender of the victim, by contrast, made virtually no difference to trial outcomes.

32. See B. Godfrey, "Prosecuting Violence in the cities of England 1888-1908", paper presented to the Department of Criminology seminar, Keele University, April 1997.

33. C. Herrup, *The common peace: participation and the criminal law in seventeenth-century England* (Cambridge: Cambridge University Press, 1987); J. Sharpe, *Crime in seventeenth-century England: a county study* (Cambridge: Cambridge University Press, 1983).

34. Beattie, *Crime*, pp. 424, 485; Herrup, *The common peace*, p. 48. Thefts of under a shilling were not felonies and could not usually therefore result in a capital conviction. The history of benefit of clergy is complex (Beattie, *Crime*, pp. 141-7) but this plea, if successful, meant that the offender was branded and then released rather than sentenced to death.

35. Herrup, *The common peace*, pp. 150, 176.

36. Sharpe, *Crime in seventeenth-century England*, pp. 95-109.

37. G. Walker, "Crime, gender and social order in early modern Cheshire" (PhD thesis, Liverpool University, 1994), p. 190.

38. Beattie, *Crime*, p. 404. Figures based on totals produced by adding the four categories of property offence listed together (i.e. capital, non-capital, forgery, fraud).

39. *Ibid.*, pp. 437-8.

40. Walker, "Crime", pp. 187, 190.

41. The evidence currently available leaves this issue open to debate. Sharpe, *Crime in seventeenth-century England*, p. 124, contains figures that suggest (using the same method as that used for Tables 2.8-2.9) that 39 per cent of male murderers in Essex were convicted compared to 29 per cent of females. The proportions of convicted offenders actually hanged were 52 and 50 per cent respectively. Herrup,

The common peace (p. 150), suggests Sussex women were less likely to be convicted of murder but the sample size is very small. Walker's forthcoming book *Crime, gender and social order in early modern England* (Cambridge University Press, in press) suggests that while women were more likely to be acquitted of murder, once convicted they were considerably more likely to hang. Infanticide cases certainly suggest a different pattern in the seventeenth century when Herrup (p. 150) suggests 53 per cent were convicted and Sharpe (p. 135) notes that 37 per cent of the female accused went to the gallows. In Surrey 1660-1719, 30 per cent of infanticide accused were sentenced to death and 11 per cent were hanged. In the period 1720-1802 the figures were 3 per cent in both cases (Beattie, *Crime*, p. 116).

42. J. Sharpe, *Instruments of darkness: witchcraft in England 1550-1750* (London: Penguin, 1996) esp. pp. 105-27, 169-89. For a European-wide overview of the predominance of women amongst those accused of witchcraft, of the high execution rates and of the decline of prosecutions after the mid-seventeenth century, see for example, B. Levack, *The witch-hunt in early modern Europe*, 2nd edition (London: Longman, 1995), pp. 23, 134, 190. All English witchcraft statutues were repealed in 1736.

43. F. Heidensohn, *Women and crime* (London: Macmillan, 1985), p. 53; A. Morris, *Women, crime and criminal justice* (Oxford: Blackwell, 1987), p. 81.

44. *The Times*, 2 March 1997.

45. Table 2.10 is based on the 1983 figures quoted in A. Bottomley & K. Pease, *Crime and punishment: interpreting the data* (Milton Keynes: Open University Press, 1986), p. 88. Broadly similar figures for 1991 and 1995 can be found in C. Hedderman & L. Gelsthorpe (eds), *Understanding the sentencing of women* (London: Home Office, 1997), p. 2.

46. Bottomley & Pease, *Crime*, pp. 88-92.

47. Morris, *Women*, pp. 85-7; Heidensohn, *Women*, pp. 60-62.

48. For an introduction to a broader debate on continuity or change as key themes, see B. Hill, "Women's history: a study in change, continuity or standing still?", *Women's History Review* 2, 1993, pp. 5-22; J. Bennett, "Women's history: a study in continuity and change", *Women's History Review* 2, 1993, pp. 173-84.

49. Anon., *An authentic narrative of the celebrated Miss Fanny Davis* (London: 1786) includes a record of the judge remarking in passing sentence that she should not expect that her sex would protect her from the hand of justice "on this occasion".

50. For overviews of some of this work, see, for example, A. Edwards, "Sex/gender, sexism and criminal justice: some theoretical considerations", *International Journal of the Sociology of Law* 17, 1989, pp. 165-84; Morris, *Women*, pp. 79-103; Heidensohn, *Women*, pp. 31-68; I. Nagel, "Sex differences in the processing of criminal defendants"; in A. Morris & L. Gelsthorpe (eds), *Women and crime* (Cambridge: Cropwood Conference Series No. 13, 1981), pp. 104-21.

51. A large literature has recently grown up around this subject. Much of it gives little space to the type of findings expressed in Table 2.10, focusing more frequently on issues not directly within the purview of this chapter, including rape trials, the judicial treatment of prostitutes, the police processing of young girls perceived to be in danger and a rich variety of other issues that reveal the gendered nature of judicial decision-making. See, for example, S. Walklate, *Gender and crime: an introduction* (London: Prentice-Hall, 1995); P. Carlen & A. Worrall (eds), *Gender, crime and justice* (Milton Keynes: Open University Press, 1987); S. Edwards, *Women*

on trial (Manchester: Manchester University Press, 1984); C. Smart, *Women, crime and criminology: a feminist critique* (London: Routledge, 1976); N. Naffine (ed.), *Gender, crime and feminism* (Aldershot: Dartmouth, 1995); L. Gelsthorpe & A. Morris, *Feminist perspectives in criminology* (Milton Keynes: Open University Press, 1990); A. Worrall, *Offending women: female lawbreakers and the criminal justice system* (London: Routledge, 1990); R. Dobash, R. P. Dobash, L. Noaks (eds), *Gender and crime* (Cardiff: University of Wales Press, 1995).

52. Morris, *Women*, p. 80.

53. Heidensohn, *Women*, p. 44, quoting D. Farrington & A. Morris, "Sex, sentencing and reconviction", *British Journal of Criminology* 23, 1983, pp. 245-6.

54. Edwards, "Sex/gender", pp. 170-71.

55. Edwards, *Women*, p. 185; Heidensohn, *Women*, pp. 43-50; Morris, *Women*, pp. 82-101.

56. Edwards, "Sex/gender", p. 171.

57. Women's occupations are very rarely recorded and men's status is also inaccurately stereotyped on most indictments. Exceptionally men's occupations are fairly systematically given in the Old Bailey records of the early 1790s but women are usually described in terms of their relationship to men - spinster, wife, widow.

58. Based on data for the period 1787-1852 in L. Robson, *The convict settlers of Australia* (Melbourne: Melbourne University Press, 1965), pp. 176-185. Information is not available for a considerable proportion of convicts - A. Shaw, *Convicts and the colonies* (London: Faber & Faber, 1981), pp. 149-52 - and these findings are therefore very tentative. The figure for women with previous convictions quoted by Oxley is lower than Robson's. This may reflect different ways of treating unknowns or the fact that Oxley's data is drawn from the period after 1826. D. Oxley, *Convict maids* (Cambridge: Cambridge University Press, 1996), p. 41. Oxley does not quote any figures for men which would allow comparisons to be made. Transportees are, of course, an untypical sample of all prosecuted offenders (*ibid.*, p. 110) and this evidence must therefore be treated with caution.

59. Zedner, *Women*, pp. 318-20.

60. P. King, "Decision-makers and decision-making in the English criminal law, 1750-1800", *Historical Journal* 27, 1984, pp. 25-58, especially pp. 36-41; P. King, "Female offenders, work and lifecycle change in late eighteenth-century London", *Continuity and Change* 11, 1996, pp. 61-90, especially p. 65; P. King & J. Noel, "The origins of 'the problem of juvenile delinquency': the growth of juvenile prosecutions in London in the late eighteenth and early nineteenth centuries", *Criminal Justice History* 14, 1993, pp. 17-41, especially pp. 21-27. Since women were overrepresented among the relatively small number of offenders in their thirties and early forties (who also received relatively lenient treatment) the juvenile effect may have been counteracted to some extent.

61. London and slave ports such as Bristol and Liverpool were the main centres of black communities in Britain in the late eighteenth and early nineteenth centuries: P. Linebaugh, *The London hanged* (London: Allen Lane, 1991), p. 135; D. Killingray, "The black presence and local history", *The Local Historian* 19, 1989, pp. 8-15, especially p. 8. The great majority were men: J. Walvin, "Blacks in Britain: the eighteenth century", *History Today* (September 1981), pp. 37-8; N. Myers "The black presence through criminal records 1780-1830", *Immigrants and Minorities* 8, 1988, pp. 292-307; N. Myers, *Reconstructing the black past: blacks in Britain 1780-1850* (London: Frank Cass, 1996), pp. 82-103.

62. For a few years after 1791 the place of birth of the accused is given for the Old Bailey accused and trial outcomes involving Irish-born offenders (a substantial minority) can therefore be studied. I hope to eventually publish this data. Early samplings have yet to reveal any significant harshening of trial outcomes in cases involving Irish accused but larger samples are clearly required before this can be confirmed and gendered differences have yet to be identified.

63. Heidensohn, *Women*, p. 43; Edwards, *Women*, pp. 1-4, 185; Morris, *Women*, p. 101; P. Carlen, "Women, crime, feminism and realism", reprinted in Naffine, *Gender, crime and feminism*, p. 433.

64. King, "Female offenders, work and lifecycle change", pp. 77-8.

65. Sample based on all female property offenders appearing in the Old Bailey Sessions Paper trial reports January to December 1792 using HO26/1-2 for further information. A third of prostitutes and just under a third of all female offenders whose trials were reported were found not guilty. This pattern may not have been true earlier in the century but as lawyers increasingly infiltrated criminal trials at the Old Bailey in the late eighteenth century a considerable number of prostitutes hired them to orchestrate their defence. The lawyers in turn soon developed a very effective defence tactic, attacking the male victim's character and thus turning the public hearing into a trial of the prosecutor himself. The parallel with the fate of many female victims in rape trials, who also effectively ended up in the dock themselves is fascinating and ironic. The effect, however, was to get a significant number of prostitutes off. See, for example, the case of Sophia Tilly, December 1792, *Old Bailey Sessions Papers*.

66. Morris, *Women*, p. 88; Edwards, *Women*, p. 177. King, "Punishing assault", p. 55. See also simple larceny figures in Tables 2.3 and 2.5 and King, *Crime, law and society*, p. 336.

67. L. Zedner, "Women, crime and penal responses: a historical account", in M. Tonry (ed.), *Crime and Justice. A Review of Research* 14, 1991, pp. 307-62, especially p. 320.

68. Hedderman & Gelsthorpe, *Understanding the sentencing of women*, pp. 26-9.

69. Edwards, *Women*, p. 187. For an interesting discussion of the ambivalent effects of some of these notions, see Worrall, *Offending women*, pp. 165-7; Walklate, *Gender*, p. 140, who also discusses the ways female defendants are frequently denied a sense of responsibility for their actions and therefore placed in a "compassion trap" in which they are presumed to have qualities associated with femininity, presumed to be more caring, nurturing and domestic. On the ways young girls can be over-policed and on the sexualization of female deviance: Morris, *Women*, pp. 96-100; Heidensohn, *Women*, pp. 48-51.

70. "A feme covert shall not be punished for committing any felony in company with her husband; the law supposing she did it by the coercion of her husband" commented Anon., *The laws respecting women* (London, 1777), p. 70. See also: W. Blackstone, *Commentaries on the laws of England* (Oxford: Clarendon, 1769), vol. 4, pp. 22-4. For further discussion, see King, "Female offenders, work and lifecycle change", pp. 67-8; Beattie, *Crime*, p. 414. For a further discussion of potential causes of the relative leniency experienced by women in the eighteenth century, see Chapter 8 of my forthcoming book *Crime, justice and discretion: law and society in England 1740-1820* (Oxford University Press, in press).

71. Deirdre Palk's current research on Bank of England prosecutions for forgery in the first quarter of the nineteenth century suggests that *feme covert* by no means

always saved wives who acted with their husbands. For the mid-nineteenth century, see Barry Godfrey's chapter in this volume.

72. Discussed in more detail in King, "Female offenders, work and lifecycle change".
73. Edwards, *Women*, pp. 7-8.
74. Feeley and Little, "The vanishing female"; Rudé, *Criminal and victim*, pp. 45-6, 50-1, 60-63; Beattie, *Crime*, pp. 240, 439.
75. Beattie, *Crime*, pp. 430-1. The use of this plea was declining, however: J. Oldham, "On pleading the belly: a history of the jury of matrons", *Criminal Justice History* 6, 1985, pp. 1-43.
76. M. Foucault, *Discipline and punish* (London: Allen Lane, 1977); R. McGowen, "Punishing violence, sentencing crime", in *The violence of representation: literature and the history of violence*, N. Armstrong & L. Tennenhouse (eds) (London: Routledge, 1989), pp. 140-55. R. McGowen, "A powerful sympathy: terror, the prison, and humanitarian reform in early nineteenth-century Britain", *Journal of British Studies* 25, 1986, pp. 312-34.
77. Radzinowicz, *A history*, vol. 1, pp. 209-13, 578.
78. A relative reluctance had existed, as we have seen, since the seventeenth century (if not before). In the late seventeenth and eighteenth centuries the proportion of capitally convicted female offenders who were hanged fluctuated. The Surrey figures were 1663-94, 27 per cent; 1722-48, 52 per cent; 1749-63, 10 per cent; 1764-75, 0 per cent; 1776-87, 29 per cent; 1788-1802, 19 per cent: Beattie, *Crime*, pp. 454, 514, 532-3. By 1827-30 only 4 of the 59 people executed in London were women and all of these had committed murder: V. Gatrell, *The hanging tree* (Oxford: Oxford University Press, 1994), p. 8.
79. Gatrell, *The hanging tree*, pp. 336-7.
80. C. Hall, "The early formation of Victorian domestic ideology" in her book *White, male and middle class: explorations in feminism and history* (Oxford: Polity Press, 1992), pp. 75-94; L. Davidoff & C. Hall, *Family fortunes: men and women of the English middle class 1780-1850* (London: Routledge, 1987); Zedner, *Women, crime and custody*, pp. 1-18 focuses on the Victorian period primarily but argues that the ideal of the angel in the house "affected all but the very lowest stratum of society". It should be noted, of course, that early modern historians have found many of the constructs associated with nineteenth-century attitudes to women's roles in earlier periods. The extent of change in the late eighteenth and early nineteenth centuries may have been over emphasized. See, for example, M. Wiesner, *Women and gender in early modern Europe* (Cambridge: Cambridge University Press, 1993), pp. 240-52; A. Vickery, "Golden age to separate sphere? A review of the categories and chronology of English women's history", *Historical Journal* 36, 1993, pp. 383-414.
81. Zedner, "Women, crime and penal responses", p. 321.
82. Zedner, "Women, crime and penal responses", p. 308. Zedner does not refer directly to the concept of "double jeopardy" in this passage but her language comes close to paralleling modern work which does: Edwards, *Women*, p. 216 - "women defendants are on trial both for their legal infractions and for their defiance of appropriate femininity and gender roles". F. Heidensohn, *Crime and society* (London: Macmillan, 1989), p. 102.
83. Between 1780 and 1830 all jurors, magistrates, assize and Old Bailey judges and Home Office officials involved in pardoning decisions were men.
84. G. Elton, "Crime and the historian", in *Crime in England*, J. Cockburn (ed.), p. 13.

Chapter 3

The trouble with boys: gender and the "invention" of the juvenile offender in early nineteenth-century Britain

Heather Shore

> He was a snub-nosed, flat-browed, common-faced boy enough; and as dirty a juvenile as one would wish to see; but he had about him all the airs and manners of a man. He was short of his age, with rather bow-legs, and little, sharp, ugly eyes. His hat was stuck on the top of his head so lightly, that it threatened to fall off every moment – and would have done so, very often, if the wearer had not had a knack of every now and then giving his head a sudden twitch, which brought it back to its place again. He wore a man's coat, which reached nearly to his heels. He had turned the cuffs back, halfway up his arm, to get his hands out of the sleeves: apparently with the ultimate view of thrusting them into the pockets of his corduroy trousers; for there he kept them. He was, altogether, as roystering and swaggering a young gentlemen as ever stood four feet six, or something less, in his bluchers.[1]

In this description of the Artful Dodger, the novelist Charles Dickens drew in minute detail a representation of the contemporary stereotyped juvenile delinquent.[2] Jack Dawkins was that curious amalgam of man and boy that was so characteristic of the schizophrenic relationship between innocence and experience in early nineteenth-century accounts of child criminality. Moreover, the conflict between his childishness and his maturity that was fundamental to such descriptions was underlined by particular constructions of gender.

This chapter will examine the gendered nature of the nineteenth-century discourse on juvenile crime, laying a central emphasis on the relationship between masculinity and maturity which occurs in portrayals of delinquent boys.[3] In using the term "masculinity", the object is to convey the association with perceived forms of male behaviour. Hence, certain forms of activities and conduct were seen as being specifically masculine. The term "discourse" is used to refer to a number of texts that started to appear with increasing frequency from the late 1810s, and which articulated a strong concern with the causes and nature of juvenile crime, and with the search for a possible solution. Moreover, these texts, I will argue in this chapter, contained a very particular representation of the male juvenile delinquent. Yet, despite this particularism, the terminology of juvenile crime was rarely consistent; juvenile offender, juvenile delinquent, juvenile criminal, young offender, criminal children and child were used interchangeably as descriptive terms. Moreover, the exact age of the juvenile delinquent in these discourses was somewhat arbitrary. The nineteenth-century debates pinpointed the early and mid-teens as the prime times for offending. However, since the legal definition of "juvenile" changed from one report to another, and from one year to another, it would be misleading to assume any definite age for a strict definition of juvenile crime. Nevertheless, the limit of 16 and under set by the Juvenile Offenders Act of 1850 may be used as a general guide.[4]

The relationship between gender and juvenile crime has been of little concern to historians hitherto, possibly because of the relative lack of any clear understanding of chronology and developing patterns of child criminality in Britain. While a narrative history of the legal and philanthropic response to juveniles has existed for some time, it is only more recently that a more rounded, and particularly more quantitative analysis of such crime has emerged. The early nineteenth century had been neglected due to the lack of consistent official statistics for juvenile crime. However, recent work by the author and by Peter King, based on detailed quantitative analysis of the Criminal Registers, a series recording indicted crime running from the late eighteenth century, has significantly opened up the field.[5] Out of this new wave of studies there has also been some focus on constructions of female juvenile crime. However, this has concentrated largely on the post-1850 period, when the industrial and reformatory schools legislation resulted in the creation of a whole bureaucracy, and a whole new set of records, which have subsequently been exploited by historians interested in the systems of classification employed by such institutions.[6] Recent articles by Linda Mahood and Barbara Littlewood, and by Michelle Cale, focusing on Scotland and England, have pointed to the equation between female juvenility and sexual knowledge as a criterion in treatment and punishment within the reformatory schools.[7] Moreover, the dichotomy between representations of boys and girls is underlined in Louise Jackson's work on child sexual abuse in this volume.[8]

Historians considering the issue of masculinity and crime have tended to concentrate on the transition from youth to adulthood, the "rites of passage" associated with becoming a man, or with the character of association, peer recognition and fraternity amongst older youths and adult males.[9] Moreover, most studies that have considered the centrality of gender and constructions of masculinity in the field of youth crime belong to the twentieth-century sociological, rather than historical, tradition; for example, the studies of "the gang", pioneered by the Chicago school during the 1920s and 1930s.[10] Most historical studies focusing on masculinity in the nineteenth century, as John

Tosh has pointed out, have been generally limited to the middle-class male.[11] This chapter will consider the associations made between masculinity, criminality and class in the early nineteenth century, as evidenced in perceptions of male juvenile crime.

The "invention" of juvenile crime and the demarcation between boy "thieves" and girl "prostitutes"

The period of the early nineteenth century formed a crucial watershed in the evolution of models of male and female juvenile criminality. At the cessation of the French wars in 1815 there was a widespread belief in the increase of juvenile crime.[12] A number of factors, such as population rise, urbanization, poverty and demobilization inter-reacted, leading to something of a moral panic about such crime. This period, it has been argued, experienced an "invention" of the juvenile delinquent; for the first time the juvenile was a definable entity.[13] Concern had been expressed about delinquent youth in previous centuries; however, it was only from the 1810s that consistent representations and inquiries started to appear.[14] As this chapter will show, the most characteristic anomaly of these chronicles was the almost invisible figure of the female juvenile offender. Indeed, when girls were considered it was from the confines of narrow descriptive categories, which stereotyped them as either prostitutes or flash-girls, comparable to a gangster's moll. Moreover, representations of young offenders were generally based on the most extreme examples of juvenile crime: children who had reached the superior courts, who awaited transportation, and who lingered in the prisons and houses of correction, children who were invariably boys. The level of experience of the juvenile boy was measured by the degree of maleness and maturity which was expressed in cockiness, boldness and aggression. The level of experience of the juvenile girl was measured by the degree of maturity and sexuality: she had the capacity to corrupt in the manner of a childish Eve. Thus, the concern over girl delinquents was generally framed in terms of their sexual immorality, accompanied by a strong emphasis on the sexual threat which they apparently posed to boys.[15] Moreover, this dichotomy between representations of male and female juveniles was underlined by the scarcity of reference to male prostitution. Jeffrey Weeks has written about the lack of commentary about male prostitution and homosexuality before the 1860s and 1870s, pointing out that "as late as 1871 concepts both of homosexuality and of male prostitution were extremely undeveloped in the Metropolitan Police and in high medical and legal circles".[16]

The division between juvenile boys and girls was expressed clearly in a document of 1816, the report of the Committee for Investigating the Causes of the Alarming Increase of Juvenile Delinquency in the Metropolis. This committee, composed of various, but mainly Quaker, philanthropists, conducted an investigation into the nature and causes of juvenile crime.[17] In *c.* 1815 several hundred boys were interviewed in Middlesex prisons and houses of correction by members of the committee in order to compile the report. Female juvenile offenders were not interviewed; typically girls were referred to only in the context of prostitution. Thus, argued the committee, boys associated with "professed thieves of mature age, and with girls who subsist by prostitution".[18] Yet this role division was hardly new; in the eighteenth century magistrate John Fielding commented that: "deserted boys were thieves from necessity, their sisters are whores from the same cause; and, having the same education with their wretched brothers, generally join the thief to the prostitute".[19]

In the commissions, reports and texts that appeared from the late 1810s the primary concern was with property crime. There was little significant discussion of other forms of crime such as indirect property crime (fraud, for example), assault, or other physical violence, and while immorality was a concern, this was rarely explicitly stated as sexual immorality, except when female juvenile prostitution was considered.[20] Consequently it seems that rather more substantial attention was lavished onto male juvenile offenders. However, other forces were at play in the concentration on male juvenile offenders. It is clear that not only did a far higher number of boys enter the criminal justice system, but that in the case of juvenile indictments the rise was much more markedly male than female. After 1813 the proportion of males was never less than 81 per cent of all juvenile indictments. The proportion of juvenile females only ever rose above 19 per cent before 1814, the rise in such prosecutions coinciding with the war.[21] This in itself raises the very question of gender bias at different stages of the criminal process. Hence, were girls more likely to be treated informally than boys? Were magistrates unhappy about committing girls for trial, preferring to recommend them to a short stay in the Bridewell? These questions will be pursued in the penultimate section of this chapter.

The construction of the male juvenile

So what form did representations of male juveniles take? Two physical "types" seem to have been most common in the contemporary texts. One was the characterization of the juvenile boy as a loutish, brutal thug. This representation seems to have been preferred in cases where juvenile boys were associated with violence, or where they had been reduced to such levels by the implied barbarity of some institutional regimes. For example, the juvenile murderer John Any Bird Bell was described thus in a report on his trial and execution in *The Times*: "His features are not good, although not expressive of any degree of ferocity or depravity, but there is about the eyes, which are deeply sunk in the head, a strong expression of cunning".[22] Again, W. A. Miles described Nicholas Bradshaw, a nine-year-old in Newgate in 1837, as a "short, thick, ill-featured urchin . . . with a dogged, animal sort of manner, both in feature and expression, was sulky and hardened". However, Miles was somewhat chastened when, on being visited by his mother, the boy "hid his face under his arm casting his whole body on one side. His neck and ears were as red as scarlet, and he was evidently crying bitterly".[23] Rather more frequently employed was the characterization of the bold, bright, cocky, alert boy juvenile, who possessed a sort of native intelligence. This was a commonly used stereotype; one that was to be employed most memorably, as we have seen, in Dickens's almost picturesque description of the Artful Dodger. In 1817 a notorious recidivist, 14-year-old John Leary, was described with a sneaking admiration by Spitalfields philanthropist Peter Bedford (incidently, Bedford was one of the main contributors to the 1816 Report on Juvenile Delinquency). Bedford describes how he encountered Leary in Newgate prison "standing in one corner of the room with his arms akimbo, looking as bold as any lion".[24] The Honourable Henry Grey Bennet, chairman of the 1817 Select Committee on Metropolitan Police, also spoke of Leary, characterizing him as good-looking, sharp and intelligent.[25] Similar physical and mental characteristics were intimated in 1832, by Thomas Wontner, the ex-schoolmaster of Newgate, who described boy pickpockets as having, "a light tread, a delicate sense of touch, combined with firm nerves".[26]

Sharpness, boldness, intelligence and firm nerves were common characteristics in representations of juvenile boys. However, a further agenda accompanied this tone of underlying admiration: it was tempered by the concerned perception that such boys were displaying a premature maturity or/and engaging in behaviour that detached them from childishness. Accordingly, in Newgate, Leary refused to go into the schoolroom, preferring to stay in the prison yard with the men, exhibiting qualities of bravado, and evincing an identification with the adult male prisoners. H. S. Cotton, the Newgate Chaplin, remarked in 1818 that boys, whilst being flogged, "were not allowed by their fellow prisoners to cry, or express any sort of feeling".[27] This sort of bravado and masculine posturing was particularly associated with male juveniles; hence, in prison surrounded by adult offenders the aspiration to manliness was emphasized. Adult felons on their way to the scaffold, many of them little more than callow youths themselves, would be exhorted by their fellow inmates to, "die hard, my boy", "remember yourself", "act like a man".[28] In 1818, J. A. Newman, an ex-keeper of Newgate, described how a boy named Cox had, at 19, eventually come to be executed. Cox:

> had received many addresses from the court, and he used jokingly to call the Recorder his godfather; he came to be executed at last; and the night before he was executed he amused himself by engraving on a plain halfpenny, the picture of a man hanging, and W. C. on the other side.[29]

Certainly, such gallows bravura and humour was not restricted to men and boys. Vic Gatrell has recently discussed the "dying game", the language of the gallows exhibited by both men and women.[30] However, while a certain defensiveness and resignation might be expressed in the words of both men and women at the gallows, to "die like a man" or "act like a man" suggests a specific association with perceptions of male bravery, boldness and courage.

Manliness, hardness and lack of emotionality were essential elements in the portrayals of male juveniles. To some extent the sort of machismo described above was a necessary requirement of male criminal lives; it is perhaps understandable that boys would "swagger" and "royster", since survival in penal institutions was not amenable to childishness. Moreover, it suggests that the distancing from childishness, indeed from childhood, that occurs in these descriptions, was particularly appropriate coming as it did from the middle- and upper-class creators of the discourse. It provided a welcome contrast between criminal children and their own children, who were increasingly perceived as childish, and informed by an innocence that was largely absent in the former. The decades of the late eighteenth and early nineteenth centuries are generally seen as crucial in the transformation of attitudes to childhood, continuing formulations of thought and ideology that had emerged during the previous century.[31] The concern over poor children was reflected in employment legislation, in the growth of institutional responses to child poverty and vagrancy, and in philanthropic endeavour, aimed at the amelioration of moral, religious, and educational needs of children. The issue of class lay at the heart of these changes and while many of these innovations were focused on working-class children, the basis of change was often rigid, circumscribing the behaviour of such children. While the convergence of concerns over juvenile crime in this period was undoubtedly shaped by more generalized concerns about the experience of childhood, it should be stressed that it was also strongly informed by fears of the criminal class and the threat of the underclass. This threat was emphasized, and perhaps made more palatable, by the delineation of working-class boys as masculine, embryonic adults. For example, although it was commonly agreed that education was essential to moral reformation, the boundaries had to be clearly set. In 1828 William Bodkin, the founder of the Mendicity Society, told a parliamentary select committee that

> with regard to the increase of juvenile delinquents . . . the facility afforded for obtaining instruction, and the consequent degree of intelligence that pervades the lower ranks of society, has caused, with respect to those boys, a sort of premature manhood.[32]

These were overwhelmingly the fears of the middle and upper classes. Given the nature of the sources, indications of working-class attitudes to juvenile crime are practically unrecoverable, underlining the distinctive class conflict within the discourses. However, a narrative from "thieves" in Coldbath Fields prison, compiled by the prison governor Mr Chesterton in 1839, did comment on local forms of summary justice:

> Boys are often caught in shops on "the sneak" for the till; and on most of these occasions receive punishment on the spot. They are sometimes horsewhipped, at other times they have their faces and hands oiled and

soot sprinkled over them . . . a boy was severely punished . . . his hands were tied behind him and he was sent about his business with a large placard pasted upon his back bearing the ominous characters of "A Thief".[33]

The theme of masculinity, and the conflict between childishness and premature maturity was emphasized in the descriptions of juvenile pastimes and actions. There were commonly references to boys smoking, drinking and gambling, to boys attending theatre, boys congregating in gangs, boys showing off, bullying, and cheeking authority. Accounts of juvenile behaviour seem caught within a conflict of the portrayal of boyish activities and that of threatening behaviour, veering on disorder. In the descriptions of young male juvenile offenders the persistence of contemporary rhetoric conveying an impression of a general level of insolence, a lack of respect, almost what could be called a "challenging" hedonism, is marked. Whichever purlieu the child inhabited, in whichever institution he resided, concern was repeatedly expressed about behaviour of this sort. Even at trial, notwithstanding the majesty and solemnity of the court, juvenile boys were described as engaging in rumbustious, impudent, bold behaviour. After a trial of April 1835 where a number of juvenile boys were appearing, *The Times* fulminated:

Several of the prisoners, the majority of whom were young persons, behaved with so much levity, that the learned recorder was compelled to recall them, and lecture them upon their indecorous and hardened behaviour. He also reminded them that transportation was not a removal to a state of comparative idleness, but a continuous course of constraint, severity and privitation [*sic*]. Some of their friends in the gallery added to the disorder by insolent exclamations towards the learned judge of the grossest kind, and others by vehement screaming and exultations.[34]

The 1816 report on juvenile crime found "habits of gambling in the streets" to be a principal cause of delinquency, and indeed this theme continues to occur in representations of male juveniles both outside and inside institutions.[35] Boys gathered together to gamble and thieving, it was said, was the natural consequence. In 1817 Samuel Furzon, the constable of St. Giles and St. George's, Bloomsbury, complained about the gangs of young boys who could be found gambling in the streets; apparently as many as 50 or 60 boys grouped together for this purpose. Furzman believed that this was an inevitable source of pickpockets and thieves.[36] In 1828 Matthew Wood, Alderman of the City of London, bemoaned such gatherings:

. . . it is a common practise for those juvenile offenders to assemble in the open spaces of ground which there are in the City and in the Borough, at Spitalfields, and places of that kind, where they are gambling from morning till night, throwing up money, and tossing into a pit.[37]

Most contemporaries recognized the inevitability of certain forms of behaviour within institutional environments as a product of what was perceived as the general malaise operating in the unreformed prisons. Lack of discipline, control and respect for the institution and for the individuals that represented it were all features of prison culture. However, juvenile boys were, once again, particularly identified with this sort of behaviour. In 1835 the Select Committee on Gaols received a statement from a 15-year-old prisoner who had been in Newgate on remand. This boy described the behaviour of the young inmates to the committee: "there was gambling carried on all day long; card-playing, pitch and toss, and chuck farthing . . . some boasting of their former robberies, some cursing and swearing, some telling of obscene stories, and some singing vile songs".[38]

Not surprisingly, gambling and gang behaviour were occasionally linked together. On the streets, gangs of boy gamblers were referred to as a general amorphous threat. They were described as "swarms", "troops", "congregations"; they "loitered", "prowled" and "paraded" the streets; a language which underscored the contemporary fears of a lurking criminal class was thus utilized. A few identifiable gangs of boys and young men were mentioned in the earlier period. For example, in 1816 magistrate William Fielding was asked about the "enormous associations in the Metropolis that went by the name of the 'Cutter lads'".[39] Throughout the whole of the period references were made to the "swell-mob". The swell-mob has been described as "pickpockets [who] . . . to escape detection, dress and behave like respectable people".[40] It would be difficult to give any accurate age range of the youths involved. However, contemporary literature suggests that members of the "swell-mob" were in their late teens and early twenties. John Gillis suggested the ages 14 to 20 for youth gangs in the nineteenth century, with a division marked by sexual activity.[41] There is a practical consideration to this, since status and belonging were generally conferred with experience and success. Certainly the popular perception was that boy thieves, and particularly pickpockets, might graduate into the ranks of the swell-mob; as Mayhew noted, "they have in most cases been thieves from their cradle".[42] A boy called Hewitt, awaiting transportation on the *Euryalus* hulk in the mid-1830s, told an interviewer that the swell-mob would often call into lodging-houses in order to recruit "go-alongs" for thieving expeditions: "boys are delighted [they] think it an honour to go with a swell-mob".[43] For example, a Superintendent of the C Division (Mayfair and Soho) told W. A. Miles of "a young man called Nelson . . . He is about twenty-three years old, of excellent address and manners and been many times in prison . . . The officers at Marlborough-street say that he makes more than any other of the swell-mob".[44] Another boy William Holland, aged 17, described the set-up used by Nelson and his more junior acolytes: "Nelson watches at Granger's and similar shops, to see where gentlemen put their purses; then gives a signal to his underling across the street, who comes over to do his work, under the shelter of Nelson, who he says has followed the line for 10 years".[45] Significantly, these gangs were explicitly male and, as suggested above, contemporary commentators saw them as providing an example of progression in the male juvenile's advance into crime. The swell-mob epitomized the rewards of a life of crime. A boy who had gained membership of the swell-mob, had, so to speak, arrived.

The construction of the female juvenile

The swell-mob were imbued with masculinity and maturity. An essential pre-requisite to assert and demonstrate such status was to have a girl. A female acquaintance was referred to by a number of designations. Whether she was his "girl", "mistress", "flash-girl", or "jomer", the presence of female company provided the step between immaturity and maturity that a boy apparently sought.[46] While it sometimes wasn't clear whether the girls were sexual part-ners, or "partners in crime", contemporary commentators seem to have gained a vicarious sexual thrill from describing the association between these young girls and boys. In 1817 William Crawford, a member of the Society for Invest-igating the Causes of Juvenile Delinquency, mentioned a 14-year-old boy who had confessed to sleeping with a number of girls of his own age; "he particularly named five".[47] In the same year several contributors to the police Select Com-mittee referred to the mistress of one Burnet, who was no more than ten at the time. In 1835, William Augustus Miles shockingly referred to a 15-year-old who, when apprehended, was in bed with three girls.[48] Girls were typically portrayed in sexual and corruptive contexts, and whilst a boy could be seduced by the example of a fellow juvenile, or by adult thieves, "women" were seen as a major downfall. In 1831 Edward Gibbon Wakefield wrote that:

> a still more effectual means of seduction is applied, viz. the precocious excitement and gratification of the sexual passion, by the aid of women in league with the thieves, and to whom is commonly entrusted the task of suggesting to the intoxicated youth, that robbery is the only means, and a safe means, of continuing to enjoy a life of riotous debauchery.[49]

"Women" generally referred to girls in their teens, or at the most, in their early twenties. Wakefield described women as posing as the boys' sisters, sug-gesting that he was not referring to females of an advanced age. Indeed, the ambiguity of this language describing the boys and their "women" or "girls" is routine in the contemporary literature.[50] There was a general inference that these female seductresses tended to be older than the boys they consorted with. Girls, who were open to corruption, were instead the corrupters; there were few references to boys corrupting girls. This stereotypical Eve relation-ship is remarkably consistent; presumably the slightly older age range of the girls made it easier to support this model of corruption. Tentative findings from sampled indictments derived from the Middlesex criminal registers between 1797 and 1847 suggest that girls entered the criminal justice system when slightly older. Thus, 45 per cent of juvenile girls were aged 16, as opposed to 34 per cent of juvenile males (83 per cent of juvenile females, and 73 per cent of juvenile males were aged 14-and-over). This pattern changed little over time.[51] However, since much "sexual corruption" presumably took place outside the justice system there is no practical way of assessing the relative ages of females. These girls were clearly defined in their gender roles. The children were not portrayed merely as boys and girls herding together, rather they were boy thieves and girl prostitutes. Moreover, the terminology clearly referred to a sexual relationship rather than one of financial exchange. Prostitute was interchangeable with temptress or seductress: the significance lay in the sexual implications of this terminology.

The subject of juvenile prostitutes caused some conflict in the representations of juvenile boys. On the one hand, sexuality and female companionship implied both masculinity and maturity; yet, on the other hand, the way in which these girls were stereotyped seemed to suggest a relative innocence on the part of the boys. Thus girls, once they were categorized as criminals, or more appropriately as prostitutes, were attributed a greater maturity than boys. This points to a strong resistance to equate sexual knowledge with female physical immaturity. Almost consistently girls were portrayed as hardened, corrupt women. In January 1831, two girls were arrested and charged at Bow Street:

> ... with walking the streets for the purpose of prostitution, and with uttering the most abominable language under the Piazzas of Covent-Garden ... although of such tender years, the defendants were hardened in vice, and the language which they were constantly in the habit of using was most obscene and disgusting.[52]

It is hard to credit that these two girls were aged 11 and 12. There seems to be an implicit suggestion that girls, unlike boy thieves, had considerably more control over their actions. This reflected the contemporary stigmatization of the "fallen" woman. Thus, once a woman (or girl) had given herself to "immorality", she was capable of far greater depths of evil and vice than her male counterparts. Moreover, once corrupted sexually, reclamation or restoration of respectability was inconceivable: hence, *she* then became the corrupter (in contrast to this was the identification of the female child as a victim of sexual corruption, illustrated by the moral panic surrounding the "white slave trade" in the later nineteenth century).[53] Mary Carpenter, well known for her work with juvenile offenders, wrote in 1872:

> The very susceptibility and tenderness of woman's nature render her more completely diseased in her whole nature when this is perverted to evil; and when a woman has thrown aside the virtuous restraints of society, and is enlisted on the other side of evil, she is far more dangerous to society than the other sex.[54]

The sense that once within the criminal justice system the woman or girl offender was worse than her male counterpart was also implied by Mrs Shaw of the Chelsea School of Discipline. When asked about the girls' demeanour, Shaw replied, "their violence is really fearful, one or two have threatened to knock me down; they doubled their little hands; however we have never suffered anything serious; its mere threat".[55]

While male juvenile behaviour was characterized by the conflict between innocence and experience, there was generally seen to be some force influencing their actions. Thus they were corrupted by parents, by other boys, by temptations, by older thieves, by women and girls. While juvenile girls had also been corrupted at some stage, what is interesting is the way in which they were treated as part of the threat to boys, rather than assessed as offenders in their own right. There was much less discussion of saving and reforming these juvenile prostitutes, rather it seems that their role within these discourses was mainly as a cipher for the actions of male juvenile offenders. Badness was transferred from the boys to their girls. Thus as one writer commented in 1835: "these boys have their girls, who are more depraved even in their habits, who live extravagantly on the produce of the plunder, urging them on to guilt, and sinking these boys as low as they can be sunk in every species of debauchery and crime".[56]

In fact, a substantial minority of girls were appearing in front of the criminal courts in their own right, charged with petty theft, pickpocketing, and other property crimes.[57] Of the 217 female juvenile indictments sampled from the Middlesex Criminal Registers, 89 per cent were indicted for larceny. Only three girls were indicted for serious larcenies (such as burglary and robbery), and four for crimes against the person.[58] The larceny figures are very similar for boys. Hence, 90 per cent were indicted for larceny.[59] There was slightly more likelihood for girls to be indicted for indirect property crimes such as coining and fencing (7 per cent as opposed to 4 per cent of boys); however, the numbers are small so that it would be unwise to draw any definite observations from this.[60] While the presence of female juveniles was lower compared to the number of indicted females overall, there is a suggestion that girl thieves were more likely to be treated informally, by the magistrate prior to the superior courts, or by some other agency.

A number of institutions existed to deal with delinquent youth. The Refuge for the Destitute and the early Philanthropic Society took in children of both sexes. At least two organizations were aimed at juvenile prostitution. For example the Society for the Suppression of Juvenile Prostitution was in operation in the 1830s, and the Birmingham Society for the Protection of Young Females and Suppression of Juvenile Prostitution in the 1840s. The Royal Victoria Asylum and the Chelsea School of Discipline in Middlesex were designated for female juveniles. At the School of Discipline, girls were not allowed skipping for exercise "since it makes them bold in their manners".[61] A set of admissions to the London Bridewell in 1835 show a healthy female presence; just under half of the juvenile inmates were girls. However, almost three-quarters of the boys had been admitted for thieving and pilfering, as opposed to just over a quarter of the girls.[62] In fact, the vast majority of the girls had entered into the Bridewell on the grounds of prostitution. For example, the Refuge for the Destitute and the Bridewell took in female juveniles, in some cases recommended by the magistrates, in others brought by their guardians.[63] Typical of entrants to the Bridewell House of Correction in 1835 were the 14-year-old, brought in by her father: "a Girl of violent, wild, and disobedient Character, quite beyond the Control of her parents"; and another 14-year-old, brought by her friends, a "young girl [who] is addicted to pilfering, has followed loose habits, and associated with very bad characters".[64] Even where "loose habits" were not expressly referred to, sexual transgression was implied. Portrayals of female juveniles were permeated with maturity, and there was little conflict with childishness in these descriptions. In 1835 Lieutenant John Silby, governor of Brixton House of Correction, posed the following rhetorical question: "What female who may, by the temptation of a vanity so natural and so fatal to the sex, have once rendered herself liable to this contamination, can for a moment be supposed capable of ever resisting its influence. [sic]"[65]

Conclusion

This chapter has explored the ways in which gender was expressed in representations of male juvenile delinquents. Moreover, it has suggested that the role of gender in constructions of criminal children in the early nineteenth century was inextricably tied to behaviour perceived as being associated with maturity, or the adult state: i.e. robust masculinity, sexual knowledge, coarse language and pastimes. Gender roles were clearly stated in the familiar mantra of the boy thief and girl prostitute. However, this was a partisan discourse that concerned itself almost wholly with male juvenile offenders. The conflicts between innocence and experience and the resonance of these themes in institutional and legislative responses to juvenile crime were based largely on a concern over boys rather than girls. Where girls were considered, their role was peripheral and sexual. Moreover, the context they were located in was at the periphery of male juvenility. This rigid exposition of the female gender was also inherent in concern over occupational issues. For example, the investigations and committees leading up to the 1842 Mines Act put considerable emphasis on the proximity of girls to boys, and on the various states of female undress. Ultimately this discourse was locked in the conflict between masculinity and boyishness, between maturity and childishness – female juvenile delinquents were of little significance. These concerns were underlined by Matthew Davenport Hill, recorder of Birmingham, and a founder of the Reformatory School movement. In 1855 he argued that the delinquent:

> is a stunted little man already – he knows much and a great deal too much of what is called life – he can take care of his own immediate interests. He is self-reliant, he has so long directed or misdirected his own actions and has so little trust in those about him, that he submits to no control and asks for no protection. He has consequently much to unlearn – he has to be turned again into a child.[66]

Statistical Appendix:
Table 3.1 Juvenile indictments, Middlesex, 1791–1848*

Year	Juveniles	Juveniles % of total	Girls only	Boys only	Girl % of juveniles	Boy % of juveniles
1791	104	7	18	86	17	83
1792	74	8	15	59	20	80
1793	60	6	11	49	18	82
1794	14	2	3	11	21	79
1796	44	5	9	35	20	80
1797	32	3	6	26	19	81
1800	83	10	15	68	18	82
1801	135	9	21	114	16	84
1802						
1803	76	7	15	61	20	80
1804	71	8	28	43	39	61
1805	68	7	32	36	47	53
1806	57	5	11	46	19	81
1807	53	5	15	38	28	72
1808	45	4	17	28	38	62
1809	100	8	34	66	34	66
1810	71	6	13	58	18	82
1811	71	6	18	53	25	75
1812	101	7	33	68	33	67
1813	100	6	25	75	25	75
1814	123	8	17	106	14	86
1815	147	7	19	128	13	87
1816	200	9	29	171	15	85
1817	286	11	21	265	7	93
1818	244	9	28	216	11	89
1819	261	10	24	237	9	91
1820	331	12	33	298	10	90
1821	322	13	40	282	12	88
1822	316	12	27	289	9	91
1823	329	13	44	285	13	87
1824	377	14	52	325	14	86
1825	368	13	47	321	13	87
1826	440	13	45	395	10	90
1827	459	14	33	426	7	93
1828	427	12	41	386	10	90
1829						
1830						
1831						
1832						
1833						
1834	602	15	102	500	17	83
1835	489	14	89	400	18	82
1836	503	15	98	405	19	81

Table 3.1 (Cont'd)

Year	Juveniles	Juveniles % of total	Girls only	Boys only	Girl % of juveniles	Boy % of juveniles
1837	396	12	63	333	16	84
1838	475	14	68	407	14	86
1839	520	14	72	448	14	86
1840	506	14	69	437	14	86
1841	502	14	74	428	15	85
1842	526	13	83	443	16	84
1843	600	14	79	521	13	87
1844	540	13	76	464	14	86
1845	725	16	93	632	13	87
1846	760	16	92	668	12	88
1847	802	15	79	723	10	90
1848	597	12	83	514	14	86

* This table gives the yearly counts and the yearly percentage distribution of juvenile offenders (0-16). It also gives counts and percentages for both female and male juveniles. There may be some very minor inaccuracies in these figures since they are based on a manual count of *all* the registers. The registers for 1791-1802 are not discrete (e.g. 1791-2 has been called 1791), and data is missing from some of these early years. The ages are missing from the registers for 1829-33. These figures come from the Middlesex Criminal Registers for 1791-1848. HO26/1-56, Public Record Office.

Notes

1. C. Dickens, *Oliver Twist* (London: Richard Bentley, 1838), p. 123.
2. For work on the history of juvenile crime, see V. Bailey, *Delinquency and citizenship: reclaiming the young offender, 1914-48* (Oxford: Clarendon Press, 1987); L. R. Berlanstein, "Vagrants, beggars and thieves: delinquent boys in mid-nineteenth century Paris", *Journal of Social History* 12, 1978-9, pp. 531-52; J. Gillis, "The evolution of juvenile delinquency in England, 1890-1914", *Past and Present* 67, 1975, pp. 96-126; E. Harvey, *Youth and crime in Weimar Germany* (Oxford: Oxford University Press, 1994); P. J. R. King & J. Noel, "The origins of 'the problem of juvenile delinquency': the growth of juvenile prosecutions in London in the late eighteenth and early nineteenth centuries", *Criminal Justice History* 14, 1993, pp. 17-41; S. Magarey, "The invention of juvenile delinquency in early nineteenth-century England", *Labour History* [Canberra] 34, 1978, pp. 11-27; M. May, "Innocence and experience: the evolution of the concept of juvenile delinquency in the mid-nineteenth century", *Victorian Studies* 17(1), 1973, pp. 7-29; A. Platt, *The child savers: the invention of delinquency* (Chicago: University of Chicago Press, 1969); L. Radzinowicz & R. Hood, *The emergence of penal policy*, vol. 5 of *A history of English criminal law and its administration from 1750* (Oxford: Stevens & Sons, 1986); P. Rush, "The government of a generation: the subject of juvenile delinquency", *Liverpool Law Review* 14(1), 1992, pp. 3-43; H. Shore, *The social history of juvenile crime in Middlesex, 1790-1850* (PhD thesis, University

of London, 1996); H. Shore, *Artful dodgers: youth and crime in early nineteenth-century London* (Woodbridge: The Royal Historical Society, forthcoming).

3. This conflict is particularly strengthened when considered in light of work on the growing tendency to feminize the child during the nineteenth century. C. Steedman, *Strange dislocations: childhood and the idea of human interiority, 1780-1930* (London: Virago Press, 1995), p. 9.

4. Juvenile Offenders Act 1850, 13 & 14 Vict. C. 37.

5. King & Noel, "Origins"; Shore, *Juvenile crime*, pp. 47-70, 161-91.

6. Reformatory Schools Act 1854, 17 & 18 Vict. C. 74; Middlesex Industrial Schools Act 1854 (Local), 17 & 18 Vict. C. 169; Reformatory and Industrial Schools Amendment Act 1856, 19 & 20 Vict. C. 109; Industrial Schools Act 1857, 20 & 21 Vict. C. 3; Reformatory Schools Act 1857, 20 & 21 Vict. C. 55.

7. M. Cale, "Girls and the perception of sexual danger in the Victorian reformatory system", *History* **78**, 1993, pp. 201-17; L. Mahood & M. Littlewood; "The 'vicious' girl and the 'street-corner' boy: sexuality and the gendered delinquent in the Scottish child-saving movement, 1850-1914", *Journal of the History of Sexuality* **4**, 1994, pp. 549-78; L. Mahood, *Policing gender, class and family* (London: UCL Press, 1995).

8. L. Jackson, "The child's word in court: cases of sexual abuse in London, 1870-1914", see Chapter 11.

9. For a discussion of the forces that shape societies' constructions of masculinity, see A. Phillips, *The trouble with boys: parenting the men of the future* (London: Pandora, 1993); on masculinity and crime, see T. Newburn & E. A. Stanko (eds), *Just boys doing business? Men, masculinities and crime* (London: Routledge, 1994). For historical discussions of masculinity, see M. Roper & J. Tosh (eds), *Manful assertions: masculinities in Britain since 1800* (London: Routledge, 1991).

10. For a discussion of the development of North American and British sociological perspectives on youth crime see, G. Pearson, "Youth, crime and society", in *The Oxford handbook of criminology*, M. Maguire, R. Morgan, R. Reiner (eds) (Oxford: Clarendon Press, 1994), pp. 1161-206.

11. J. Tosh, "What should historians do with masculinity? reflections on nineteenth-century Britain", *History Workshop Journal* **38**, 1994, pp. 179-202.

12. King & Noel, "Origins"; Shore, *Juvenile crime*, pp. 47-70.

13. Magarey, "Invention".

14. For the later eighteenth century, see: J. Hanway, *An account of the Marine Society, recommending the piety and policy of the Institution, and pointing out the advantages according to the nation ... The sixth edition, adapted to the present time* (London: 1759); J. Fielding, *An account of the receipts and disbursements relating to Sir John Fielding's plan, for the preserving of distressed boys, by sending them to sea, as apprentices in the Merchants service ... and a short account of the sending boys on board men of war ... in the year 1756* (London: W. Griffin, 1771).

15. See W. A. Miles, *Poverty, mendicity and crime*, H. Brandon (ed.) (London: Shaw & Sons, 1839), p. 45; E. G. Wakefield, "Facts relating to the punishment of death in the metropolis", in *The collected works of Edward Gibbon Wakefield*, M. F. Lloyd Pritchard (ed.) (Glasgow: Collins, 1968), pp. 187-267, particularly pp. 200-1.

16. J. Weeks, *Against nature: essays on history, sexuality and identity* (London: Rivers Oram Press, 1991), pp. 46-67, especially p. 50. See also Jackson, "Child's word".

17. *Report of the committee for investigating the causes of the alarming increase of juvenile delinquency in the metropolis* (London: Dove, 1816). Cited in "Select Committee on the state of the police of the metropolis" (hereafter SCP), "2nd report", *PP*, 1817, pp. 433-9.

18. SCP, "2nd report", *PP*, 1817, p. 434.

19. J. Fielding, *A plan of the asylum; or, house of refuge for orphans and other deserted girls of the poor in this metropolis* (London: printed for R. Franklin, 1758), cited in W. B. Sanders, *Juvenile offenders for a thousand years: selected readings from Anglo-Saxon times to 1900* (Chapel Hill: University of North Carolina Press, 1970), p. 57. For a discussion of delinquent youth in the early modern period, see P. Griffiths, *Youth and authority: formative experience in England, 1560-1640* (Oxford: Clarendon Press, 1996).

20. Shore, *Juvenile crime*, pp. 71-97.

21. See Appendix.

22. *The Times*, 30 July 1831, p. 4, c. b.

23. Miles, *Poverty*, pp. 106-7.

24. W. Beck, *Friends, ancient and modern* (London: Friends Tract Association, 1908), pp. 26-7.

25. SCP, "2nd report", *PP*, 1817, p. 542.

26. T. Wontner, "The school master's experience in Newgate", *Fraser's Magazine* 5, 1832, p. 363.

27. SCP, *PP*, 1818, p. 173.

28. *Ibid.*, pp. 181-2.

29. *Ibid.*, pp. 181-2.

30. V. A. C. Gatrell, *The hanging tree: execution and the English people, 1770-1868* (Oxford: Oxford University Press, 1994), pp. 35-6, 110, 138, 144.

31. On childhood and youth, see P. Ariès, *Centuries of childhood* (London: Jonathan Cape, 1962); H. Cunningham, *The children of the poor: representations of childhood since the seventeenth century* (Oxford: Blackwell, 1991); H. Cunningham, *Children and childhood in western society since 1500* (Harlow, England: Longman, 1995); A. Davin, *Growing up poor: home, school and street in London, 1870-1914* (London: Rivers Oram Press, 1996); L. De Mause, *The history of childhood* (New York: PsychoHistory Press, 1974); J. Gillis, *Youth and history: tradition and change in European age relations, 1770-present* (London: Academic Press, 1974); H. Hendrick, *Images of youth: age, class, and the male youth problem, 1880-1920* (Oxford: Oxford University Press, 1990); M. Mitterauer, *A history of youth* (Oxford: Blackwell, 1992); G. Pearson, *Hooligan: a history of respectable fears* (London: Macmillan, 1983); I. Pinchbeck & M. Hewitt, *From the eighteenth century to the Children's Act 1948*, vol. 2 of *Children in English society* (London: Routledge & Kegan Paul, 1973); L. Rose, *The erosion of childhood: child oppression in Britain,1860-1918* (London: Routledge, 1991); J. Springhall, *Youth, empire and society* (London: Croom Helm, 1977); J. Springhall, *Coming of age: adolescence in Britain, 1860-1960* (London: Gill & Macmillan, 1986); Steedman, *Strange dislocations*.

32. SCP, *PP*, 1828, p. 68. London's Society for the Suppression of Mendicity was founded in 1818 by William Bodkin. For discussion of the Society, see L. Rose, *"Rogues and vagabonds": The vagrant underworld in Britain, 1815-1985* (London: Routledge, 1988), p. 18.

33. "First report of the commissioners appointed to inquire as to the best means of establishing an efficient constabulary force in the counties of England and Wales", *PP*, 1839, Appendix 6, p. 206.

34. *The Times*, 15 April 1835, p. 6, cc. d & e.

35. SCP, "2nd report", *PP*, 1817, pp. 360-1; *Committee for investigating the causes . . .* cited in Sanders, *Juvenile offenders*, p. 104.

36. SCP, "2nd report", *PP*, 1817, pp. 360-1.

37. SCP, *PP*, 1828, p. 84.

38. "Select Committee on gaols and houses of correction in England and Wales" (hereafter SCG), "1st report", *PP*, 1835, p. 307.

39. SCP, *PP*, 1816, p. 129.

40. E. Partridge, *A dictionary of the underworld* (Ware, Hertfordshire: Wordsworth, 1989, originally published by Routledge & Kegan Paul, 1950), p. 707.

41. See Miles, *Poverty*, pp. 136-7, 142-3; Wontner, "School master's experience", pp. 352-3; Gillis, *Youth and history*, p. 62. Gender/gang issues have also been discussed by A. Davies, "Youth gangs and street violence: Manchester and Salford, 1870-1900", paper presented at the international conference "Gender and crime in Britain and Europe: early modern and modern", Roehampton Institute London, England, 1995.

42. H. Mayhew et al., *London labour and the London poor*, vol. 4 (London, 1861-2), p. 308.

43. Evidence of Hewitt, loose manuscript notepads, vol. 3, HO73/16, Public Records Office (PRO).

44. Miles, *Poverty*, p. 137. William Nelson, aged 23, was sentenced to transportation for seven years at the Westminster Sessions, 8 December 1836. Middlesex Criminal Registers, HO26/42, 1836, PRO.

45. Miles, *Poverty*, p. 114.

46. Jomer = a girl, a mistress, a fancy girl. Partridge, *Dictionary of the underworld*, p. 371.

47. SCP, "2nd report", *PP*, 1817, p. 430.

48. *Ibid.*, p. 440, 542; Evidence from W. A. Miles, SCG (secret), p. 4, HO73/16, PRO. This evidence contributed to the Select Committee was not released for publication.

49. Wakefield, "Facts relating to the punishment of death", p. 200.

50. *Ibid.*, p. 201; Miles, *Poverty*, pp. 45-6.

51. HO26/5, 13, 23, 33, 43, 53, PRO. For further insight into female and male offender age distribution, see Shore, *Juvenile crime*, pp. 66-8; King, "Female offenders, work and life-cycle change in late eighteenth-century London", *Continuity and Change* 11(1), 1996, pp. 61-90.

52. *The Times*, 26 January 1831. See Jackson, "Child's word", for discussion of the connection between the "immoral" child and vocabulary.

53. For discussion of the stigmatization of criminal women, see L. Zedner, *Women, crime and custody in Victorian England* (Oxford: Oxford University Press, 1991), pp. 40-50. For the female child as victim, see J. Weeks, *Sex, politics and society: the regulation of sexuality since 1800* (Harlow, England: Longman, 1981), pp. 86, 90, 92. For discussion of "The maiden tribute of modern Babylon", W. T. Stead's famous 1885 exposé of child prostitution, see J. Walkowitz, *City of dreadful delight: narratives of sexual danger in late-Victorian London* (London: Virago, 1992).

54. M. Carpenter, *Reformatory prison discipline* (London: Longman, 1872), p. 68.
55. SCG, "4th & 5th report", *PP*, 1835, p. 487.
56. *Ibid.*, "4th & 5th report", 1835, p. 513.
57. See Appendix.
58. Middlesex Criminal Registers, HO26/5, 13, 23, 33, 43, 53, PRO; Shore, *Juvenile crime*, especially pp. 47-70.
59. *Ibid.*
60. *Ibid.*
61. SCG, "4th & 5th reports", *PP*, 1835, p. 485.
62. SCG, "3rd report", 1835, pp. 419-25.
63. See the Minutes of the Refuge for the Destitute (1819-47) at the Rose Lipman Library, Hackney Archive Department.
64. SCG, "3rd report", *PP*, 1835, pp. 419-25.
65. SCG, "1st report", *PP*, 1835, p. 150.
66. M. D. Hill, "Practical suggestions to the founders of the reformatory schools", in J. C. Symons, *On the reformation of young offenders* (London, Routledge, 1855), p. 2.

Women and crime in Imperial Russia, 1834–1913: representing realities

Stephen P. Frank

The construction of nineteenth-century "female criminality" within the context of a medicalized discourse on gender and agency has been widely discussed in an impressive body of literature on the development of modern criminology and social control, as has the critical role played by anxieties over moral and public disorder in this process. Much less known is how legal and medical professionals utilized judicial statistics to sustain their belief that the criminal woman represented not only a social and cultural deviant but also a moral, psychological or biological aberration.[1] Statistical evidence, specialists argued, served to confirm that gender itself determined the nature and parameters of criminality while also explaining why women perpetrated so few crimes and such a narrow range of offences. Crime constituted a largely male domain in Imperial Russia, much as it did across Europe, not only in theory or ideology but also in the very production of documents like criminal statistics. As a result, with the exception of offences committed almost exclusively by women (abortion and infanticide) and crimes (murder of spouses or sexual offences) in which women deviated from their traditionally assumed roles as passive, religious, maternal and moral models, professional literature dating from the 1860s and after paid scant attention to female perpetrators, and virtually all who proffered written opinions leaned heavily upon judicial statistics to support, refine and perpetuate culturally constructed stereotypes concerning women's involvement in the criminal process.[2] Yet their analysis was seriously flawed by misinterpretation of these very sources.

This chapter offers an interrogation and critique of the primary documents upon which Russian criminologists and jurists relied in their depictions of female criminality, and questions their peculiar image of women and crime in Imperial Russia. Above all it seeks to uncover the narrative embedded in these sources as opposed to the narrative that a small group of mostly male professionals fashioned from them. I argue here that the processes through which sociological illusions of the criminal were produced only become evident within the broader context of Russia's highly fluid court jurisdictions. Through an analysis of tsarist judicial statistics for the period 1834–1913, I show that shifting jurisdictions over certain offences (especially property infractions), the exclusion of most misdemeanours from discussions of crime, and changes in both the law and patterns of prosecution combined to determine the statistical appearance of women's criminality and its subsequent interpretation. These points are supported by an examination of female perpetrators' social, occupational, and geographical profile (that is, the profile drawn by published data), for here, too, the structure of court jurisdictions ensured that women from the urban labouring poor were far more likely to end up in the statistical compilations, while peasant women remained grossly undercounted. Class thus emerges as another defining feature of "criminality".[3]

The findings of this study emphasize the historicity of crime and point out how criminality and official responses to it were shaped by a confluence of factors previously ignored. Along with the important issue of court jurisdictions, it is clear that changing occupation patterns among women and an upsurge of paternalistic and moral concerns over such changes decisively affected the types of offences for which women were prosecuted and convicted. The wildly fluctuating prosecution of fornication perhaps best exemplifies how public and class anxieties define or alter the picture of criminality. Equally significant, as the state focused increasingly on problems of social order and fiscal needs late in the century, prosecution rates showed a rapid shift toward offences within these categories. In short, the statistical records reflect socially constructed definitions of given behaviours that appeared threatening at particular historical moments, as well as the vulnerability (or juridical isolation) of certain occupational, age and gender populations. Although the influence of these phenomena can readily be located within Russia's judicial statistics, none was noted by contemporary specialists precisely because explanations of female criminality had already been formed, and published data thus served merely to confirm and buttress established knowledge.

Patterns of growth in female crime

Specialists concerned about law and order after Emancipation (1861)[4] focused most attention on the male segment of Russia's "dangerous classes" for the simple fact that, as elsewhere in the modern world, men constituted the overwhelming majority of defendants before criminal courts. The studies by those few who did venture to write on women and crime were fraught with problems. None analysed the growth of female crime, for example, or undertook comparisons of pre- and post-reform data. Far more significant, contemporaries ignored misdemeanours despite their critical importance to understanding the perceived nature of women's crime. This fact accounts in large parts for the way in which such crime was depicted.

Russians who examined female criminality sought above all to explain the apparently low level and limited range of offences committed by women. The answers they proposed, of course, were shaped by prevailing cultural images of women, but they also served to reinforce broader views about "female crime" that saw women as most likely to commit homicide (particularly murder of spouses), infanticide and fornication. Female felons were also portrayed as disproportionately urban and young, although at the same time it was claimed that the more violent a given crime, the more likely its perpetrator was to be a peasant. As we shall see, the fact that contemporaries ignored all misdemeanour data from peace and *volost'* (township) courts lent especially strong support to the prevailing stereotype. These attitudes, as expressed in the contemporary literature, reflect the peculiar mingling of patriarchal, religious and imported Western views of women and crime, most of which drew from traditional stereotypes prevailing in Russia and abroad, and all of which had their followers within educated society. Yet Russian criminologists comfortably mixed elements from various schools of thought precisely because each defined the criminal woman as having crossed moral, social, biological or environmental boundaries beyond which "normal" women did not venture. Thus the moralist perspective on crime remained dominant throughout the imperial era and beyond, as it did in western Europe and the United States.[5] When such arguments were combined with readings of the criminal statistics they gave stark definition to women's crime.

The definition of crime as a male domain placed women's criminal activity at the periphery while denying it either a history or a dynamic. Certain types of illicit behaviour on the part of women have, historically, escaped classification as "crime", and at other times authorities shunted female perpetrators to lower courts for prosecution, one important result of which is the static nature of women's crime that emerges from contemporary writings based on judicial statistics. This seemingly changeless character of female criminality has only recently received serious challenge. Analysing crime in London between 1687 and 1912, for example, Malcolm Feeley and Deborah Little demonstrate that women constituted three to four times the proportion of felony defendants during the first half of the eighteenth century as in the modern era, with most of this decline occurring in the nineteenth century. Studies of Britain, Canada, France, Holland and colonial Massachusetts all concur with these findings.[6] While existing data from imperial Russia only reach back to 1834, they nevertheless provide evidence of a similar, albeit less dramatic, decline in women's proportional representation, and also reflect a close connection between crime and socio-economic position.

The number of criminal offences for which Russian women were tried grew steadily throughout most of the 80 years examined in this study, but women as a proportion of accused felons reflected movement in the opposite direction (see Figure 4.1). While averaging 15.3 per cent of all persons tried between 1834 and 1861, with a high of almost 20 per cent as late as 1855, women declined to only 11.3 per cent in the decade 1861–70 and reached a low point

Figure 4.1 Women's proportion among criminal defendants, 1834-1913

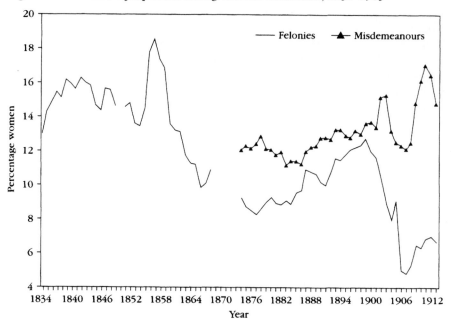

of 8.3 per cent by 1877. Although the percentage crept upwards at the end of the 1870s and jumped substantially between 1891 and 1897, achieving a post-reform peak in 1899 at the height of a still unexplored upsurge of fornication prosecutions, pre-Emancipation levels for felonies would not be matched again during the imperial era. They dropped consistently after 1897, plummeting to as low as 4.9 per cent in 1907 and averaging just 6.1 per cent between 1906 and 1913. During the First World War and the first decade of Soviet rule female felons also remained at a lower proportional level than was found in the 1840s, roughly approximating that of the mid-1890s.[7] Thus the 50 years following the Great Reforms witnessed a smaller proportion of women coming before higher courts than in the last decades of serfdom.

Figure 4.1 shows a quite different pattern for misdemeanours prosecuted before justices of the peace, where women consistently made up a larger percentage of persons tried than they did in circuit courts. During the post-Emancipation era women averaged 13.5 per cent of recorded peace court convictions and, especially from the 1890s, their proportion increased steadily to a peak of nearly 18 per cent in 1912. Records from local *volost'* courts – which tried petty offences among the peasant population and heard well over half of all criminal cases in Russia – suggest an even greater level of female participation, with women representing from 25 per cent to 40 per cent of total defendants in some localities.[8] While sufficient data do not exist to chart convictions in *volost'* courts over time, it would certainly appear that the lower we move down the jurisdictional ladder, the larger was the proportion of women. It is also clear from peace courts convictions that the proportion of women amongst those convicted for misdemeanours was increasing at the same time as female representation amongst convicted felons was decreasing.

Shifts of this sort are most commonly linked to changes in the laws or patterns of policing and prosecution, and to social change. A decline in the percentage of women coming before courts in North America and Europe, for example, was closely related to new types of social control which made women "less subject to the criminal sanction as other forms of more private control emerged."[9] These included institutions such as reformatories, "invisible" social, cultural and economic mechanisms of constraint developed by middle-class societies, and moral reform movements aimed at controlling female sexuality. But in late nineteenth-century Russia, patriarchal and familial forms of control over women remained strong, especially in the countryside, though they usually left no mark on the statistical record. At the same time, modern non-juridical controls that would have removed women from the judicial process (and from the criminal statistics) were emerging far more slowly than in countries like England or France. Reformatories, for example, had only just begun to develop near the turn of the century, leaving gaol, prison and other correctional institutions as the primary means of sanction against female offenders. As for moral reform movements, it is reasonable to presume that their efforts actually resulted in a higher number of women charged with infractions like fornication during the 1880s and 1890s.[10] Nor did changing laws on prostitution (or patterns of enforcement) influence the proportion of women among total convicts either before or after the great reforms, since the state regulated prostitution administratively and tsarist statistics do not include it among criminal offences. Unregistered prostitution was most often tried in lower courts, or else disguised as public health violations and disturbing the peace.[11]

Changing proportions of women within Russian judicial statistics can be explained most fully by a confluence of shifting jurisdictions over property offences and the decriminalization (or redefinition) of behaviours previously prosecuted in substantial numbers. The sharpest and earliest decline mirrored an easing of prosecutions for religious offences and fornication, which began in the mid-1850s after reaching a peak earlier that decade. Then a law of 18 May 1882, shifted up to half of all burglaries and a great number of petty theft cases from circuit to peace courts. The reforms of 1889 next abolished most justices of the peace, redistributing their cases among land captains and *volost'* courts. Taken together, these changes pushed the proportion of female felons steadily downward while accounting for faster growth in women's misdemeanour convictions, much as occurred somewhat earlier in England and France.[12] Overall female proportions barely reflected this shift in property crime cases, however, because convictions for fornication began to increase at precisely the same time, thereby masking a sharp fluctuation in the data. The final plunge (abetted by a drop in prosecution of women during the 1905 revolution) followed the 1903 decriminalization of fornication, emphasizing again the importance of how crime is defined at given historical moments.[13]

A combination of legal and jurisdictional changes, therefore, greatly effected women's percentage of the known criminal population. The expanded jurisdiction of peace courts and, after 1889, *volost'* courts over property offences (a category in which women were most prominently represented) resulted in an increase of women's already higher proportionality among persons convicted by these courts, especially as compared to felonies. Yet because Russian criminologists focused solely on felonies, they did not note this fundamental relationship between circuit and peace court convictions. Instead, they found a small - even shrinking - proportion of women tried and convicted, which buttressed their peculiar understanding of female criminality. In the process, they also overlooked several significant facts about women's crimes.

The most notable of these is that, despite the small proportion of women within the enumerated criminal population, growth rates for female crimes exceeded those of males in both the pre- and post-reform eras. The seeming paradox here is explained by the vastly greater number of men in the convict population at the start of our period, even a moderate increase of which would have masked a faster growth rate for women. Given that the low starting point for women's crimes makes their numerical growth appear particularly impressive, the importance of such differences should certainly not be overstated.[14] Yet women's growth rates do speak to a dynamic of change that belies images of relative stasis. Indeed, this "invisible" dynamic is striking when contrasted with the contemporary picture of female crime, since it was not limited to the "traditional" categories of fornication, infanticide or spouse murder.

During the period 1834-59 the annual rate of growth among women convicted by Russia's criminal courts (*ugolovnye sudy*) averaged 1.6 per cent, but only 0.5 per cent for men.[15] This difference was particularly notable within certain segments of the population, such as among female crown, factory and household serfs, whose crimes rose at the striking average annual rate of 13.9 per cent in contrast to an otherwise impressive 8.4 per cent for men from these same groups. Growth rates of all female and male peasants convicted were 2.6 per cent and 1.2 per cent, respectively. Although these figures do not include peasants judged outside official courts for petty crimes (by their masters and communal courts in the case of seigniorial serfs, or in village and appellate *volost'* courts established for state peasants in 1838), they nevertheless demonstrate that for serious infractions of the criminal law in the three decades before Emancipation, virtually all growth occurred among the rural population.

Following Emancipation, aggregate data indicated a much faster increase of men's crimes. But the constant addition of new courts throughout the empire combined with revolution in 1905 to distort the real movement of trials and convictions.[16] Still, even adjusted figures for the years 1874 to 1913 seem to suggest that growth rates were twice as high among male felons, averaging 1.7 per cent annually as compared with 0.8 per cent for women. Yet this difference stemmed entirely from a 14.9 per cent annual increase in the number of men convicted during the 1905-7 revolution. Thus between 1874 and 1900 women's felony convictions grew at an average yearly rate of 2.4 per cent, but the figure for men reached only 1.0 per cent, and following the 1905 revolution, women's rate exceeded that of men by nearly three times (6.9 per cent compared with 2.6 per cent). This same dynamic is equally visible in peace court convictions, where women's annual rate of growth (2.9 per cent) also exceeded that of males (2.1 per cent). Per capita felony rates tell much the same story, appearing slightly higher among men than women when calculated for the entire period 1874-1913 (1.7 per cent and 1.4 per cent, respectively). From 1874 to 1900, however, female felonies increased at a per capita rate of 2.1 per cent, while those of men averaged 0.6 per cent. Similarly, if we exclude the revolutionary years 1905-7, the per capita rate among women surpassed that of men by four times (1.2 per cent and 0.3 per cent, respectively). In sum, whatever way we measure growth rates of criminal convictions, the same conclusion emerges. Except for the years 1905-7 when the state's military, police and judicial apparatuses were strained to their limits by arrests and prosecutions aimed at restoring order, the most rapid growth occurred among Russian women.[17] It must be stressed again that these higher rates for women are neither unexpected nor extraordinary, given a much lower numerical starting point. Such growth takes on greater significance, however, when we turn to consider the areas of "female criminality" that increased most rapidly.

The nature of women's crime

Tsarist statistics reveal that, except for sex-specific offences such as infanticide or rape and crimes in public office, the types of felonies for which women were charged during this period did not differ dramatically from those perpetrated by men. Moreover, the pattern of women's convictions was far from static, but, as Table 4.1 shows clearly, changed over time as a direct result of shifting court jurisdictions, changes in the laws, state concerns over public order and loss of revenue, evolving social and labour conditions, and anxieties about immorality among occupationally mobile women. Prior to the reform era of the 1860s criminal courts convicted women most frequently for theft, followed by religious offences (primarily deviation from the Orthodox faith or entering a sect of the old belief), fornication, murder, infractions of fire safety rules, vagrancy and violation of passport regulations, bootlegging, abandonment or concealing the corpse of a newborn, arson and adultery. By contrast, men were convicted for twice as many property offences as women, although nearly 70 per cent of these consisted of illegal wood-cutting in state or private forests, a crime for which few women were prosecuted. Misuse of public office took a distant second place among male crimes, followed by bootlegging, deviation from the faith, passport violations, and murder. These data from the second quarter of the nineteenth century, in fact, show a distribution of female felonies broader than that found in the post-reform era.

Table 4.1 Felony trials and convictions of women, 1837–1913 (As percentage of all women tried and convicted)

Crime	1837–46 Tried	1837–46 Convicted	1847–56 Tried	1847–56 Convicted	1861–69 Tried	1861–69 Convicted	1874–83 Tried	1874–83 Convicted	1884–93 Tried	1884–93 Convicted	1894–1903 Tried	1894–1903 Convicted	1904–13 Tried	1904–13 Convicted
Religious crimes	9.48		18.48	16.98	3.67	3.78	0.45	0.57	1.24	1.50	1.28	1.25	0.78	0.96
Sacrilege	0.39		0.23	0.19	0.11	0.15	0.31	0.25	0.25	0.23	0.15	0.12	0.25	0.23
Perjury and giving false evidence	0.16		ND	1.56	0.03	0.04	0.75	0.65	1.05	0.75	1.13	0.76	1.06	0.70
Uprisings and resistance to authorities	1.04		1.76	1.34	1.04	1.53	1.57	0.87	5.16	3.60	4.03	4.00	8.10	8.14
Insulting and disobeying authorities	ND		0.12	0.07	0.39	0.61	4.90	6.17	6.96	8.65	5.14	6.07	4.81	7.10
Infractions of passport regulations	7.59		ND	5.82	5.01	7.16	1.67	0.76	1.36	1.57	1.35	1.83	0.82	1.30
Forgery	ND		0.51	0.15	1.08	0.28	0.68	0.43	0.74	0.50	0.88	0.36	1.02	0.50
Infractions of customs regulations	0.47		ND	ND	0.28	0.28	0.47	0.63	1.41	1.64	1.56	1.75	3.80	5.03
Infractions of liquor regulations	3.37		6.77	5.72	1.46	1.87	1.36	1.99	2.54	2.92	0.69	0.74	1.04	1.33
Infractions of forest regulations	0.39		2.33	2.04	2.08	2.69	0.25	0.16	0.18	0.19	0.25	0.18	0.32	0.27
Organized gangs	ND		ND	0.25	0.17	0.11	0.23	0.21	0.16	0.13	0.08	0.06	0.30	0.26
Other crimes against safety and peace	1.92		ND	8.15	4.93	6.09	0.31	0.38	0.11	0.11	0.10	0.11	0.13	0.14
Fornication	7.57		8.79	12.28	2.91	4.46	2.16	3.49	8.80	11.67	15.31	20.06	0.00	0.00
Murder of spouse and relatives	0.29		ND	ND	ND	ND	2.06	2.52	1.60	1.69	1.45	1.32	2.14	1.77
Infanticide	1.96		ND	ND	ND	ND	2.20	1.26	2.87	1.63	2.53	1.51	2.50	1.00
Poisoning	0.81		ND	ND	ND	ND	0.77	0.71	0.75	0.60	0.46	0.36	0.36	0.20
All other murder	ND		ND	ND	ND	ND	4.39	4.39	4.63	4.58	3.05	2.78	3.60	2.98
(Total murder)	7.83		3.25	7.48	4.44	5.34	9.42	8.89	9.85	8.50	7.50	5.97	8.59	5.95
Abandonment and concealing corpse of newborns	0.90		0.45	2.91	1.33	2.04	5.86	9.23	9.21	13.99	9.26	13.51	8.28	13.75
Mortal injury	ND		ND	ND	ND	ND	0.72	0.54	0.72	0.56	0.68	0.61	1.25	1.01
Bodily injury	0.49		1.85	1.42	1.82	1.68	3.12	2.46	6.09	4.31	9.96	7.63	6.65	6.42
Insult (by word and deed)	1.72		ND	1.24	9.26	7.39	0.09	0.05	0.27	0.12	0.35	0.16	0.90	0.51
Adultery	0.49		1.86	2.31	0.93	1.03	0.80	0.68	1.31	1.05	2.56	1.69	1.33	0.87
Incest	0.42		0.73	0.48	0.24	0.28	0.94	0.76	1.18	1.04	0.97	0.72	0.53	0.40
Arson	4.36		3.62	2.84	1.51	1.03	3.21	1.23	3.16	1.15	1.75	0.57	2.08	0.55
Robbery	1.23		0.66	0.59	0.91	0.79	3.07	2.68	1.68	1.26	1.10	0.71	2.20	1.33
Burglary	ND		ND	ND	ND	ND	19.95	15.76	4.76	3.50	3.46	2.44	5.04	3.42
Dealing in stolen goods	ND		ND	ND	ND	ND	2.43	2.07	1.22	0.89	0.99	0.65	1.98	1.38
All other theft	24.25		29.81	21.63	36.35	28.17	27.03	29.13	22.85	21.17	19.97	17.60	29.11	27.51
(Total theft)	26.26		32.79	24.26	39.34	31.65	52.48	49.64	30.41	26.72	25.53	21.40	38.33	33.64
Swindling	1.65		1.84	0.98	4.36	2.99	0.41	0.34	0.26	0.23	0.24	0.21	0.34	0.32
Other	23.28		18.24	4.37	14.94	19.17	10.89	10.67	10.54	9.77	10.71	10.50	10.95	10.63

Several notable movements occurred in these patterns over the first two decades following the great reforms. Most significant, prosecution of sectarians before criminal courts fell sharply, and by the early 1870s the previously sizeable proportion of women convicted for religious crimes (18.5 per cent during the years 1847–56) fell to under 1 per cent of all female convicts. Insult and slander as indictable felonies likewise plummeted from 9.3 per cent to less than 1 per cent of women's total convictions during the 1860s, remaining at that level until the end of the old regime; in peace courts and *volost'* courts, however, such charges accounted for a much larger percentage of female *and* male offences.[18] Fornication witnessed a remarkable drop of five and a half times its pre-reform level (to a low of only 1.6 per cent of all women tried and 2.4 per cent of those convicted in the period 1874–8), and did not begin rising again until the early 1880s.[19] Here we can see clearly how socially or ideologically contrived definitions of threatening forms of sexual activity influenced the portrait of women's crime. Prior to Emancipation, Church persecution of schismatic marriages increased recorded cases of fornication substantially, since marriage to a sectarian and unregistered sectarian marriages were viewed as illegitimate, constituting a state of illegal cohabitation. As official persecution of schismatics declined, we find a corresponding drop in prosecutions of illegal cohabitation. Though by no means unknown before the 1860s, "free marriages" as practised within certain occupation groups appeared to grow thereafter in direct conjunction with the rising number of female outworkers and labourers, presenting another form of fornication subject to punishment under Russian law.[20] Most important for the post-reform era, beginning in the 1880s and continuing for nearly two decades until fornication's decriminalization in 1903, the fervent response by moral reformers to what they perceived as a frightening rise in illicit sexuality found clear reflection in the upsurge of convictions for this crime, much as was true throughout the industrializing world.[21]

Other categories of female felony convictions, most notably theft, murder, and concealing the corpse of a newborn, rose considerably in the wake of Emancipation. By the mid-1870s, theft had grown to over 50 per cent of all felonious offences for which women were tried and convicted, and remained at that level until the 1882 law shifted many burglaries and thefts to the peace courts' jurisdiction, creating a significant but entirely artificial change in the crime pattern thereafter. Since large numbers of Russian women were prosecuted for minor property offences, their proportion of felonious thefts declined sharply as a result, falling to a pre-reform level of 21.2 per cent during the years 1899–1903. A low growth rate for property offences also reflected this change, since "real" growth occurred in peace and *volost'* court convictions largely as a result of changing jurisdictions. Theft remained the largest group of women's recorded felonies throughout our period, however, with total property offences averaging 40 per cent of all convictions – slightly less than the 44.3 per cent for men. Nevertheless, contemporaries read into the statistics a low ratio of female crimes against property and a rising percentage of sexual and violent offences, particularly in the countryside.[22] By transferring the vast majority of property infractions from circuit to lower courts, the state itself gave a unique colouring to felonies. From the 1880s on, jurisdictional changes made crime – especially women's crime – seem increasingly sexual, violent and urban, and this in turn reinforced the growing concerns of upper- and middle-class society about vice and disorder among lower-class migrants then flooding Russia's cities and factory towns.

For reasons still unclear, prosecution of women also increased for homicide and infanticide between the 1860s and 1870s, though here some qualification is necessary.[23] Excluding infanticide, murder accounted for 7.3 per cent of all women convicted in the years 1874-8, compared to only 4.5 per cent of males. When examined by specific types of homicide, it becomes clear that the major difference in these figures resulted from the greater percentage of women tried and convicted for murdering their spouses – a crime that constituted 18.4 per cent of women's murder convictions. Among men, this figure averaged 5.3 per cent. The per capita growth rate in convictions of female spouse murderers, however, only slightly exceeded that of their male counterparts (4.3 per cent versus 4.1 per cent), while men registered a higher rate among persons tried (4.2 per cent versus 3.8 per cent), suggesting a greater commission rate as well, but also indicating an already high level of spousal homicides perpetrated by women earlier in the century.

Murder of spouses made up only 1.8 per cent of the total felonies for which Russian women were tried in the post-Emancipation period, but it remained one of the few female offences (together with infanticide) that attracted the attention of jurists, criminologists, professional journals and newspapers.[24] Spousal homicide, it seemed, represented one of the rare felonies to which women (particularly peasants) were prone, distinguishing female murderers from their male counterparts. As·one criminologist claimed in 1887, unlike men who committed homicide, women murderers "are led to their crime by sexual passion".[25] Even more popular in Europe at the time, this notion helps to explain why spouse murders fascinated and frightened Russian society. The heinousness of such deeds not only ran counter to women's perceived nature (as a result of which psychological examinations of accused murderesses became standard procedure as early as the 1860s), but opposed the basic principles upon which Russia's patriarchal social order rested. Others, by contrast, suggested that murder of husbands symbolized the defects of that very order, because Russians had little recourse to divorce before 1917 and legal separation proved difficult to attain as well.[26] Despite these legal barriers, however, women still struggled to free themselves from domestic violence. Peasant wives, for example, filed endless petitions requesting to live apart from abusive husbands. When land captains replaced peace courts in 1889, they received the right to grant passports to women against the wishes of husbands; in effect, during its counter-reforms, the state circumvented Church strictures on divorce by allowing for *de facto* abrogation of marriages through administrative separation. Even though this measure did not permit remarriage, the number of peasant women petitioning land captains for passports grew rapidly immediately thereafter, attesting that rural women possessed a greater know-ledge of the law and legal change than previously granted, and demonstrated an unquestionable willingness to use and challenge the legal process in their own interests.[27] By no means were all such petitions satisfied, of course (sample cases from Riazan' and Moscow provinces suggest an approval rate of between one-half to two-thirds), and some educated circles continued to argue that the absence of legalized divorce in the face of widespread domestic brutality led directly to women murdering their husbands. The statistics cannot confirm whether this was the primary reason for such homicides, but cases I have examined implicate it as a leading cause.[28]

Infanticide, too, substantially raised the proportion of female murderers, averaging 25 per cent of women's homicide convictions from 1874 to 1913. While convictions for infanticide remained constant as a percentage of felonies, Russian criminal statistics, like their European counterparts, also contained the category of "concealing the corpse of a newborn" for cases of suspected infanticide.[29] This latter group increased sevenfold from 1834 to 1893, drop-ping off modestly during the years 1909-13. Conviction also proved more likely for this lesser offence than it did with infanticide. Courts convicted an average 88.8 per cent of all women brought to trial on charges of concealing an infant's body in the post-Emancipation period – the highest rate for any female crime; by contrast, only 31.1 per cent of those charged with infanticide were found guilty.[30] Such a sharp difference in conviction rates is largely explained by judicial procedure, since most cases of concealment (86 per cent) were tried in courts without jury, where judges proved more willing to convict. Women accused of infanticide, however, stood trial before juries, and defence attorneys as well as defendants utilized both the jury's well-known sympathies for victims of circumstance and its aversion to imposing the harsh punishment prescribed by law for this crime.[31] But in cases of concealment tried by juries, women stood as great a chance of conviction as they did before courts without juries. Other factors, then, helped to differentiate how these two charges were viewed. Religious concerns might have influenced judges, for in concealing her dead infant a woman not only broke state law but also sinned against Church stricture and canon law by denying the newborn a Christian burial with proper rites. Moralization, too, may have been an import-ant element, as it was elsewhere, particularly after the state increased property qualifications required for jury service.[32] Most important, the less severe penalt-ies for concealment certainly likely made jurors more willing to convict for an offence that they, too, felt to be symbolic of moral decline and sexual danger. Russia's male juries and judges both actively played the role of moral guardian in this instance as well as others, at a time when the Church itself fretted that it was losing a bitter struggle against secular values and widespread lower-class immorality.

Patterns of prosecution changed once again in the mid-1880s, when disobedi-ence and resistance to authorities emerged as the third most frequent felony for which circuit courts convicted women in the decennial 1884-93, followed closely by illegal cohabitation. Attesting to the influence of moralization on patterns of arrest and prosecution, fornication moved briefly into first place during the late 1890s and remained only slightly behind theft until 1903. But it is the high and growing percentage of women charged and convicted for resistance to authorities that is most intriguing, given contemporary views of female crime and the ideal passive and submissive Russian woman. Indeed, during both the pre- and post-reform eras, women accounted for a larger proportion of convictions for resistance and disobedience to or insulting authorities than they did among total felonies. No criminologist ever commented on the phenomenon, but at a time when educated Russians were expressing serious concern about a breakdown of morality, family and authority, especially among the growing numbers of younger women moving from villages to towns in search of employment, this trend in prosecutions should not be surprising.[33] As occupational changes brought women into more frequent contact with authorities, such encounters created increased occasions for disputes. Fear of the unsupervised woman stemmed in large part from the realities of social change, resulting in a greater number of women charged for "aggressive" acts as well as sexual offences. Such cases involved a multiplicity of petty insults inflicted on lower-level officials or police and therefore resisted ready characterization; but this fact, too, reveals broad fears of the "unruly woman."[34] The peasant who cursed or attacked a minor official, the working-class woman engaged in protest, the shopkeeper disobeying police orders, and the housewife involved in a violent altercation at the market: all stepped beyond the margins of what was deemed permissible for women. Such acts represented nothing new, of course, but by the early 1880s, at a time when many middle-class Russians and state officials sought to regulate more closely the boundaries of permissible female conduct, it appears that an increasing number of lower-class women were violating accepted norms of behaviour. In an atmosphere of political and social insecurity that witnessed simultaneous efforts by the state to strengthen patriarchal authority while moral reformers sought to bring "respectability" to the lower classes, crimes of this nature seemed far more worrisome. Indeed, although Russian courts convicted women at a lower overall rate than men (57.6 per cent and 65.4 per cent respectively), rates for insulting and disobedience to authorities were nearly equal for both groups. From 1889 to 1898, and again during the post-revolutionary years 1909–13, women's conviction rate for this offence actually surpassed that of men.[35]

To summarize the overlooked dynamics within women's crime that emerges from post-reform judicial statistics, let us examine per capita felony growth rates, for it is here in particular that a picture emerges quite different from that drawn by contemporaries who utilized these sources. As Table 4.2 illustrates, the most dramatic rate of increase in crimes for which circuit courts convicted women came among infractions of customs regulations (smuggling, avoiding customs duties, resistance to customs officials),[36] followed by peace and safety offences (public health violations, disturbing the peace, and others), resistance to authorities, infraction of passport regulations, and bootlegging. Of particu-

Table 4.2 Average per capita rate of increase for selected felonies, 1874-1913

Crime	Accused		Convicted	
	Men	Women	Men	Women
Infractions of customs regulations	21.1	30.9	24.1	53.2
Crimes against peace and safety	12.5	33.9	24.2	42.8
Rape	10.9		30.3	
Uprisings and resistance to authorities	14.0	10.7	18.6	26.8
Infractions of passport regulations	1.9	3.2	5.9	15.0
Infractions of liquor regulations	5.9	14.8	5.0	14.8
Mortal Injury	4.0	5.5	5.0	12.9
Fornication*	11.1	11.9	11.5	11.2
Assault	4.3	5.1	5.1	8.5
Dealing in stolen goods	3.5	4.0	6.2	6.7
Infanticide		3.7		4.7
Abandonment and concealing corpse of newborns		3.2		4.3
Insulting and disobeying authorities	2.0	3.0	3.7	4.1
Murder of spouse and relatives	3.8	3.7	3.7	4.1
Adultery	5.9	4.8	7.9	3.7
Incest	2.8	2.9	3.4	2.7
Total theft	1.1	0.9	0.7	0.5
Arson	1.6	1.2	0.7	0.2
Robbery	1.7	2.9	0.8	0.1
Total murder	3.2	0.8	3.0	-0.3

* 1874-1903 only

lar interest is the much lower growth among those crimes to which women were supposedly most inclined. Infanticide and concealing the corpse of a newborn, for example, rose modestly when compared to the above offences. With the exception of murdering spouses and relatives, total female homicide conviction rates actually declined. In the case of adultery, the rate for male convicts almost doubled that of females, increasing at a slightly faster pace for incest as well. The growth rate of fornication was also virtually identical among men and women. Indeed, if these figures are ranked from high to low, we find remarkable similarities between sexes. Apart from rape for men and mortal injury for women, felonies that grew most rapidly remained much the same within each group. Equally important, crimes that witnessed the fastest per capita increase among Russian women were those that proved especially harmful to state revenues (i.e. customs, tobacco and liquor taxes), followed by resistance and disorder.[37] With its limited police resources, a constant need to sustain or raise revenue, and fear of revolution, the state thus played yet another key role in determining the shape of felonies (and, perhaps, their growth rates as well) through a selective pattern of policing and prosecution.

A closer look at the social makeup of female convicts will bring these findings into sharper focus.

Female offenders: a social and occupational profile

Members of the peasant estate constituted the majority (65 per cent) of women tried by circuit courts between 1834 and 1861, nearly identical to the 67.8 per cent figure for men, although both accounted for substantially less than the 85 per cent peasant proportion of Russia's population. Roughly 17 per cent of these women and 7 per cent of men were non-farming peasants (most working in factories or as servants), and this group increased in number among female criminals throughout the pre-reform period, accounting for just under 24 per cent by 1857. Following Emancipation, the proportion of female farming peasants convicted on felony charges continued its plunge, averaging only 27.5 per cent for the years 1874–1913 (compared with 36.0 per cent for men), and reached an astonishing low of 12.2 per cent in 1913. These figures were even smaller for misdemeanours, reflecting the peace courts' more urban character and the fact that, for minor offences, most peasants stood trial before *volost'* courts or land captains. The proportion of peasant farmers prosecuted before state courts, then, had been slowly declining since the 1830s, and this process accelerated after Emancipation. This decline occurred not because of any substantial change in the proportion of female farming peasants during our period, but above all because of a reformed court system that excluded peasants from its jurisdiction unless they committed serious offences. The apparent parallel rise in women's urban crime was due in large part to their occupational mobility with its greater social visibility and vulnerability, and was fuelled by growing anxieties about the absence of familial supervision over women working in non-traditional settings. Although criminologists were certainly aware that the absence of *volost'* court data greatly skewed urban-rural ratios, they nevertheless chose to characterize female crime as disproportionately urban.[38]

Russian women engaged at occupations that took them outside the village and away from the potential protection of family, kinship, or other local networks stood a far greater chance of coming into contact with the criminal law and the regular courts. Occupational data available for the period following Emancipation confirm what had already been evident even before industrialization began to reshape the division of labour within Russian society. Women engaged in trade, for example, made up 5.2 per cent of all female felons between 1874 and 1913, a figure that rose to 7.6 per cent for the years 1909–13. Domestic servants accounted for 11.4 per cent of all felony and 22.6 per cent of recorded misdemeanour convictions among women. Indeed, domestics made up the second largest female occupational group convicted by the peace court administration – a not unexpected finding, given that domestic servants were by far the largest female occupation group in towns. Also striking, day labourers and hired agricultural workers combined to equal the proportion of peasant farmers among female felons for the years 1874-1913, and exceeded that proportion in the case of misdemeanours.

Offences, too, differed significantly according to occupational group, and both their patterns and ratios confirm the close relationship between occupation and social visibility, on the one hand, and prosecution by circuit courts, on the other. Among female peasant farmers, theft made up a mere 20 per cent of post-Emancipation felony convictions, a figure not at all surprising since the overwhelming majority of rural property offences were tried by *volost'* courts. Prior to 1889, peasants came before circuit courts for theft only if they had committed this crime twice before; that is, not until their third offence would they be sent before a higher court. The counter-reforms of 1889 transferred most cases of third theft to land captains for summary trial, thereby removing still more property offences from the judicial statistics.[39] This fact not only explains the tiny percentage of rural property crimes found in official records but, more importantly, promoted the erroneous impression that bloodshed and violence best characterized rural criminality. Hence we find that infanticide ranked in second place among peasant women's felony convictions, followed by murder, insulting and showing disrespect to officials, assault, insurrection or resistance to authorities, fornication, and customs or liquor offences. Contemporaries who depicted infanticide as a quintessential *peasant* crime were deceived, however, by their pre-existing views of female criminality and peasant society.[40] Indeed, more incidents of uprising and resistance to authorities occurred among women in rural settings than did cases of infanticide, yet no criminologist argued that this was above all a female peasant crime. Nor did any examine who perpetrated infanticide in the countryside. Female peasant farmers actually constituted only 30 per cent of infanticide convictions (equal to their proportion of the convict population but far less than their proportion of Russia's total female population); by contrast, female hired agricultural workers accounted for fully 20 per cent of all cases, women engaged as day labourers 18 per cent, and female domestic servants 16 per cent. As elsewhere, servants were the most over-represented group convicted for infanticide, stressing the extent to which occupation influenced prosecution patterns.[41] In the case of female agricultural workers infanticide took first place, with theft close behind, then fornication, murder, insulting officials, bodily injury, and resistance to authorities. Property crimes ranked highest among day labourers and domestics, as did fornication. For domestic servants, in fact, theft, infanticide, and fornication together made up 83.7 per cent of their total convictions - a result, one criminologist explained, of the fact that domestics were "spoiled," had no real authority over them, and therefore lacked moral fortitude.[42]

During the period 1874-1913, slightly less than half of male and female felons fell below 30 years of age, and 37 per cent were single. Widows accounted for a striking 13.7 per cent of female felons and 17 per cent of peace court convicts; by contrast, this proportion stood at roughly 3 per cent for male convicts. Similarly, women in the over-30 age group tilted more toward the elderly end of the scale than did their male counterparts. Yet these figures, too, fluctuated tellingly over time, especially for youthful offenders. From 1884 to 1903, precisely in the years when authorities again vigorously prosecuted fornication, women in the under-30 age group made up a larger percentage of total female convicts than did men of the same cohort. Indeed, 40 per cent of all women convicted for fornication were 16 to 20 years old. Between 1889 and 1893, 52.1 per cent of female felons fell below the age of 30, compared to 43.3 per cent of males. This group reached its highest level in the years 1894–98, then declined to a much lower percentage immediately following the decriminalization of "illegal cohabitation". A strong relationship thus existed between prosecution patterns for this offence and changes in the proportion of younger female felons, who correspondingly represented the fastest growing cohort within the general convict population, with an average annual growth rate of 3.8 per cent for those under 20 years old (most rapid in the 17–20-year age group, and during the mid-1880s and late 1890s).

When considered together with occupation, these data indicate the very close link between Russian women's economic situation and the likelihood that they would be prosecuted by circuit courts for activities that were criminalized. As a substratum of Russia's labouring poor, women employed as day labourers, hired agricultural workers, or domestics led an often precarious existence. Employers frequently fired domestics over petty disputes, for instance, or brought them to court on charges like theft or immoral conduct (charges that could also serve as a means to avoid paying wages). More importantly, with seasonal unemployment common and wages low, women unable or unwilling to return to their village found supplemental income in theft, smuggling, bootlegging, prostitution, or other illegal activities. As V. A. C. Gatrell has noted, the boundaries between employment, unemployment, poverty and crime remained highly porous during the nineteenth century, and the labouring poor crossed them on numerous occasions.[43] That widowed, unmarried, and young women accounted for such high proportions of the female convict population, therefore, should not be unexpected. Married women (particularly those with children) tended toward greater caution when faced with hardship. For others in professions such as day labour and domestic service, or in situations like widowhood that left them more vulnerable to the brutalities of the economy and with a limited range of choices, the decision to step from poverty to crime was perhaps no less difficult, but their options, too, proved fewer.

As for nineteenth-century claims about the more urban character of female crime, such assessments can be confirmed by data on the geographical distribution of felony convictions *only* if we ignore entirely the existence of separate court jurisdictions for peasants and the nature of prosecution within Russia's reformed court system. Statistics do show that during the post-Emancipation era 34.6 per cent of female felons perpetrated their offences in urban areas, compared to 28.4 per cent of male convicts.[44] Not surprisingly, the more industrial judicial circuits of tsarist Poland and the Baltic provinces contained the largest proportions of women among total felons; circuits like Kiev, Iaroslavl' and Khar'kov similarly convicted above-average numbers of urban women. It is of more than passing interest that after 1894, when data from tsarist Poland was included in the criminal statistics, an average 20.3 per cent of all female convicts were Polish, while 25.1 per cent were Catholic. Polish and Catholic territories also recorded the greatest number of offences with which the state was especially concerned, smuggling and bootlegging in particular. Agricultural provinces like Tambov, Samara, Saratov and Voronezh, by contrast, contained the lowest proportions of female felons. These figures, however, mask faster growth rates for felonies committed by women in rural areas, where female convictions increased at a 1.5 per cent annual rate in contrast to only 0.6 per cent for males (urban rates stood at 0.9 per cent and 0.6 per cent, respectively). The highest per capita growth rates for women's felony convictions could be found in the black-earth province of Tambov (12.6 per cent, compared to 2.5 per cent for male felons), to note only the most striking. Rates remained lowest in major urban centres like Moscow and St. Petersburg. Growing felony conviction rates among rural women similarly corresponded to their increased participation in outwork, day labour, and other occupations concentrated in the countryside. Over the period 1874 to 1913, growth rates for female agricultural workers and day labourers averaged 5.6 per cent and 4.2 per cent, respectively, but actually declined by 0.7 per cent for female farming peasants.

In effect, official data from reformed courts merely confirm a situation that was already evident during the reign of Nicholas I earlier in the century: that is, urban women and those with non-farming occupations proved most likely to be caught and prosecuted for felonies, and thus ended up with disproportionate representations in the criminal statistics. It should also be emphasized that the "dark figure" of unreported and unsolved crimes was far higher in the countryside than in cities, and rural growth rates offered above are therefore quite conservative. The published sources reflect, yet again, the way in which jurisdiction shaped the statistical and subsequent sociological profile of female offenders, since the vast majority of rural crimes were adjudicated before *volost'* courts and therefore remain part of the dark figure. The data do suggest, however, that as the state grew increasingly concerned over what it defined as a rising tide of violence and administrative infractions in rural areas – particularly resistance and disobedience to its appointed officials – both rural men and women employed away from the village stood an ever greater chance of falling foul of the law. Yet it was the urban women and those with income sources outside of farming who appeared most visible to criminologists reading the statistics in search of confirmation for their explanations of female criminality.

Conclusions

This picture of Russian women's encounters with the tsarist judicial system bears little resemblance to the female criminal commonly portrayed in nineteenth-century legal and medical journals. Rather, growth rates, the dynamics and patterns of criminal convictions, and the social position of perpetrators all attest that what was termed "female criminality" by professionals mirrored several developments in Imperial Russia that had little at all to do with the narrow discourse of contemporary criminology. On the one hand, there was an unquestionable relationship between occupation and occupational change, social status and the likelihood of conviction by circuit or peace courts. Female felons were most often dependent upon such non-farming occupations as domestic service, hired agricultural labour, day labour, or factory work for their incomes, a trend that stretched from at least the early 1830s to 1913 and beyond. During the post-reform era, women convicts tended to be somewhat older than their male counterparts (especially those charged with misdemeanours), while a large proportion were widows apparently lacking even the limited range of opportunities open to younger women. Throughout the period examined here poor pay, frequent bouts of unemployment and poverty kept property offences in first place among women's crimes, despite the skewed statistics. That far more widows perpetrated misdemeanours than felonies, for example, suggests a strategy of survival rather than a search for greater material gain. Likewise, housewives without regular employment engaged in crimes such as bootlegging or smuggling not only because they were less liable to be caught, but also because these activities provided a source of income and could be flexibly adapted to the tedious schedule of domestic chores. For their part, domestic servants proved especially vulnerable to charges of theft, fornication and infanticide because the very nature of their work placed them under close and often constant supervision, leaving them isolated and more vulnerable to exposure and denunciation.

Women's increasingly visible presence among the country's labouring poor also drew correspondingly greater attention from police, judicial authorities and educated Russians concerned with the moral state of the lower classes, a fact more broadly reflected in efforts to regulate popular life by imposing respectability, decorum and order. This appears to have been true to some extent before the Great Reforms, though the scale and level of concern proved far greater thereafter. While the agents of these efforts had changed somewhat by the 1870s, with professionals and moral reformers partly displacing their clerical predecessors, their goals remained similar. Even more important, judges appear to have served a crucial role as regulators of public morality, much as did other officials placed in positions of authority. Although occupational and social change can be singled out as primary factors accounting for the faster growth rates of women's crime, we cannot neglect the part played by official and unofficial guardians of public morality in this increase, or their influence on the very definition of crime.

State anxieties about crime also found clear expression in patterns of prosecution and sentencing. Whether the accused was female or male, conviction rates grew most rapidly for offences injurious to the government's fiscal requirements and those perceived to threaten the established order. Indeed, when the government of Alexander III began removing cases and entire categories of crimes from the competence of juries during the 1880s, one overriding purpose was to raise conviction rates for offences against state interests.[45] Through its interventions into the reformed judicial administration the state thus helped to determine faster growth rates of certain offences and to shape patterns of "female criminality" by defining or redefining these crimes.

The findings of this study stress above all that the nature of Russia's criminal justice system must be carefully considered if we are to understand crime and its statistical representations in Imperial Russia. We have seen, above all, that the apartheid-like court system imposed on the countryside following Emancipation kept the overwhelming majority of peasant offenders out of the judicial statistics, much as did pre-reform rural justice. The delimitation and division of jurisdictions over certain behaviours and offences likewise skewed the way professionals viewed, discussed and portrayed crime patterns, particularly since they focused on felonies alone. Perhaps most important, the exclusion of vast numbers of peasant crimes from the regular courts and shifts in jurisdiction over property offences falsely served to depict rural crime as consisting largely of violent and brutal acts, a perspective that meshed especially well with late nineteenth- and early twentieth-century images of peasant life. But women too were swept into this same distorted imagery, thereby reinforcing longstanding views on female criminality. Beginning in the 1880s, in particular, Russians who studied judicial statistics found ready evidence to support the image of women's crime as both static and timeless. In their view, "female criminality" was an unchanging reflection of gender rather than of economic and social factors, court structures and jurisdictions, or the very way in which crime was defined and culturally constructed. Neither followers of modern criminology nor those within the various strands of moral reformism saw the interconnected causes that linked their ideas and activities to the shifting boundaries of jurisdiction and resulting patterns of prosecution. Indeed, immediately following the movement of minor property crimes to the peace courts' jurisdiction, women appeared in the criminal statistics with ever more disturbing rates of murder, infanticide and fornication than in the past. These sources thus provided "scientific" confirmation for a mythical portrait of the female criminal, thereby reifying the very narrative responsible for creating this myth.

Notes

1. In addition to secondary works cited below, see also Ann-Louise Shapiro's chapter in this volume and her *Breaking the codes: interpretations of female criminality in fin-de-siècle Paris* (Stanford: Stanford University Press, 1984); Ruth Harris, *Murders*

and madness: medicine, law and society in the fin-de-siècle (Oxford: Oxford University Press, 1989); H. Boritch & J. Hagan, "A century of crime in Toronto: gender, class, and patterns of social control, 1859-1955", *Criminology* **28**, 4, 1990, pp. 567-99; L. Zedner, *Women, crime and custody in Victorian England* (Oxford: Oxford University Press, 1991); J. Kermode & G. Walker (eds), *Women, crime and the courts in early modern England* (Chapel Hill: University of North Carolina Press, 1994); R. Schulte, *The village in court: arson, infanticide, and poaching in the court records of Upper Bavaria, 1848-1910* (Cambridge: Cambridge University Press, 1994). To date, there are virtually no historical studies of women and crime in Russia. On prostitution, see L. Bernstein, *Sonia's daughters: prostitutes and their regulation in Imperial Russia* (Berkeley: University of California Press, 1995). Infanticide is treated in D. Ransel, *Mothers of misery: child abandonment in Russia* (Princeton: Princeton University Press, 1988). L. Engelstein, *The keys to happiness: sex and the search for modernity in fin-de-siècle Russia* (Ithaca: Cornell University Press, 1992), examines representations of women criminals by certain groups of Russian professionals.

2. Of the few published works, see P. Mullov, "Zhenshchina kak podsudimaia i prestupnitsa po russkomu zakonodatel'stvu", *Zhurnal Ministerstva Iustitsii* [hereafter: *ZhMIu*] 3, 1861, pp. 540-86; M. Filippov, "Kharakter spetsificheskikh zhenskikh prestuplenii i nakazanii", *Russkoe slovo* 5, 1863, pp. 1-36; E. N. Tarnovskii, "Prestupleniia protiv zhizni po polam, vozrastam i semeinomu sostoianiiu", *Iuridicheskii vestnik* 10, 1886, pp. 276-97; I. Ia. Foinitskii, "Zhenshchina-prestupnitsa", *Severnyi vestnik* 2, 1893, pp. 123-44; 3, 1893, pp. 111-40; M. Ratov, *Zhenshchina pered sudom prisiazhnykh* (Moscow, 1899); Nikolai Zeland, *Zhenskaia prestupnost'* (St. Petersburg [hereafter: SPb], 1899); P. N. Tarnovskaia, "Zhenskaia prestupnost' v sviazi s rannimi brakami", *Severnyi vestnik* 5, 1898, pp. 133-49; Tarnovskaia, *Zhenshchiny-ubiitsy* (SPb, 1902); M. N. Gernet, *Sotsial'nye faktory prestupnosti* (Moscow, 1905); N. Davydov, *Zhenshchina pered ugolovnym sudom* (Moscow, 1906).

3. All data used in this article are drawn from *Otchet Ministerstva Iustitsii* (1834-68), 35 vols. (SPb, 1835-71); and *Svod statisticheskikh svedenii po delam ugolovnym* (1872-1913), 43 vols. (SPb, 1874-1916). The only long-term published study is E. N. Tarnovskii, *Itogo russkoi ugolovnoi statistiki za 20 let* (1874-94 gg.) (SPb, 1899), which can be supplemented by his "Dvizhenie prestupnosti v Rossiiskoi imperii za 1899-1908 gg.", *ZhMIu* 9, 1909, pp. 52-99. In the period following the judicial reforms of 1864, felonies were tried before circuit (*okruzhnyi*) courts with or without juries, while misdemeanours were dispersed among peace (*mirovoi*) courts or township (*volost'*) courts. Judicial statistics included data for only about 8-10 per cent of peace court cases, while crimes tried by township courts were not enumerated in any published source.

4. The Emancipation of 1861 abolished serfdom in Russia and began the era of the "Great Reforms" (1861-73), which included the judicial reform of 1864 that introduced Western-style higher courts, justices of the peace and trial by jury, among other things. All references in this study to "pre-" or "post-reform" use the standard date of 1861 to divide the two periods.

5. L. Zedner, "Women, crime, and penal response: a historical account," in Michael Tonry (ed.), *Crime and justice: a review of research*, vol. 14 (Chicago: University of Chicago Press, 1991), pp. 311-12, 335-6, argues persuasively that the European "shift in criminological understanding from the 'moral' to the 'medical' . . . was less

marked than has been thought. For, in relation to female criminality at least, the questions, methods, and . . . findings of the new medical and psychiatric approaches to crime remained bound by the traditional moral framework." Indeed, these interpretations were so successful "for the very reason that they appeared to provide 'scientific' confirmation of existing assumptions about 'normal' and 'deviant' women." See also Zedner, *Women, crime and custody*, ch 2.

6. M. M. Feeley & D. L. Little, "The vanishing female: the decline of women in the criminal process, 1687-1912", *Law and Society Review* **25**, 1991, pp. 719-57.

7. In 1916 women accounted for 15.5 per cent of total convictions, and 14.7 per cent during the period 1922-8. Gernet, *Prestupnost' i samoubiistva vo vremia voiny i posle nee* (Moscow, 1927); Gernet, *Prestupnost' za granitsei i v SSSR* (Moscow, 1931), p. 141.

8. For examples from Riazan' and Moscow provinces, see *Gosudarstvennyi Arkhiv Riazanskoi Oblasti* (GARO), f. 76, op. 5, sv. 3, d. 6, l. 89; op. 7, sv. 3, d. 12, l. 64; and f. 1256, op. 1, d. 12, ll. 25-29ob.; *Tsentral'nyi Gosudarstvennyi Istoricheskii Arkhiv goroda Moskvy* (TGIAgM), f. 28, op. 1, d. 19, ll. 2, 5, 6-6ob., 7ob.

9. Feeley & Little, p. 741. See also M. J. Wiener, *Reconstructing the criminal* (Cambridge: Cambridge University Press, 1990), especially pp. 129-31; E. S. Abelson, *When ladies go a-thieving: middle-class shoplifters in the Victorian department store* (New York: Oxford University Press, 1989); D. J. Pivar, *Purity crusade: sexual morality and social control, 1868-1900* (Westport, CT: Greenwood Press, 1973); C. A. Nathanson, *Dangerous passage: the social control of sexuality in women's adolescence* (Philadelphia: Temple University Press, 1991), chs. 6-7.

10. In 1897 Russia had only 27 juvenile institutions with 1,414 inmates. Tarnovskii, "Prestupnost", in *Rossiia v kontse XIX veka*, V. I. Kovalevskii (ed.) (SPb, 1900), p. 935. On moral reform movements, see S. P. Frank, "Confronting the domestic other: rural popular culture and its enemies in *fin-de-siécle* Russia", in *Cultures in flux: lower-class values, practices, and resistance in late Imperial Russia*, S. P. Frank & M. D. Steinberg (eds) (Princeton: Princeton University Press, 1994), pp. 74-107; J. R. Gusfield, "Moral Passage: The Symbolic Process in Public Designations of Deviance", *Social Problems* **15**, 1976, pp. 175-88.

11. For examples, see GARO, f. 717, op. 52 (1902), sv. 85, d. 1; op. 53 (1903), sv. 86, d. 8; op. 54 (1904), sv. 87, dd. 3, 8, 18.

12. S. Budzinskii, *Zakon 18 maia 1882 g. o krazhe* (Warsaw, 1886); E. Frantsesson, "Po povodu zakona 18-go maia 1882 goda 'o nakazaniiakh za krazhu so vzlomom' ", *Sudebnaia gazeta* **3**, 12, 1884, pp. 12-15. I. N. Aristov, comp., *Volostnoi sud po zakonu 12-go iulia 1889 goda* (Kazan', 1893), pp. 56-60. In France, women's declining representation among felonies stemmed from an identical shifting of property crimes to lower courts as well as changing prosecutions for forest infractions. M. Perrot, "Delinquency and the Penitentiary System in Nineteenth-Century France", in *Deviants and the abandoned in French society*, R. Forster & O. Ranum (eds) (Baltimore: Johns Hopkins University Press, 1978), pp. 220-1. On England, see Clive Emsley, *Crime and society in England, 1750-1900* (London: Longman, 1987), pp. 24-5.

13. P. Anan'ev, "Po povodu otmeny 994 st. ulozheniia o nakazaniiakh", *ZhMIu* **9**, 6, 1903, part 2, ch. 10, sec. 3, pp. 154-68; A. Popov, *Sud i nakazaniia za prestupleniia protiv very i nravstvennosti po russkomu pravu* (Kazan', 1904), pp. 397-407.

14. Higher growth rates for women were, in fact, numerically dwarfed by moderate increases among male convicts. In the period 1834-59, for example, while female

crimes rose at three times the rate of those committed by men, numerical growth registered an increase of 2,973, but 8,051 for men.

15. Growth rates in this paragraph are calculated from data in *Otchet Ministerstva Iustitsii*, vols. 1-16.

16. The judicial reform was introduced gradually, with new courts and circuits being added throughout the years 1874-1913. The following discussion is based on data controlled to exclude courts added after 1874, thereby eliminating the largest amount of artificial growth. Population data are drawn from *Svod statisticheskikh svedenii*, part 3.

17. That repression of the revolution focused primarily on men is readily apparent. In 1906, the number of men convicted on felony charges rose by 60.7 per cent, but fell 15.2 per cent for women.

18. GARO, f. 721, op. 1, sv. 3, d. 167, ll. 192ob.-193; f. 1256, op. 1, d. 12, ll. 7-8, 19-19ob., 22-23ob., 25-29ob.

19. Fornication, or illegal cohabitation, was defined under article 994 of the *Code of Criminal and Corrective Punishments* as two unmarried persons (man and woman) living together by mutual agreement, but most people thus charged did not reside together; rather, their actual offence was engaging in non-marital sex. For examples, GARO, f. 640, op. 51, sv. 152, d. 538; sv. 155, d. 589; sv. 163, d. 685; sv. 182, d. 992. Attesting to the continued mixture of sin and illegality within Russia's reformed judicial system, Church penance was the only punishment imposed for fornication. *Svod zakonov ugolovnykh*, part 1 (SPb, 1885), p. 200; Sereda, "O liubodeianii po russkomu zakonodatel'stvu", *Sudebnyi zhurnal* 17(5-6), 1875, pp. 1-24; (7-8), 1875, pp. 25-58; V. Volzhin, "O protivozakonnom sozhitii", *Iuridicheskii vestnik* 22, 1890, pp. 646-63; Ia. Orovich [Ia. A. Kantorovich], *Zhenshchina v prave*, 2nd ed. (SPb, 1896), p. 131.

20. *Sel'skii vestnik* 2, 1895, p. 13. "Illegal cohabitation" also represented a protest against the high fees charged by local clergy to perform marriages; a growing number of peasants either could not afford or simply refused to pay the required fee. "Volostnye sudy Vitebskoi gubernii", *S-Peterburgskie vedomosti* 187, 1865, p. 2; "Sl. Orlovka. (Braki u popa-rasstrigi)", *Nizhegorodskii listok* 243, 1896, p. 3. On free marriages, see, for example, I. Orshanskii, "Narodnyi sud i narodnoe pravo", *Vestnik prava* 3, 1875, pp. 103-4; E. Nagibin, "Na volostnom sude", *Permskie gubernskie vedomosti* 88, 1884, p. 3; "G. Ufa", *Volzhskii vestnik* 27, 1899, p. 3.

21. D. N. Zhbankov, "Polovaia prestupnost'", *Sovremennyi mir* 7, 1909, pp. 54-91. The powerful element of sexual control in nineteenth-century moral reform crusades is already well known in European and American studies, but has yet to be examined for Russia, where contemporaries simply assumed a "meteoric rise" of sexual offences. For further discussion, see S. Frank, *Cultural conflict and criminality in rural Russia, 1861-1900* (PhD thesis, Brown University, 1987), ch. 3. Compare Engelstein, *Keys to happiness*, p. 99, citing R. C. Sutton, *Crime and social change in Russia after the great reforms: laws, courts, and criminals, 1874-1894* (PhD thesis, Indiana University, 1984), esp. pp. 232-3. Among numerous Western examples, see M. Valverde, *The age of light, soap, and water: moral reform in English Canada, 1885-1925* (Toronto: McClelland & Steward, 1991); E. D. Gelfand, *Imagination in confinement: women's writing from French prisons* (Ithaca: Cornell University Press, 1983).

22. See, for example, Tarnovskii, "Raspredelenie prestupnosti po professiiam", *ZhMIu* 9, 1907, pp. 58-9, claiming that "urban women [steal] twice as much as rural

women"; and Foinitskii, 3, pp. 121-3, noting the "extremely high number of bloody crimes" among peasant women, despite having pointed out in a footnote that the low level of property offences was attributed to the *volost'* courts' jurisdiction over most of these cases.

23. As was true in other crime categories, this increase may have been directly related to the serfowners' loss of judicial power after 1861. Cases previously tried on landed estates began, by the mid-1860s, to come before regular courts and, hence, were reflected in the statistics.

24. GARO, f. 7, op. 1, d. 95, ll. 12ob., 88ob.; d. 535, ll. 21ob., 43ob., 76; d. 613, 1. 76ob; "Karachev", *Orlovskii vestnik* 5, 1888, pp. 2-3; "G. Kozmodem'iansk, Kazanskoi gub. (Muzheubiistvo)", *Volzhskii vestnik* 27, 1899, p. 3; "Iz zaly suda", *Riazanskaia zhizn'* 9, 1911, p. 4, for examples. Women accounted for 43.8 per cent of all persons tried and 39.3 per cent of those convicted for spousal homicide between 1874 and 1913, though Russian women were unexceptional in this regard. Compare Margo I. Wilson and Martin Daly, "Who kills whom in spouse killings? On the exceptional sex ratio of spousal homicides in the United States", *Criminology* 30(2), 1992, pp. 189-215. See also Chapter 10 of this book.

25. Tarnovskii, "Prestupleniia protiv zhizni i usloviia obshchestvennogo byta", *Iuridicheskii vestnik* 8, 1887, p. 506.

26. Among many examples, see 'Protsessy zhenshchin-muzheubiits i ikh obshchestvennoe znachenie", *Russkoe bogatstvo* 4, 1888, section 3, pp. 143-5; Ratov, *Zhenshchina pered sudom prisiazhnykh*.

27. I. P. Kupchinov, *Krest'ianskoe samoupravlenie*, 2nd ed. (Moscow, 1905), p. 20. For examples, see GARO, f. 72, op. 15, dd. 8, 10, 14; op. 16, d. 54; TsGIAgM, f. 803, op. 1, dd. 530, 609, 614, 615, 648, 650-1, 653, 655, 745-6, 748, and others.

28. Following a beating by her drunken husband one evening in 1911, a peasant woman waited until he was asleep, then murdered him with an axe, chopped off his head and threw it into the stove. *Sankt-Peterburskie vedomosti* 199, 1911, p. 3. For further discussion, see Frank, *Crime, cultural conflict and justice in rural Russia, 1856-1914* (Berkeley: University of California Press, 1999), ch. 5.

29. Defendants usually claimed the infant was stillborn or had died soon after birth. GARO, f. 7, op. 1, d. 535, ll. 6, 14-14ob., 17ob., 25, 75ob.; d. 584, ll. 17, 21ob., 42ob., 72ob., 81, 103-103ob. While infanticide was classified and prosecuted as a specific crime separate from homicide, contemporary discussions of murder often included this offence as a means of distinguishing female and male offenders more sharply.

30. This was the lowest conviction rate among all felonies. For men, the crimes least likely to bring convictions were adultery (40.9 per cent convicted) and rape (44.3 per cent). Here an important shift had occurred over time; in the early nineteenth century male conviction rates were highest for adultery.

31. For examples, see GARO, f. 640, op. 51, sv. 154, d. 577 (1895); sv. 164, d. 713 (1901); sv. 180, dd. 947-948 (1907). Identical tactics were used in European infanticide trials, but acquittal rates were far higher in Russia. See R. G. Fuchs, *Poor and pregnant in Paris* (New Brunswick: Rutgers University Press, 1992), p. 206, pp. 211-14. The most severe punishment allowed for infanticide under post-Emancipation law was exile to Siberian settlement with loss of civil rights. Concealment of an infant's corpse, by contrast, was punishable by four to eight months in prison. *Svod zakonov ugolovnykh*, 296, art. 1460. Among women convicted of infanticide, 20 per cent were sentenced to Siberian exile, 50 per cent to prison terms, and the remainder (before 1884) to work houses.

32. Alexander K. Afanas'ev, "Jurors and Jury Trials in Imperial Russia, 1866-1885", in *Russia's great reforms, 1855-1881*, B. Eklof, J. Bushnell, L. Zakharova (eds) (Bloomington: Indiana University Press, 1994), pp. 214-30. Compare J. M. Donovan, "Justice unblind: the juries and the criminal classes in France, 1825-1914", *Journal of Social History* **15**(1), 1981, pp. 89-107.

33. In Europe and the United States, too, periods of rapid social change and heightened anxiety over disorder and immorality witnessed sharp increases in prosecutions. M. E. Odem, *Delinquent daughters: protecting and policing adolescent female sexuality in the United States, 1885-1920* (Chapel Hill: University of North Carolina Press, 1995); V. A. C. Gatrell, "The decline of theft and violence in Victorian and Edwardian England", in *Crime and the law: the social history of crime in Western Europe*, in V. A. C. Gatrell, B. Lenman, G. Parker (eds) (London: Europa Publications, 1980), p. 255; Emsley, *Crime and society*, pp. 28-32; Wiener, *Reconstructing the criminal*, pp. 257-307.

34. To take but one mundane example, the peasant Ekaterina Nikitina from Moscow province was found guilty of insulting a police officer when, after he had knocked her to the ground and struck her daughter, she called him a "swindler". TsGIAgM, f. 62, op. 3, d. 892 (1899), ll. 1-1ob., 4-5ob., 8-9ob.

35. For the large number of peace court convictions on public disorder and assault charges, see *Otchet Ministerstva Iustitsii za 1866 g.* (SPb, 1869), pp. 14-16; D. A. Liapunov, *Pervoe desiatiletie Tverskikh mirovykh sudebnykh uchrezhdenii 1866-1876* (Tver', 1876); M. I. Pokrovskaia, "O zhenskoi prestupnosti", *Zhenskii vestnik* **1**(10), 1905, p. 294.

36. Smuggling of a wide variety of goods, including narcotics, was especially prevalent along the Polish border, accounting for as much as 80 per cent of all female felony convictions in this region. See *Svody*, part 2; "Vmesto vodki", *Volzhskii vestnik* **58**, 1892, p. 3.

37. The more vigorous prosecution of bootlegging as well as smuggling followed the establishment of a state monopoly over liquor sales, and efforts to protect the new monopoly played no small role in shaping the statistical picture of "crime". See, for example, GARO, f. 5, st. 1, op. 2, d. 3061, ll. 1-118.

38. Among many examples, see "Prestupleniia i prestupniki Arkhangel'skoi gubernii", *Izvestiia Arkhangel'skogo Obshchestva izucheniia Russkogo Severa* **4**, 1912, p. 387; V. Kopiatkevich, "Prestupnost' v Olonetskoi gubernii za piatnadtsatiletie 1897-1911 g.g.", *Izvestiia Obshchestva izucheniia Olonetskoi gubernii* **5-6**, 1913, pp. 108-11.

39. E. G., GARO, f. 721, op. 1, sv. 3, d. 167, ll. 42ob., 45, 192ob.-193. On jurisdiction, see Aristov, *Volostnoi sud*, p. 56.

40. This depiction is found in, among other works, Foinitskii, "Zhenshchina-prestupnitsa", 3, p. 121.

41. On infanticide among servants, see D. L. Ransel, *Mothers of misery: child abandonment in Russia* (Princeton: Princeton University Press, 1988), ch. 8; R. Schulte, *The village in court* (Cambridge: Cambridge University Press, 1994), pp. 79-118; Margaret L. Arnot, *Gender in focus: infanticide in England 1840-1880* (PhD thesis, University of Essex, 1994).

42. Foinitskii, "Zhenshchina-prestupnitsa", 3. pp. 117-18.

43. It was not professional criminals who swelled nineteenth-century court records, V. A. C. Gatrell argues, but "'ordinary' men and women whose depredations upon each other had been built into an immemorial way of life and survival, and whose

depredations upon their betters, when these were possible, were in their eyes legitimized by the brutal facts of existence." Many were "people in employment who supplemented their income with theft". Gatrell, "Decline of theft and violence", p. 265. See also Schulte, *Village in court.*

44. Urban-rural ratios remained similar at least into the late 1920s, with urban crimes accounting for an even larger proportion of total female offences. M. N. Gernet, "Statistika gorodskoi i sel'skoi prestupnosti", *Problemy prestupnosti* 2, 1927, pp. 15-24.

45. This point is discussed in N. V. Davydov & N. N. Polianskii (eds), *Sudebnaia reforma*, vol. 2 (Moscow, 1915), pp. 47-53; Afanas'ev, "Jurors and Jury Trials", p. 228; W. G. Wagner, "Tsarist legal policies at the end of the nineteenth century: a study in inconsistencies", *Slavonic and East European Review* 54(3), 1976, pp. 381-2; J. W. Atwell, Jr., *The jury system and its role in Russia's legal, social, and political development from 1857 to 1914* (PhD thesis, Princeton University, 1970), pp. 137-47.

Chapter 5

✦

Crime against marriage?
Wife-beating, divorce and the law
in nineteenth-century Hamburg

Lynn Abrams

Divorce laws

In the summer of 1826, Catharina Nix divorced her husband Johann in the St. Pauli district of Hamburg just two years after the couple had obtained an official separation on the grounds of Johann's intolerable behaviour. Shortly after the separation Johann promised to mend his ways, "to treat his wife in an orderly way, live with her in love and peace and to refrain from his dissolute way of life", but his "pious assurances . . . were nothing but words" and Johann quickly returned to his old ways, which included demanding that his wife "dress elegantly, give his parents one Mark every week, pay the rent, look after his clothes and underwear, also to send him a good meal every midday and evening".[1] In return Johann was "brutish, his vice was terrible, and the plaintiff was in danger from the defendant's brutal treatment." Moreover, in addition to stating that her husband's main vice was his "frequent drunkenness, his dissolute lifestyle and adultery", Catharina described struggles over control of the household finances that culminated in his brutality towards her. On two separate occasions he had poured hot water from a kettle over her head because she refused to give him the money he demanded.[2]

The relative ease with which ordinary German citizens like Catharina Nix were able to obtain a divorce in the nineteenth century often comes as a surprise to historians who are more familiar with the authoritarian and illiberal facets of German society and politics of the period. In contrast with France where, following a brief flirtation with liberal divorce laws during the revolutionary years, French citizens were denied access to divorce until 1884, and England where, prior to the 1857 Divorce Act, a separate Act of Parliament was required in order for a man or a woman to obtain a dissolution of marriage, in most German states divorce was available to all classes of the population and both sexes for most of the century.[3] Moreover, in most German jurisdictions, marital cruelty was acknowledged as a legitimate ground for a divorce or at least an official separation. In Prussia, for example, the divorce law of the Prussian civil code (*Allgemeines Landrecht*, ALR) of 1794 permitted divorce on no fewer than 11 grounds, including persecution, attempt on a spouse's life, endangering life or crude and wrongful offence to [a person's] honour as well as the violation of the personal freedom of the other spouse.[4] Here, divorce was seen as a civil procedure which was necessary in order to permit unhappy spouses to remarry and procreate thus supporting Frederick the Great's population policy. Under the French Code Napoléon which constituted civil law in the Prussian Rhine Province and Baden, victims of domestic violence were able to obtain a divorce on the grounds of assault, mistreatment and serious insult, in addition to the grounds of wilful desertion and adultery although the adultery clause incorporated the double standard which somewhat inhibited women's use of this ground for divorce.[5]

In the city state of Hamburg, the primary focus of this chapter, a husband or wife could file for a divorce on the grounds of adultery, desertion or imprisonment of one party. Cruelty was only grounds for an official separation. Paragraph 138 of Hamburg law stated: "A separation from bed and board may be permitted when the cohabitation of the spouses has become an intolerable burden as a result of mistreatment, threats or abuse by one party."[6] In the case of a formal separation being granted, neither partner could marry again, a date was set for a reconciliation and, in theory, the husband was obliged to maintain his wife for the duration of the separation. In 1875 an imperial German divorce law was introduced throughout the empire based on the Prussian law which liberalized the situation in states like Hamburg, permitting cruelty to be cited as a ground for divorce but it would be wrong to interpret this legislation as an indication of a commitment to uniform liberalization of divorce law. When, in 1900, the new civil code for the unified Germany (*Bürgerliches Gesetzbuch*, BGB) was implemented, female victims of domestic violence found their escape route obstructed. The new law relegated cruelty to what was called a "relative" ground for divorce which meant a court was obliged to consider all the circumstances of the case presented, including the severity of the abuse, and was not always willing to grant a full dissolution, as opposed to the absolute grounds of adultery, bigamy, wilful desertion, attempted murder and unnatural intercourse which, if proven, would automatically result in a divorce being granted. Divorce by mutual consent and on the grounds of "insurmountable aversion" was abolished and the divorce process also became more adversarial with the guilt of one party a necessary precondition for the granting of a divorce. In contrast with other European states that did liberalize their divorce laws – in England and Wales the 1857 Divorce Act permitted divorce on the grounds of adultery, or aggravated adultery in the case of a female plaintiff, and the 1884 Naquet Law in France recognized several grounds which were equally applicable to men and women, including cruelty – Germany chose to restrict access to divorce. For almost a century, German women had been using the courts to escape violent and abusive marriages and in the process had brought the issue of marital violence into the public arena. And yet the BGB failed to recognize this.

One of the ways in which gender difference was perpetuated and rein-forced in nineteenth-century Germany was by means of legal practice. The legal arena was "a contested site of power" and what happened in the divorce court was a guide to dominant ideology regarding gender roles as well as serving to perpetuate prevailing notions of sexual difference and inequality.[7] The story told by Catharina Nix, recounted at the beginning of this chapter, was replicated many times throughout the century by countless women who, desperate to escape a brutal marriage, utilized a language of difference based on prevailing notions of what constituted femininity and masculinity in order to bolster their claims to be heard and believed in court.[8] However, while providing an avenue of escape for female victims of domestic violence, the law failed to acknowledge the disparity of power relations within marriage in physical and financial terms – a disparity graphically illustrated by the struggle in the Nix household – and it left many women with an impossible dilemma.[9] If a woman was successful in gaining a separation from a violent husband, she placed herself in a potentially insecure position, unable to remarry and lacking financial support if her husband denied her maintenance. If she decided to leave the marriage, she could be divorced by her husband for desertion and risk losing her property and guardianship of any children.

Notwithstanding the gendered character of the law and its application – a state of affairs common across Europe in the nineteenth century – in Germany the comparatively liberal and tolerant divorce laws before 1900 appear to have nevertheless represented a distinct freedom unavailable to women in the rest of Europe and North America, particularly women who were victims of cruelty and domestic violence.[10] It has been suggested that women, and particularly lower-class women, were the beneficiaries of these German law codes. Dirk Blasius, the primary advocate of this standpoint describes divorce as acting as a "safety-valve" for female victims of assault.[11] Yet, while not denying the greater availability of divorce in Germany and the fact that many more women than men initiated divorce proceedings,[12] it would be wholly inaccurate to describe the situation as a "true paradise for wives" as one conservative com-mentator described Prussia.[13] In Germany spousal cruelty or wife-abuse, rather than being treated as a crime against the person, was regarded as a crime against the marriage institution; marriage being regarded as a social and sexual contract within which women consented to obey their husbands in return for protection. As Anna Clark has pointed out, this contract justified the denial of individual rights to women on the grounds they would be protected by their husbands, a fiction which worked in the interests of maintaining and reinforc-ing patriarchy.[14] In Prussia and in Hamburg, physical chastisement of a wife was not a criminal offence – a remnant of British and European legal tradition that defined a wife as part of her husband's property – and therefore it was not possible for a woman to bring an independent criminal prosecution against a violent spouse.[15] Husbands may have believed it was their right, under the sexual contract, to beat their wives since the law gave them *de facto* control over their wives' services and property and ultimately their persons too.[16] German women were treated by the law as the property of their husbands; under the Prussian *Allgemeines Landrecht*, for instance, a married woman was subject to her husband's authority in respect of her right to take employment, sign a contract or appear in court.

It was a married woman's lack of basic rights, her lack of citizenship, which meant that a female victim of domestic violence had no basis from which to challenge her husband's power. And indeed, it has been acknowledged that the husband's duty to protect his wife was largely symbolic whereas "his right to obedience has great practical significance in everyday life."[17] Some husbands asserted their right to this obedience by abusing their wives both physically and verbally. In Hamburg, although a married woman possessed quite extensive rights to engage in trade and commerce she was not regarded as an independent legal entity and was obliged to be represented by a man or legal guardian in court. Men, therefore, were granted patriarchal rights to women in both the private and public spheres. Despite the apparent progressive nature of the German laws, in practice the legal process perpetuated patriarchal relations within marriage. By permitting a few women relief from an abusive or adulterous marriage there was no need to question the fundamentally unequal basis of conjugal relations. Indeed, the existence of the liberal divorce law appears to have been a site for the bolstering of patriarchal marriage, a point made by Roderick Phillips in respect of the general liberalization of divorce laws in Europe who writes that "divorce laws were part of a complex of paternalistic legislation that sought to protect women from the most harmful implications of their inferior status without attempting to change their status significantly."[18]

Discourse on marital violence

The cases referred to below are drawn from a sample of around 130 divorce and separation petitions heard before the Hamburg lower court between 1816 and 1879.[19] During its period of operation over 2,500 couples had their cases heard in this court, with 60 per cent of cases initiated by women. In addition another 1,081 couples sought a formal separation and no fewer than 84 per cent of the petitioners in these cases were female, which probably indicates that this route was more likely to be followed by female victims of domestic violence as well as women who claimed their husbands failed to provide for them financially.[20] The total number of cases rose year on year although the increase would appear to be in line with Hamburg's population expansion of the late nineteenth century.[21] Hamburg's predominantly Protestant population would suggest that the divorce rate here was somewhat higher than other parts of the country and after 1900 official statistics show that Hamburg was second only to Berlin in having the highest divorce rate in Germany.[22] Cases were brought by all classes of Hamburg's population and although artisans and labourers were overrepresented this was most likely a reflection of the stigma of divorce in middle- and upper-class circles.[23] Divorce was not necessarily an expensive process for the plaintiff; those who could not afford legal fees had recourse to the poor relief fund to pay their costs, although the guilty party was often charged with making maintenance payments following a divorce decision. As we shall see, domestic violence, contrary to the prevalent contemporary view articulated by numerous campaigners against wife abuse, was not a lower-class phenomenon aggravated by poor living conditions – and although cruelty cases were somewhat less frequent than in jurisdictions where mistreatment was grounds for a divorce, women appear to have utilized Hamburg's legal system by obtaining a legal separation agreement and then returning to the court some years later for a divorce on the grounds of desertion.[24]

It is clear from women's separation narratives that exist within a discourse centred on the family as a sacred institution at the centre of the state that the legal system prioritized the preservation of the family over the protection of the individual. Thus, while the women whose stories we read evidently believed their husbands to have committed a "crime" against the person as well as against the institution of marriage, their narratives of abuse are characterized by the women positioning themselves as dutiful wives and mothers, as fulfilling their role within marriage and thus implicitly arguing that their husbands had no justification for such violent acts. Many of the women also attempted to embellish accounts of their husbands' violence with descriptions of their drunkenness, laziness, failure to provide and so on. Violent acts alone, despite the wording of the law, were seemingly insufficient grounds for the granting of a separation. The women were also on trial and being judged according to the rules of the sexual contract; only women who conformed to the ideal of the submissive and dutiful wife were worthy of their husbands' protection and if this were not forthcoming then the legal system was entitled to step in.

On the other hand, historians of marriage and divorce have recently suggested that in Britain and North America in the mid- to late nineteenth century marriage was subjected to much greater critical public scrutiny with the focus on those aspects of conjugal life not compatible with middle-class norms of domesticity.[25] Increasing attention was paid particularly to those elements of masculine behaviour, such as wife-beating, that were regarded as unrespectable or rough and unacceptable. Robert Griswold has argued that the "feminization" of male attitudes towards marital violence resulted in a challenge to prevailing notions of what constituted acceptable masculine behaviour and James Hammerton suggested that this questioned the location of authority within the family. This redefinition of the masculine role within marriage was carried out on two fronts. On the one hand, in the "public" arena feminist campaigners challenged male dominance and female subordination within marriage (and in Britain and the United States these campaigns explicitly drew attention to the lack of protection for female victims of domestic violence). On the other, in the "private" sphere, women were challenging their husbands' use of violence and thereby articulating a new marriage ideal.[26] This is not to say that the patriarchal model of marriage gave way to a more companionate one, but women's resistance in both domains did shape a discourse on marriage which resulted in some welcome legislative change and change in attitude. In Britain the 1878 Matrimonial Causes Act, said to be the direct result of Frances Power Cobbe's campaign against wife-beating, gave magistrates the power to grant a separation to female victims of spousal abuse and the 1895 Summary Jurisdiction (Married Women) Act allowed a wife to apply to the magistrates' court for a separation and maintenance order on the grounds of "persistent cruelty". In the northeastern states of the United States, with the exception of New York, liberalization of divorce legislation introduced grounds of cruelty and intolerable hardship and by 1860 all the states that formed the Confederacy widened the definition of cruelty to encompass abusive treatment and verbal threats.[27]

In Germany a rather different situation is apparent. In contrast with early radical liberal writers on the woman question such as Louise Dittmar and Hedwig Dohm, who regarded the law as the very foundation of women's subordination within marriage, late nineteenth-century German feminists and jurists were seemingly unwilling to confront the unpalatable issue of wife-abuse. Choosing to reject a radical stance on marriage – Dittmar and Dohm had recognized that women's equality under the law was a prerequisite for all other improvements in women's position[28] – the moderate feminists of the late nineteenth century, who might have been expected to take a stand, made a virtue out of difference and sanctified the family. More surprising, though, is the fact that the notion of the husband's protection (and thus ownership) of the wife within marriage was never fundamentally questioned by the majority of German feminists or jurists until the 1920s. Although from the 1860s the General German Women's Association (*Allgemeine Deutsche Frauenvereine*, ADF) addressed the position of women within marriage and family law in general, these moderate feminists did not stray from the belief that the institution of marriage (albeit a reformed institution that gave women property and guardianship rights) offered the wife and mother the best guarantee of protection.[29] For these women wife-beating was an inconvenient problem that threatened to explode the myth of conjugal harmony in domesticity. To admit to wife-beating as located within unequal marital relations would have meant admitting that the institution of marriage was tantamount to legalized slavery, and this they could not do.

For feminists of a more radical persuasion, it would seem that although the problem of domestic violence was not publicly addressed, the campaign for the vote around the turn of the century was regarded as a necessary precondition for further and far-reaching changes in women's position, including those within marriage. Furthermore, the concern of the radicals with issues of sexual morality, particularly prostitution, and initiatives involving the setting-up of women's centres which dispensed advice on all matters, indirectly benefited all women, including victims of cruelty.[30] Although socialist feminists were conscious of the discourse on the alleged degeneration of family life by the factory system and women's work in particular – indeed even August Bebel, leading socialist ideologue and author of the best-selling *Women under Socialism*, published in 1878, adhered to this belief – there would appear to have been little acknowledgement by socialist women of the problem of marital cruelty amongst the working class.[31] And as Kathleen Canning points out, the Social Democratic women's movement not only accepted a traditional household role for women but also echoed the bourgeois women's movement in its idealization of motherhood.[32]

In Hamburg and elsewhere, the task of placing this uncomfortable fact of marriage on the social and legal agenda was left to ordinary women. Female victims of domestic violence and other forms of behaviour interpreted as intolerable did bring their cases into the public and in doing so they signalled their rejection of male violence within marriage and articulated an alternative model of marriage based on reciprocal obligations and mutual respect.

Narratives of wife abuse

While moderate feminists were largely ignoring the issue of wife abuse, in Hamburg and elsewhere women were seemingly willing to expose their violent marriages to public scrutiny. Their narratives both describe their anger and hurt at the abuse they were receiving and their belief in a more equal or reciprocal marriage. But although the law did empower women, enabling them to dissolve a marriage and expose their husbands' behaviour to public scrutiny, their language in court was necessarily a gendered language. Women's accounts were informed by dominant notions of sexual difference and gendered marital roles. In short, women spoke a language the courts recognized and understood.[33]

In 1879 Emilie Beil attempted to gain a formal separation from her husband of five years on the grounds of cruelty. Her statement, in which she placed great emphasis on her fulfilment of marital obligations whilst she was being abused by her husband Friedrich, began with the words:

> the couple did not encounter the anticipated marital harmony and the relationship became increasingly intolerable from one year to the next, particularly as [Friedrich] began to pursue a life away from home and every evening returned home drunk.

Emilie endured this situation for some time and:

> despite the attempts of her husband to . . . cast aspersions on her fidelity in the coarsest terms, she was not swayed from dutifully caring for the common household. When the defendant finally lost his head and hit his wife and physically mistreated her . . . she abandoned her hope for a resurrection of a tolerable situation and left the house the next morning with the child . . .[34]

Henriette Bucke, married for just two years to Theodor, a Hamburg publican, stated in her separation deposition in 1860 that despite the appalling behaviour of her husband, she had:

> always been conscious of being a faithful and loving wife. That she was, at the same time, a conscientious wife is demonstrated by the fact that she ran the household without a servant girl even though she had five lodgers to look after, and she worked in the defendant's business - a public house and *Krüperei* - a burden she had carried since the birth of her child and which she had done for a year without help.[35]

Theodor Bucke had been so bold to call his faithful, hardworking wife "a cursed slut [*Luder*], a beast and so on" and he failed to protect her when his relatives "jostled her, threatened her with blows and chided her with abusive language."[36] The mere existence of a cruelty provision within the law permitted women like Henriette Bucke and Emilie Beil to draw attention to wife abuse but without direct reference to more fundamental legal inequalities.

It has been suggested by a number of historians and sociologists that the isolation of beaten wives from "traditional" networks and community surveillance became more noticeable during the late nineteenth century, an argument that has some relevance to urban Hamburg in the later nineteenth century in contrast with a more rural region of Germany. As authority over domestic affairs was vested increasingly in the state and in the heads of each privatized household, and rituals of community regulation - such as "rough music" - were replaced by state regulation, "for the most part, women who were struggling against violence had to rely upon fragments of the traditional community response and elements of a supportive female culture."[37] As community intervention receded it may be that, as Susan Dwyer Amussen has suggested for the early modern period, "women were forced to rely on an ideology of individual respect and love for their protection".[38] Family support and community surveillance had protected women (and still did in rural communities) but increasing emphasis on the privatized family may have isolated many women from these sources of support. We know that community shaming rituals, such as *Katzenmusik* or charivari, were used to regulate marital and social stability right up until the end of the century but it seems unlikely that such elaborate rituals would have been performed in cases of common domestic violence, despite the fact that knowledge of violent marriages was often in the public domain. The idea that marriage was a social contract in which wives obeyed their husbands in return for protection may have isolated women rather than providing them with legal redress.

Certainly in Hamburg neighbours and relatives appear to have intervened only reluctantly, leaving formal intervention to the police, a situation contrasting strongly with a rural area where female support networks were well developed and beaten women were readily taken in and supported and witnesses were willing to testify against husbands in court.[39] In the rural district of Cleve, near

Düsseldorf, the case of the short and profoundly unhappy marriage of Catharina to Bernhard Riess, a baker, is a good example of the support given to women in a rural community. The couple married in 1838, and Catharina asked for a divorce the following year on account of her husband's cruelty which began on their wedding night when he drank to excess, and continued in the form of threats to her life. During their eight-month cohabitation the neighbours as well as the police had repeatedly intervened on Catharina's behalf. The day after the wedding the young wife had fled to her parents following a bitter exchange of words if not blows, but three days later she returned to her husband accompanied by two female neighbours. Thereafter Riess's brutality was witnessed by Bernhard's apprentice baker and the servant girl. One night Catharina called the neighbours and the police when she found a sharpened knife lying in an unfamiliar place - the policeman placed it back in its sheath and removed it from the house without laying charges - and on the final occasion, when Riess threw a chair at his wife's head which sent her running for help, a local carpenter along with three others heard her cries and helped her climb a wall to a neighbour's house where she was attended by a doctor.[40] Household servants, apprentices, neighbours, chance passers-by, the police, a doctor and Catharina's parents intervened in the violent Riess marriage. All of them came to Catharina's aid, provided sanctuary and thereby implicitly demonstrated their disapproval of Bernhard's behaviour.

When women cried for help in these small towns and villages, neighbours came running to their aid. Hendrina Kutsch was able to rely on the testimony of five witnesses to her coppersmith husband's cruelty as well as "many others who were called forth by the cries for help".[41] As the shopkeeper Johann Leun repeatedly hit his second wife Elise over the head and back with a thick stick, her cries summoned the neighbours to her aid.[42] And when the customs officer Johann Jacobs seized his wife round the throat and proceeded to hit her head against the wall, she took refuge in another room in the house inhabited by the Vogels and their daughter. It was the daughter who prevented further mistreatment by slamming the door in Johann's face.[43]

In contrast, in the city of Hamburg, neighbourly intervention appears to have been far more non-committal throughout the whole period under investigation, 1816-79. For example, when Bertha Kallmes's case against her husband Moses on the grounds of cruelty was heard in 1879, a number of witness statements were used by the plaintiff to support her claim that he had severely mistreated her and specifically that on one occasion, without reason, Moses

> suddenly seized [his wife] around the neck, shook her with both hands, hit her head with great force against the door, beating the plaintiff in the coarsest way on the chest and accompanied this outbreak of the worst brutality with the words, "you cursed *Pöbelweib* [vulgar woman], cursed whore . . ."

One female witness who lived one floor above the couple testified: "We live one flight of stairs above the parties and as the floors are not locked I very frequently heard on the landing of my apartment how the plaintiff was abused and scandalized by the defendant in deplorable ways." Yet, she made no mention of intervention, although the fact that the Kallmeses were ostensibly a fairly wealthy couple - Moses was said to own a large business - may have conditioned the neighbours' response.[44] The apparent tolerance for many years of dangerous levels of cruelty and abuse by a number of women here also suggests neither community nor police intervention was always forthcoming. Magdalena Frohmeyer endured 28 years of marriage to her abusive manservant husband, during which time she delivered eight children. When she decided to request a legal separation in 1879 only four of her children were still at home and she must have calculated that she could survive on her earnings from cleaning and renting a room. Indeed, Magdalena had been independently supporting her family for some time; one of her complaints against her husband was that he did not bother himself with the household, she had to take care of everything. However, she added, "she would gladly take care of everything if the defendant would conduct himself like a husband."[45] In no Hamburg cruelty case did neighbours or kin intervene directly to prevent wife assault occurring, in a period when mistreated wives in rural Cleve in the Rhine Province were actively supported at home and in court. While in Hamburg outsiders were frequently on hand to prevent the violence taking a more dangerous turn, they did not call upon the forces of the law; it was not until the end of the century that the state increasingly began to regulate what were hitherto regarded as private affairs and communities began to use the police instead of informal means of regulation.[46] And yet, in a situation where official emphasis on the privacy of the family incorporating paeons to domesticity was coupled with the absence of a law outlawing spousal abuse, the decline of community intervention threatened to leave abused wives in a vacuum of inaction.

The ideology of domesticity and, associated with this, companionate marriage that espoused new ideals of manhood based upon hard work, self-control and rational behaviour and which therefore no longer tolerated violent behaviour towards a spouse, was simultaneously an ideology that constricted abused wives. As Myra Glenn observed in the case of mid-nineteenth-century America: "These women had to model their behaviour after a narrow and distorted view of femininity in order to gain public sympathy and legal help."[47] A woman's right to redress against an abusive husband was not unconditional. Similarly, Nancy Tomes in her study of working-class women in nineteenth-century London suggested that having "repudiated the idea that women were aggressive, fit partners for combat, they had no alternative but to embrace the middle-class view of women as weak, fragile, passive creatures who needed 'natural protectors'."[48]

Such domestic rhetoric would certainly have appealed to the male lawyers and judges and was almost certainly employed deliberately by female plaintiffs in order to achieve the desired result, but in the longer term these women's narratives had no significant impact on the shaping of marriage and divorce law in Germany. The case of Johanna Behr, heard by the Hamburg court in 1860, illustrates the dilemma of a victim of domestic violence who appears to have been a prisoner of domestic ideology. Johanna married her businessman husband in 1848 and both brought limited property to the marriage but shortly afterwards Johanna's parents died leaving her a very sizeable sum which was invested.

> In the first years of the marriage, in contrast with later years, the plaintiff lived *fairly* peacefully with her husband, however the defendant went so far as to box his wife's ears, but because the defendant is hot-headed the wife passed over this in silence, didn't tell her relations and kept quiet about similar incidents in order not to create a family scandal.[49]

Johanna described how there were often arguments and fights between the couple, but "mindful of her duty as wife she endured it in silence in the hope of better times." However, as the beatings became worse, culminating in Behr hitting his wife with a plank of wood, Johanna became ill and "it became clear to her that her husband had only married her for her property and he had never really loved her."[50] Johanna was unwilling to expose her marriage to the scrutiny of relatives, suggesting she may have been concerned to preserve the illusion of marital harmony in order to maintain respect within the family and the community. The veil of silence which Margaret Hunt has described as being created around respectable families, the identification of domestic violence with the lower classes in public discourse and the increasing association of middle-class marriages with companionship and harmony meant that only the most extreme cases of cruelty in middle- and upper-class marriages reached the public domain.[51] Voluntary organizations were slow to step into the gap left by the breakdown of community regulation, in contrast with the plethora of charitable organizations active in the field of child poverty and abuse in Hamburg. In Hamburg it was not until 1897 that a legal advice centre run by the *Allgemeine deutsche Frauenvereine* (ADF) was established, which dispensed free advice on a variety of matters including marriage, separation and divorce, and even this was unable to come to the aid of all female victims of domestic violence as one woman's experience shows.[52] In 1897 Frau B. approached the centre and explained that her husband frequently mistreated her but she had no witnesses. "We advised her to return to her husband and allow him to hit her in front of witnesses" was the record in the log book.[53]

Women were indicating their unwillingness to tolerate their husbands' cruel behaviour by filing for a separation, but at the same time they often articulated an alternative model of marriage based on principles of respect, reciprocity and sometimes what might be described as companionship. Anna Kopmeyer, who had been married once before, said that with this marriage "she had hoped she had found in the defendant a man whom she believed to be sincere, who would treat her well and would manage things carefully and in an orderly way." She was, however, to be "bitterly disappointed."[54] Her husband proved to be neglectful of his business and of his wife, his behaviour culminating in Herr Kopmeyer mistreating his wife "in the most atrocious way" one night when he returned home drunk that Anna was forced to call the watch who arrested her husband when he continued this "brutal behaviour".[55] Emilie Beil spoke of "anticipated happiness and marital harmony" which never materialized.[56] Charlotte Bunge's divorce deposition read:

> The hopes which the plaintiff has held until this day, shall never be real-
> ized. Instead of the anticipated happiness, dissension soon arose between
> the newly married couple, even though the wife tried by patience and
> strong fulfilment of duty to bring about a better relationship, even though
> the marriage was blessed with a child, after 6 years of marriage it came
> about that the wife found that her husband was almost never at home at
> night, that he no longer supported her and her child while he increased
> his business with a concubine.[57]

These women were publicly announcing that acceptable marriage relations were characterized by harmony and happiness that in turn were achieved by mutual fulfilment of conjugal responsibilities. While some women spoke of love - Johanna Behr appeared to have harboured a wish for a marriage based on love as opposed to property considerations, stating that "it became increasingly clear, that her husband had only married her for her property and that he had never really loved her"[58] - most would have been content with harmonious, reciprocal relations and, of course, the absence of violence. The legal system was prepared to come to these women's aid for a number of reasons. Male violence within the family was now unacceptable. Women had to be protected by the courts from these brutes who were threatening the very institution of marriage. Women who presented themselves as submissive, weak, in need of protection, were given that protection. Moreover, the state wished to promote the institution of marriage and the procreation of children by allowing remarriage. Permitting a few women access to the divorce court did not, however, bring into question the patriarchal, hierarchical model of marriage relations.

Feminist responses

The law provided a platform for the articulation of women's grievances and ideals. Is this the explanation for the virtual absence of any public debate in Germany on the issue of domestic violence? The provision of an escape route for female victims, in contrast with the situation in Britain until 1878, perhaps stifled further consideration of the problem. Yet, the inaction of the moderate women's movement, the ADF (later the *Bund deutscher Frauenvereine*, BDF)

129

is better explained by its overall attitude towards marriage and the family. In 1867 the ADF singularly failed to act on information it had at its disposal regarding the real everyday experiences of many women within marriage. Having asked female readers of *Neue Bahnen*, the ADF's newspaper, to write in with their experiences, Louise Otto-Peters declined to publish the material it had received saying: "our pen declines to dip into this filth, and it is impossible for us to overcome our shame, repulsion and disgust."[59] And despite evidence to the contrary, they apparently continued to believe that wife-beating was a deviant act carried out by disturbed, drunken individuals who had no control over their actions.[60] It was much easier to portray the wife-beater as patholo-gical, as a drunken brute, that is, to individualize the situation, and thereby deal with the individual in the courts without recourse to a debate on the fundamental nature of marriage and the family. Indeed, abusive husbands were commonly portrayed by their legal representatives in such terms. In a case from Hamburg in the 1850s, Jacob Müller was described as having "little by little brought himself with such ease to a state of drunkenness" and as getting into such a state "in which he no longer knows who he is . . . and for more than six months has lived in a state of such perpetual fuddle that he can no longer be brought to his senses."[61] Friedrich Beil was similarly described as "losing his head" when he beat his wife, implying an absence of responsibility on his part owing to his drunkenness.[62]

Once more it is valuable to note the contrast with the tactics – if not some of the sentiments – of the most notable British campaigner for women's rights and against wife-abuse, Frances Power Cobbe, who spoke out against violence against women in her influential article entitled "Wife-Torture in England" published in the *Contemporary Review* in 1878 and who placed incontro-vertible evidence of wife-beating before parliament, thus shocking men with details of the actions of members of their own sex.[63] During the 1890s a new generation of German feminists did begin to challenge the ideology of "spiritual motherhood" developed by the first wave of activists. The new generation, later known as "radicals", continued to emphasize maternal values but their critique of women's legal position was informed by an interest in sexual issues such as prostitution, pornography and illegitimacy. During the 1880s and 1890s when the ADF was provided with a golden opportunity to address and influence the position of women under civil law during the draft-ing of the new civil code even its radical wing continued to defend women's rights as the rights of mothers rather than the rights of the individual.[64] It made a decision to reject the language of rights and citizenship inherited from early nineteenth-century feminist writers such as Louise Dittmar and Hedwig Dohm, in favour of a campaign for improvements to women's rights as wives and mothers within the context of a belief in motherhood as a source of strength and marriage as a means of protection for women.

When the new Civil Code saw the light of day it was clear that the posi-tion of women was in some respects less favourable than it had been under some of the codes it superseded. The more restrictive divorce law indicated that greater priority was placed on marital stability than individual protection and thus the legal system appeared to be implicitly reinforcing male authority within the family, if not explicitly condoning violence. The women's movement focused criticism of the BGB on the paragraphs relating to parental guardianship and property that, although pertinent to separated and divorced women – (abused wives amongst them) – still reinforced a marriage model based on difference and therefore inequality. Feminists' – moderates and radicals – defence of the rights of mothers was at the expense of an individualist conception of rights that would have provided some protection for beaten wives.

Conclusion

Women used the legal system to challenge a patriarchal model of marriage while articulating new models of conjugal relations. However, despite the apparent liberality of the German legal system before 1900 in empowering female victims of domestic violence, there was no questioning of the fundamental inequalities that subordinated women within marriage. Women were still objects of protection, if not by their husbands, then by the courts, and this new system of regulation of conjugal relations may have imprisoned women more than it liberated them. In Germany ordinary women who used the legal system to gain protection, but also to protest against a marital hierarchy which did not coincide with their expectations, received little support from the German women's movement which placed preservation of marriage and the family ahead of the emancipation of individual women; it did not engage with the material and political circumstances that were at the centre of the wife-beating problem. The state also demonstrated its priorities in 1900 when the new civil code placed greater emphasis on marital stability at the expense of female autonomy. Ordinary women who were victims of domestic violence continued to take their marriages to the courts but now, even more so than before, they were dependent on the generosity of individual judges. The gradual rise in the divorce rate after 1900 suggests some judges at least were interpreting the cruelty paragraph of the law in women's favour.[65] Women's words, however, continued to ensure that domestic cruelty was placed on the legal agenda.

Notes

1. Staatsarchiv Hamburg (StAH), Bestand 411-2, Patronat St. Pauli, III 268: Catharina *contra* Johann Nix, 17 July 1826.
2. *Ibid*.
3. For a comprehensive survey of divorce law in the rest of Europe, see R. Phillips, *Putting asunder: a history of divorce in western society* (Cambridge: Cambridge University Press, 1988). In England and Wales, before the 1857 Divorce Act, parliamentary divorce on the grounds of adultery was the only way of securing a

dissolution and this avenue was rarely open to women: there are only four recorded cases of women being granted divorce by Parliament. See L. Holcombe, *Victorian wives and property: reform of the married women's property law in nineteenth-century England* (Toronto: Toronto University Press, 1983), p. 96. On the practice of the law in England before 1857, see L. Stone, *Uncertain unions and broken lives: marriage and divorce in England 1660-1857* (Oxford: Oxford University Press, 1995). In France, following the introduction of divorce by the revolutionary government in 1792 and a more restrictive law in the form of the Code Napoléon, divorce was abolished in 1816 not to be reintroduced until 1884 when the Naquet Law allowed men and women equal access to divorce; see G. L. Savage, "Divorce and the law in England and France prior to the First World War", *Journal of Social History* **21**, 1987, pp. 499-513.

4. However, the notion of persecution had a class dimension. It would have been difficult for a member of the lower classes to have obtained a divorce on the grounds of verbal insult alone. ". . . ein wohlerzogenes Frauenzimmer wird durch eine Ohrfeige empfindlicher beleidigt als die Tochter eines Schubkärners". See S. Weber-Will, *Die rechtliche Stellung der Frau im Privatrecht des Preussischen Allgemeines Landrechts von 1794* (Frankfurt am Main: Peter Lang, 1983), p. 144.

5. Articles 229 and 230 of the Code Napoléon stated: "The husband can demand a divorce on the grounds of his wife's adultery. The wife can demand a divorce on the grounds of the husband's adultery if he has lived with his concubine under the roof of the matrimonial home."

6. Dr. L. Niemeyer, *Hamburger Privatrecht* (Hamburg: W. Manke Söhne, 1898).

7. C. Smart, *Feminism and the power of law* (London: Routledge, 1989), p. 138.

8. See L. Abrams, "Restabilisierung der Geschlechterverhältnisse: Konstruktion und Repräsentation von Männlichkeit und Weiblichkeit in Scheidungsprozessen des 19. Jahrhunderts", *Westfälische Forschungen* **45**, 1995, pp. 9-25.

9. On the contestation of power in marriage, see L. Abrams, "Whores, whore-chasers, and swine: the regulation of sexuality and the restoration of order in the nineteenth century German divorce court", *Journal of Family History* **21**(3), 1996, pp. 267-80.

10. For example, see D. Blasius, "Scheidung im 19. Jahrhundert: zu vergessenen Traditionen des heutigen Scheidungsrechts", *Familiendynamik* **9**, 1984.

11. D. Blasius, "Bürgerliches Rechtsgleichheit und die Ungleichheit der Geschlechter", in *Bürgerinnen und Bürger*, U. Frevert (ed.) (Göttingen: Vandenhoek & Ruprecht, 1988), p. 78. It should also be pointed out that men also used the cruelty paragraph to divorce their wives, but in much smaller numbers. For example, Constantin Steben from Hamburg complained that his wife Maria was "so quarrelsome and spiteful, that it is impossible to live with her in peace." StAH, Bestand 211-5, Niedergericht, 207: Constantin Steben *contra* Maria Steben, 1820.

12. The sex-ratio of petitioners was influenced by the terms of the legislation but where men and women had equal access to separation and divorce the majority of petitioners are generally female. For a comparison between England and France in this respect, see G. L. Savage, "Divorce and the law".

13. J. G. Schlosser (1789) cited in U. Gerhard, "Bürgerliches Recht und Patriarchat", in *Differenz und Gleichheit*, U. Gerhard et al. (eds) (Frankfurt: Ulrike Helmer Verlag, 1990), p. 197. In fact the main benefit to married women was the maintenance provision of the ALR which awarded maintenance to the not-guilty woman in a divorce case.

14. A. Clark, "Humanity or justice?: wifebeating and the law in the eighteenth and nineteenth centuries", in *Regulating womanhood*, C. Smart (ed.) (London: Routledge, 1992), p. 191.

15. Wife-beating was always treated differently from other assaults since the marriage relationship was regarded as private and to some extent immune from legal intervention. See Clark, "Humanity or justice?", pp. 187-206.

16. I have argued elsewhere that it was precisely when husbands felt this authority to be under threat that they sought to reinforce their patriarchal power by assaulting their wives and frequently seeking to control the female domain of the household economy. See L. Abrams, "Companionship and conflict: the renegotiation of marriage relations in nineteenth-century Germany", in *Gender relations in German history*, L. Abrams & E. Harvey (eds) (London: UCL Press, 1996), pp. 101-20.

17. H. Dörner, *Industrialisierung und Familienrecht. Die Auswirkungen des sozialen Wandels dargestellt an den Familienmodellen des ALR, BGB und des französischen Code civil* (Berlin: Duncker & Humbolt, 1974), p. 143.

18. R. Phillips, *Untying the knot: a short history of divorce* (Cambridge: Cambridge University Press, 1991), p. 172.

19. The lower court (*Niedergericht*) operated between 1815 and 1879 when it was abolished, and consisted of both professional and lay persons.

20. It impossible to state how many of the divorce or separation cases were cases of assault and domestic violence without consulting every single case file as the archival index merely gives the date of the case and the name of the complainant.

21.

Years	Divorces	Separations
1816–1820	23	23
1821–1830	46	104
1831–1840	105	140
1841–1850	252	133
1851–1860	287	147
1861–1870	623	314
1871–1878*	1,192	220

* 1878 was the last year for which complete figures are recorded.

StAH, Bestand 211-5, Ehescheidungen 1816-79; Bestand 211-6, Präturen 1816-79.

22. In Hamburg in 1905 there were 607 divorces or 70.2 per 100,000 inhabitants while in Berlin the figures are 1,424 and 70.2. In 1911 the rate in Hamburg had increased to 89.5 while Berlin's rate was 96.2. *Statistisches Jahrbuch für das deutsche Reich* **28**, 1907, p. 22 and **34**, 1913, p. 27.

23. Although the majority of cases consulted involve couples from the artisan and labouring classes it is not possible to state the percentage categorically owing to the absence of information regarding the male occupation in many cases.

24. For instance, in the Frankfurt/Oder jurisdiction under the *Allgemeines Landrecht* drunkenness and assault was the most common ground cited and in the Cleve district of the Rhine Province between 1818 and 1870 almost three-quarters of cases cited Article 231 of the law permitting divorce on the grounds of cruelty, mistreatment or serious insult. D. Blasius, "Bürgerliche Rechtsgleichheit", pp. 77-8; Hauptstaatsarchiv Düsseldorf, Rep 7, Cleve Landgericht.

25. See, for example, A. J. Hammerton, *Cruelty and companionship: conflict in nineteenth-century married life* (London: Routledge, 1992); R. L. Griswold, *Family and divorce in California, 1850-1900: Victorian illusions and everyday realities* (Albany: State University of New York Press, 1982); L. Gordon, *Heroes of their*

own lives: the politics and history of family violence (London: Virago, 1989), p. 253. On Germany, see A-C. Trepp, *Sanfte Männlichkeit und selbständige Weiblichkeit: Frauen und Männer in Hamburger Bürgertum zwischen 1770 und 1840* (Göttingen: Vandenhoek & Ruprecht, 1996).

26. See Hammerton, *Cruelty and companionship*, and J. Snell, "Marital cruelty: women and the Nova Scotia divorce court, 1900-1939", *Acadiensis* **18**, 1988, pp. 3-32.

27. For details of divorce laws in the United States, see Phillips, *Untying the knot*, pp. 139-53.

28. L. Dittmar, *Das Wesen der Ehe* (Leipzig, 1849); H. Dohm, *Der Frauen Natur und Recht* (Berlin, 1876). On Dohm's attention to the negative effects of women's dependence on men within marriage, see C. Weedon, "The struggle for women's emancipation in the work of Hedwig Dohm", *German Life and Letters* **47**, 1994, pp. 182-92.

29. The most vocal proponent of this position was Marianne Weber in her work *Ehefrau und Mutter in der Rechtsentwicklung* (Tübingen: J. C. B. Mohr, 1907) and her collected writings, *Frauenfragen und Frauengedanken* (Tübingen: J. C. B. Mohr, 1919). Woman's primary role as wife and mother was regularly reinforced by articles in *Die Frau*, the journal of the bourgeois women's movement; see, for example, R. Hinsberg, "Das Erziehungsrecht der Mutter", *Die Frau* **5**, 1898, pp. 257-63, and E. Friedberg, "Die Unterhaltungspflicht nach dem Bürgerlichen Gesetzbuch", *Die Frau* **7**, 1899/1900, pp. 455-61.

30. See U. Gerhard, *Unerhört: die Geschichte der deutschen Frauenbewegung* (Reinbek bei Hamburg: Rowohlt, 1990), pp. 243-64.

31. See K. Canning, *Languages of labor and gender: female factory work in Germany, 1850-1914* (Ithaca: Cornell University Press, 1996), especially Chapter 3.

32. Canning, *Languages of labor and gender*, p. 151.

33. On the meaning of legal narratives, see L. Gowing, *Domestic dangers: women, words and sex in early modern London* (Oxford: Clarendon Press, 1996), Chapter 7.

34. StAH, Bestand 211-6, Präturen, II B 171: Frau Emilie Beil gegen Friedrich Wilhelm Beil, 1879.

35. StAH, Bestand 211-6, Präturen II B 542: Henr. Cath. Bucke gegen Theodor F. Bucke, 19 January 1860.

36. *Ibid*.

37. For example, R. P. Dobash & R. E. Dobash, "Community response to violence against wives: charivari, abstract justice and patriarchy", *Social Problems* **28**, 1981, p. 573.

38. S. D. Amussen, " 'Being stirred to much unquietness': violence and domestic violence in early modern England", *Journal of Women's History* **6**(2), 1994, p. 84.

39. See Hauptstaatsarchiv Düsseldorf (HStAD), Rep 7, Cleve Niedergericht. Also R. Phillips, "Gender solidarities in late eighteenth-century urban France: the example of Rouen", *Histoire sociale - Social History* **13**, 1980, pp. 325-37.

40. HStAD, Rep 7/249: Ehescheidung - Catharina Baus gegen Bernhard Riess, 15 January 1839.

41. HStAD, Rep 7/246, 2 November 1838: Ehescheidungs-Sache Kutsch v. Kutsch.

42. HStAD, Rep 7/283, 7 October 1858: Ehescheidung Leun v. Leun.

43. HStAD, Rep 7/244, 26 June 1838: Ehescheidungs-Sache Jacobs v. Jacobs. See also cases 7/245, 1838; 7/247, 1839; 7/249, 1839; 7/253, 1842; 7/255, 1844; 7/261, 1846; 7/264, 1848.

44. StAH, Bestand 211-5 Niedergericht, 5477: Bertha Kallmes *contra* Moses Kallmes, 12 July 1879.

45. StAH, Bestand 211-6, Präturen, II S 700: Ehescheidungsklage Magdalena Frohmeyer gegen F. Frohmeyer, 18 June 1879.

46. The police were increasingly being used as mediators in domestic disputes and as arbiters of public morality. On the increasing role of the police in the community, see E. G. Spencer, *Police and the social order in German cities* (Dekalb, Ill.: Northern Illinois University Press, 1992) and L. Abrams, "Concubinage, cohabitation and the law: class and gender relations in nineteenth-century Germany", *Gender and History* 5, 1993, pp. 81-100.

47. M. Glenn, "Wife-beating: the darker side of Victorian domesticity", *Canadian Review of American Studies* 15, 1984, p. 31.

48. N. Tomes, "A 'torrent of abuse': crimes of violence between working-class men and women in London", *Journal of Social History* 11, 1978, p. 342.

49. StAH, Bestand 211-5, Niedergericht 1733: Johanna Behr *contra* J. H. Behr, 1860.

50. *Ibid.*

51. M. Hunt, "Wife beating, domesticity and women's independence in eighteenth-century London", *Gender & History* 4, 1992, p. 27. The most notable and celebrated upper-class marriage to reach the divorce court in Germany was that of Sophie von Hatzfeldt and her husband the Graf von Hatzfeldt, a case of unparalleled brutality and adultery. See L. Abrams, "The personification of inequality: challenges to gendered power relations in the nineteenth-century divorce court", *Archiv für Sozial-Geschichte* XXXVIII, 1998, pp. 117-31.

52. By 1901 there were 56 *Rechtschutzstellen* in Germany. See H. Lange & G. Bäumer (eds), *Handbuch der Frauenbewegung* vol. 5 (Berlin, 1901).

53. StAH, Bestand 611-20/20: ADF B1, 13 April 1897.

54. StAH, Bestand 211-5, Niedergericht 759: Anna Kopmeyer *contra* S. W. Kopmeyer, 4 June 1840.

55. *Ibid.*

56. StAH, Bestand 211-6, Präturen II B 171: Frau Emilie Beil gegen Friedrich Beil, 1879.

57. StAH, Bestand 211-5, Niedergericht 1729: Charlotte Bunge *contra* Carl Bunge, 22 May 1860.

58. StAH, Bestand 211-5, Niedergericht 1733: Johanna Behr *contra* J. H. Behr, 1860.

59. Cited in R. J. Evans, *The feminist movement in Germany 1894-1933* (London: Croom Helm, 1976), p. 25.

60. On the attitude of the moderate feminists towards alcohol consumption, see E. Meyer-Renschhausen, *Weibliche Kultur und soziale Arbeit: Eine Geschichte der Frauenbewegung am Beispiel Bremens 1810-1927* (Cologne: Böhlau, 1989), Chapter 3.

61. StAH, Bestand 211-5, Niedergericht 1221: Anna Catharina Müller *contra* Jacob Müller, 23 March 1850.

62. StAH, Bestand 211-6, Präturen II B 171: Frau Emilie Beil gegen Friedrich Wilhelm Beil, 1879.

63. See C. Bauer & L. Ritt, " 'A husband is a beating animal': Frances Power Cobbe and the wife-abuse problem in Victorian England", *International Journal of Women's Studies* 6, 1983, pp. 107-10; C. Bauer & L. Ritt, "Wife-abuse, late-Victorian English feminists and the legacy of Frances Power Cobbe", *International Journal of Women's Studies* 6, 1983, pp. 195-207. Although Power Cobbe was exceptional in placing

the issue of wife-abuse on the public agenda, she too had a tendency to ascribe such behaviour to the artisan and labouring classes.

64. A. T. Allen, *Feminism and motherhood in Germany 1800-1914* (New Brunswick, NJ: Rutgers University Press, 1991), pp. 135-45.

65. Blasius suggests that judges tended to make use of one of the more flexible paragraphs of the BGB, paragraph 1568, which recognised profound marital disorder as a "relative" ground for divorce to permit a dissolution of marriage. D. Blasius, *Ehescheidung in Deutschland im 19. und 20. Jahrhundert* (Frankfurt: Fischer, 1992), pp. 156-7.

Chapter 6

Workplace appropriation and the gendering of factory "law": West Yorkshire, 1840–80[1]

Barry Godfrey

> Taking our Mills, generally . . . a female who has no value for reputation
> or character, is already a lost woman. So precious, is the preservation of
> female purity, that a single error herein is a blemish for life.
>
> Reverend William Scoresby, *A sermon preached to
> the Bradford female factory operatives*, 1846[2]

Men constitute the overwhelming majority of those prosecuted for property
offences. Both historical and modern studies have found large disparities in
the rates of males and females prosecuted both in England[3] and Continental
Europe.[4] It has been suggested that similar "gender distinctions were woven
into the fabric of industrial capitalism"[5] when textile workers were gathered
together in vast centralized work areas in the mid-nineteenth century. These
differences were evident in the gender segregated occupations, supervisory
structure, and unequal wage rates in the factory system, and are equally prevalent in the statistics of workplace appropriation.[6] The surviving petty sessions
records for the West Riding of Yorkshire show that few women were prosecuted for appropriation in the minor courts. Similarly, the records of the
Worsted Committee and their Inspectorate (a private policing and prosecution
agency established for the benefit of textile manufacturers) show that only
15 per cent[7] of those prosecuted between 1844 and 1876 were women.[8] West
Riding quarter sessions tell a similar tale. In those records only 6.8 per cent of
those tried for appropriation were female.[9] Although studies of eighteenth-
century criminality have shown women property offenders to be a much smaller
group than men,[10] the proportion of female to male workplace appropriators
in this later period is extraordinarily low, even by these standards. Fortunately,
some explanation for these figures can be found in the West Riding quarter
sessions depositions, local newspapers and the records of the Worsted Committee, which together form a rich and textured source of information for the

period when factory production had become the dominant form of manufacturing in West Yorkshire.

This article will suggest that this disparity in prosecution figures for male and female workers can be explained in three ways. First, women were less inclined to commit acts of "theft" within their workplace; secondly, the barriers placed against workplace appropriation were particularly effective against women; and lastly, ideological constructions of femininity, reinforced by legal doctrine in the form of *feme covert*, combined to depress the numbers of women workers forwarded to the courts for prosecution.

First, however, we must dismiss the most obvious explanation for the differential prosecution statistics of workplace appropriation: that there was a simple imbalance in the proportions of men and women who toiled in the West Riding textile industries. Female labour was consistently important to textile employers throughout the nineteenth century. For the larger factory masters, women represented a cheaper and more docile workforce than men, and were to be employed as machine minders whenever possible. For the smaller masters, who lacked capital resources, a female workforce was often the only means of competing with large fully mechanized concerns. In the main geographical focus of this study, Bradford, women constituted 73.7 per cent of the worsted factory workforce. A similar figure was recorded in Bradford's woollen factories, which had replaced their predominantly male workforce with a predominantly female workforce between 1830 and 1850.[11] The prosecution figures are almost inversely proportional to the gender structure of the factory.

Was it the case, therefore, that women were less inclined than men to commit acts of workplace "theft"? Certainly there existed strong motivational factors for women to supplement their income by illegal means. Appropriation of workplace materials potentially allowed women more freedom than was usual for them in a patriarchal society. For example, the sale of appropriated goods could have contributed towards a woman's financial independence from her husband and family, over and above that offered by the weekly wage. The independence granted by women's employment was, in itself, problematic for contemporary commentators. For example, in 1868 Mr Baker Smith, a prominent member of the National Association for the Promotion of Social Sciences (NAPSS) stated that factory employment:

> leads a girl to a spirit of independence . . . Wages have become a greater power than natural affection. Then again, affected by the state of trade, by the seasons of the year, by fashions which chase each other through a thousand currents that ebb and flow according to circumstances over which they have no control, the factory girl is to-day rich, to-morrow poor. To-day her labour is everything to be desired, to-morrow it may be worthless.[12]

His words seem to suggest that factory women would try and "grab" what they could, whenever they could, as their employment could cease with a sudden downturn in the market. The Victorian historian L. O. Pike also suggested that the independence of working women, together with the experience of living in industrializing areas, and competing freely with men in the labour market, led to a masculinization of women, and therefore a "masculine" attitude towards achieving material gain through theft.[13] Pike's opinions were in keeping with the dominant ideological construction of femininity as a quality to be treasured and protected from the contamination of working conditions.[14] But there is another easily understood reason why some women had an incentive to appropriate although they may not have acted upon it. Family responsibilities may have played a more prominent part in the minds of female workers than male workers, and the necessity of providing food and clothing for children may have driven some mothers to steal.[15] These factors seem unlikely to have overcome women's fears of the triple penalty: imprisonment; separation from children; and loss of present and future employment.[16] It must be remembered that the stigma attached to a woman after a period of imprisonment was even greater than that attached to a man, and it assumed real importance when it came to finding future employment since many millowners operated an unofficial cartel whereby known appropriators, prostitutes, or "troublemakers" were never employed. The "game" may simply not have been worth the candle. However, it remains the case that there is little contemporary discourse concerning female appropriators, and it is very difficult to gain a sense of offenders' lives as they are only glimpsed through criminal records. These records tend to portray offenders as people who are acted upon; they are rarely identified as agents in control of their fate, or even with an identity outside of the criminal justice system. Arguably, female workers are even less visible, since the diaries and journals of women do not survive as those of men occasionally do, and so their lives and motivations remain in the historical shadows.

Allied to the strong possibility that many women were deterred from appropriating because of the penalties involved is the likelihood that opportunities for workplace appropriation were especially limited for women in the mid-Victorian factory system. That system had fundamentally altered the physical geography of production, and it also limited the workers' freedom of movement and actions within the working environment. The disciplinary hierarchy was staffed by men - foremen, as the term suggests, were invariably male in this period, although mature trusted women occasionally acted as under-foremen in a small number of factories - and the supervisory structure impressed itself mainly on female workers.

In 1868 a contributor to the journal of the NAPSS suggested three ways of controlling female labour. First, women of "staid character" should be placed in all rooms; secondly, privacy must be made impossible, every spot being open to public view, so as to spot any misbehaviour; and thirdly, each room must have, in addition to a departmental overlooker, a general superintendent, a foreman or manager whose duty it was to visit each room regularly but without warning.[17] In fact, the author only outlined a situation that had already existed in many of the large factories for a number of years, and a position to which many smaller firms had aspired.

Male workers - warehousemen, porters and labourers, who by virtue of their jobs had more mobility around the factory - had better opportunities to appropriate than the women did. They could, for example, leave appropriated goods about the factory to be collected at a better time, or they could throw the goods over the factory walls to be picked up by accomplices, or by themselves after work. Those appropriations (which were detected and pro-secuted) that were committed by women took place not in the heavily super-vised working areas (in which desirable goods were plentiful) but in the less regulated areas where raw material was handed in or given out.[18] Considering the relatively restricted movement of women around the factory it is not surprising that their preferred way of taking materials from the factory (as with many other larcenies committed by women) was to conceal them on their person. Depositional evidence reveals that all of the prosecuted female offenders secreted the goods on their person, whereas only 54 per cent of the men did so.[19] As searchers at the factory gates were male (constables, Worsted Inspectors and foremen) they may not have been able to search women as thoroughly as they could other men. However, since Esther Mitchell was found by a Worsted Inspector to have cloth hidden in her cleavage, some searches were clearly intimate in nature.[20] Moreover, since, in a few factories, additional personal searches were carried out in the weaving rooms by female supervisors, most of the hidden goods must have been detected before the factory gates were even in sight.[21]

The scarcity of good opportunities to appropriate, the threat of detection posed by overseers, and the disproportionately heavy penalties for female appropriators may well have dissuaded many women from attempting to re-move workplace materials. However, more importantly, Worsted Committee minute books reveal that some of the women who risked appropriation, and whose act was discovered, never went on to be prosecuted. Were more informal methods of punishment preferred by employers to formal court actions?

When apprehended, an appropriator's actions were limited: she or he could beg forgiveness, offer compensation, or negotiate in some other way. Foremen and employers had greater flexibility in their programmes of action: they could impose fines, dismiss the culprit, or initiate a prosecution. However, whereas men received these more formal punishments, foremen favoured more retribut-ive, visible and physical forms of control for women, at least until the final quarter of the century when over-physical supervisors began to be prosecuted by their victims in significant numbers, possibly as a result of unionization.[22] To take two typical example prosecutions from the mid-Victorian period: a millowner had recently hired an unpopular overlooker, and this man was regularly "hooted" and jeered by the workers as he walked home. Annoyed by such a public demonstration of lack of deference, on one occasion the millowner came out to "box the ears" of the culprits. He hit two passing mill girls so hard that one was made permanently deaf.[23] In another case, a foreman was accused of assaulting on two separate occasions an 18-year-old described as being "weak in mind".[24] The assaults, possibly of a sexual nature, were reported to the girl's father by another worker. Despite being offered £5.00 to "square it", the father successfully prosecuted the foreman. The irony of imposing a £5.00 fine was apparently lost on the magistrate.

The foremen who were accused of assault gave a variety of explanations for their behaviour. Aside from simple denial, they usually alleged that physical discipline was a part of working life, and implied that they enjoyed the same rights as parents in disciplining young workers. For example, one foreman seized a woman employee by her hair and hit her on the head because she was not attending to her work. Previously she had been dismissed for inattendance, but her mother had pleaded for her reinstatement. The foreman contended that he had been given permission to discipline the girl by her mother. He was, nevertheless, fined 5s and 10s costs.[25]

Some magistrates considered it their duty to protect female workers from physical abuse, others sympathized more with factory management. For example, when an overlooker made improper remarks to a 16-year-old mill girl, his advocate asserted that "there is no case to answer because if overlookers who had good characters were to be convicted on such evidence they would never be safe."[26] The case fell. The general attitude of the magistracy in these cases can be summed up in this statement by a magistrate in 1874: "Overlookers", he said, without irony, "must always be protected from their hands".[27] Even when assaults were proved, female workers could be cautioned on their behaviour. For example, when a foreman was convicted of assault he pleaded for mitigation on the grounds that the victim had provoked him by swearing. The magistrate fined him 2s, but also chastised the woman for using such foul language to her overlooker.[28]

Women workers clearly faced informal, unpredictable and capricious forms of physical punishment for their misbehaviour in the factory. But, as newspapers and Worsted Committee records show, many of those punished in these ways had infringed less serious factory rules than the offence of workplace theft. Those who had broken two important nineteenth-century trusts – the first to God, as laid down by scripture, and the second to the master, who gave her waged labour[29] – faced either prosecution, or more usually dismissal from work for female workers. Women were quickly replaced because weavers, spinners and piecers were relatively unskilled compared to male master spinners and weavers. The dismissal of offenders may have been preferable to prosecution since the outcome of a legal prosecution was never certain. Successful prosecutions against women, for example, may have been jeopardized by the impact of the social construction of femininity.

Many contemporary commentators regarded women factory workers as a group "at risk". Expressed through journal articles, the fears of middle-class reformers concentrated on the moral well-being of female factory workers, fearing that "natural femininity" would be perverted by the corrupting effect of factory toil and workplace associations:[30]

they listen to the gossip of experiences which are criminal from ignorance . . . evil communications . . . It is never so much the men that corrupt the women, but the women the women; and thus the cycle goes on from year to year. Experience shows the sisterhoods of vice are as strong as adamant.[31]

Such "sisterhoods" were cited by the defending advocate of Fanny Whitehead, a power loom weaver who had been "encouraged by some evil advisers, ignorant of the Worsted Acts, not to return her work."[32] The *Bradford Observer* also warned of "the corrupting associations into which they [female weavers and spinners] are necessarily thrown by their occupations."[33] Together with other members of the NAPSS, Mr Baker-Smith used his lectures to discuss sexual morality within factories and the neglect of the children of factory workers, a regular concern of these commentators.[34] He was not the first to comment on such matters, indeed public discomfort over the behaviour of factory women had led to the establishment of the Committee for Improving the Morals of Female Factory Operatives in 1846 in Bradford to improve and preserve good behaviour inside and outside the factory.

However, by 1868 Baker-Smith had codified public concerns into a list of factory women's inadequacies, moral and practical. First, he argued that ex-factory women were impossible to train in domestic duties; secondly, that millwomen could easily be corrupted by their association with work colleagues of bad character; and lastly, that the workers would lose their feelings of modesty and purity, through being obliged to work under immoral supervisors. In fact his complaints joined a great number of evils that were ascribed to the transforming power of factory labour, as one contributor to the *Bradford Observer* explained: "they [factory women] are supposed to be slatternly, coarse in speech, and gross in their amusements, without feeling, delicacy, or perception, irreligious, undomesticated, ill-mannered and 'unfeminine'."[35] It is clear from such comments that paternalistic feelings fostered on patriarchal paradigms of care and protection were apparently mixed with certain ambiguities about the masculinization, and even brutalization, of the factory women by the industrial system in which they worked. It seems that factory reformers intended to reclaim for women a femininity they had been deprived of at the factory gate. Nineteenth-century cultural expressions echoed these sentiments. For example, one poem written about the factory suggested:

> The daughters too no moral precepts know,
> And from their hearts a train of evils flow.
> All noxious weeds spring up and grow apace,
> Shorn of their beauty, and each native grace,
> Far from the paths of virtue gone astray,
> Fair modesty's soft blush is fled away.[36]

Similar conceptions of femininity fuelled a justice system that punished women for perceived immorality as much as criminality, and legitimated a system which made drunkenness and prostitution[37] the most prevalent offences for women since these offences against "morality" were perceived to deserve legal sanctions. Yet female appropriators were rarely prosecuted, a phenomenon partly explained by the persistence of an eighteenth-century legal convention.

> A Feme covert shall not be punished for committing any felony in company with her husband; the law supposing she did it by the coercion of her husband. But the bare command of her husband be no excuse for her committing a theft if he was not present; much less is she excused if she commit a theft of her own voluntary act . . . And such coercion is always presumed until the contrary appears in evidence.[38]

Was this convention interpreted by the magistrates and prosecutors of the nineteenth century in a way which lessened women's chance of conviction, and therefore dissuaded victims from using the courts to prosecute female appropriators?

In the early factories, the proximity of the husband, which was of obvious importance in determining the freedom of the woman to act on her own volition, meant that women who worked near their husbands may have been "immune" to prosecution. Immunity for this reason, however, must have become invalid when the factory system ceased to reproduce familial structures within its walls later in the century. Is it possible that the authority figure of the family was replaced by the authority figure of the factory, and that the foreman could have assumed legal responsibility for the actions of those women serving under him, making informal sanction the only option open to the employers?[39] This would be consistent with the theory of the organization of patriarchal industrial capitalism that some have suggested.[40] Quarter sessions depositions and Worsted Committee records show that, for men but not for women, the foreman was an important factor in the route to trial. Approximately a third of all male offenders admitted their guilt to the foreman, and another third to the arresting policeman. But no women are recorded as admitting their guilt to the foreman (roughly a tenth admitted guilt to a policeman, and a tenth admitted to a Worsted Inspector).[41] Female offenders did not by-pass the foreman's authority, but failed to progess any further on the route to prosecution because the foreman was responsible to the manufacturer for the behaviour of the women under him, and matters of discipline were dealt with internally by him. It also seems unlikely that the courts would accept that the foreman legally "covered" the female workers under him, and since the husbands were not present in the same area of the factory as their wives due to occupational segregation, the convention would have had to bear a much wider interpretation in order to cover married factory women. Was the husband's influence or coercion over his wife's actions taken as an implicit factor of the authority structure of marriage, and did this protect the sixth of the factory workforce who were married women?[42]

This appears to be an easy question to answer given that, first, large numbers of female appropriators were prosecuted and imprisoned in the eighteenth century with *feme covert* seemingly playing no part.[43] Moreover, the convention only applied to felonies, whereas most cases of workplace appropriation were tried summarily. However, the convention was certainly heeded by particular magistrates in the eighteenth century,[44] and, once established in the minds of the magistrates, the convention may have influenced proceedings in both the minor and the major courts[45] at a date when the convention was not cited by legal textbooks as a valid defence. In 1840, for example, Mary Haigh stated in her voluntary deposition that she had stolen three bobbins "for her husband", and was acquitted at quarter sessions. The depositional evidence does not state whether she had been questioned as to whether she had been instructed to take them, or had acted for her husband's benefit on her own initiative.[46] The mere fact of her married status was sufficient to ensure her release, a point the Worsted Inspectors had grasped, if not certain employers:

> I told the gentleman and his manager that she was a married woman and although not living with her husband the magistrate would not commit her if she told them she was married, nevertheless they felt desirous to try it, she being so very stupid.[47]

Since her marital status was established by the court from the outset of the case, she was immediately discharged by the magistrate.

Such experiences did not persuade the Worsted Inspectorate to limit themselves to the pursuit of men, however. Indeed, Styles conversely suggests that the Worsted Inspectorate in its initial phase was primarily a policing agency of a female workforce,[48] and was later used in the nineteenth century to collect evidence for employers to prosecute exemplary cases of appropriation in order to intimidate female workers. One employer, for instance, ensured that all of his weavers were present in court to hear him say that he would drop the case against some female employees if they promised not to re-offend.[49] Similarly, in 1870, the Worsted Inspector recorded that:

> I collected sufficient evidence to make a case of Felony against her and she having several former convictions proved against her the court ordered her to be kept in penal servitude for seven years. I then consulted as to the desirability of giving publicity to this case in the newspapers in order to deter others from doing the same.[50]

Those cases came when the influence of *feme covert* was probably waning due to the increasing difficulty of claiming coverture. However, in the early to mid-century, similar cases were not pursued. For example, a male worker persuaded Anne Gallimore to steal some goods from the warehouse and give them to him. This she did, and he put the goods under his hat and left the factory. He was arrested and prosecuted, but she was not.[51] Perhaps *feme covert* protected her from prosecution or possibly her employers felt that the magistrates would seek to show leniency to a woman. It was certainly true that employers, as well as the Worsted Inspectorate, were keen to select the "best" cases for prosecution to over-ride the perceived leniency of the bench.

They were not always successful, however, as this letter to the *Bradford Observer* complained:

> For some time we suspected embezzlement in our concern; at last we decided on two offenders whose characters on inquiry we find certainly don't merit much sympathy, and who were earning fairly good wages. We bring one of them to justice hoping thereby to deter others whom we suspect but could not detect. And what is the result? The woman pleads "guilty" and "poverty" and the Mayor allows a plea of "poverty" as an excuse for "theft", slightly reprimands the woman, and discharges her; thereby, we submit, instead of checking dishonesty absolutely encouraging it in the future. Under such ruling as this masters have little protection from the robbery of their workpeople.[52]

As Mr. Waud pointed out in his letter, the plea of poverty provided a useful defence, though a limited one, if, as said before, the facts of the case were clear, or the scale of the theft was deemed too serious for clemency to be granted. For example, the female employee of James Kaye who had "brought at different times, in her pockets 40 lb weight of worsted yarn and worsted waste", had committed the crime too often, and had taken too much, for any plea for leniency to be heard, and she was imprisoned for one month.[53] Similarly, Sarah Wagstaff's appeal for mercy fell on deaf ears. She pleaded that she was "out of work many months before I went to Glossop and Nutt . . . I was left with three small children and I took these goods to buy things to make myself and my home comfortable".[54] This was ignored when the bench was told that she had pawned 90 yards of cloth from the warehouse, and also a gold and pearl ring from Glossop's house, where she occasionally swept the floors.[55] Had Sarah been a young woman, rather than a mature mother of three, she may have fared better since magistrates were often at their most lenient when dealing with young women.[56] To take one typical example, a 17-year-old girl who was caught taking waste from the factory was convicted, but the magistrate imprisoned her only until the court rose as "she was young and did not deserve jail".[57]

The contradictory and partial information provided by newpaper court reports and records of the Worsted Committee make a proper assessment of the impact of *feme covert* problematic: it is always easier to explain why offenders have appeared in the courts than why they have not. The prosecution practices of the employers and of the Worsted Inspectors are not sufficiently systematically recorded to allow conclusive statements to be made about their attitudes towards the prosecution of female appropriators. The use of a legal convention may have reduced the numbers of women being sent to court and convicted, but it is not an adequate explanation for the huge discrepancies in the proportions of male and female appropriators being dealt with by the courts. Moreover, if both legal conventions and magistrates' sympathies protected women from the rigour of the law, then one would expect a low conviction rate for female appropriators. In fact, the conviction rate for female appropriators in the West Riding was 88.5 per cent, compared to 75.5 per cent for men.[58] Even allowing for the employers' care in only selecting very good cases for prosecution, this figure seems to be at odds with their views concerning the leniency of the magistrates. Magistrates may have felt bound to convict women when the facts of the case were proven, albeit reluctantly. For example, in one case alleging receipt of stolen goods, a magistrate said it was impossible for the bench to ignore the fact a woman had bought appropriated goods. He added that it was "most painful to us that we are obliged to convict . . . I am glad, however, that our decision can be appealed against" (the appeal was not forthcoming, and a £20 fine was paid to the court).[59]

The impact of *feme covert* was, therefore, uneven. It did not automatically protect married women from prosecution. However, it did encourage employers to turn to informal methods of discipline for women in an attempt to punish women the manufacturers felt were receiving lenient treatment from the courts. Their beliefs may not have accurately reflected the reality of the situation – no doubt the majority of magistrates had ceased to respect the clauses of the convention by the mid-nineteenth century. Nevertheless, while *feme covert* maintained its reputation in the minds of manufacturers, it acted as a barrier to prosecution for a proportion of female factory offenders.

To summarize, there may have been a lower base of female offenders, due to family responsibilities or a disinclination to commit crimes for other reasons. Those women who did have a criminal disposition had little opportunity to appropriate goods due to the considerable supervision of female labour in the factory. Male workers, being employed in occupations that involved moving around the factory, were not so closely monitored, and therefore had more opportunities to purloin goods. Men were also more likely to be prosecuted than women for two reasons: women could be punished by simple dismissal because they were easier to replace than men; and some women may have been difficult to convict due to legal convention.[60] Lastly, the overseers were much more likely to treat female offenders informally, as they were directly responsible for female weavers' behaviour. It may also be that women had some manoeuvrability within the factory authority structure since overlookers may have needed to tolerate a certain level of appropriation in order to maintain good labour relations with the spinners and weavers under them. Women may also have had further strong negotiating positions that were much less likely to be open to men. For example, when the appropriation was detected by the foreman, sexual favours may have been offered by the woman, or demanded by the foreman, in order to keep the offence from progressing further in the disciplinary process. Moreover, female factory workers could have employed various successful strategies to destabilize and rework the unofficial "rules" that governed gender and class relations within the factory in a way which would enable them to negotiate a better position in the complex inter-relationship between foreman and those under him (a relationship which formed a separate subculture within the dominant factory culture of time and work discipline). For example, foremen who had developed a relationship

146

with the workers under their supervision may have been sympathetic to offending women who pleaded poverty for themselves and their children. Nevertheless, the character and personal philosophy of individual foremen may still have been the most influential factor in the decision to prosecute female workplace offenders. Prosecution remained more likely if the route from detection to prosecution did not involve the foreman, or if he decided that the offence was "worth" a punishment other than dismissal, a fine, or physical assault.

Women clearly faced many disincentives to appropriate workplace materials, ranging from the physical and the supervisory structures of the factory, to the deterrence of punishments which were particularly severe for women – the loss of children, and future employment, for example. A significant proportion of those women who ignored the risks, and subsequently had their "offence" detected, were never prosecuted, first because foremen and employers prefered to use informal punishments; secondly, because the victims of appropriation feared that legal conventions made the conviction of women too problematic to risk a prosecution. With fewer and fewer women progressing through each stage of the journey, from committing the "crime" to a formal prosecution, it is little wonder that the percentages of female to male appropriators were so disproportionate.

Notes

1. I am grateful for the comments of Peter King and Clive Emsley on an earlier draft of this chapter.
2. W. Scoresby, *The condition and prospects of the female operatives: a sermon preached at the parish church, to the Bradford female factory operatives, on Sunday, November 15th, 1846* (London: James Nisbet, 1846).
3. See L. Zedner, *Women, crime and custody in Victorian England* (Oxford: Clarendon, 1991), and modern studies by P. Carlen, *Women, crime and poverty* (Oxford: Open University, 1988) and F. Heidensohn, *Women and crime* (London: Macmillan, 1985).
4. See F. Heidensohn, "Women and crime in Europe", in *Crime in Europe*, F. Heidensohn & M. Farrell (eds) (London: Routledge, 1991), pp. 55–71.
5. S. O. Rose, *Limited livelihoods: gender and class in nineteenth-century England* (London: Routledge, 1992), p. 185.
6. Workplace appropriation, or the taking home of work materials, often referred to as "embezzlement" by legal authorities and employers, was widely practised in most industries, and frequently defended by its adherents as a customary right. Therefore, the words "appropriation" and "appropriators" have been used in this article in preference to value-laden terms, such as "embezzlement" and "theft". See B. Godfrey, "Law, factory discipline and 'theft': The impact of the factory on workplace appropriation in mid- to late nineteenth-century Yorkshire", *British Journal of Criminology* **38**(1), 1999 (forthcoming).
7. All figures in this chapter are calculated to one decimal place.
8. Worsted Committee registers, West Yorkshire Archives: Bradford (WYAB). For a history of the organization and operation of the Worsted Committee in the mid- to late nineteenth century, see B. Godfrey, " 'Policing the factory': The Worsted Committee, 1840–1880", *Criminal Justice History* **17**, 1996, pp. 1–33.

9. Quarter sessions, West Riding, 1840-45 (QS1840-80) West Yorkshire Archives: Wakefield (WYAW).

10. See P. J. R. King, "Female offenders, work and lifecycle change in late eighteenth-century London", *Continuity and Change* 3(1), 1996, pp. 61-90; J. Beattie, "The criminality of women in eighteenth-century England", *Journal of Social History* 8, 1975, pp. 80-116, p. 91.

11. *Bradford Observer*, 22 February 1855.

12. R. Baker-Smith, "Social results of the employment of girls and women in factories and workshops", *Transactions of the National Association for the Promotion of Social Science (Trans NAPSS)*, 1868, p. 542.

13. L. O. Pike, *A history of crime in England*, [4 vols] vol. 2 (London: Smith Elder, 1876), p. 527.

14. The impact of the social construction of femininity is considered later in the chapter.

15. *Bradford Observer*, 26 September 1875.

16. See E. Johnston, *Autobiography: poems and songs of Emily Johnston, "The Factory Girl"* (Glasgow: unknown publisher, 1867).

17. Baker-Smith, "Social", pp. 538-49.

18. QS1840-80, WYAW.

19. QS1840-80, WYAW.

20. July 1841, Wakefield Court, QS1840-80, WYAW.

21. Report of Saunders, 12 April 1842, *PP*, (410) vol. 22, p. 21.

22. There are numerous reports in the Bradford newspapers in the 1870s of foremen and some manufacturers being prosecuted for a range of physical abuses on workpeople. Possibly because of the growing unionization of female millworkers in the 1875-1914 period, assaults on workpeople were more likely to go to court. See B. Godfrey, " 'That's the history of the mills': sources for studying the working experiences of mill women, 1840-1950", *Women's History Notebooks* 5(1), 1998, pp. 16-21; See S. D'Cruze, *Crimes of outrage: sex, violence and Victorian working women* (London: UCL Press, 1998).

23. *Bradford Observer*, 7 November 1874.

24. *Bradford Observer*, 20 August 1875.

25. *Bradford Observer*, 1 June 1878.

26. *Bradford Observer*, 15 September 1873.

27. *Bradford Observer*, 27 June 1874.

28. *Bradford Observer*, 19 November 1875.

29. Blackstone stated the "three great relations in private life are, 1. That of Master and Servant . . . 2. That of Husband and Wife . . . 3. That of Parent and Child": W. Blackstone, *Commentaries on the laws of England, book the first* (Oxford: Clarendon Press, 1765) p. 410.

30. See D. Valenze, *The first industrial women* (Oxford: Oxford University Press, 1995), pp. 85-112 and I. Pinchbeck, *Women workers and the industrial revolution, 1750-1850*, 3rd edn (London: Virago, 1985), pp. 196-201.

31. Baker-Smith, "Social", p. 539.

32. *Bradford Observer*, 1 July 1852.

33. *Bradford Observer*, 8 October 1847.

34. See B. R. Parkes, "The balance of popular opinion in regard to women's work", *Trans NAPSS*, 1862, pp. 808-9; E. Faithful, "Some of the drawbacks connected with the present employment of women", *Trans NAPSS*, 1862, pp. 809-10; and

M. Tabor, "On the condition of women as affected by law", *Trans NAPSS*, 1862, pp. 910-11.

35. *Bradford Observer*, 15 June 1874.

36. Anon., *The factory child: a poem* (London, 1831).

37. For example, on average, 20 per cent of the women appearing at the Bradford courts between 1866 and 1871, and 31 per cent of the women tried summarily at Leeds between 1878 and 1883 were prosecuted for drunkenness. Chief Constable's Reports, Judicial statistics, 1866-83, BBC1/2-5, WYAB.

38. Blackstone, *Commentaries*, vol. 1, 1765, pp. 27-8; J. Johnson, *Laws respecting women* (London: unknown publisher, 1777), pp. 70-1. See also J. Beattie, *Crime and the courts in England, 1660-1800* (Oxford: Clarendon, 1986), p. 414.

39. 24 September 1866, among many others, in the Worsted Committee Minute Books, 56D.88/1/5, WYAB.

40. Rose states that the family structure was used as a template for paternalistic management structures. See Rose, *Limited*, p. 34; B. Hill, *Women, work and sexual politics in eighteenth-century England* (Oxford: Blackwell, 1989), p. 263; S. Horrell & J. Humphries, "Women's labour force participation and the transition to the male-breadwinner family, 1790-1865", *Economic History Review* **48**, 1995, pp. 89-117.

41. QS1840-55, WYAW.

42. *Bradford Observer*, 8 October 1846.

43. See R. Soderlund, *Law, crime and labour in the worsted industry of the West Riding of Yorkshire, 1750-1850* (PhD thesis, Department of History, University of Maryland, 1992).

44. The Worsted Committee had fought with magistrates who had refused to punish female embezzlers in the eighteenth century. H. Heaton, *The Yorkshire woollen and worsted industries from the earliest times to the eighteenth century* (Oxford: Clarendon, 1920), p. 429.

45. One way for employers to circumnavigate *feme covert* was to take cases to the civil jurisdiction of the County Court where *coverture* did not apply. For example, appropriation of workplace materials could be prosecuted through the County Courts under master and servant legislation for breach of contract. Many women could have been dealt with in these courts. However, Yorkshire County Court records are not sufficiently detailed to identify cases of appropriation - were they so, our conception of the route to prosecution for female appropriators may have been radically different. However, since there is no mention of men or women being pursued through the County Courts in either the newspapers, or the Worsted Committee records, it seems unlikely that these courts were much utilized.

46. Quarter sessions, Leeds, 1840, QS1/180/10, WYAW.

47. 24 September 1866, Worsted Committee Minute Book, 56D.88/1/5, WYAB.

48. J. Styles, "Policing a female workforce: the Worsted Inspectors, 1760-1810", *Bulletin for the Study of Social History* **52**, 1987, pp. 39-41.

49. *Bradford Observer*, 15 May 1862.

50. *Bradford Observer*, 12 January 1870.

51. Quarter sessions, Doncaster, 1840, QS1/179/2, WYAW. On similar occasions, the giver-out had been prosecuted.

52. Sent by a leading manufacturer, *Bradford Observer*, 12 May 1880.

53. March 1877, Worsted Committee Minute Book, 56D.88/6, WYAB.

54. Quarter sessions, Sheffield, 1842, QS1/181/18, WYAW.

BARRY GODFREY

55. *Ibid*.
56. It is possible that *feme covert* was being interpreted in its very widest sense - that married women were under the authority of their husbands, and also that young girls were under the "coverage" of their fathers until the age of majority. Indeed, some authorities interpreted *coverture* in an even wider context: "An ancient authority has assured us that all women in the eye of the law, are either married or about to be married" Anon., *A treatise on feme covert, or the lady's law* (London: unknown publisher, 1732). It must also be remembered that women were not allowed to launch a master and servant case in their own name. A case could only be made by a husband on his wife's behalf, or a father on behalf of his children under the age of 21 (J. Burn, *The justice of the peace and parish officer* [5 vols], vol. 5 (London: Stevens & Sons, 1837), p. 549). Unfortunately, the number of women workers who were under 21 (the age of majority) cannot be determined. However, Factory Inspectors record that women under 19 years old constituted approximately a third of the worsted factory workforce. If this figure is added to the proportion of married women, almost one half of the female workforce could have been protected from prosecution by *coverture*.
57. *Bradford Observer*, 3 December 1875.
58. Worsted Committee Registers, 56D.88/4/2-3, WYAB. Nationally, the female proportion of those convicted (all offences) between 1860 and 1875 is consistently 11 per cent lower than the proportion of males convicted, Zedner, *Women*, p. 308.
59. *Bradford Observer*, 24 May 1849.
60. Which, as has already been stated, may have led to the careful selection of prosecutions, so that only the strongest cases against women reached the courts.

Chapter 7

♨

Consuming desires: female prostitutes and "customers" at the margins of crime and perversion in France and Britain, *c.* 1836–85

Bertrand Taithe

A comparison of the historiography of prostitution and regulationism produced in the nineteenth[1] and twentieth centuries illustrates how insular and nation-based narratives of sexuality and gender have become recently.[2] Nineteenth-century texts tended to cover and compare several nations and ages, often with the intention of showing that prostitution was ahistorical and that any medical regulation abided by centuries-old wisdom and practice. While not subscribing to this particular agenda, a comparative study of France and England provides useful insights on attitudes towards prostitution. It also demonstrates the fundamental inter-relationship between the two countries. Attitudes to prostitution were integrated to a more global discourse on European problematic urban reality. The regulationists and anti-regulationists who produced this comparative literature on prostitution also read widely and travelled across Europe but principally between France and Britain. Building on the work of Judith Walkowitz and Alain Corbin,[3] to name but two, one can use a comparative framework to highlight how female prostitution became the object of a repressive "melodramatic fix" in Britain while it became the centre of a fundamentally different nosology of perversion and decadence in France.[4] This article argues that from a relatively common basis two stories developed and completed each other in a reflexive manner and through constant references to the other country. In Britain after 1864 the Contagious Diseases Acts (CDA) failed to focus fear of degeneracy on prostitutes. Instead the anti-CDA movements succeeded in associating stories of prostitution with older and more politically sensitive forms of melodramatic representations within the British radical tradition. In France, regulationism survived the extreme left's assaults inspired by the British literature and tradition. Indeed, the French practice of regulation was renewed and reinforced by the fears of national decline revived by the 1870-71 wars against Germany and the Commune.[5] Eventually the

British and the French narratives achieved remarkably similar results and contributed to define, segregate and persecute women who sold themselves. This chapter will thus start with the common platform of legal, medical and social representations of prostitution. It will then show how the "melodramatic fix" described in Christina Crosby's work took a greater hold in Britain and failed in France between 1870 and 1885.[6] The French situation differed in that there was more focus on venereal danger in a discourse about decadence and male unfitness. In their different ways both sets of representations went through a shift of emphasis from women to men. By 1885, excesses of male sexuality, be it male homo-eroticism or venal promiscuity, became denounced as and assimilated to prostitution. Prostitution had long channelled masculine desires and sexual urges, but through the anti-regulationist or regulationist scaremongering campaigns it became the unacceptable expression of what was essentially wrong with unrestrained masculine sexuality.[7]

Definitions and social problems

The large literature on prostitution published in both countries from the 1830s onwards defined prostitution as a crime of sorts. If it was not a legally sanctioned crime, it was a moral and social one. Since the "oldest profession" predated even the beginnings of history, it was defined in an essentialist rather than relativist way. Henry Mayhew's 1851 reluctant definition of prostitution was an interesting attempt to solve this riddle. In spite of his encyclopaedic intentions, Mayhew's definition had to introduce nuances and relativist views, taking into account prostitutes' conditions of existence and the circumstances of their crime or "fall". His radical political views forced him to discuss the nexus of financial, legal and sexual relationships at the heart of prostitution:

> The offensiveness of an act of unchastity to the moral taste or sense constitutes the very essence of prostitution; and it is this moral offensiveness which often makes the licensed intercourse of the sexes, as in the marriage of a young girl to an old man for the sake of his money, as much an act of prostitution as even the grossest act of libertinism.[8]

Mayhew constantly oscillated between the emotive religious militancy of contemporary evangelical writers,[9] and the aloofness of "scientific" approaches modelled on Parent-Duchâtelet's work which inspired William Acton and shaped the Contagious Diseases Acts.[10]

These religious/scientific polarities proceed from a loose epistemological category, a form of necessary generalization. One could for instance see a moral common ground between Josephine Butler (the deeply religious campaigner against the CDA) and Yves Guyot (the fiercely moralistic anticlerical Radical who opposed regulation) and associate them under the "evangelical" label. Those who endorsed a "scientific" approach usually followed the French medical school and A. Parent-Duchâtelet's work. Philippe Ricord,[11] Alfred Fournier[12] and Jean Jeannel[13] later promoted the cause of a medical regulation of prostitution. They found a model of social policy in the earlier French, more specifically Parisian, rationalization and regulation of prostitution. The difference between the two approaches could not have been greater than it was in the 1850s and 1860s. The moral and religious approach dealt with prostitutes' immortal souls and their corrupting influence; the scientific lobby claimed to deal purely with the mortal body of prostitutes. The two systems of representation did not share a common definition of prostitution, nor did they wish to address directly those men who paid prostitutes, abused them, "protected" them or lived with them.[14] However, these male customers were the vacuous centre of both discourses: they were either to be protected from the contagion, or, as the cause of prostitution, they were the source of moral contagion. It was their masculinity and their sexual identity that were threatened and threatening. The prostitute herself was a supposedly willing subject spreading corruption by providing for a market of sexual urges, and/or an object and victim of violence and exploitation. Between the 1830s and 1860s, the crime of the "fallen woman" or prostitute was to provide physically, socially and morally tainted sex.

At a later period, I would argue, this system of representation had weakened, the prostitute was predominantly perceived to be "sinned against" or/and was placed at the heart of a nosography of perversion or of a melodramatic narrative. The pivotal period in this shift seems to be 1870-71 in France and Britain. In both countries the role of men became more explicit as the cause of prostitution and less attention was paid to the "prostitutes' crime" and more to the provision and "consumption" of prostitution, which implied greater scrutiny on male responsibility while always stopping short of criminalizing consumption. The years 1870-71 mattered in France because the experience of military defeat was compounded with the civil war and a general critique of the Parisian police, while in Britain 1870 signals the beginnings of well-organized resistance to the principle and extension of the CDA.

This shift of emphasis from women's criminal dispositions to men's animal and criminal instincts did not only operate in time but also arguably in social space and within the relationship between women and the men. The issue of prostitution became increasingly complex as the moral framework weakened to be replaced by a critique of the morality of capitalist exchanges and a denunciation of exploitation. Moreover, this shift entailed a reversal of influence between practice and representation. In the period before 1870, practice preceded theorization and fed into new representations of prostitution that grew out of it. After 1870, the French theory of regulation was reinforced and enriched by notions of national decline. Under new political pressure this medical rationale justified afresh the regulation of prostitution in France. On the other hand the repression of prostitution and customers that took place in Britain after the repeal of the CDA was the direct application of a set of melodramatic representations of vice and virtue: the theory preceded the practice. These themes will be treated chronologically in two phases, one covering the period 1830 to 1870, the second starting in 1870 and finishing in 1885.

Regulationism in the making

Mayhew's wide definition of prostitution quoted above illustrates the many ambiguities of the relationship between sex and money. In 1851, one of the readers of *London labour and the London poor*, named as the "Clerk in the City", wrote to Mayhew to define his common-law wife as a good ex-prostitute. He used her story to defend the "unfortunate women in London" from what he perceived to be unfair attacks. This couple had met in an ill-famed casino. She seemed to have had a protector and occasional clients when she decided to seduce him, dine him and entertain him.[15] The situation changed when she lost her source of income and protector and moved in with the "Clerk in the City" to lead a lower middle-class life. The clerk presented this story as a case of unspectacular "redemption". This narrative is not improbable and seems consistent with Françoise Barret-Ducrocq's account of the material from the London foundling hospital.[16] Mayhew's answer was to advise a prompt official marriage, which would redress the situation and extirpate the clerk from the ranks of "fancy men of the metropolis". The social unease arising from moral definitions of prostitution came from the fact that these included a variety of relationships which went from the street-walker to the common-law wife. The clerk himself accepted these definitions and did not deny that his common-law wife was still "an unfortunate woman", albeit a "good one". The basic definition of prostitution came from the fact that common-law wives were subversive of wedlock while street-walkers and brothel prostitutes were selling themselves in a parody of wedlock. The unease with prostitution proceeded from what the trade revealed by analogy about the gender struggle and the mercenary economy of even the most respectable marriage. The words used to describe street-walkers and freelance prostitutes in French echoed this anxiety: *femme publique, femme à tout le monde*, do not simply translate as public woman. *Femme* before a name in the French lower classes often signified a married or mature status; *prendre femme* also means to become married. *Femme* meant the equivalent of *Madame* for their Bourgeois counterparts.[17] A prostitute was everybody's wife. The exchange of money threatened the more stable and long-term conventions of marital exchange and household management.

In this context, the clerk, who defined himself as coming from a respectable middle-class family, had initially failed to establish a moral compact with his partner when he was her "fancy man", and by failing to marry her he simply changed her status from a street-walking prostitute to a common-law wife prostitute. In Mayhew's middle-class terms there could only be a redemption through a permanent and legal contract.

In commercial terms, leaving aside the implications of such transgressive relationships, the concept of a "punter" was really that of a "customer" led by a sex drive which, Thomas Laqueur has argued, was one of the best models of consuming hunger in early political economy thinking.[18] Prostitutes negotiated with this sexual demand by developing survival strategies in which they were simultaneously producers, products and retailers. They were the object of the commercial transaction but they were also responsible for the nature of the transaction. This economic definition grew in France within the framework of municipal regulationism.[19] French regulationism originated from a police spying measure of the late *ancien régime*[20] turned into a Utopian project of purification by Restif de la Bretonne in his *Pornographe*.[21] The utilitarian aspect of this regime of summary examination by second-rate doctors in a crowded room prevailed over the theory.[22] One had to wait for Parent-Duchâtelet and the 1830s to find a retrospective justification of regulationism.[23] The examination of prostitutes became increasingly compulsory and tied to "administrative" condemnation to short periods in prison lock-hospitals during the first half of the nineteenth century. The police used regulation primarily to maintain law and order in Parisian streets,[24] and to prevent social climbing and the violation of class boundaries.[25] Police registers fixed prostitutes under a clear and communicable label that would prevent them from mingling and marrying "above their station" in life. This form of social danger found in many of Balzac's novels should not be confused with the more sinister fears of social decay one can find in Zola's *Nana*.[26] In *Nana*, published in 1878, the high-class prostitute of the late Second Empire is dangerous because she carries mayhem and fatal diseases. In her own family tree and in the diseases she communicates, she best illustrates the hereditary danger to the French race that is one of the key themes of Zola's work.[27] Unlike a British melodramatic heroine victim of circumstances and ultimately redeemable, Nana is more predatory; she does not want to and cannot settle. Her whole being is dangerous. In 1830s French writings, on the other hand, prostitutes could be the source of social status, the affirmation of their protectors' wasteful wealth. The fact that their social climbing was impeded by the Police registration office did not prevent them from being the image of social climbing itself. The *demi-mondaine*, the high-class prostitute was an ornament constantly monitored by the police, on the margins of registered prostitution, and under a constant threat of being dragged back into it.[28]

For the police, prostitutes were often potentially useful as informers and as go-betweens between the twilight of a dangerous world and respectability. Their notorious propensity to associate with students could give to politically minded policemen a useful insight into the most troublesome quarters. Significantly, the services in charge of regulation in Paris did not originally belong to the criminal or sanitary services, but to the political branches of the police.[29] The strident emphasis on the dangers of syphilis that became much louder as the century went along and especially after 1870 did not originate from the police administrators.[30] They managed another set of issues. The prostitutes they regulated belonged to the shady areas of semi-crime, semi-unrest, semi-vice. Yet the police slowly associated them with the retailing trades for all purposes, including taxes. The prostitute belonged socially to the fringes of the criminal world, but her official tormentors in Paris treated her like a fishmonger. She was fined, locked in, inspected as the owner of a stall would be, with the sole difference that she sold herself and that it was she who might be judged unfit for sale and confiscated. Brothel keepers, always female by law, were vetted by the police who assessed their honesty and their docility. They remained easily removable unpaid agents of the regulationist machinery. The prostitutes' legal status was that of merchandise but their fiscal status was that of a retailer. Only medical practitioners fantasized them as a "seminal sewer".[31] Policemen administered a trade, a crime perhaps, but not really an epidemic. In all circumstances they privileged their law-enforcement mission over their sanitarian one:

> To increase the enforcement of the control of medical visits is apparently to improve the necessary guarantees to Public health; in reality, it makes registering [prostitutes] more difficult, it provokes considerable resistance and it increases the need for repression.[32]

Far from being a system simply imposed from above, regulationism permeated the relationship between prostitutes and customers. They denounced each other[33] and sometimes protected each other.[34] Prostitutes denounced corrupt doctors who treated them in secret,[35] but more importantly they denounced other, unregistered prostitutes. Regulationism was absolutely internalized and functioned routinely as the coherent, threatening and reassuring framework of venal sexual intercourse. Prostitutes knew to whom they could send their letter denouncing a corrupt policeman, the vicious punter, the shabby doctor who did not disguise their syphilis well enough. They could act within regulation almost as much as they were acted upon. In Britain, regulated prostitutes similarly used the system and 326 "Queen's girls" petitioned parliament in 1872 to defend the CDA.[36]

Parisian prostitutes also exploited the loopholes of the legislation and gradually freed themselves from the brothels or closed houses (*maisons closes*). Policemen were unable to control this move into the open and the geographical space of this trade. By 1870, 50 per cent of the 4,000 or so registered prostitutes worked freelance and their number was matched by that of illegal prostitutes. This evolution atomized the neat geography of brothel prostitution in Paris and opened the trade to rife competition, to street-walking and to complex territorial struggles. Registered prostitutes and brothel keepers called in the police against all the strangers, foreigners, under-age girls, casual and unregistered workers who competed cheaply to undercut them. The policemen unwittingly became the protectors of the prostitutes' "goodwill" and of their "*clientèle*".

The moral dimensions of prostitution were remarkably absent from all French legal documents and archives. Regulation solved the issue of prostitution in that it shifted the debate from the nature of the prostitutes' lifestyles to the social and physical innocuousness of the product they sold. Even within this economic analytical framework, observers, sometimes triggered by voyeurism, could not help creating a typology of the prostitute. Parent-Duchâtelet in the 1830s, like Mayhew in the 1850s, classed them according to "their" customers, according to their niche in the market. Their part-time or full-time status also positioned the prostitute towards the underworld. The unregistered *grisette*, Henri Murger's bohemian's friend, or Mayhew's implicitly tolerated needle-workers and occasional prostitutes shared with the soldiers' women a transient set of survival practices that had allegedly little in common with fully regulated French brothel prostitutes. Parent-Duchâtelet also observed the changes prostitution inflicted on a woman through drinking and sex. Their gender characteristics became noticeably altered, their voice became hoarser and their walk more masculine. He combined these observations with his study of "tribadism" among prostitutes.[37] If there were any deviance in his relatively cold account of the "trade", it lay entirely with the prostitute, even though this behaviour was also accounted for as a romantic form of gender solidarity in a world of unambiguous sexual polarities. These remarks on the gradual confusion of femininity and masculinity in prostitutes did not address what prostitution did to the customer.[38] The unspoken assumption of regulationism was that prostitution was a necessary safety valve in a society in which men tended to marry late.

As Corbin rightly emphasized, Parent-Duchâtelet's work framed most medically minded analyses of prostitution and assimilated regulationism to public health[39] in a powerful paradigm which remained unchallenged for the following 40 years in France and, to a slightly lesser extent, Britain.[40] Mayhew, for instance, tried to associate his own observations with Parent-Duchâtelet's, to combine his pro-Chartist political agenda with scientific rigour. He apportioned the guilt of crime to prostitutes according to their social origins. There could be no fall when one was a "born prostitute". Where there was a crime it was "truly and really, women's crime", the crime of envy and consumerism. Mayhew dealt with anecdotal evidence but he also tried to survey the police authorities of Britain with a questionnaire that included questions such as: "Number of prostitutes, well-dressed, living in brothels? Number of prostitutes well dressed walking the streets? Number of prostitutes, low, infesting low neighbourhoods?"[41]

He wished to emphasize the prostitutes' and customers' social status by encouraging a description of their outfits. He wanted to identify their aspirations and spending patterns as well as their geographical distribution within the town. His emphasis on the localization of prostitutes, on the geography of vice in Victorian cities reflected the priorities of sanitarian reformers. Mayhew shared their concern about the rookeries, the slums and the dens of the modern city.[42] In his account the dirty neighbourhood, the destitute and un-educated social context made the early Victorian prostitute and was to bear the responsibility for her crime. The fourth volume of *London labour and the London poor*, which was almost entirely farmed out to mercenary journalists, abandoned any such class analysis and was rightly denounced by Florence Nightingale for using sensationalism to serve a regulationist agenda. This agenda gathered impetus after the Crimean war and culminated in the British regulationist Acts of the 1860s. While it remains difficult to identify clearly who was "behind" the Contagious Diseases Act and regulationism when it was passed in 1864,[43] it is, however, easier to identify the campaigners who attempted to promote the Acts and to extend them to the whole of the United Kingdom between 1865 and 1885. They were mostly members of the establishment: army officers, Anglican clergy and medical practitioners. The CDA, a national form of legislation (as opposed to the French municipal regulations), came at a crucial time of consolidation for the Metropolitan Police[44] and after 20 years of renewed medical work on venereal diseases. Most of this research came from Paris and presented regulationism as a fundamental sanitary measure on which the science of venereology rested. Unlike the French case, the British practice of regulation had from the start a medical rationale.[45] Beyond improved military efficiency, other secular and religious uses could be found in the Acts. Policemen in plain clothes, uncomfortably similar to French *agents provocateurs*, could use them to control prostitutes and their friends. Missionaries had a literally captive audience to hear calls of redemption. The regulation package was not unlike the French model with perhaps more emphasis on redemption. It suffered from its national and centralized legislative backing, however, and could not be extended locally.[46] From 1869 to 1884, as Linda Mahood has shown, the CDA affected indirectly even areas of Britain that were not regulated and boosted the often flagging support for local lock hospitals[47] and veiled police regulation.[48] However, this influence was circumscribed and 1869 was the apex of regulationism in Britain. For the following 16 years the promoters of the Contagious Diseases Acts found themselves unable to make Parliament agree to any more metropolitan legislation.[49]

Regulationism and abolitionism after 1870

In the history of representations it is always difficult to choose a "watershed" or a significant turning point. Most contemporaries' accounts tend to retrospectively structure a heroic narrative precisely around a momentous date. Those who campaigned against regulation and their hagiographers were no exception.[50] In Britain and France, isolated opponents to regulationism had voiced their opposition since at least the early 1850s. In 1870–71, however, a conjunction of events enable us to choose that year as significant in the history of regulationism. The Franco-Prussian war is one of them. During the siege of Paris the Préfecture de Police was almost abolished; prostitutes themselves petitioned the government to obtain the end of what they perceived to be purely repressive medical examinations.[51] During the Commune prostitution was officially "abolished" and made redundant to the new social order. The Commune either repressed, regulated or tolerated according to local authorities controlling the various areas of Paris.[52] Medical examination was abandoned and only the policing core of regulationism survived. This illustrates how unimportant in the public eye the medical discourse had been in the justification of police regulation until 1870.

In 1870 also, the London-based Ladies' National Association manifesto began the more vociferous campaigning against the British CDA. While this association was only one movement among many devoted to the cause of repeal, its manifesto was an important symbolic gesture launching organized repeal. Josephine Butler, Henry Wilson, Jacob Bright, Benjamin Fowler, A. J. Mundella, Benjamin Lucraft, liberals and socialists, feminists and evangelical religious preachers led a very varied and sometimes violent political campaign in Parliament and in the constituencies against identified Liberal promoters of the CDA.[53] By the mid-1870s the repeal campaigns developed complex forms of rhetoric. While early repeal documents emphasized repetitiously the innocence of wrongly convicted women persecuted by undercover officers in breach of *habeas corpus*, later propagandists started to tackle the issue of prostitution on the grounds of sentimental representations and using the arguments of the anti-slavery movement.[54]

The early repeal campaigns had been prisoner of the semantics and legal paradigms of the Contagious Diseases Acts. Daniel Cooper's pamphlet *A dear remedy* published in 1869 at the origin of the repeal campaign still relied on the medical language and issues of the Acts.[55] The medical discourse emphasized since the 1830s centred on debates on the nature of syphilis and progressively made regulationism devoid of any debate on the nature of prostitution. To redefine the debate on prostitution and on prostitutes' life-stories, opponents of regulation in Britain and later in France used the medium of melodrama. These sentimental rhetorical tropes were first developed in the English-speaking world before repealers in France attempted in vain to make them relevant to the French political context. In this sense Britain served as the centre of the anti-regulationist movements of Europe.

Melodramatic images of prostitution pre-dated the Contagious Diseases Acts. Some of H. Mayhew's correspondents, for instance, travelled down to the Great Exhibition of 1851 in the hope of finding out for themselves the environmental causes of prostitution. They haunted the dens of vice to meet and rescue unwilling "fallen women". One such well-intentioned voyeur from Glasgow chose to track down a casino prostitute and was narrated, possibly to escape his zeal, the tragic story of her life. Hers was a story of abandoned youth corrupted under the influence of alcohol and seduction in her sleep.[56] This pattern of seduction she had to re-enact night after night in spite of herself. Other correspondents were not impressed. Londoners who had "studied" prostitution, some of them admittedly as customers, recognized in this melodramatic plot the "officer's daughter's tale", a common narrative in the folklore of the underworld.[57]

As Amanda Anderson and Tom Winnifrith have argued, melodramatic accounts of the "fall" into prostitution were codified early on for the theatre and cheap novels alike.[58] The core of the story was that a naïve girl, sin-free, drank either alcohol, or a drugged beverage, to wake in the morning tainted and unable to avoid a cycle of alcohol and vice: drinking to forget a sin committed under the influence of drink. This set of codified representations operated in novels, paintings or on the stage and within a definite sentimental space for an anticipating audience. The practice of melodrama may have had cathartic purposes for the audience but melodrama remained restricted to the medium used. When the screen fell down in the East End or on *boulevard du Crime*, prostitutes carried on their business under the eye of the police, regulated or tolerated as ever. Spectators may have seen them redeemed in ideal homes, but deep down they knew that melodrama only addressed their fantasies and domestic nostalgia.[59] The Contagious Diseases Acts first produced narratives of persecution that fitted well with these earlier melodramatic narratives. Mrs Percy who committed suicide in March 1875 was a very good example.[60] A cabaret singer, she was often seen drinking with soldiers, and was repeatedly harassed by the police. She wrote a desperate letter to the *Daily Telegraph* and threw herself into the canal and drowned.[61] While the police denounced the case as a sordid accident, a sad drunk falling into a canal, the repealers refined the stereotype of a woman hunted to death by the state. To exploit stories like these the repealers created a specialized network of journals and newsletters. This emphasis on simple narratives that attempted to make simple cases for complicated legal or moral discussions of the nature of prostitution forced the repealers to seek more material abroad. In spite of a number of British cases, the martyrology of European police forces was a much richer seam and provided the *Shield* and the many titles of the repeal press with the news material they needed to fill their columns and reach as wide an audience as possible, even if that implied an adulteration of the message through increased sensationalism.[62]

The editors of those titles gradually became pornographers (*porne-graphos*, depicting prostitutes) whose stories probably titillated the voyeurism of virtuous readers. Suicides, drunken men and innocent girls wrongly arrested formed the core of the material published in the *Shield*, or the *National League Journal* (the weekly of the Working Men's League published between 1875 and 1884), which eventually merged in 1884 with the Dyer Brothers' social purity paper, the *Sentinel*.[63]

Of all the repeal publicists the Dyer brothers and Hugh Price Hughes, editor of the *Methodist Protest*, were the most enthusiastic to use melodramatic stories from the mid-1870s onwards. The most direct consequence of focusing on stories of prostitution rather than on the *erreurs judiciaires*, was a focus on prostitutes themselves, and this time not solely on the cases of mistaken identity. These campaigns also found a rich seam of images on the theatre stage. One example was *The new magdalen* adapted from Wilkie Collins's novel and set during the Franco-Prussian war. It used some material from Mayhew's own articles of 1849 on needlewomen. The heroine, Mercy, a needleworker-prostitute who, rescued, became a war nurse, says in the first act:

> I sometimes ask myself if it was all my fault. I sometimes wonder if society
> had no duty towards me, when I was a child selling matches in the streets

- when I was a hardworking girl, fainting at my needle for want of food. Now Society can subscribe to reclaim me - but Society can't take me back . . . Will you hear the story of Magdalen - in modern times?[64]

This play was staged in 1873 and again in 1884 without any changes because the plot and the pathos of melodrama had the enduring qualities and the limitations of a recognized genre. Taking the image of the prostitute from this theatrical context to introduce it with a great sense of controversy in the political world, the Dyer brothers and their friends shifted the repeal campaign in the direction of evangelical and social purity revivals. They also took responsibility away from the prostitute. From retailer and trader of herself as sexual commodity, she became a simple object, a recipient of charity and redemption with all the helplessness of a theatrical heroine. There was a certain vacuity in the prostitute's part. She was one minute full of guilt and social unease, and later, after a dramatic atonement, often at death's door, full of gratitude, redemption and humility. This vacuity fitted within the domestic romance of the Chartist traditions upheld by the Working Men's League.[65] The stray daughters lost their adult identity to regress into dependence and immaturity.[66] While the "fall" became the central episode of all portrayals of prostitution, it was almost always under the influence of love or narcotics that diminished the prostitute's responsibility but paradoxically not the sentimental appeal of a scene of redemption.

This type of narrative did not undermine significantly the consumerist nature of prostitution but re-shuffled the roles and changed the apportionment of guilt.[67] From traders prostitutes became the object of the trade. The parallel with the slave trade resulted from an attempt to identify the repeal movements with successful international campaigns such as American abolitionism. The United States was the Holy Land for many British repealers. There the anti-slavery movement had spectacularly triumphed a few years before, women had organized themselves in influential political groups and the Christian revival was strongest. The British temperance and teetotal movements were also transatlantic.[68]

In America "women have stood with the Negro, thus far, on equal ground as ostracized classes outside the political paradise".[69] Organized women's rights activism[70] originated from the early days of the anti-slavery cause.[71] Elizabeth Blackwell, one of Britain's first women doctors, had trained in the United States, and, unlike Elizabeth Garrett who had trained in France,[72] she opposed re-gulationism.[73] Suffrage campaigners involved in the repeal campaign, such as Mrs Bright Lucas or, to a lesser extent, Millicent Fawcett, were in touch with American activists and received numerous supportive visits.[74] Americans had also led the way in the repeal cause by successfully combating municipal regulation in Louisville between 1872 and 1874.[75] Unlike their British or French counterparts, the majority of American doctors had not supported regulation in their annual meetings.[76] After a fact-finding mission in the United States, the cause of repeal became associated with the abolition of slavery and repealers subsequently called themselves "abolitionists".[77] This was a fundamental strengthening of the repealers' discourse. Abolition had been a triumphant cause and a prestigious crusade for over a hundred years.[78] With the term "abolitionist" came the corresponding term for prostitute: "white slave".[79] This analogy with slavery reinforced the fundamental point that repealers had been making in arguing that the Acts were as unjust as slavery, but it also diminished the environmental argument which made prostitution a necessary element of slum culture.[80] These women were not simply poor, they were *white* slaves. In a period of ethnocentrism and vexed national and racial identities, their whiteness made their slavery doubly abhorrent. The ethnocentrism of anti-slavery campaigners discussed by Catherine Hall about missionaries of the 1830s was a central feature of the white slave discourse.[81] It played on xenophobic reflexes and articulated the debate on prostitution as another expression of national competitiveness and struggle for life.[82] Adding to the "slum culture", it set it as the European equivalent of the African captives, with the women as the "negroes" and the worst men as the traders/consumers. The image of customers as a debased form of men satisfying cheaply the most animal part of their physical identity slowly emerged from this discourse.

The logic of this metaphor was such that abolitionists' discourse on prostitution preceded Alfred Dyer's quest for evidence in 1878: "When there was slavery, there will be a slave trade."[83] This constituted a revolution in the perception of the problem. It minimized the prostitutes' individual responsibility and implied a whole pattern of economic circumstances, turning the "fall" into economic exploitation, turning seduction stories into an international traffic sanctioned by regulationists. At the heart of this traffic was the existence of a market, of a male demand for fresh flesh and of a criminal male-dominated international network which had to be fought across Europe. This global perspective developed through contacts at a European level in 1875 when Josephine Butler visited France, Italy, Switzerland and Belgium. The pornographic trade also provided a model for this theory of international traffic.[84] Since the eighteenth century,[85] pornographic material printed in France, the Netherlands and in England ignored national borders.[86] The individuals she met in Switzerland and France, like Pastor Borel in Geneva or the Radical publicist Yves Guyot in Paris, were interested in setting an international organization that could match the international medical networks and the *cordon sanitaire* advocated by Dr Jeannel of France.[87] For the sake of her cause Josephine Butler relied too heavily on her Protestant contacts in Catholic countries like Italy and France. When she reached out beyond these narrow circles, she focused energies and helped Guyot lead an important and radical campaign with his newspaper *La Lanterne* against the Préfecture de Police.[88] Butler and Guyot's main target was Lecour, an experienced and well-established policeman from the Imperial age whose management of regulation in Paris had been ruthless. Yves Guyot, a journalist on the extreme left of French politics, seized the issue in 1876, six months after the "state of siege" enacted in 1871 ended, to attack the repressive administrations in Paris and the stuffy *ordre moral* which followed the Commune repression. The prostitution issue was an ideal tool to undermine both Lecour, who resigned in 1878, and then the Prefect of Police himself. The political debate in France meant that this first campaign signalled more the return of the extreme left to politics after five years of silence than real empathy with the religious ideals of Josephine Butler and her handful of Protestant preachers.[89] If anything, the emphasis on the legal sexual exploitation of working-class women by religious middle-class men, however distant from the reality this image might be, served an anti-Catholic political agenda. In spite of these contradictions, Butler's work in France enabled a political opening to the left and contributed to the early days of French organized feminism, particularly with the work of Maria Deraismes and Léon Richer.[90] The Geneva congress of 1877 which created the Fédération Britannique et Continentale pour l'Abolition de la Prostitution changed the abolitionist agenda from the repeal of regulationism to the abolition of prostitution, a prohibitionist aim only ever tried by the Commune of Paris. After Prefect of Police Andrieux's resignation under the pressure of the Paris council, Yves Guyot's book on prostitution in Paris signalled the climax of French left-wing abolitionist thinking.[91] In spite of his high-profile campaigning, the municipal structure of French regulationism meant that, apart from the departure of a handful of Parisian policemen, the abolition of the vice squad but not of their functions, abolitionists had achieved remarkably little practical progress by 1885. French parliamentary politics also meant that the socialists remained on the margins of the political world and could not emulate their British radical counterparts who played on the divisions of the Liberal party to obtain a vote in parliament and the gradual repeal of the CDA in Parliament between 1883 and 1886.[92] As mentioned earlier, the medical emphasis on the hereditary nature of syphilis, on syphilitic insanity and on the decline of the French nation had reinforced regulationism from without and turned it into a symbol of medical power in the aftermath of the 1870 defeat.

If the French left learnt a lot from the British abolitionist movement, the British brought back from the continent a greater emphasis on rescue work.[93] The rescue of "Magdalenes",[94] which was an important part of the social work of Roman Catholic religious orders, was far more common in southern Europe than in Britain.[95] Josephine Butler and her friends in the Salvation Army put a lot of their energy into rescue work from the late 1870s onwards.[96]

The combination of this rescue work and the fears of an international trade of women led to the "Maiden Tribute to Modern Babylon"[97] published in William Stead's *Pall Mall Gazette* in 1885.[98] This scandal and the agitation that followed were enough to push through the 1885 Criminal Law Amendment Act which is the boundary of this article and the real conclusion of the anti-regulationist fight in Britain, while also the beginning of a new phase in British sexual politics as Lucy Bland has shown.[99] William Stead wrote his articles on the evidence provided by Alfred Dyer and on his own investigation, which included the abduction of a young girl for which he went to prison.[100] By 1885 the repealers had emphasized the foreign origins of vice and forms of moral protectionism promoting social purity that also reflected growing national and economic uncertainties in the face of foreign competition.[101] From libertarians and defenders of the *Habeas Corpus* in 1869, the repealers had become legislators with a vengeance. Brothel keepers, lodgers, friends and families of prostitutes, exploiters and normal social networks fell under the new rigours of the law. The paradoxical Labouchère amendment also made homosexuals the victims of legal actions.[102] As Jeffrey Weeks has argued, this condemnation of homoerotic behaviours seems to proceed less from the construction of a specific entity named homosexual, than from the ultimate perversions of a debauchee.[103] This assimilation of homoeroticism to a continuum of excessive heterosexuality shows how central concerns about male sexuality had become. While in France the prostitute had first been sexualized up to perversion in medical accounts, the customer became sexualized to the same extent in British repealers' texts.[104] The perversion of the sexuality expressed in venal inter-course meant that the debate itself became perverse:

> the individual who has the effrontery to tell me that prostitution is a necessity, has learnt it from his own experience, from his own inability to control and conquer his own vile passions . . . whatever their exterior they *are rotten to the core*.[105]

The assimilation made with melodramatic plots put the emphasis on the seducers, the semi-professional fiancé taking the innocent woman on a trip abroad, down the sexual ladder. Across the Channel, the ultimate victory of the French medical discourse reinforced the regulation of prostitution but also strongly put an emphasis on heredity through male sexuality and on the moral imperatives of sexual continence. Hygienists and moralists could co-exist in a republican project that intended to reshape Frenchmen and, with the combined effort of education and medicine, regenerate the French race. In practice, around 1885, the promises of a new race did not really apply in the police services. Regulation remained, more repressive than previously, certainly more anxious about the dangers of prostitution but as compromised and badly funded as ever.

Conclusion

The conflicting discourses produced by the repeal agitation and the medicalization of regulation interacted with the legal framework to structure deviancy and crime. The medical literature cultivated alarmist accounts of an all-pervasive syphilis carried by prostitutes to the heart of middle-class homes.[106] The troubling nosology of perversions applied to a few observed cases in Parisian hospitals was re-deployed with increasing strength and rigidity to sexualized men, sexualized customers both in France and in Britain.[107] In British sexology and in French psychiatry of the *fin de siècle* male sexuality became increasingly scrutinized and subdivided in nosological categories of abnormality.[108] The clear set of moral answers promoted by the abolitionist movement defined the criminal space of prostitution and the perversion of prostitutes' punters by opposition to a central domestic sphere. "Normal" male sexuality implicitly excluded such excesses in the company of strangers in a criminal space.

The criminal nature of the intercourse between prostitutes and customers also perceivably shifted. Prostitutes in Orléanist Paris were on the margins of crime because they associated with criminals and political opponents; in early Victorian England they were tolerated on the fringes of the same criminal world. While coming late, the British Contagious Diseases Acts were undoubtedly more essentially medical than French regulation.[109] The paradox then is that while French regulationism became increasingly justified in medical terms, criminalizing the transmission of diseases, the prohibitionist tactics of the British police after 1885 took a leaf or two from the French policing books.[110] The Criminal Law Amendment Act criminalized everyone living near a prostitute, the social and geographical space of prostitution. From the regulationist environment remained the policing, but a form of punitive and blind policing that kept prostitutes in a social limbo more than ever before.[111]

Notes

1. For instance, the widely translated F. Buret, *Syphilis today and among the ancients* (Philadelphia: Davis, 1891).
2. For instance, M. Mason, *The making of Victorian sexual attitudes* (Oxford: Oxford University Press, 1994); M. S. Micale, "Hysteria male/Hysteria female: reflections on comparative gender construction in nineteenth-century France and Britain", in *Science and sensibility, gender and scientific enquiry, 1780-1945*, M. Benjamin (ed.) (Oxford: Basil Blackwell, 1991), pp. 200-42.
3. A. Corbin, *Les Filles de noce: misère sexuelle et prostitution (19ème siècle)* (Paris: Aubier 1978); J. Walkowitz, *Prostitution and Victorian society* (Cambridge: Cambridge University Press, 1980).
4. The treatment of male prostitutes differs in many important areas. See J. Weeks, *Against nature: essays on history, sexuality and identity* (London: Rivers Oram, 1991), pp. 46-68; R. Aron & R. Kempf, *La Bourgeoisie, le sexe et l'honneur*, 2nd edn (Brussels: Complexe, 1984); M. Duberman, M. Vicinus, G. Chauncey (eds) *Hidden from history: reclaiming the gay and lesbian past* (New York: Meridian Books, 1990); G. Mosse "Masculinity and the decadence" in *Sexual knowledge, sexual science: the history of attitudes to sexuality*, R. Porter & M. Teich (eds) (Cambridge: Cambridge University Press, 1994).
5. R. Nye, *Crime, madness and politics in modern France* (Princeton N.J.: Princeton University Press, 1984), pp. 132-70; C. Digeon, *La Crise allemande de la pensée française 1870-1914*, 2nd edn (Paris: Presses Universitaires de France, 1992).
6. C. Crosby, *The ends of history: Victorians and the "woman question"* (London: Routledge, 1991), pp. 69-109.
7. On masculinity, see J. E. Adams, "The banality of transgression? Recent works on masculinity", *Victorian Studies* 36, 1993, pp. 80-87; G. Mosse, *The image of*

men: the creation of modern masculinity (Oxford: Oxford University Press, 1996); M. Roper & J. Tosh, *Manful assertions: masculinities in Britain since 1800* (London: 1991), pp. 1–24; B. Taithe, "La question du genre: l'approche du masculin", *European Review of History / Revue européenne d'histoire* 1(2), 1994, pp. 233–9.

8. H. Mayhew, *London labour and the London poor*, [4 vols] (New York: Dover, 1968), vol. 4, p. 36.

9. For links with Evangelical movements and Temperance groups, see W. Logan (1813–79), *Prostitution in London, Leeds, Rochdale and Glasgow, or the great social evil*, 2nd end (London: Hodder & Stoughton, 1871) and *Early heroes of the temperance reformation* (Glasgow: Scottish Temperance League, Houlston & Son, 1873).

10. A. J. B. Parent-Duchâtelet, *Essai sur les cloaques ou égouts de la ville de Paris, envisagés sous le rapport de l'hygiène publique et de la topographie médicale de cette ville* (Paris: Baillière, 1824); *De la prostitution dans la ville de Paris, considérée sous le rapport de l'hygiène publique, de la morale et de l'administration* (Paris: Baillière, 1836). On William Acton, see L. Hall's summary of the debates, L. Hall & R. Porter, *The facts of life: the creation of sexual knowledge in Britain, 1650–1950* (New Haven & London: Yale University Press, 1995), pp. 141–4.

11. C. Eginer, *Philippe Ricord: sa vie son oeuvre* (Paris: Le François, 1939).

12. A. Fournier, *De la contagion syphilitique*, (Paris: Delahaye, 1860); Fournier, *L'Hérédité syphilitique* (Paris: G. Masson, 1891); Fournier, *Danger social de la syphilis* (Paris: Delagrave, 1907); A. Auzias-Turenne, *De la contagion syphilitique à propos de la thèse de M. A. Fournier* (Paris: J. B. Baillière, 1860); H. Mireur, *Essai sur l'hérédité de la syphilis* (Thèse de médecine, Paris University, 1867); P. Yvaren, *Des métamorphoses de la syphilis* (Paris: J. B. Baillière, 1854); C. Quétel, *History of syphilis* (Cambridge: Polity, 1990).

13. J. Jeannel, *De la prostitution dans les grandes villes au XIXème siècle et de l'extinction des maladies vénériennes* (Paris: Baillière et Fils, 1868).

14. See J. Termeau, *Maisons closes de province* (Le Mans: Cénomane, 1986), pp. 175–90.

15. See "Answers to the Correspondents" in B. Taithe, *The essential Mayhew: representing and communicating the poor* (London: Rivers Oram, 1996), pp. 248–9.

16. F. Barret-Ducrocq, *Love in the time of Victoria: sexuality, class and gender in nineteenth-century London* (London: Verso, 1991).

17. By a nice linguistic twist, a "madame" in English is also a brothel keeper.

18. T. W. Laqueur, "Sexual desire and the market economy during the industrial revolution", in *Discourses of sexuality: from Aristotle to AIDS*, D. C. Stanton (ed.) (Ann Arbor: University of Michigan Press, 1992), pp. 185–215.

19. Each town has therefore a different story to tell: L. Amiel, *La prostitution à Bordeaux du début du dix-neuvième siècle au début du vingtième siècle* (Cahier de l'IAES 8, Institut Aquitain d'Études Sociales, 1994); B. Clais, *La prostitution à Amiens au dix-neuvième siècle* (Amiens: Bibliothèque Municipale, Eklitra, 1993); B. Coussec, *Petite histoire de la prostitution Lilloise* (Lille: Raimbeaucourt, 1995).

20. E-M. Benabou, *La prostitution et la police des moeurs au XVIIIème siècle* (Paris: Perrin, 1987); J. Harsin, *Policing prostitution in nineteenth-century Paris* (Princeton N. J.: Princeton University Press, 1985).

21. Nicolas Restif de la Bretonne (1734-1806) was a very prolific and disorderly author of the low enlightenment. His utopian *Pornographe ou idées d'un honnête*

homme sur un projet de règlement pour les prostituées (London & The Hague: Gosse Junior et Pinet, 1769) anticipated the policing of prostitution in Paris.

22. This medicalization was often the result of private initiatives like Dr Jeannel's dispensary project which was frowned upon: *Rapport à M. le Préfet*, 18 April 1874, Archives de la Préfecture de Police de Paris, (APdP) Da 232.

23. P. Sabatier, *Histoire de la législation sur les femmes publiques et les lieux de débauches* (Paris: n.p. 1828); C. Béraud, *Les Filles publiques de Paris et la police qui les régit* (Paris: n.p. 1839); J. Garin, *De la police sanitaire et de l'assistance publique dans leurs rapports avec l'extinction des maladies vénériennes* (Paris: Masson, 1866).

24. *Circulaire*, 7 Sept. 1830, APdP, Da 223, a detailed regulation of authorized streets and hours. J. Tulard, *Paris et son administration, 1800-1830* (Paris: Imprimerie Municipale, 1976), pp. 105-38.

25. See C. J. Lecour, *Les Attaques contre la Préfecture de Police, envisagées surtout du point de vue du service des moeurs* (Paris: P. Asselin, 1881), pp. 31-5.

26. P. Wald-Lasowski, *Syphilis: essai sur la littérature Française au dix-neuvième siècle* (Paris: Gallimard, 1982).

27. C. E. Russett, *Sexual science: the Victorian construction of womanhood* (Cambridge Mass.: Harvard University Press, 1991), p. 64; D. Pick, *Faces of degeneration: a European disorder, c. 1848-c. 1918* (Cambridge University Press, 1989).

28. C. Bernheimer, *Figures of ill-repute: representing prostitution in nineteenth-century France* (Cambridge Mass.: Harvard University Press, 1989).

29. See Lecour, *Les Attaques contre la Préfecture de Police*, pp. 31-5.

30. Termeau, *Maisons closes de province*, pp. 19-23, 96-8.

31. A. Parent-Duchâtelet, who coined the phrase, was a hygienist whose seminal work on sewers was well known before he tackled the issue of prostitution. On Parent-Duchâtelet's intellectual milieu, see: Elizabeth A. Williams, *The physical and the moral* (Cambridge: Cambridge University Press, 1994), pp. 151-66.

32. *Rapport à monsieur le Préfet de Police*, 3 September 1874., A.P.d.P., Da 232. On epidemiology in France, see F. Delaporte, *Le Savoir de la maladie: essai sur le choléra de 1832 à Paris* (Paris: Presses Universitaires de France, 1990), pp. 135-76.

33. Customers denouncing unregistered prostitutes, *Rapport*, 24 June 1877; Prostitutes denouncing unruly soldiers, *Doléance 43701*, Police Municipale, Femme Vincent, 10 August 1870, all in APdP, Da 225. In early 1866, for instance, Marie denounced Antonie, "A neighbour" denounced Marie's purchase of medication at the chemist, a girl denounced Dr Guillard who treated and protected women. In 1862 Dr Rossignol was denounced and sacked. APdP, Da 230.

34. "Behind each of those girls there is a whole group of ex-lovers, current lovers, of fools, of protectors and parasites, of suppliers, of landowners and disguised pimps who seek to make them avoid registering", Note de Lecour, 7 July 1868, APdP, Da 225.

35. *Rapport à M. le Préfet*, 18 August 1873, APdP, Da 232.

36. "Something new in English history!" (London: *The Shield*, 1872). These four petitions were always seen as dubious but there is some evidence that they were genuine.

37. A. Corbin (ed.) *La Prostitution à Paris au dix-neuvième siècle* (Paris: Seuil, 1981), pp. 114-15.

38. For a later period, see Russett, *Sexual science*, pp. 49-61.

39. See A. F. La Berge, "Edwin Chadwick and the French connection", *Bulletin of Medical History* **62**, 1982, pp. 23-41, especially p. 31; M. Ramsey, "Public health in France", in D. Porter (ed.), *The history of public health and the modern state*, Clio Medica (Amsterdam: Rodopi, 1994), pp. 45-118.

40. See W. Acton, *Prostitution considered in its moral social and sanitary aspects in London and other large cities* (London: John Churchill, 1857). This book relied heavily on Trébuchet and Poiret-Duval's 1857 enlarged edition of Parent-Duchâtelet's work: (see Acton, p. ix); J. Peterson, "Dr Acton's enemy: medicine, sex and society in Victorian England", *Victorian Studies* **29**, 1986, pp. 569-90.

41. Taithe, *Essential Mayhew*, pp. 184, 195-6.

42. G. Goodwin, *London shadows: a look at the homes of the thousands and town swamps and social bridges*, 2nd edn (Leicester: Leicester University Press, 1972), p. 42; T. Beames, *The rookeries of London* (London: Thomas Bosworth, 1850), p. 196; J. Greenwood, *The seven curses of London* (London: Stanley Rivers, 1869), pp. 173-212; G. Stedman-Jones, *Outcast London: a study in the relationship between classes in Victorian England*, 2nd edn (Harmondsworth: Penguin, 1992), p. 167.

43. J. G. Gamble, *The origins, administration and impact of the Contagious Diseases Acts from a military perspective* (PhD thesis, University of Southern Mississippi, 1983) is very inconclusive in this respect.

44. V. Bailey (ed.), *Policing and punishment in nineteenth-century Britain* (London: Croom Helm, 1981), pp. 94-124.

45. F. D. Lowndes, *The extension of the Contagious Diseases Acts to Liverpool and other seaports practically considered* (Liverpool and London: Holden, Churchill, 1876).

46. B. Taithe, *From danger to scandal: debating sexuality in Victorian England* (PhD Thesis, University of Manchester, 1992), pp. 58-87.

47. J. T. Wyke, "The Manchester and Salford lock hospital 1819-1917", *Medical History* **19**, 1975, pp. 73-83.

48. L. Mahood, *The magdalenes: prostitution in the nineteenth century* (London: Routledge, 1990), pp. 137-52.

49. Colonial ordinances did not have the same problem. Beyond this the British army abroad organized regimental brothels comparable to the French army's lasting well after the repeal of the Contagious Diseases Acts. R. Hyam, *Empire and sexuality: the British experience* (Manchester: Manchester University Press, 1990), pp. 117-21; K. Balhatchet, *Race, sex and class under the Raj: imperial attitudes and policies and their critics, 1793-1905* (London: Weidenfeld & Nicolson, 1980).

50. See E. Moberly Bell, *Josephine Butler: flame of fire* (London: Constable, 1962); G. Petrie, *A singular iniquity: the campaigns of Josephine Butler* (London: Macmillan, 1971).

51. Lecour, *De la prostitution*, p. 310.

52. G. Da Costa, *La Commune vécue* [3 vols] (Paris: Quantin, 1903), vol. 2, pp. 295-310; *Journal officiel de la République*, Édition de la Commune, 4-15 April 1871; various files in APdP, Da 225-30.

53. See J. Butler, *Personal reminiscences of a great crusade* (London: Horace Marshall & Son, 1911); H. Bell, H. J. Wilson & B. Scott, *Copy of a rough record of events and incidents connected with the repeal of the* CDA *in the United Kingdom* (London: Association for the Social Hygiene, 1906).

54. B. Scott, *A state iniquity* (London: National Association for the Repeal of the CDA, 1871); S. Amos, *The policy of the Contagious Diseases Acts 1866-1869* (London:

J. Churchill, 1870); Amos, *Laws for the regulation of vice* (London: J. Churchill, 1870).

55. See D. Cooper, *The remedy worse than the disease* (London: Rescue Society, 1869).

56. On comparable literary scenarios in France, see J. Matlock, *Scenes of seduction: prostitution, hysteria and reading difference in nineteenth-century France* (New York: Colombia University Press, 1994).

57. Taithe, *Essential Mayhew*, pp. 211-13.

58. A. Anderson, *Tainted souls and painted faces: the rhetoric of fallenness in Victorian culture* (New York: Cornell University Press, 1993); T. Winnifrith, *Fallen women in the nineteenth-century novel* (London: Macmillan, 1994).

59. See P. Brooks, *The melodramatic imagination: Balzac, Henry James, melodrama and the mode of excess* (New Haven, Ct.: Yale University Press, 1976); P. Joyce, *Visions of the people* (Cambridge: Cambridge University Press, 1992), Ch. 2.

60. See Butler, *Personal reminiscences*, p. 112.

61. Capt. Harris, *Annual report of the chief commissioner of police*, 1876.

62. B. Nevins edited *The Medical Enquirer* in Liverpool 1878-83, H. Price Hughes edited *The Methodist Protest*, later *The Protest*, 1876-83; the Ladies National Association had *The Shield* 1870-85; A. Dyer edited both *The National League Journal*, 1875-84 and *The Sentinel*, 1880-85.

63. See B. Taithe, "Working men, old Chartists and the Contagious Diseases Acts", in *Social conditions, status and community*, K. Laybourn (ed.) (Stroud: Sutton Publishing, 1997), pp. 200-24.

64. *The new magdalen*, staged at the Olympic Theatre May 1873, and April 1884; W. Collins, *The new magdalen* (Stroud: Alan Sutton Publishing, 1993).

65. A. Clark, *The battle for the breeches: gender and the making of the British working class* (London: Rivers Oram, 1995), pp. 220-32; J. Schwarzkopf, *Women in the Chartist movement* (London: Macmillan, 1991).

66. Work on incest proves how much more complex this relationship with their home was. See L. Mahood, *Policing gender, class and family: Britain, 1850-1940* (London: UCL Press, 1995), pp. 106-12.

67. L. Nead, *Myths of sexuality representations of women in Victorian England* (Oxford: Blackwell, 1988), pp. 129-35.

68. See B. Harrison, *Drink and the Victorians: the temperance question in England 1815-1872* (London: Faber & Faber, 1971), pp. 20-30.

69. E. Cady Stanton, *Eighty years and more (1815-1897): reminiscences of E. Cady Stanton* (New York: European Publishing Company, 1898), p. 255.

70. Stanton, *Eighty years and more*, pp. 80-81.

71. C. Midgley, *Women against slavery: the British campaigns, 1780-1870* (London: Routledge, 1992), pp. 121-77.

72. Y. B. Potter, *Justina's letter in reply to Miss Garrett's defence of the Contagious Diseases Acts* (London: Pall Mall Gazette, 1870).

73. E. Blackwell, *Wrong and right methods to deal with the social evil* (London: William Hastings, 1883). S. Holton, "State pandering, medical policing and prostitution: the controversy within the medical profession regarding the Contagious Diseases legislation 1864-1886", *Law, Deviance and Social Control* 9, 1988, pp. 149-70.

74. See M. Mackenzie, *Shoulder to shoulder* (New York: Random House, 1975), pp. 12-29.

75. See J. & R. Haller, *The physician and sexuality in Victorian America* (Urbana: University of Illinois Press, 1974), p. 242.

76. J. M. Sims, *Legislation and the contagious diseases*, inaugural address delivered before the AMA 25th meeting June 1876, p. 13. Sims's address, which summed up the medical rationale of regulationism, was ultimately rejected by the AMA. "They [authorities] now have the power of hunting out small pox, and of sending it to hospitals for treatment; and they should have the same power of searching out the abode of syphilis and of sending its victims to hospitals for treatment."

77. J. Stuart, *The new abolitionists: a narrative of a year's work* (London: Dyer Brothers, 1876).

78. J. Addams, *A new conscience and an ancient evil* (New York: Macmillan, 1912), pp. 5-7.

79. The term "white slave", meaning children and women, had been coined during the 10 hours bill agitation in Great Britain. In the British political context the emphasis on slavery had a very emotional echo. The "Rule Britannia" anthem and much of the radical literature was built on the defence of free-born Englishmen's and women's rights. In the 1870s the term came back via Switzerland. In France and in other continental countries the term referred much more directly to orientalist myths and to the colonial empire. In Britain it had the conotations mentioned above and also referred to the century-old and deep-rooted anti-slavery movement.

80. See F. Finnegan, *Poverty and prostitution: a study of Victorian prostitutes in York* (Cambridge: Cambridge University Press, 1979).

81. C. Hall, *White, male and middle class: explorations in feminism and history* (Cambridge: Polity, 1992), pp. 205-54.

82. Jews were especially targeted. See E. J. Bristow, *Prostitution and prejudice: the Jewish fight against white slavery, 1870-1939* (Oxford: Clarendon Press, 1982). In the regulated empire ethnicity and masculinity became interdependent. M. Sinha, *Colonial masculinity: the "manly Englishman" and the "effeminate Bengali" in the late nineteenth century* (Manchester: Manchester University Press, 1995) pp. 153-4.

83. Pastor T. Borel, *The white slavery of Europe*, J. Edmonson (ed.) (London: Dyer Brothers, 1876), p. 45.

84. R. C. Collingwood, *The French regulation of immorality at the bar of public opinion* (London: Campbell, 1877).

85. G. S. Rousseau & R. Porter (eds), *Sexual underwords of the Enlightenment* (Manchester: Manchester University Press, 1987) pp. 1-17.

86. I. McCalman, *Radical underworld: prophets, revolutionaries and pornographers in London, 1795-1840*, 2nd edn (Oxford: Clarendon, 1993), pp. 204-31; G. Legman, "Introduction" in *The private case; an annotated bibliography of the private case erotica collection in the British Library*, P. J. Kearney (ed.) (London: Jay Landesman, 1981), p. 45.

87. J. Jeannel, *De la prostitution dans les grandes villes au XIXe siècle*. A *cordon sanitaire* is a system of quarantine.

88. *La Lanterne* had been Henri Rochefort's newspaper and an important Communard newspaper. B. Noël, *Dictionnaire de la Commune*, [2 vols] (Paris: Flammarion, 1978), vol. 2, pp. 218-19.

89. See *Chartes de l'association pour l'abolition de la prostitution réglementée* (Paris: Association pour l'abolition de la prostitution réglementée, 1879).

90. Corbin, *Les Filles de noce*, p. 340. C. House & A. R. Kenney, *Women's suffrage and social politics in the French Third Republic* (Princeton N.J.: Princeton University Press, 1984).

91. Y. Guyot, *Étude de physiologie sociale, la prostitution* (Paris: Charpentier, 1882); Guyot, *Études de physiologie sociale, la police*, 2nd edn (Paris: Charpentier, 1884); Guyot, *La Traite des vierges à Londres* (Paris: Charpentier, 1885); L. Andrieux, *Souvenirs d un préfet de police* [2 vols] (Paris: Jules Rouff, 1885), vol. 2, pp. 24-32; L. Fiaux, *La Police des moeurs en France, son abolition*, 2nd edn [2 vols] (Paris: Félix Alcan, 1921); J. M. Berlière, *La Police des moeurs sous la Troisième République* (Paris: Le Seuil, 1992), pp. 131-66; J. Butler, "introduction" in her *Souvenirs personnels d'une grande croisade* (Paris: 1900).

92. P. McHugh, *Prostitution and Victorian social reform* (London: Methuen, 1980), pp. 216-25.

93. See Termeau, *Maisons closes de province*, pp. 168-71.

94. E. J. Bristow, *Vice and vigilance: the purity movements since 1700* (Dublin: Gill & Macmillan, 1977), p. 64.

95. About Ireland, see M. Luddy, *Women and philanthropy in nineteenth-century Ireland* (Cambridge: Cambridge University Press, 1995).

96. G. Ball, *Practical religion; a study of the Salvation Army social services for women, 1884-1914* (PhD thesis, University of Leicester, 1987), p. 239.

97. See J. Walkowitz, *City of dreadful delight* (London: Virago, 1992), pp. 81-134; R. L. Shults, *Crusader in Babylon: W. T. Stead and the Pall Mall Gazette* (Lincoln: University of Nebraska Press, 1972).

98. Shults, *Crusader in Babylon*, p. 130.; W. T. Stead, *Speech at the central criminal court, by W. T. Stead* (London: Vickens for the Moral Reform Union, 1885); Stead, *Why I went to prison!* (London: Reprinted from the *Review of Reviews*, 1911). Also see *Pall Mall Gazette* articles of 7 July 1885.

99. L. Bland, *Banishing the beast: English feminism and sexual morality, 1885-1914* (Harmondsworth: Penguin, 1995), pp. xiv-xv, 297-8.

100. H. R. F. Fox Bourne, *The English newspapers: chapters in the history of English journalism* [2 vols] (London: Chatto & Windus, 1887), vol. 2, p. 392.

101. B. Scott, *Is London more immoral than Paris or Brussels?* (London: Dyer Brothers, 1883).

102. F. B. Smith, "Labouchère's amendment to the Criminal Law Amendment Bill", *Historical Studies* 17, 1970, pp. 165-73. R. Dellamora, *Masculine desire: the sexual politics of Victorian aestheticism* (Chapel Hill: University of North Carolina Press, 1990), pp. 200-1.

103. J. Weeks *Sex, politics and society*, 2nd edn (London: Longman, 1989), p. 106.

104. See A. S. Dyer, *Facts for men on moral purity and on health* (London: Dyer Brothers, 1884).

105. *National League Journal*, 1 February 1878.

106. See H. Ibsen, *Ghost* (London: W. Scott, 1890); A. Corbin, "Hereditary syphilis or the impossible redemption: a contribution to the history of morbid heredity", in his *Time, desire and horror: towards a history of the senses* (Cambridge: Polity Press, 1995), pp. 111-34; B. Nevins, *On hereditary syphilis* (Liverpool: The Medical Enquirer, 1878); Quétel, *History of syphilis*, pp. 160-75.

107. In literature, see W. Greenslade, *Degeneration, culture and the novel, 1880-1940* (Cambridge: Cambridge University Press, 1994), pp. 211-33.

108. E. Showalter, *Sexual anarchy: gender and culture at the fin-de-siècle* (New York: Viking, 1990), pp. 169-71; Hall & Porter, *Facts of life*, pp. 154-202.

109. F. B. Smith, "Ethics and disease in the later nineteenth century: The Contagious Diseases Acts", *Historical Studies of Australia and New Zealand* **15**, 1971, pp. 118-35; F. B. Smith, "The Contagious Diseases Acts reconsidered", *Social History of Medicine* **13**, 1990, pp. 197-215.

110. G. S. Meyer, "Criminal punishment for the transmission of sexually transmitted diseases: lessons from syphilis", *Bulletin of the History of Medicine* **65**, 1991, pp. 549-64. The British did investigate the French system during the Royal Commission on the CDA. Letter 21 November 1878, APdP, Da 232.

111. The abolition of regulationism in France in 1946 resulted in an even more inflexible sanitarian inspection policy abrogated in 1960, which in turn gave way to more repressive policing practices in place since. Berlière, *Police des moeurs*, pp. 167-8.

Chapter 8

♨

Male crime in nineteenth-century Germany: duelling*

Ute Frevert

This chapter deals with duelling, a criminal act committed exclusively by men. Although the gender-specific nature of this act was recognized by nineteenth- and early twentieth-century contemporary society, its criminalization provoked continued protests and resistance. The criminal law was perfectly clear: under the Reich penal code of 1871 and its various precursors duelling was a crime. However, wide sections of the German middle and upper classes did not share this view: they considered duelling in certain circumstances to be as honour-able as it was inevitable.

In the following I want to ask (and possibly answer) three questions. First: why - and by whom - has duelling been considered a crime in modern German society? How has the "criminal energy" of duelling been described by contemporaries? What was the status of duelling in the legal system of civil society established in the nineteenth century? Secondly: how did duellists themselves perceive their action? Did they accept it as being criminal? Why did they behave in the way they did? How did their social peers react? And thirdly: what did duelling have to do with gender? How far was masculinity defined by this kind of honourable - or criminal - action? Could women engage in a duel? How did the practice of duelling enforce gender norms in society and culture?

The crime of duelling

A duel was defined in a German encyclopaedia of 1750 as a "serious com-bat between two equal parties aiming at the preservation of a certain good". That this good was called honour, the author of the article did not mention.

* Translated by the author and Cornelie Usborne

Obviously he found it difficult to discover honourable motives in the early modern duels to which he referred. This interpretation is supported by the fact that the article used the word "duel" synonymously with "single combat", "scuffle" and "rowdy fight".[1] These synonyms were equally adopted by the first mandates and edicts that had been issued in the seventeenth century by German princes and statesmen in order to ban and criminalize duelling. They referred to empirical cases marked by a chain of action linking offence, physical combat/revenge and reconciliation (or death). These actions were generally performed by military men, noble courtiers and students who sought and preserved honour in fighting one another.

This kind of private combat between two men seems to have become more frequent throughout the early modern period. In the German territories duelling was apparently supported by the turmoil of the Thirty Years' War. In the mercenary armies of the enemy, which often formally allowed "scuffles", there was ample opportunity to indulge in more or less serious conflicts. Not surprisingly, the Grandduke of Brandenburg issued his first edict against duelling in 1652, four years after the long war had ended. The edict not only reacted to the obvious rise of challenges, rowdy fights and scuffles. It also expressed the Grandduke's willingness to suppress any form of "self-revenge, offence, disturbance of peace, and duelling" among his subjects, whether they were nobles or not.[2] Absolutist rule that came to be established in most German states after the end of the Thirty Years' War could not accept any erosion of its monopoly of power. That men deliberately used force to settle their disputes violated the state's claim to exert supreme authority. They performed a kind of self-justice that counteracted and negated official legal procedures.

If we look at it more closely, duelling constituted a two-fold challenge (and threat) to state power. First, it embraced physical force and violence potentially leading to serious wounding, even to the death of its participants. As such, it opposed the state's function to protect its subjects from inner strife and injury and to guarantee their physical integrity. Secondly, the duel objected to the state's claim to settle conflict among its subjects in a peaceful and legally controlled manner. The more the early modern state defined itself as being a state under the rule of law (*Rechtsstaat*), the less it could put up with people insisting on their right to self-regulation and autonomous behaviour.

It is interesting to note that this latter challenge to state authority was taken even more seriously than the first. Mandates and edicts issued in the late seventeenth and eighteenth centuries were not so much directed against the so-called "rencontres", i.e. more or less spontaneous combats without further preparation. Rather, they took offence at formal duels that were characterized by a high degree of institutionalization and organization. Before a duel was fought, cartels and challenges had to be exchanged, conditions of combat had to be agreed on, seconds had to be involved. A duel thus was a carefully and intentionally planned operation whereas a "rencontre" was attributed to sudden fury and uncontrolled passion. The theme of violence itself was apparently not enough to provoke state action and regulation. The criminal energy attributed to duellists was not found in their attacking the other's physical integrity. The early modern state itself did not judge this integrity a basic and final value, as can be seen from the use of torture to obtain confessions in the legal process.

The early modern construction of duelling as first and foremost a crime against the state's monopoly of force continued into the revolutionary period. The Prussian Civil Code (*Allgemeines Landrecht*) enacted in 1794 interpreted it this way. Duellists were seen to violate the "first principle of civil society which urges their members to settle conflicts not by autonomous private force, but by the laws of the state".[3]

A totally different perspective was taken by the post-revolutionary French legal system which was then exported to the Rheinbund states, e.g. Bavaria, as well as to the Prussian Rhineland. Rhenish legal officials in the early nineteenth century claimed that it was not the state that was attacked by private combat; instead, the duel was perceived as a private act threatening the physical integrity of the duellists. As, however, this threat was agreed upon by the opponents, the state had to stand back and refrain from prosecution. Only in the case of a fatal outcome could the state step in and punish a duellist for causing bodily injury or for homicide. But even then the jury might decide against punishment if "mean intentions" and "disorderly behaviour" could be excluded. As a private act, the duel expressed the "free will" of the participants, and the state therefore had no right to intervene.[4]

This liberal attitude that emphasized the free choice of the individual and its quasi-contractual reciprocity went hand-in-hand with the notion of the male individual whose freedom of action ought to be hindered or disturbed as little as possible. His private sphere was merely to be protected by the state but not to be controlled and certainly not curtailed. It was part of the male individuality, as it was defined in the late eighteenth and nineteenth century, to exert one's own interests, whether material or immaterial, decisively and independently. The "male character", so it was continuously asserted, distinguishes himself by the fact that he "realizes his plans with firm and honest vigour" and "is neither a slave of men nor even less of women".[5] Thus, public respect was said to depend on "his ability to assert his independence".[6]

This self-assertion was neither to be undermined by state nor civil society which could only derive advantage from this ideal of masculinity. This was because it was held that men who defended their private interests courageously and decisively would also act strongly as public figures, as members of civil society and fight against any kind of despotism. "Public spirit", that central guiding principle of liberal policy statements, presupposed "civic virtue" and civic honour; it required "civic courage" and "civic energy", all attributes which men could only develop in an environment free from state tutelage.[7]

If manliness and civic respectability were proved by men standing up courageously, strongly and virtuously for their personal honour and the honour of the nation, it would not do to criminalize duelling as an expression of that same integrity. Many lawyers and politicians therefore advocated the exemption of duelling from criminal prosecution as "the last asylum of individual freedom" and thus its protection from the reach of the "omnipotent state".[8] In 1838 the liberal parliamentarian Friedrich Römer declared in the Wurttemberg Diet that he could not and would not "grant the State the right to hinder me through the executioner to be master of my body, my life or my health".[9] And in 1847 his political companion Carl Welcker described "the control over a self-reliant personal honour and law of honour and of a manly valiant mind and the capability for its defence" as "one of the most glorious aspects of our entire recent culture" that must on no account be allowed to be damaged by state intervention.[10]

In Berlin this liberal attitude met with strong objection. Yet even here it was conceded that duellists had honourable motives and it was therefore not easy to subsume them among common criminals. The draft of a new penal code which came into force in 1851 therefore classified duelling not as a "crime and offence against life"; instead it was given its own "title".[11] Thus, like infanticide, duelling gained the status of a special penal offence; yet, as a rule it remained punishable. The Prussian bureaucracy thereby stayed loyal to the principle that duels as such (and not just their results, as the French or Bavarian codes wanted it) constituted a crime against state and civil order and that they should therefore be prosecuted and punished regardless of their results. With the passing of the Reich penal code in 1871 this legal interpretation became binding for the entire German Reich.[12]

"Crime of honour": the noble art of self-defence

The special character of the duel, which had been legally acknowledged and guaranteed, was rooted in its motives and social environment. The duel was held to be a "crime of honour", resulting from noble motives. A duellist did not act meanly and maliciously; he did not intend to harm his opponent but to protect his own honour and moral integrity. The ultimate goal of a duel was not, to be sure, the death or injury of the man involved. Rather, it served to demonstrate the noble character of the two partners who did not hesitate to risk their lives in order to preserve their honour. Thus, in the words of a high Prussian official of the early nineteenth century, duels displayed something "sublime and highly respectable" which rendered them useful and worthwhile to the monarchical state.[13] Such a state was utterly dependent on the loyalty and service of its nobility. As long as this nobility claimed honour to be its vital essence, the state was well advised to credit and protect this essence - as long and as far as it did not interfere with its own prerogatives.

Since the late eighteenth century, state legislation found it more and more difficult to come to grips with this problem. On the one hand, it criminalized duelling as a challenge to the state's monopoly of force and justice. On the other hand, it respected duelling as an extraordinary and "elevated" practice by granting it a special position in the codes of law. Additionally, duellists who had been prosecuted and condemned in an official court case could trust the sovereign's mercy. Almost any verdict of guilty was softened by the king's intervention in favour of noble duellists, apart from cases where there were serious traces of viciousness, in which case the convicted had to serve his penalty. In general, however, social and political elites conceived of duelling as a kind of gentleman's agreement. The act itself was enobled by the social status of its participants as well as by their high motives. Duelling, as the Prussian minister of justice Friedrich von Savigny put it in 1844, stemmed from "love of honour and courage". To punish it with defamatory penalties would therefore not be acceptable.[14] Consequently, duellists did not have to go to prison, but enjoyed privileged confinement in a fortress.

Taking all this into account, it cannot come as a surprise that duellists themselves did not feel as if they were committing a crime or behaving like criminals. Although they knew that their behaviour violated state rules, they did not take this disobedience very seriously. For them, the practice of duelling was rooted in and legitimized by a long tradition of noble self-defence. As long as this tradition lived on, duellists felt accepted by their social peers. For them, this acceptance mattered far more than the highly ambivalent rules of the legal system. This held especially true for the officer corps of the German armies. In 1896 one could read in the official journal of the military elite:

How we have to act as officers is prescribed by orders, regulations and the stable manners and traditions of our estate. Those are our laws and authorities. If by obeying them we get into conflict with the laws of the Reich, we are ready to take the consequences.[15]

The Bavarian Minister of War expressed the same opinion in 1912:

Everybody who is a commissioned officer knows by education and tradition that he must not only display personal courage on the battle field but also, if necessary, defend his honour with the weapon in his hand. Tacitly he complies with those demands of his estate which serve the preservation of the highest virtues of a man.[16]

But it was not only officers who gave priority to the rules of their social and professional milieu. Among civil servants, too, the duel was held in high esteem; even members of the legal profession did not hesitate to repair their damaged honour by an act which was officially forbidden by the law they themselves had to represent. A fine example was the Prussian junior barrister Heinrich Simon who in 1828 shot a friend and colleague in a duel. Sixteen years later he did not hesitate to challenge a conservative colleague who had attacked and offended him because of his liberal opinion on judicial independence. In his view, there was no alternative way to solve the conflict: "Among a hundred thousand men, all but one would have acted the way I did."[17] Probably he was right. This was demonstrated by the fact that the brother of the man he killed came to visit him in prison. In other cases, the fathers of dead duellists wrote letters of mercy for the men who had killed their sons.

Duellists were by definition "men of honour", and a fatal result did not exclude them from respectable society. Rather, the opposite was true.

Exclusion, however, came nearly automatically whenever a man whose honour was injured did not take the right steps of action. In this sense, the junior barrister Gilow argued in 1843 that he simply had to accept the challenge to a duel because otherwise he would have been ostracized. To refuse to duel would have been interpreted as a "lack of courage and would have made him the object of disdain and contempt by his opponent and his colleagues". This argument was fully backed by his superiors who all voted against a criminal prosecution that would harm the duellists' careers. In addition, they explicitly appreciated the motives and actions of Gilow and von Mettingh (who, by the way, were both sons of high state officials). If Gilow had turned the challenge down, this would have destroyed his "social existence amidst his peers". Almost everyone else, declared the Prussian Ministers of Justice, of the Interior and of Finance unanimously, would have behaved likewise.[18]

"Almost everyone else" – this phrase must not be understood to have encompassed any man (or woman) of this time. Behaviour according to the rules of honourable conduct was reserved for men of the upper and middle classes of society. Originally, the group of potential duellists had been even smaller. When the Prussian legal code of 1794 defined the crime of duelling it took it for granted that duellists were nobles. When a man belonging to a lower class wanted to fight a duel, his act was not defined as duelling but (depending on the outcome) as murder or bodily injury. Thus duelling was regarded as a class privilege of the aristocracy. This was explained by the fact that the typical cause for a duel – the insult to personal honour – was only perceived as an existential attack by aristocrats (and officers). Again and again it was held that a sense of honour was only sufficiently strongly developed within the "status of honour" of the aristocracy that an insult had to be expiated with blood. In contrast to the nobility, "people of common rank" (and the "upper bourgeoisie" counted among these) possessed less honour and therefore a correspondingly less developed sense of honour. Consequently, they were less sensitive to insults to their honour and had no reason to respond to these with a duelling request.[19]

Starting in the early nineteenth century, this strict line of social differentiation gradually broke down. More and more often, middle-class men became engaged in duelling and even were accepted by nobles as duelling partners. With its stronghold in the military and among students, the duel soon found its most ardent followers in the educated middle classes. Here it enjoyed an enormous prestige based largely on its claim to individuality and personal autonomy. Many university professors, writers, lawyers and doctors praised it as a means of demonstrating personal integrity and independence. In this sense Carl Welcker in 1847 underlined the "fine results" of duels embodying a "reflection of virtuous freedom".[20] Ten years later, Karl Marx in his London exile found nothing wrong in the idea that, given the conditions of "bourgeois society", men could only maintain their "individuality" by referring to "feudal forms". As long as the duel helped to solve important personal conflicts it could be justified; only if people merely complied with social pressure, were they performing an empty *Standeszeremonie*, an exclusive ceremonial act without any personal commitment and logic.[21]

In Marx's words the duel constituted a "feudal form" of the human longing for "individuality", i.e. for a value system typically rooted in the modern middle classes. This does not mean that the middle-class value system was totally compatible with duelling. Quite obviously, important virtues and guidelines of the middle classes - like work, efficiency, rationality - did not live in harmony with the *point d'honneur*. Other parts of middle-class identity, however, were well at ease with the noble art of self-defence. To take responsibility for oneself, to behave independently, to claim individuality and integrity, to free oneself from state control and concern - all these attitudes gained support from the duel and its philosophy.

In this way duelling stressed and strengthened the demand of the educated classes to constitute an aristocracy of their own, equipped with exclusive manners and a strong sense of individual and social honour. At the same time, it promised to draw a strict borderline between middle and lower classes who were definitely excluded from the honourable art of self-defence. This exclusion took place in several stages: first the so-called circles that were qualified to duel did not recognize men of lower social classes as equal partners. Insults by lower-class men were not perceived nor treated as such. Thus the liberal politician Georg von Vincke declared in 1847 that even in the case of a violent attack by a day labourer or a journeyman he would

> not take notice, not get involved in a discussion with such a person, a person who is placed too far below me and who is not equal to me as regards honour, that is a person who is not even deserving of my touching him with the stick. Rather in this case my honour would have remained entirely intact.[22]

Even if members of the lower social classes duelled against each other, as was very rarely the case, among the upper classes this was not recognized as a noble duel. Thus in 1871 two waiters from Berlin were, it is true, convicted for a duel with pistols; but they were refused the otherwise customary honourable confinement in a fortress, as well as their request for clemency. After all, argued the Prussian Justice Minister, "respect" for their honour and their reputation had not necessitated their "involvement in a duel and therewith a violation of the law unlike other similar cases which are then taken into consideration in favour of the convicted".[23] Another sign that the aristocracy and bourgeoisie reserved for themselves alone the honour to duel was in their continuous and determined attempts to distance themselves from the typical rituals of conflict of the lower classes. Fistfights and knife battles within the working-class milieu were never regarded as an equivalent to duelling but as evidence that those men did not possess a genuine sense of honour.

From the vantage point of the workers this attitude appeared discriminatory and hurtful. One worker from Hamburg offered the view in 1896 that "the honour of a nobleman was no different from that of any other citizen. 'Often many a worker possesses more honour than a nobleman.'" A colleague agreed and criticized the German justice system very severely because it operated a double standard in this respect. If "educated people and those of high status" had been involved in a duel, judges handled them with kid gloves; but a worker or craftsman

> who is possibly mortally insulted by one of his colleagues in a pub and who picks a fight with him on the way home so that this then assumes a serious character and the one or the other remains on the battle ground there follows an indictment of manslaughter or even murder.

There was general agreement about the necessity to abolish the duelling clause of the penal code.[24]

This was also advocated by the Social Democratic Party which voiced continuous and strong objection in newspapers and parliaments against the privilege of honour of the bourgeois-aristocratic classes. It denounced duelling as an excess of German militarism and feudalism and tried to expose the handling of it by the state as an example of undisguised class discrimination. Left-liberal and catholic circles also voiced their criticism, the first by pointing to the legal principle of civil equality, the latter by emphasizing the unchristian nature of the duel and by drawing attention to the strict ban of duelling that popes and council congregations had renewed again and again.

From the turn of the century the women's movement joined the duelling critics. In these circles duelling was held to be "reprehensible, barbarian" as well as deeply misogynist. According to Helene Lange, president of the General German Women's Association, the honour defended in a duel was a purely egotistical "male honour" which degraded women to objects without any "personal responsiblity".[25] Minna Cauer, editor of the journal *Die Frauenbewegung*, appealed in 1909 to her women readers to reject the concepts of honour that were at the basis of duelling and to replace them with "a true sense of honour":

> We demand that women rely on themselves and know how to preserve their own honour not only in their relations with men but in all situations of life. We conceive of a wide meaning of honour. It is not only limited to sexuality but should also include integrity and purity in every action.[26]

Duelling and the gender system

Duelling, as Helene Lange put it, was after all not only a "question of class" and an expression of "class mores" but also a sign of "patriarchy".[27] Indeed, duelling did not exhaust its meaning in patterns of social differentiation or anti-state rebellion. There was more to it, and the essence of this surplus value was not at all concealed, but very openly displayed.

In 1864 the judge and president of the Berlin provincial court, Adolph von Kleist, put it bluntly: the most important, in fact the only purpose for which a duel could be rationally justified was the verification of manly dignity. "Male dignity", he wrote in an anonymously published newspaper article, "requires above all manliness, that is, the consciousness of personal courage. The demonstration of this characteristic seems to us to be the principal aim of the duel."[28] In 1907 the Prussian Minister of Justice, Beseler, equally thought "our opinion of the duel does not merely rest on the fact that the honour is injured but indirectly also on the fact that the manliness of the injured party is attacked and that he now seeks to restore his disputed manliness through duelling".[29]

The language of masculinity was present in all documents that can be collected on the philosophy of duelling as well as in empirical duelling cases in the nineteenth century. Terms like "manly consciousness", "manly pride", "manly virtue", "manly dignity" and even "manly holiness" were used to describe the identity and motivational structure of duellists. Duels were not only genuine "male affairs" (*Männergeschichten*, as Heinrich Heine put it in 1837)[30] taking place only ever between men; furthermore duels also represented acts which allowed male "gender characteristics" to be displayed and a disputed manliness to be restored.

It was precisely this function that an 1896 pistol duel had. It took place in Königsberg between the junior barrister Ernst Borchert and a second lieutenant, Seidensticker. The background to the story was as follows. On 2 February there was a big masked ball for the urban middle classes. The 28-year-old Borchert attended this dressed up as a sailor and thus conveyed not only his enthusiasm for the imperial navy policy but also his yearning for faraway places, his desire for independence and erotic frivolity. Suddenly the unspeakable occurred: a man who was also in costume but heavily drunk and who sat on a neighbouring table, pinched Borchert's "behind coarsely" and bade him to bring him a glass of beer. Gesture and tone were plain: this was behaviour generally reserved for a waitress.

The junior barrister understood the enormity of the offence in a flash. He told the other angrily that he behaved like a *Louis*. With this expression Borchert placed the assailant into the disreputable demi-monde mileu of pimps and homosexuals and thus for his part now dealt him a gross slander. On top of this he threatened to slap him in the face, i.e. threatened him with the kind of violence that, according to the academic-military code of honour, belonged to the category of gross insults which simply demanded a duel. Had Borchert's opponent known about and followed this code of honour he would have had to demand satisfaction of the barrister. Since he did not Borchert concluded he was dealing with somebody unqualified to duel. Therefore he considered the matter as closed. But presently he heard that his offender was an officer. This delighted him so much that he exclaimed: "Isn't that good, isn't that great!". He gave Seidensticker an ultimatum and urged him to name his second so that he could convey to him his request for a duel. When the drunken lieutenant tried to placate him, declaring him "crazy", Borchert applied even stronger means: he slapped his opponent's face several times. The following day Seidensticker's second delivered a challenge to a duel with pistols. The duel took place the morning of 6 February and ended with the death of the officer.[31]

All this had begun with a joke that had misfired. Seidensticker's pinching of Borchert's bottom had offended the honour of the civil servant. One could treat a waitress like this but not a man dressed up as a sailor. Obviously Borchert regarded being pinched as a gross contempt of his male honour. In fact, two boundaries had been transgressed: one of gender and another of social class. A man was permitted to pinch a woman's (yet not every woman's) bottom but not that of a man. The gesture signalled male indecency, sexual interest and availability of the female body. The pinching of a woman's bottom was an act of superiority that presupposed male power and female submission as much as it represented it. Structurally it was one-sided: women could not reciprocate. The act also had a class dimension, signifying as it did social domination and subordination. The male bourgeois visitor to a pub was permitted to treat the proletarian waitress like this but not the daughter of a good family. Towards her, a potential future wife, he had to adopt a more restrained, less direct and more strictly coded behaviour.

Seen in this light, Seidensticker's pinching of Borchert's backside meant a double humiliation. Borchert must have felt offended and degraded both in his masculinity – that is, his male honour was affronted – and in his social status. Extremely irritated by this, he got even with his offender by accusing him of behaving like a *Louis*. A *Louis* was in contemporary language a kind of pimp, a man who moved in dubious circles and who made women work for him. But *Louis* could also mean a homosexual, a man who blatantly contradicted contemporary notions of masculinity and who threatened to blur the generally sharply drawn gender boundaries. Although such a person was hardly a man, he nevertheless posed an extreme threat to other's masculinity and had to be checked by further emasculation by, for example, threatening him with a slap in the face.

Had the second lieutenant been in the possession of his full senses and not completely drunk he would have had to answer such an affront immediately with a request for a duel. This was the only way he, as a representative of a profession who took and had to take honour especially seriously, could counter the insult adequately. Duelling offered him the only chance to restore his honour that had been under attack by Borchert's slander. At the same time this would have allowed him to demonstrate that he was man enough to stamp out all doubts about his masculinity. Since manliness was identified with courage the readiness to risk one's life and to face up to the opponent's drawn pistol was considered as evidence of the highest form of manliness. The same logic had motivated Borchert's behaviour: he could restore his offended manliness among his peers only by fighting a life-threatening duel.

This logic based on potential death was central for the behavioural culture of duelling as it evolved among middle- and upper-class men of the nineteenth century. The deadliness of the weapons therefore played a correspondingly large role and helped to differentiate between the genders. In the same way as one denied that brawls and fistfights of the working-class males were honourable and fit to incite a duel, one mocked female pseudo-duels. In 1864, for example, a conservative newspaper reported on a ladies' duel with a mixture of open disgust and sensual voyeurism:

> Fortunately, the weapons did not consist of either sabres or pistols, but of two pliant canes; a friend of one of the duellists acted as impartial observer of this strange duel, which ended with both ladies discarding their canes and throwing punches at each other until several men intervened to separate them . . . Both these emancipated creatures were in such a sorry state that they had to be driven home in hackney-carriages to avoid an even bigger scandal.
>
> The editor's comment: "Another step forward, but definitely not one which redounds to the honour of these two ladies!"[32]

Ladies' duels - marginal as they were - obviously were regarded as insincere and ridiculous. At the same time, however, they were seen as threatening male social power. They tended to undermine the gender system that only allowed women to provide the motive for duelling without granting them the right to defend their honour the same way men did. But women who took up the sword did not simply cross the borderline which separated them from men; they also demasculinized men by making inroads into a domain which was so unanimously claimed a masculine preserve.

In any case, there were only a few women who went so far. Most ladies of the middle and upper classes did not step out of the value system that praised male courage and honour as prime facets of gender typing. They even paid reverence to this system by admiring and celebrating men who had displayed that kind of behaviour. As a Roman Catholic newspaper put it in 1907:

> Not rarely, one finds Catholic daughters - even of a higher age - who look down on a Catholic student who, by orders of his church, was not allowed to fight duels with disdain and even scorn. In contrast, they idolize those corporated students whose faces are decorated with duelling wounds.[33]

A man like Heinrich Simon who had shot his duelling partner and was confined for some time in the fortress of Glogau enjoyed the "manyfold interest namely of Glogau's female population".[34]

These female interests were unquestionably expected, even taken for granted by men. As one contemporary put it, "one also has an eye to the admiring favour of women when one takes up a weapon".[35] Very many if not most duelling conflicts among men arose in a social situation that was characterized by the prominent presence of women. Favourite locations for duels to be arranged were social events such as balls, afternoon dances, private festivities when both sexes mixed. Especially in view of the relatively sharp separation of male and female spheres in the bourgeois society of the nineteeth century, which was also clearly expressed in gesture, language and gaze, it apparently was intriguing to parade the entire range of masculine "gender characteristics" at such encounters. Under the watchful eye of potential future brides men sought to outmatch each other's manliness and to present themselves as heroes.

Furthermore, women were educated to hold physical vigour and courage in high esteem and "to look up to the man as a hero who has defended his honour with blood".[36] Respect of weapons and admiration of the bearer of arms increased as the nineteenth century declared all men as destined to defend the nation and put them in the "king's coat" for a certain period of their life. Universal conscription introduced in Prussia in 1813/4 universalized man's function as a warrior and upgraded military service as every man's obligation that both contained and procured honour. This conferred a new, unmistakable gender identity on men and at the same time drew new and sharp boundaries between masculinity and femininity.[37] Since they were excluded from universal military service, women were given the status of helpless objects of male protection. The topos of female weakness that corresponded to male power thus received a new, hitherto unknown intensity and resonance.

Against this background the much noted female adoration of duelling heroes at this time takes on a certain logic. Again and again men emphasized the analogy of war and duelling since, as the argument went, on both occasions they sacrificed their life for honour. They protected the honour of the defenceless, namely the honour of the "disgraced" fatherland and the "disgraced" woman respectively. This reference to an altruistic motive was one of the strongest and most suggestive arguments that supporters of duels put forward and it rarely failed in its effect.

But what was the reality like? "The duellist", complained critics of duelling, "defends only his own interests. Even when he defends the honour of a woman he fights only for himself."[38] That was most clearly shown in all those cases in which wives or fiancées had been seduced or molested by other men; whereupon their "natural protector" challenged the aggressor to a duel. It then turned out very quickly that women were generally not the winners, but the victims of a duelling affair. If a woman's moral conduct initiated a duel, her own honour was lost forever. If the men who fought the duel were injured or killed, it was the woman who was found guilty. Even if the men survived, the woman's guilt was not contested. Instead, it was doubled, as her faulty behaviour had, as it were, forced men to risk their lives.

This is well illustrated by a case of 1902 that occurred near Hanover. Adolf von Bennigsen, a 41-year-old *Landrat* (district administrator) had heard rumours that his wife Elisabeth, 11 years his junior, had an intimate relationship with the tenant farmer Oswald Falkenhagen. He confronted his wife and challenged Falkenhagen to a pistol duel. The deadly bullet hit the *Landrat*. Falkenhagen was sentenced to several years' confinement in a fortress but

Elisabeth von Bennigsen was also punished severely. She was forced to leave house and children and was disowned by her original as well as her husband's family. She subsequently earned her living by giving piano lessons. She was forbidden to have contact with her five children; only when her daughters were of age were they allowed to visit their mother. They were cared for by the sister of their father, a governess and a domestic servant who, as the family chronicle noted dryly, were "unequal to this task".[39]

Elisabeth von Ardenne suffered a similar fate. As wife of the colonel Armand von Ardenne she had had a love affair with the judge of the *Amtsgericht* (lower district court) in Düsseldorf, Emil Hartwich. When her husband, who was a friend of Hartwich, learnt of this, he challenged him to a pistol duel. This duly took place on 27 November 1886 in Berlin. Hartwich was hit in the abdomen and died a few days later. The killer marksman was sentenced by a court marshal to two years' confinement in a fortress of which he only served a few weeks. He had sued for a divorce from his wife beforehand. The marriage was dissolved in 1887 and the father was granted custody of the two children. While her ex-husband continued his career without a break Elisabeth von Ardenne had to build herself a new life. She was bereft of her former social circle since everyone had repudiated her. But unlike Effi Briest, the heroine in Theodor Fontane's novel whom she had inspired, she managed to win a new purpose in life and proved, as Fontane knew, "an excellent carer in a large sanatorium".[40]

At this point, it becomes very clear that duelling indeed was a "male affair". The repeated argument that duellists stepped in to protect female honour was a profound lie. They only protected their own honour that had come to harm by the action of another man. Male honour, not female honour, was at stake in a duel. A woman who had lost her honour could not repair it by the duel that somebody fought as a consequence. Her honour remained violated and this was even more the case since the male combat had turned this loss into a public fact and a topic for public discussion. A woman's lapse was therefore the talk of the town and she suffered the consequences just like Elisabeth von Bennigsen and Elisabeth von Ardenne.

Their husbands, however, were in a different situation. For them, duelling meant retaining and regaining their honour that had been damaged by the opponent's encroachment. Since their ownership had been disputed they had to purify themselves both before themselves and before the usurper of the disgrace and humiliation which they had suffered. The seduction of a married woman meant, according to the prevailing opinion, "a very serious offence" for her husband and almost forced him to demand a duel. In this sense the War Minister von Falkenhayn described in 1914 the break-up "of the peace of his house", (a paraphrase for adultery), as a blatant "disrespect" of a man, as doubting his "manliness and fitness for combat".[41] The "cuckolded" (deceived) husband could remove this doubt only by means of a duel. By challenging the other to combat he proved to himself and to the public that he was man enough to defend his rights and his honour. Even if and especially since his wife had not brought honour upon him but dishonour, he was able to divest himself of the tarnish of his honour by publicly avowing his readiness to fight physically.

Duelling thus was one of the cornerstones of gendered behaviour. First, it separated men from women by separating male rules of conduct from female ones. In addition, it represented and enforced male command over women in that it placed pressure on women to adjust to men's rules. Apart from that, it was best at mystifying gender relations: even today, collective memory still sees duelling as a representation of knightly behaviour when the hero sacrifices his life for a beloved lady.

To destroy this myth does not mean to deny the fact that there were of course sacrifices, death and injury, fear and personal hardship. Few men seem to have shown cold blood or even temper in a duel which carried the risk of death or serious injury. Nevertheless, open resistance to duelling within the ranks of society where duelling was justified remained only marginal up to the First World War. Even those men who were engaged in the Anti-Duelling League (established in the early twentieth century) claimed their right to fight a duel whenever they thought it was inevitable. Quite obviously, the personal and social benefits of demonstrating courage and honourable conduct outweighed the disadvantages.

Moreover, the social and political structures of Imperial Germany all strengthened duelling as an icon of middle- and upper-class manliness. Apart from the fact that it was outlawed *de jure* though not always *de facto*, opposition came only from outsiders: from the Catholic church (which, however, could not prevent its own flock from getting involved in this unholy practice); from some leftist Liberals who untiringly stressed the illegal nature of duelling; from Social Democrats who criticized it as a class privilege, and from parts of the women's movement which denounced duelling as a patriarchal sin.

To cut a long story short, it needed the radical breakdown of traditional sociopolitical networks and structures after the First World War to deprive duelling of its social foundations, its political support and its mythical aura. The "new man" of the Weimar Republic could very well do without this old-fashioned icon of manliness, and so could the "new woman".

Notes

1. J. H. Zedler, *Grosses vollständiges Universal-Lexicon aller Wissenschaften und Künste*, vol. 64 (Leipzig, 1750), pp. 1330–1430. For more details, see U. Frevert, *Men of honour. The social and cultural history of the duel* (Oxford: Polity Press, 1995).

2. Quoted in E. Fleck (ed.), *Die Verordnungen über die Ehrengerichte im Preußischen Heere* (Berlin, 1865), pp. 149–50.

3. H. Conrad, G. Kleinheyer (eds), *Vorträge über Recht und Staat von Carl Gottlieb Svarez* (Cologne, 1960), p. 411.

4. HStA Düsseldorf, OLG Köln, no. 11/1183: report of Boelling (c. 1822).

5. C. F. Pockels, *Der Mann. Ein anthropologisches Charaktergemälde seines Geschlechts*, vol. 2 (Hanover, 1806), p. 337.

6. M. Aschenbrenner, *Über das Verbrechen und die Strafe des Zweykampfes* (Würzburg, 1804), p. 29.

7. C. Welcker, "Bürgertugend und Bürgersinn", in *Das Staats-Lexikon*, vol. 2 (Altona, 1847), pp. 762-71.

8. O. H. A. v. Oppen, *Beiträge zur Revision der Gesetze* (Cologne, 1833), p. 44 (Oppen was president of the Cologne provincial court); H. Wagener (ed.), *Staats- und Gesellschafts-Lexikon*, vol. 23 (Berlin, 1867), p. 200.

9. *Verhandlungen der Kammer der Abgeordneten des Königreichs Württemberg auf dem Landtage von 1838*, vol. 4 (Stuttgart, 1838), p. 66.

10. C. Welcker, "Infamie, Ehre, Ehrenstrafen", in *Das Staats-Lexikon*, vol. 7 (Altona, 1847), pp. 377-404.

11. Strafgesetzbuch für die Preussischen Staaten und Gesetz über die Einführung desselben vom 14. April 1851 (Berlin, 1851).

12. P. Allfeld (ed.), *Die Strafgesetzgebung des Deutschen Reichs* (Munich, 1900), pt. I.

13. Geheimes Staatsarchiv Berlin-Dahlem, Rep. 84 a, No. 8034: E. F. Klein's report of 17 August 1809.

14. *Ibid.*, no. 8035: von Savigny's memorandum of 18 September 1844.

15. "Der Zweikampf", in *Militär-Wochenblatt* **37**, 1896, p. 1040.

16. Bayerisches Hauptstaatsarchiv Munich, Abt. IV, M Kr No. 11097: Note of 29 December 1912.

17. J. Jacoby (ed.), *Heinrich Simon*, vol. 1 (Berlin, 1865), p. 68.

18. Deutsches Zentralarchiv Merseburg (DZM), Rep. 77, Tit. 114, no. 223, vol. 1: ministerial report of 11 May 1844.

19. *Zeitschrift für die Criminal-Rechts-Pflege in den preußischen Staaten* **17**, 1831, pp. 150-93.

20. Welcker, "Infamie".

21. K. Marx/F. Engels, *Werke*, vol. 29 (Berlin, 1970), pp. 331, 336, 562f.

22. E. Bleich (ed.), *Der Erste Vereinigte Landtag in Berlin 1847*, pt. 2 (Berlin, 1847), p. 261.

23. DZM, Hist, Abt. II, 2.2.1. no. 17834: excerpt from examination procedures, 12 July 1871.

24. R. J. Evans (ed.), *Kneipengespräche im Kaiserreich. Stimmungsberichte der Hamburger Politischen Polizei 1892-1914* (Hamburg, 1989), p. 187.

25. H. Lange, "Die Duelldebatten im Reichstag", in *Die Frau* **19**, 1912, pp. 513-18.

26. *Die Frauenbewegung* **15**, 1909, p. 110.

27. H. Lange, "Zum Duellmord von Insterburg", in *Die Frau* **9**, 1901/2, p. 139; Lange, "Duelldebatten", p. 517.

28. (A. v. Kleist), "Kleine Mittheilung über Duelle", in *Militärische Blätter* **6**, 1864, p. 62.

29. Stenographische Berichte über die Verhandlungen des Preussischen Herrenhauses in der Session 1907 (Berlin, 1907), p. 173.

30. H. Heine, *Briefe 1831-1851* (Berlin, 1970), p. 204.

31. DZM, Hist. Abt. II, 2.2.1., no. 17838: ministerial report of 28 August 1896.

32. *Neue Preussische Zeitung*, no. 204, 1 September 1864.

33. Quoted in O. F. Scheuer, "Studentenmensur und Sexualität", in *Zeitschrift für Sexualwissenschaft und Sexualpolitik* **15**, 1929, p. 465. See also E. Heilborn, "Das Duell, eine Frauenfrage", in *Die Frau* **3**, 1895/6, pp. 500-502.

34. Jacoby, *Heinrich Simon*, vol. 1, p. 83.
35. Heilborn, "Das Duell", p. 502.
36. *Ibid.*, pp. 500, 502.
37. U. Frevert, "Das Militär als 'Schule der Männlichkeit'", in Frevert (ed.), *Militär und Gesellschaft im 19. und 20. Jahrhundert* (Stuttgart: Klett-Cotta Verlag, 1997), pp. 145–73.
38. Heilborn, "Das Duell", p. 501.
39. DZM, Hist. Abt. II, 2.2.1. no. 17839: Extract from the pre-trial records, 12 September 1906. Information from the Bennigsen family chronicle has been kindly supplied by Walther von Bennigsen (Springe), a grandson of Adolf and Elisabeth von Bennigsen.
40. *Vossische Zeitung*, 3 December 1886; *Berliner Tageblatt*, 3 December 1886, p. 4; G. Erler (ed.), *Fontanes Briefe*, vol. 2 (Berlin, 1989), p. 375; H. W. Seiffert (ed.), *Studien zur neueren deutschen Literatur* (Berlin, 1964), pp. 255–300.
41. Geheimes Staatsarchiv Berlin-Dahlem, Rep. 84a, no. 8037: Falkenhayn's report of 22 April 1914.

Chapter 9

♨

Dutch difference? The prosecution of unlicensed midwives in the late nineteenth-century Netherlands

Willem de Blécourt

Historiography

In feminist historiography the image of the disempowered midwife, expelled by obstetric doctors and eventually male gynaecologists from her natural domain of helping women in childbirth, has been used to symbolize female oppression in general. The subjugation of midwives proved such an adroit symbol because, as Ludmilla Jordanova pointed out, "midwives, being generally women with children themselves, and being associated with birth, were at the centre of feminine stereotypes".[1] Since the middle of the eighteenth century midwives have indeed been forced to succumb to the growing influence of the medical profession.[2] Yet, this gloomy picture may be too sweeping and too anglocentric. At least research on the Netherlands seems to indicate that Dutch midwives were not methodically driven out of their jobs by power-hungry doctors. In fact the Netherlands are often singled out as the glorious example of the survival of the midwife. "Advocates of midwifery in the United States point to the Netherlands as a model for midwifery care. They note that Dutch midwives have a good deal of autonomy, that they are free to work with little supervision".[3] Today midwives still attend about 30 per cent of all births in the Netherlands. To quote Hilary Marland: "In the 1990s the Dutch system of obstetric care is unique in the Western world for the predominance of midwife-attended births, the high level of home delivery, and the low rate of intervention in the birthing process." She continues: "Many see the Dutch system as a model to be followed, because it gives the pregnant woman more choice of where, how, and with whom she will give birth, and the midwife a higher level of professional autonomy".[4]

This rosy representation is now the received opinion, even if its features are occasionally exaggerated. For example, the medical historian Irvine Loudon claimed that:

189

The Netherlands persisted longer than any other country with a policy of home deliveries by midwives. Hospital deliveries accounted for only 26 per cent of total deliveries in 1957, 33 per cent in 1965, and they were still less than half (47.4 per cent) in 1970.[5]

A careful check of his sources shows his conclusions to be erroneous because he has confused the statistics concerning place of delivery with those of birth attendants. In 1957, doctors attended 61 per cent of all deliveries, midwives only 38.5 per cent (which is still relatively high, but a far cry from the 74 per cent suggested by Loudon).[6] The error arose because Dutch midwives also attended at clinical births and many Dutch medical practitioners helped women in their own homes. In fact, if one considers the professional qualifications of persons attending births to be the most important measure of change, the halfway mark, when midwife-attended deliveries had fallen to 50 per cent of all deliveries, was reached in the Netherlands in the mid-1930s, not the 1970s.[7] If Loudon's American and British figures are to be trusted, it means that the Netherlands reached this watershed even earlier than Britain or the rural parts of the USA. The most significant distinction between Dutch and British midwifery, concluded a British Departmental Committee in the 1930s, was the Dutch tendency to send abnormal cases to hospitals. According to these findings the position of the Dutch midwife differed mainly from her British colleagues in that her help was restricted to the birth itself and post-natal care was left to others.[8]

In this chapter I wish to question some of the commonplace assumptions about midwifery in general and the Dutch system in particular. I want to show that midwives were not necessarily models of femininity and regarded as close allies by women in childbirth. By stressing the relevance of illegal midwifery in the Netherlands I hope to adjust the image of the Dutch situation as the glorious exception to the rule and instead show that it was not necessarily so different from other Western countries.[9] The examination of the criminalization of a specific form of childbirth attendance also highlights differences in conceptions of crime between different professional groups and different social classes. As very peculiar criminals unlicensed midwives have not attracted much attention either in criminal, or in medical history. "Midwives practising without a formal education and licence, and thus in effect outside of the law, remain in just as much obscurity in Holland as in other countries", Van Lieburg and Marland remarked in their ground-breaking article on nineteenth-century Dutch midwifery, indicating that they left unlicensed midwives out of consideration.[10] Yet is does not seem very logical to compare Dutch legal midwives with nineteenth-century US or British female birth attendants who had not undergone any formal training and whose craft was not subject to regulation.

The forgotten story of Dutch illegal midwifery can be approached from different angles. It had a legal as well as a medical context. Moreover, it had its practitioners and "patients". It was a crime by definition, but who actually considered it as such? How widespread was unlicensed midwifery in the Netherlands and who used it and why? How was it related to official midwifery? What does it tell us about the power relations between medical practitioners of different professional status and between men and women? How did this affect the masculinization or feminization of a skill that was dominated by female practitioners and female patients? In the following sections I attempt to answer these questions.

The criminalization of unlicensed midwifery

Many Dutch cities had already regulated the practice of midwifery in the early eighteenth century. Several rural areas followed around 1800, and when in the early nineteenth century the Netherlands were united into the Kingdom as it still exists today, midwifery was subjected to national criminal law.[11] Practising medicine (including midwifery) without a license thus became a crime, liable to a fine, starting with 25 guilders (the equivalent of several weeks' subsistence for a lower-class family) and rising to 50 and 75 guilders and eventually gaol if the offence was repeated.[12] From 1865 onwards, a new Medical Act stipulated that judges determine the amount of the fine. Overall this resulted in much lower fines against women practising midwifery illegally, usually a few guilders. When in 1886 the Criminal Law was finally reformed, practising medicine without a licence was redefined as a misdemeanour. This, however, had no perceptible effect on either the prosecution or the level of fines imposed; it merely delegated the cases to lower courts.

The criminalization of irregular midwifery was directly linked to the professionalization of medicine. Unlicensed midwifery was created and thus defined by regulation. Ideally the laws set out to support public health by defining the field of competence for health practitioners. The laws also restricted people's, in this particular case women's, actions and can be seen as part of ongoing attempts to "civilize" society. The medical rhetoric of the "common good" thus provided the legitimation to prevent individual women assisting other women at a time of need. The women themselves, often neighbours but also dry nurses and "handy women", thought of this as ordinary "neighbourly duty" and as an act of humanitarianism. As one of them told the judge in 1893: "In the absence of a doctor I had to help the woman, if I did not want her to die". Another said "that it would be a shame to abandon a woman in need to her fate".[13] The medical stereotype of the illicit midwife meanwhile included images of incompetence, superstitious traditions, filth and death (but, as far as I have been able to find out, no reference to abortion). In the view of the official midwives' journal at the beginning of the twentieth century, for instance, illegal help with deliveries would inevitably result in the death of the mother.[14] According to this extreme opinion, the crime of practising midwifery without a licence equalled murder. This was only confirmed by the odd, exceptional case. Neither medical inspectors nor later researchers could establish a correlation between mortality and unlicensed midwifery.[15]

By the turn of the century official midwifery had outgrown the repertoire of negative labels.[16] These had not disappeared altogether but had now become attached to lay midwives. Midwives who had undergone a two-year training, on the other hand, were regarded as the champions of hygiene as not only did they bring new life into the world but also demonstrated a new way of dealing with it.[17] In this they were subjected to the control of male doctors, who determined training, examination, organization, as well as the practice of midwifery itself. What is more, the actions of official midwives were restricted to "normal" births. They were not allowed to use instruments or administer medicines, and at the merest sign of complications they were obliged to call for a (male) medical practitioner. "The battle for the demarcation of the professional domain was mainly fought in the eighteenth century and had been partly lost by the midwives", concluded the historical anthropologist van der Borg,[18] and, if anything, this is an understatement. Official midwifery had become nothing less than an extension of male medicine. The certified midwife was admonished not to consider a doctor as a competitor, but as "someone who is more qualified, someone who she can trust to help, assist and advise her, and who she can call for assistance and support, without it being in conflict with her self-interest".[19]

Such was the theory, at least. In practice there was genuine competition between doctors and official midwives. Especially in times of scarcity of patients when the doctors were young and trying to get established locally they were known to use their attendance at deliveries as a lever to become the family doctor. Also, in most places official midwives were limited to attending lower-class births, while doctors took care of the more affluent ones. There hardly seems to have been any protests on the midwives' part. They were not renowned for their militancy, nor were they among nineteenth-century feminists;[20] significantly, they were almost forgotten when it came to showing examples of female employment in the National Woman's Exhibition of 1898. Their unions, founded at the end of the century, were headed by male gynaecologists who also edited their journals.[21] Midwifery has been rightly sociologically classified as a sub-profession and this label applies even more when gender relations are taken into account. How then should we consider official midwives in terms of contemporary perceived gender characteristics? Should they be considered as representatives of female values simply because they happened to be born women? Or had they been incorporated into a male medical culture to such an extent that they both behaved in a masculine way, and were perceived as more male than female? The study of illegal midwives may throw some light on this problem.

Prosecuting unlicensed midwives

Complaints about the practice of unlicensed midwives were usually tabled by official midwives and doctors. As the Dutch Medical Society (from which official midwives were excluded) stated in 1881, the incidence of unlicensed midwives demeaned the status of doctors and midwives alike.[22] From 1865 onwards these complaints were addressed to the regional inspector of Medical State Supervision, the official body concerned with public health. The inspector could then reprimand the accused, or instruct the mayor of her community to do so, or inform the public prosecutor and in this way initiate a criminal trial. A trial could also be achieved by having a policeman draw up an official report, directly or under orders from the mayor. Before 1865 a similar line of action was followed, with a provincial medical committee in the place of the inspector. When a public prosecutor decided to prosecute, obviously a conviction or an acquittal would follow. (The Dutch judicial system operated without a jury.) Appeal was theoretically possible until a case reached the Supreme Court. A convict could also request clemency, which depended on the advice of the inspector. In practice, the system was open to different interpretations at many stages. The law provided for exceptions that were especially applicable in the case of childbirth. Lay medical intervention was permitted when no doctor or midwife could reach the expectant mother in time. Quite a few cases were quashed because of such immediate need.

Statistics of midwife prosecutions in the Netherlands are sketchy. National figures are only available from the annual reports of the chief health inspector, covering the period 1865-1905. He in turn had to rely on the information of the regional inspectors who were dependent on what the courts told them.[23] In the course of this process mistakes could easily have crept in. Also not every inspector distinguished clearly between the unlicensed practice of medicine in general and the unlicensed practice of midwifery in particular. Checking the original court records (mainly verdicts) is thus imperative, also in order to differentiate between the number of offences and the number of offenders. After 1886 when these cases were settled in the lower courts this becomes rather difficult, due to the large number of these courts and the poor state of some of their archives and indexes. Given these limitations, the overall number of prosecutions between 1865 and 1905 can be put at a little over 200 (including the roughly 20 cases identifiable as recidivism). This is a high number compared to the prosecution of other illegal providers of health care in the same period. In this sense the prosecution of unlicensed midwives can be characterized as fierce. Besides, women appearing in court cases only form an (unknown but probably small) proportion of the total number of lay midwives, as can be glimpsed from the cases in which an official warning sufficed or those in which one woman was singled out as a local deterrent to others.[24]

When we look at the prosecution from a regional perspective, a similar picture of severity emerges. In the countryside of the province of Groningen, for instance, cases against unlicensed midwives constituted about 35 per cent of all cases against illegal medical practitioners.[25] In the town of Groningen, on the other hand, there were no such cases in the second half of the nineteenth century; the last official complaint dated from 1827. A more refined view of the material shows this distinction between town and countryside to be valid for the whole of the Netherlands. By the middle of the nineteenth century cases were restricted to the countryside. But the distribution was still fairly uneven and it concerned only certain parts of the countryside. Prosecution mainly occurred in the eastern and the southern provinces of the Netherlands. Within those provinces, however, considerable local diversity can be discerned. This geography of unlicensed midwifery, based as it is on court cases, is further supported by the early twentieth-century birth statistics.[26] Although they measure the absence of official birth attendants rather than the presence of unlicensed help, it can be presumed that in most cases someone was indeed present, if only to cut the umbilical cord and to remove the placenta.

In the courtroom

When considering whether a lay midwife was guilty or not, judges had to find answers to the following four questions.

1. Is the accused licensed to practise midwifery?
2. Has the accused provided midwifery assistance?
3. If so, has she done this out of necessity?
4. Was it part of a trade?

The regional inspector usually provided the answer to the first question by consulting the official lists of licensed midwives. For the other questions witnesses were required. This was easier said than done. In other cases of the illegal practice of medicine the police often resorted to provocation; they consulted practitioners about fake complaints and consequently reported the treatment they received as an offence. This was out of the question in cases of "healthy illness" (the colloquial for births), if only because the police force consisted of men. Policemen could only find out what happened by talking to the woman who had given birth and anybody else who had been present. Doctors and official midwives who wanted to instigate a prosecution met with similar difficulties. Often the inspector had to ask them for more detailed information, which they as a rule did not or could not furnish, thereby undermining their own attempts to eliminate competitors. Most of the time the prosecuting attorney had to base his case on hostile witnesses. Many cases could have been known or were even reported yet were quashed because not enough people were willing to testify. A judicial fact had to be confirmed by two witnesses (one of whom could be the perpetrator), and evidence of a trade needed to be based on several distinct facts, although there was some flexibility in the interpretation. Some judges found it sufficient to have proof of money being promised, but others thought, for instance, that only helping two neighbours did not establish proof of a trade. In one particular case from the province of Zeeland a woman declared in court that she had been delivered 13 times by the same unlicensed midwife, but her statement did not play any part in the judges' considerations.[27] A woman in Frisia was acquitted, although it was proven that she had helped six women in child-birth, because she had acted as a neighbour or a good friend and did not ask for any financial reward.[28]

The issue of "necessity", or "emergency", was even more open to discussion. Courts could go to some lengths to find out how far away the nearest doctor or midwife lived and whether he or she was booked in advance. Male witnesses, on the other hand, recounted journeys they had to undertake at night, in snow storms or rain, and how they had attempted in vain to borrow a horse or a wagon to fetch official help. Somehow there always seemed to have been a lack of time and babies were always born before the doctor or the legal midwife had arrived. No wonder that unlicensed midwives resorted to the defence that they also arrived too late (as this removed them from the scene of the "crime" this was contested). Finally, judges could take mitigating circumstances into account, such as the advanced age of the defendant and her former conduct. Sometimes there was some overlap between the legal points. For example, the unavailability of medical personnel could be considered mitigating as well as belonging to the arguments about "necessity".

One of the most astonishing findings is that in several places, in different areas of the country, unlicensed midwives acted in full agreement with the local council or even the local doctor.[29] On one occasion the practice of midwifery was redefined to this end. Cutting the umbilical cord, stated a Groningen doctor in court, was only a simple operation, which anyone present at a birth was obliged to perform in the absence of official help.[30] For the councils (who had to provide the official midwife's salary), the main argument was that lay midwives were cheaper (they used the same argument in the case of veterinarian support). It was only when state funds became available at the end of the nineteenth century, that they were willing to employ a certified midwife. The attitude of the medical profession seems contradictory at first. While the inspectors were primarily concerned with raising the number of trained midwives and strongly opposed illegal ones, some of the local practitioners condoned the assistance of unlicensed midwives, as we have seen. In the final analysis these two were in pursuit of the same goal: to free general practitioners from the time-consuming care of routine deliveries which in their view could easily be supervised by less learned female assistants. As one regional inspector formulated it: "When a general practitioner is forced to practise midwifery as well, he often faces the dilemma of whom to leave without any care: one of his patients or a mother in childbed".[31] This, of course, could only occur in situations with an artificial scarcity of medical personnel.[32] The unlicensed practice of midwifery was one of the few occasions when the argument made sense that the use of lay medicine was due to the distance people lived from official medical services.

Judges usually acquitted the unlicensed midwife if it was clear that a doctor was willing to vouch for her and take responsibility for her action. Otherwise, when all the four legal requirements were met, they had to convict her. In accordance with the prosecutor, however, judges could show leniency as to the fine, especially after 1865. It is simply impossible to evaluate every financial decision, but generally it seems that the crime of unlicensed midwifery was not taken very seriously by prosecutors and judges. Women were usually let off with a fine of a few guilders, the same amount as they received for one or two deliveries. As prosecutors left the initiative to prosecute to the local physicians and midwives, we can conclude that it was primarily the medical profession (or at least its leading representatives) who sought the criminalization and punishment of lay midwifery.

Prosecuting licensed midwives

Prosecution under the Medical Act was aimed at restricting the crossing of boundaries of competence. This referred not so much to medical skill as to legal requirements. Although it was presumed that registered practitioners were skilled, what counted was in what capacity they were registered, not how capable they were. In the nineteenth-century Dutch medical system distinction was made between several sorts of medical practitioners (medical doctors, surgeons, midwives) and it was also of significance whether one practised within a town or in the countryside. Amongst others, the separation of qualifications implied that medical doctors could also be prosecuted for illegally practising midwifery if they did not have the qualification as obstetric doctor. As it turned out, a penalty clause was left out in this particular section of the law and offenders could not be punished.[33] This extraordinary incident was probably due to sheer negligence, but it also illustrates the difference in attitude towards the (then) exclusively male medical doctors and the female lay midwives. Surgeons, on the other hand, who practised midwifery without being legally qualified were also liable to prosecution (and not exempt from fines). The New Medical Act of 1865 purported to abolish these inter-professional boundaries by dissolving the separate qualifications. Since this depended on further or new examinations, which not everyone took or succeeded in, Dutch general practitioners possessed uniform qualifications only at the beginning of the twentieth century.[34]

From 1865 onwards all male medical practitioners were categorized under the title *arts* (doctor). Licensed midwives, however, were still considered as a lower species and the sheer idea of granting them the possibility to train as a doctor would have been preposterous at the time.[35] They, too, could breach medical law and occasionally did so. From the reports on the policing of licensed midwives a rather revealing picture arises. To start with, there were only about 20 cases involving licensed midwives, even though there were over 800 of such women in the second half of the nineteenth century.[36] In most of these cases a warning from the medical inspector sufficed; only a handful of them reached the courts. The concept of necessity, for instance, made it possible for licensed midwives to operate in ways otherwise restricted to obstetric doctors, as long as they reported this to the inspector. Thus a midwife in the (Catholic) province of Limburg was given a 50-cents fine for not report-ing a caesarian she had performed. The operation itself could not have been delayed.[37] Undoubtedly, Catholic dogma that stressed saving the child also played its part here.

Licensed midwives were admonished for not calling in a doctor during complicated deliveries, for using instruments, and for administering drugs (usu-ally ergot, because it eased the delivery). On one occasion "punishable actions while practising" were mentioned,[38] which probably referred to abortion, a crime not everyone was willing to mention explicitly. Midwives only became involved in it at the end of the nineteenth century, when some of them were attracted by the teachings of the Neo-Malthusian League. From an investigation of the prosecution of abortionists (which fell outside medical law), only a few official midwives appear to have resorted to what their union considered as the "unnatural" antithesis to midwifery.[39] The amount of public attention they drew nevertheless contributed to a linguistic connection, as commercial abor-tionists advertised as "midwives", without possessing any licence whatsoever.[40]

Prosecuting official midwives for trespassing the boundaries of their com-petence thus differed greatly from prosecuting unlicensed ones for transgress-ing into the domain of the others. The main difference was, of course, the very low prosecution rate of licensed midwives and the relatively high rate for their unlicensed colleagues. In part the comparison is misleading since every unli-censed midwife was, strictly speaking, committing a crime and was therefore open to prosecution. But in part, the low prosecution rate of official midwives could either point to them as very law-abiding, or it could imply that they were allowed some freedom, as long as they stayed within patriarchal control.

Why were so many unlicensed midwives prosecuted?

Amongst all unlicensed healers who faced criminal charges for illegally practis-ing medicine, women suspected or accused of unlicensed midwifery stand out quantitatively. The number of court cases against them exceeded those against any other category of healer. About three times as many unlicensed midwives as unlicensed dentists were prosecuted and about six times as many as magnetists, to mention only the two other largest groups of illegal healers. Despite being an easy target for the inspectors of Medical State Supervision, unlicensed midwives were hardly visible to the general public. Amongst others, this had to do with the local character of lay midwifery. The Dutch Society for the Repression of Quackery, for one, took hardly any notice of them, as their trade (if it were one) was not commercialized and they were obviously not committing any fraud.[41] The lack of commercialism is most blatantly shown by the lack of male participation in lay midwifery. If there had been any profit in it, men surely would have become involved.[42] Lay midwives were not out to corner a firm position in the medical market, even though they attempted sporadically to join the ranks of the certified midwives. Some of them set up (a temporary) practice after they failed their exams. This is illustrated by the case of an unlicensed midwife in the province of Overijssel. She was granted clemency because the inspector could imagine "the difficult position she must find herself in when, although she had been taught midwifery, she had to refuse to help her fellow-inhabitants on whom she depended because of her poverty". When she was convicted a second time, clemency was refused on the ground that her first conviction should have given her an excuse to refuse help. It also appeared that people had arranged for her assistance beforehand and that the emergency clause thus did not apply.[43] This case indicates, in my view, that lay midwives were interested not only in profit however small it was, but also in establishing their place within the communities they lived in as trusted carers. It also shows that to the convicted clemency and nominal fines signalled an approval rather than a prohibition.

There were several reasons why there were so many prosecutions. Among the unlicensed practitioners midwives were the weakest in socio-economic terms. Their activities were neither financially nor medically interesting enough to attract a licensed practitioner to shield them with his licence, as was often the case with magnetists or herbalists. (The instances of medical practitioners making use of lay midwives were structurally different. They only "permitted" the unlicensed practice; unlicensed healers on the other hand took the initiative themselves to hire a doctor or a surgeon.) Nor would rich patients step forward to pay the fines. Midwifery as it was practised by the unlicensed was not a field of medicine of which new results were expected. It was "only" a necessary action that did not invite a lucrative specialism. Because of the urgency of attendance, midwifery could only be practised locally. As far as treatment was concerned, pregnancy differed from illness and this implied that the number of deliveries each midwife handled was far lower than the average number of consultations of healers. A licensed midwife would have attended about 100 deliveries a year, an unlicensed one far fewer. By comparison, a modestly popular lay healer could easily attract about 20 patients a day, which could eventually add up to tens of thousands of consultations overall. Even a licensed midwife could never hope to equal that. Conversely, far more people were needed to attend at deliveries than to provide cures for illnesses. With a lack of licensed midwives, there were many more unlicensed practitioners than in other branches of the medical enterprise. Unlicensed midwives were vulnerable because they were women and because of their numbers.

Numbers, however, do not provide the whole explanation. In those days almost every single village or hamlet had its own (unlicensed and usually male) healing specialist, who was consulted in case of sprains, warts, burnings, toothache, and the like. Most of these so-called blessers applied the laying on of hands. Simultaneously they mumbled spells or prayers that they kept secret from their patients. Local doctors certainly knew about their existence, but they only combated those few who overstepped the local boundaries and went to give consultations in the cities. On the whole these blessers were left alone, as they were not direct competitors to doctors and culturally too far removed from mainstream medicine. The dearth of official medicial practitioners in the Dutch countryside was also important here. But women who provided help in childbirth and who did not otherwise dabble in medicine were not so easily tolerated by the medical profession. Medical definitions rather than issues of gender appear to have been decisive here. For if the medical wrath had been directed at women, women blessers would have been subjected to prosecution. They were not, although the inhabitants of the Calvinist countryside generally disapproved of them: this was shown by passing the tradition of blessing down the male line, not by resorting to legal measures.

The popularity of unlicensed midwives

A somewhat superficial collective biography of the unlicensed midwives in the second half of the nineteenth century reveals them to be older women, past child-bearing age, often widowed, lower class, and invariably living in the less prosperous, small and remote places of the Dutch countryside, close (geographically as well as culturally) to the women they were asked to assist. Many (but not all) of them were handywomen, who prior to the birth had agreed to come over for nine days or so to help in the household. As a rule they could be found in those areas that lacked certified midwives or doctors. Yet the unavailability of medical personnel was not the only reason for their popularity. As one judge remarked, necessity was often artificially produced.[44]

Most witnesses did not say so explicitly but only showed implicitly that they favoured a lay midwife above a certified midwife or doctor. Some of them told the judges that they had chosen the woman because she was known to practise midwifery, or because "everybody used her". Others found the certified midwife too expensive and yet others only remarked that they did not want any official help, without giving any specific reason (if they did, it was not preserved in writing).[45] Or it was said that the doctor cost too much and that the midwife was unwanted. Judges were not interested in underlying rationales even if their informants had been able to word them; in the court records it is only very occasionally alluded to that pregnant women were afraid of certified midwifes. They found them too rough and unpleasant.[46] This was also why male doctors were not called.[47] In the view of at least some pregnant women, the image of certified midwives overlapped with that of doctors.

Certified midwives certainly differed from local lay midwives. Most of them were trained in Amsterdam or Rotterdam. They had a middle-class or lower middle-class social background, they were younger (at least during the first decade of their practice), often unmarried and outsiders to the village in which they practised. Besides, they were independent working women, who would travel some distance on their own at any time of the day or night (by bicycle, of course). It does not seem far-fetched to presume that more male than female characteristics were ascribed to them and that they were contrasted with the more motherly, handy women to whom the care of the rural family was entrusted.

Conclusion

Seen from the perspective of the unlicensed midwife, most of the differences between the Netherlands and the Anglo-Saxon countries dissolve. The demise of the granny and immigrant midwife in the United States and the disappearance of the handy woman in Great Britain is mirrored in the Netherlands.[48] In the Netherlands the percentage of births occurring without official attendance had shrunk to a mere 0.2 per cent of all births by the middle of the 1930s.[49] It is, however, unlikely for the prosecution of unlicensed midwives to have played a big part in this. Changes in the infrastructure and the advance of maternity and infant care, penetrating far into the countryside and replacing the local handywomen, were probably much more important.[50] Lay midwives simply fulfilled a necessary function and when they were not required any more they quietly left the field. Childbirth became medicalized in the Netherlands as everywhere else. But to end with a speculation: lay midwives, answering to popular demand, may have contributed to the survival of woman-centred births, especially home deliveries. If that has been the case, it would show criminalization to be ineffective whenever it runs counter to deeply rooted customs, in this case the place of women in Dutch rural society.

Notes

1. L. Jordanova, *Sexual visions. Images of gender in science and medicine between the eighteenth and twentieth centuries* (New York: Harvester Wheatsheaf, 1989), p. 32.
2. See the historiography in: J. B. Litoff, "Midwives and History", in R. D. Apple (ed.), *Women, health and medicine in America* (New Brunswick: Rutgers University Press, 1992), pp. 435-50.
3. R. G. DeVries, "A cross-national view of the status of midwives", in E. Riska & K. Wegar (eds), *Gender, work and medicine. Women and the medical division of labour* (London: Sage, 1993), pp. 131-46, p. 142.
4. H. Marland, "The guardians of normal birth: the debate on the standard and status of the midwife in the Netherlands around 1900", in E. Abraham-Van der Mark (ed.), *Successful Home Birth and Midwifery. The Dutch Model* (Westport/London: Bergin & Garvey 1993), pp. 21-44, p. 21.
5. I. Loudon, *Death in childbirth. An international study of maternal care and maternal mortality 1800-1950* (Oxford: Clarendon, 1992), pp. 155-6.
6. Centraal Bureau voor Statistiek, *1899-1989 negentig jaren statistiek in tijdreeksen* (Den Haag: CBS, 1989), p. 34.
7. *Rapport over de positie van de vroedvrouw in Nederland* [offprint of *Verslagen en mededelingen betreffende de volksgezondheid* 10/11 (1963)], p. 23.
8. Ministry of Health, *Final report of the departmental committee on maternal mortality and morbidity* (London: His Majesty's Stationery Office, 1932).
9. See also W. de Blécourt, *Het Amazonenleger; irreguliere genezeressen in Nederland, c. 1850-1930* (Amsterdam: Amsterdam University Press, forthcoming), especially Chapter 3.

10. M. J. van Lieburg & H. Marland, "Midwife regulation, education, and practice in the Netherlands during the nineteenth century", *Medical History* 33 (1989), pp. 296-317, p. 316.

11. Dutch law derived from the French, cf. Matthew Ramsey, "The politics of professional monopoly in the nineteenth century: the French model and its rivals", in G. L. Geison (ed.), *Professions and the French State* (Philadelphia: University of Philadelphia Press, 1984), pp. 225-305.

12. Since a brush with the law apparently deterred lay midwives from the continuation of their practice (I have not found any cases of repeated recidivism) they merely faced imprisonment if they failed to pay the fine (plus the administrative costs).

13. Algemeen Rijksarchief, hulpdepot Schaarsbergen, archief kantongerecht Zaltbommel, inv. nr. 53, nr. 68; Rijksarchief in Drenthe, archief arrondissementsrechtbank Assen, inv. nr. 41, nr. 4662 (1875).

14. *Tijdschrift voor praktische verloskunde* 8 (1904), p. 208; 10 (1906), p. 28; 13 (1909), p. 243; 14 (1911), p. 393.

15. See, among others: Johann Heinrich Hagenbeek, *Het moederschap in Overijssel* (Zwolle: Tulp, 1936), p. 89.

16. Cf. E. van der Borg, "Beeldvorming over vroedvrouwen in de noordelijke Nederlanden (1600-1900)", *Verzorging. Tijdschrift van de vakgroep verzorgingssociologie* 3(3) (1988), pp. 2-17; *idem*, "De vroedvrouw in de historie: beeld en werkelijkheid", *Tijdschrift voor verloskundigen* 18 (1993), pp. 103-107.

17. About midwifery in the Netherlands during the early twentieth century, see the series of articles by Hilary Marland, "Questions of competence: the midwife debate in the Netherlands in the early twentieth century", *Medical History* 39 (1995), pp. 317-37; "De missie van de vroedvrouw. Tussen traditionele en moderne kraamzorg in de begin van de twintigste eeuw", in M. Gijswijt-Hofstra (ed.), *Op zoek naar genezing. Medische geschiedenis van Nederland vanaf de zestiende eeuw* (Amsterdam: Amsterdam University Press, 1995), pp. 67-86; "'A broad and pleasing field of activity'? The payments, posts and practices of Dutch midwives in the early twentieth century", in J. Woodward & R. Jütte (eds), *Coping with sickness: historical aspects of health care in a European perspective* (Sheffield: EAHMH Publications, 1995), pp. 67-91.

18. E. van der Borg, *Vroedvrouwen, beeld en beroep. Ontwikkelingen in het vroedvrouwschap in Leiden, Arnhem, 's-Hertogenbosch en Leeuwarden, 1650-1865* (Wageningen: Wageningen Academic Press, 1992), p. 102.

19. M. Niemeijer, *De vroedvrouw in de praktijk. Beknopte handleiding der vroedkunde, in vragen en antwoorden* (Purmerend: Steensma, 1899), p. 97.

20. For a discussion of lower-class participation in feminist circles around 1900, see M. Everard, "Het burgerlijk feminisme van de eerste golf: Annette Versluys-Poelman en haar kring", *Jaarboek voor vrouwengeschiedenis* 6 (1985), pp. 106-37.

21. L. Schoon, *De gynaecologie als belichaming van vrouwen. Verloskunde en gynaecologie 1840-1920* (Zutphen: Walburg Pers, 1995), pp. 121-3.

22. *Handelingen Nederlandsche Maatschappij tot Bevordering der Geneeskunst*, 1881, p. 10.

23. There were about 30 regional courts in the Netherlands at that time; the number varied because of reorganizations.

24. See, for instance, M. Pruijt, "Roeien, baren en in arbeid zijn. Vroedvrouwen in Noord-Brabant, 1800-1960", in M. Grever & A. van der Veen (eds), *Bij ons moeder*

en ons Jet. Brabantse vrouwen in de 19de en 20ste eeuw (Zutphen: Walburg Pers, 1989), pp. 122–42, especially p. 128.

25. Here the other main groups were veterinarians and semi-licensed doctors. See Willem de Blécourt, "De afstand tot de ander. Onbevoegde genezers op het Groningse platteland, tweede helft negentiende eeuw", in F. Huisman & C. Santing (eds), *Medische geschiedenis in regionaal perspectief: Groningen 1500-1900* (Rotterdam: Erasmus Publishing, 1997), pp. 161–78, especially 164.

26. C. van Tussenbroek, *De ontwikkeling der aseptische verloskunde in Nederland* (Haarlem: Bohn, 1911), p. 182.

27. Rijksarchief in Zeeland, archief arrondissementsrechtbank Goes, inv. nr. 172, nr. 233 (1872).

28. *Verslag geneeskundig staatstoezicht* 1874, p. 278.

29. Cf. *Maandblad voor Praktische Verloskunde* 2 (1898), pp. 34–5; *Tijdschrift voor Praktische Verloskunde* 24 (1920), p. 83.

30. Rijksarchief in Groningen, archief arrondissementsrechtbank Winschoten, inv. nr. 110, nr. 101 (1861).

31. *Verslag provincie Gelderland* 1874, p. 508. Shame on the part of the doctors is nowhere mentioned.

32. H. van der Velde, "Overvloed en schaartse. De verspreiding van geneeskundige hulp in Nederland in de negentiende eeuw", *Gewina* 19 (1996), p. 210-30.

33. De Blécourt, "De afstand tot de ander", p. 165.

34. M. J. van Lieburg, "De tweede geneeskundige stand (1818–1865). Een bijdrage tot de geschiedenis van het medisch beroep in Nederland", *Tijdschrift voor Geschiedenis* 96 (1983), pp. 433–53.

35. When at the end of the century women started to be admitted to university courses in medicine, it concerned upper-class or upper-middle-class women who could have studied as a teacher before. Cf. M. Bosch, *Het geslacht van de wetenschap. Vrouwen en hoger onderwijs 1878-1948* (Amsterdam: SUA, 1994).

36. Van Lieburg & Marland, "Midwife Regulation", p. 302.

37. *Verslag geneeskundig staatstoezicht* 1879, p. 319. Rijksarchief in Limburg, archief arrondissementsrechtbank Maastricht inv. nr. 469, nr. 54.

38. *Maandblad voor Praktische Verloskunde* 1 (1898), p. 142.

39. I have not found any unlicensed midwife performing criminal abortions. This is hardly surprising, as in the Dutch countryside only men dealt with terminating pregnancies. When a country woman wanted to be helped by another woman, she had to go to a city.

40. W. de Blécourt, "Cultures of abortion in The Hague, early twentieth century", in F. Eder, L. Hall & G. Hekma (eds), *Sexual cultures in Europe* (Manchester: Manchester University Press, 1999), in press.

41. The Society, founded in 1880, employed a special definition of quackery, that is to say "the willing exploitation of people's money and resources in matters of health care for the benefit of one's own gain". Quackery thus overlapped but did not equal the unlicensed practice of medicine. See about the Society: Gerrit van Vegchel, *Medici contra kwakzalvers: de strijd tegen niet-orthodoxe geneeswijzen in Nederland in de 19e en 20ste eeuw* (Amsterdam: Het Spinhuis, 1991).

42. They did so in the case of abortion; see De Blécourt, *Het Amazonenleger*, Ch. 8.

43. *Verslag geneeskundig staatstoezicht* 1877, p. 332; 1878, p. 304.

44. Rijksarchief in Overijssel, archief kantongerecht Almelo, inv. nr. 11, nr. 147.

45. The most apparent place for this information to be found are police records. Some of them may have been kept locally, but they were not included in the trial records I have consulted.

46. For instance: Rijksarchief in Drenthe, archief kantongerecht Emmen, inv. nr. 58, nr. 529 (1900).

47. Rijksarchief in Zeeland, archief arrondissementsrechtbank Goes inv. nr. 182, nr. 45 (1875).

48. N. Leap & B. Hunter, *The midwife's tale. An oral history from handywoman to professional midwife* (London: Scarlet Press, 1993); E. R. Declerq, "The nature and style of practice of immigrant midwives in early twentieth century Massachusetts", *Journal of Social History*, 1985, pp. 113-29; C. G. Borst, *Catching babies: the professionalization of childbirth, 1870-1920* (Cambridge, Mass.: Harvard University Press, 1995).

49. *Verslagen en mededeelingen betreffende de volksgezondheid* 1936, p. 570.

50. See H. Marland, "The medicalization of motherhood: doctors and infant welfare in the Netherlands, 1901-1930", in V. Fildes, L. Marks & H. Marland (eds), *Women and children first. International maternal and infant welfare 1870-1945* (London & New York: Routledge, 1992), pp. 74-96.

Chapter 10

ક

"Stories more terrifying than the truth itself": narratives of female criminality in *fin de siècle* Paris

Ann-Louise Shapiro

In *fin de siècle* Paris, the female criminal had become an evocative marker of a crisis in modern urban society, generating considerable attention among social scientists, jurists, criminologists, psychiatrists and journalists. Building on a familiar model of nineteenth-century social criticism that interpreted urban pathologies through the prism of sensationalized images of disorderly working-class women,[1] various experts and popularizers focused on the criminal woman as the mirror through which society could recognize itself; the problem of female criminality served as an interpretive tool for assessing the viability of contemporary mores and institutions. This was a time, however, of low/stable or declining rates of female crime, and nothing in the criminal statistics of these decades can account for the burgeoning preoccupation with criminal women.[2] It is my purpose here to explore the meaning of this attention to the figure of the criminal woman, to consider what was at stake for contemporaries in the discussion of female criminality, and to discover how the criminal woman came to be a powerfully resonant figure for expressing contemporary concerns.

Mary Poovey has suggested that "those issues that are constituted as 'problems' at any given moment are particularly important because they mark the limits of ideological certainty", pointing to cultural tensions and ongoing struggles.[3] Following this lead, I am arguing that the "problem" of female criminality was less a problem of women's crime than a code that condensed an array of anxieties about the nature of modern life, anxieties that derived especially from a newly unstable gender hierarchy and from a perceived moment of cultural anarchy in which traditions and traditional authorities seemed to be losing their hold.[4] By the closing decades of the century, the concerns of French criminologists extended beyond earlier preoccupations with the alleged pathologies of working women (thieves, prostitutes, abortionists, unmarried mothers) to include female criminals who belonged to the established classes: murderesses, adulteresses and kleptomaniacs who, through their criminal acts, stepped out of their protected social positions and became the centrepieces of notorious *causes célèbres*. This expanded cast of criminal types pointed not just to particular crimes identified with women, but to an apparent state of disequilibrium: to a dangerous instability in the traditional family; to shifting and unstable gender identities; to the insecurity of traditional authorities in a mass democracy. *Fin de siècle criminal women* embodied and symbolized a particularly modern malaise.

The words of the anthropologist Henri Thulié in 1885 provide a fairly complete description of a set of linked concerns, provoked and made visible by criminal women, that had gained general credibility:

> Scientists have finally aroused public attention. Cries of alarm are heard everywhere: the size of the population is diminishing; infant mortality is increasing; infanticide and abortion have become, as in America, routine phenomena of daily life; prostitution is growing; people seek shameful and sterile pleasures; the vitality of France has been undermined . . . [w]omen defend themselves against men with vitriol and with the revolver. They no longer seek legal justice which does not have the power to protect them; hence they take vengeance. This weakening of the nation, these vices and violences, are symptoms of a profound sickness from which France is suffering.[5]

National anxieties were, in Thulié's analysis, collected around the "vices and violences" of women as the malaise of modernity became indistinguishable from the malady of the modern female. The new divorce law of 1884, reintroducing divorce after nearly a century in which it had been illegal, raised the spectre of domestic chaos. And, as national anxieties in the *fin de siècle* became increasingly focused on the size of the population, the female-identified crimes of infanticide and abortion and the apparent growth of unregulated prostitution (the pursuit of shameful and sterile pleasures) seemed to be at the heart of issues of national strength, a particularly fraught theme in the aftermath of military defeat and civil war in 1870-71.[6] Women's demands for enlarged rights in marriage and greater protection for irregular liaisons, including the right to bring paternity suits (*la recherche de la paternité*), as well as the emergence of a small, but nevertheless worrisome feminist movement, confirmed anxieties about a growing tendency toward gender slippage. All threatened profoundly to destabilize traditional family patterns and masculine authority. The female offender could be seen, then, as a threat to both home and nation, the instrument and sign of domestic disorder and national debility.

In analysing the meanings of these images, I want to look beyond the highly charged descriptions of female deviancy that leap off the page in order to ask more specifically how these images worked in cultural and political terms. What gave particular representations of criminal women cultural weightiness? Even as they reiterated recurrent myths, how were they also timely, linked to specific contemporary concerns? How and where did the stories told about female criminals inform social behaviours and institutional practices?

By seeking to tease out the relationships between texts and contexts, these questions speak to broader issues in writing cultural histories. They direct attention not only to the meanings generated by particular texts, but also to the processes that anchored these meanings and to the places where the meanings mattered. Because criminal narratives were produced in several different sites – in the courtroom, in medical and social scientific journals, in popular theatre and the serialized novels of mass circulation newspapers – and because they circulated widely through different genres and among different groups, they offer a rich opportunity to explore diverse kinds of cultural interchanges. In tracking the construction and diffusion of what were essentially formulaic stories of female deviance, I want to demonstrate *how* and *why* these representations mattered in *fin de siècle* Paris.

My goal is to follow familiar images as they crisscrossed through different media and institutions, identifying the cultural work accomplished by their incorporation in particular narratives. In so doing, I hope to suggest a kind of cultural analysis that focuses on the ways in which these narratives expressed and sought to manage cultural tensions. My interest is not, finally, to describe either the hegemonic authority of dominant groups or the resistance of the socially marginalized; rather, I want to suggest a more kaleidoscopic model of cultural negotiation and exchange in which the different narratives of women's crime emerged as ways to make sense of and respond to specific contemporary problems.

By linking criminal narratives to larger national issues, I want further to contribute to a feminist critique of the public/private divide in the writing of history. For two decades, feminist scholars have argued that historians' use of the concept of distinct public and private spheres reproduces in the writing of history the very phenomena that need to be analysed. In Carolyn Steedman's words, the concept of separate spheres is "too much the anxious repetition of nineteenth-century society's deepest ideological hope to be entirely satisfactory as a category of historical inquiry".[7] Because it was/is both a trope and a means to control aspects of lived experience, operating at once descriptively, pre-scriptively and instrumentally, the public/private divide is particularly slippery. It is necessary, then, for historians to examine the implications and effects of the concept of separate spheres as used in the past, and, equally important, to move beyond those usages in our own analyses. In this essay, I am addressing both pieces of that agenda, arguing that the significance of women's crime in *fin de siècle* Paris, for contemporaries and for historians writing that history, is located precisely in the mobility of gender issues between intimate and political realms.

We can only understand the cultural resonance of female criminals if we recognize the ways in which they traversed the boundaries between public and private life, forging inescapable links between domesticity and politics. As objects of investigation, as the subjects of literature and the popular press, and as defendants passing through the criminal justice system, criminal women drew public attention to specific instabilities and uncertainties in contemporary life. Individual women who pursued their seducers and demanded retribution from the fathers of their children underscored both women's economic vulnerabilities and the inadequacies of the legal codes and practices that regulated women's rights in domestic and public life, while demonstrating their determination to fight for their rights in ways that were disturbingly at odds with the perceived feminine ideal. Women who poisoned their spouses were understood as enacting a kind of domestic treason that mirrored the public challenges of feminists to male authority. Women charged with infanticide and abortion in effect produced a discourse that ran parallel to public discussions of depopulation and its links to laws that prohibited women from initiating paternity suits. Women who shoplifted in department stores raised questions about female autonomy, economic dependency and the uses of new public spaces. Female violence that turned on adultery and betrayal generated and reflected growing dissatisfaction among reformers with the provisions in the civil code that regulated marriage. The domestic dramas recounted in women's crimes attested to shifting beliefs about such issues as the responsibilities of paternity, (double) standards for judging adultery, and the social codes that governed heterosexual relations, pitting the emerging force of popular opinion against established customs and traditional authorities.

Criminal stories thus mobilized sentiment around issues of private life that were spilling into the public domain, as the judicial system provided an arena for addressing perceived domestic and public disorder. In order to see precisely how this worked, we need to look closely at the processes through which particular narratives of women's crime became credible and effective, producing a recognizable criminal type and a cultural referent that could become part of a wide-ranging discussion of contemporary mores and institutions. Let us begin with the crime of poisoning which, perhaps more than any other offence, suggests how and why a small number of criminal women became pivotal figures in the social imagination.

Contemporaries universally identified poisoning as *the* female crime *par excellence*. If women were to be criminals, poison would be their weapon of choice. In fact, since the middle of the nineteenth century, the number of suspected poisonings had decreased continuously, and by the period 1886–1900 there were only about eight prosecuted cases per year in all of France; of this number, slightly more than half of the defendants were women.[8] But in spite of the relative insignificance of the crime, the symbolic importance of poisoning persisted and anxieties about the possibility of being poisoned remained high.

According to one commentator in 1894, "suddenly poison is on the scene again, spreading horror everywhere, multiplying suspicions, and creating *stories that are more terrifying than the truth itself*".[9] This unusual formulation – linking poison not to death but to stories and to escalating anxieties – seems to cry out for clarification. What was the relation between "stories more terrifying than the truth itself" and actual poisonings? And if there were a disparity between terrifying stories and reality, who was telling these stories, what did they mean and how were they ascribed with these meanings in the *fin de siècle*? Did these horrifying stories convey something that was at least as important as the more elusive "truth itself"?

In order to understand the ways in which poison *was* "on the scene again", it is useful to examine the kinds of terrifying stories that were emerging. Here are two exemplary cases that appeared in 1891 - one the account of an actual *cause célèbre* and the second a piece of fiction published nearly simultaneously in the prominent literary journal *Revue des deux mondes*.

In May 1891 Jeanne Daniloff Weiss was arrested for attempting to poison her husband; her lover, Roques, who had allegedly provided her with the poison, was also arrested and immediately took his own life.[10] The marriage had apparently been a happy one, producing two children, until Mme Weiss became infatuated with Roques. Over a period of months, she continued to pour *liqueur de Fowler*, a derivative of arsenic, into the medicine Weiss had been taking for a stomach ailment, until a friend, suspecting foul play, intercepted correspondence between Mme Weiss and Roques and exposed the plot. She was tried, convicted and condemned to 20 years of forced labour.

The story had all the elements to bring it instant notoriety. The defence argued that Mme Weiss had become a love slave to Roques, losing her will and her ability to resist his demands, obeying orders. In her prison notebooks, fragments of which appeared in the popular and professional press, she wrote of passion and madness: "M. R— had made me into a woman of whom I was unaware, a woman violently passionate, passively submissive; not only did he turn my life inside out, but he turned inside out my entire essence."[11] The emotional charge of this melodramatic scenario was heightened by depictions of Mme Weiss as a devoted mother whose previous behaviour had been irreproachable, by the presence in the courtroom of the wronged husband, by Mme Weiss's expressions of profound regret, and, in the final *coup de grâce*, by her dramatic suicide on the night of the verdict. A funeral cortège carrying her open coffin moved slowly through the town, inviting viewers to speculate on the wages of sin.

This image of the dishonoured mother/repentant wife/punished adulteress was, indeed, a compelling one that circulated widely in contemporary fiction as well as in more journalistic and scientific accounts. I want to emphasize here not the morality tale, but the way in which this case reinscribed all of the stereotypes around the crime of poisoning, and revitalized the figure of the "poisonness" at a time when the actual number of cases of criminal poisoning was rapidly declining. The daily newspaper *Gazette des tribunaux* introduced its report on Mme Weiss's case in the following terms:

> Of all crimes, poisoning is perhaps the one that at times denotes the greatest perversity and the most determined perseverance in evil. The guilty person watches day by day the progressive worsening caused by his

detestable acts; he is present for the slow agony of his victim while no moment of remorse arrives to awaken his conscience and inhibit the hand that is preparing death.[12]

Although the pronoun was masculine, the familiar formula referred to a crime that was, in contemporary minds, unquestionably feminine. Criminologists wrote of the odiousness of what was, in essence, domestic treason, committed by the person one trusted the most; it was a specifically female "affective perversity" that allowed the perpetrator "to slowly torture the person with whom one lived, with whom one shared meals, whose confidences one heard, while watching the slow agony of the victim that could last for hours, for days, or sometimes for weeks".[13] They made explicit their conviction that, in its combination of emotional disorder and calculated deceit, "even when it is a man's act, the crime remains feminine".[14]

My second story, the fictional poisoning, has a somewhat different emphasis, using anxieties about poison to underscore the problem of high rates of acquittal for female defendants: a flaunting of the authority of the judicial system that produced, like poison, another kind of systemic pathology. "Le Poison", written by Jean Reibrach, presents the story of Marie Morisset, a woman accused of poisoning her husband while conducting an adulterous affair.[15] Throughout the judicial investigation, she had remained impassive - no feeling, no tears, no denials - wanting only to take her own life. As a result of an impassioned defence by her lawyer, Daguerre, Marie Morisset was acquitted, evoking an ovation in the courtroom. Daguerre rescued Morriset from her despair, married her, and restored her to respectability, having established with her an "ideal love" based on "the weakness and gratitude" of the woman and the "strength and protectiveness" of the man. She gradually banished her awful memories, seeing only at a great distance "the pride that had allowed her to usurp the powers of justice".[16]

But, the text warns, she became more and more aware of a vague malaise, "a force, a continuous presence, not to be appeased, that soon became inexorable".[17] The return of the repressed, sinister echoes of an unpunished crime came in the parting words of a servant who had been dismissed: "I will not stay to be poisoned!"[18] Soon, press reports of another case of poisoning seemed to exhume Morisset's past, assaulting her with memories. The conviction of this unknown woman, her condemnation to 20 years of forced labour, shattered the calm of Marie Morriset's life. She became nervous, bizarre, swinging between torpor and forced gaiety. Her husband began to doubt her happiness and her love for him, suspecting that, perhaps, once again, she had taken a lover. The "bad seed" was bearing fruit. In anguish, he became obsessive about his health, compulsively cataloguing his symptoms and checking the pallor of his skin. He retrieved Morriset's criminal dossier, rereading each piece, searching for signs of his own blindness and finding, he believed, with a belated clarity, the truth that had eluded him: "Of the woman, nothing remained but the adulteress. Of the novel, nothing but odious machinations;

of the poetic heroine, only the criminal, a common criminal, the most cowardly of all, the most worthy of contempt, *une empoisonneuse*."[19] Inevitably, their life together became silent, oppressive, as each became imprisoned by anxieties that could not be alleviated. While Morriset suffered from her crushing guilt, Daguerre wondered to himself, "Is she perhaps . . . a monomaniac of poisoning?"[20]

In the *dénouement* that becomes increasingly inevitable, Daguerre refused to drink the coffee that his wife had prepared, examining its colour and odour with a look of disgust, and finally suggesting with some malice that he was tempted to have it analysed. Pushed by her own profound despair, Morriset insisted on an explanation. "It was in the coffee, wasn't it," Daguerre asked with ferocious irony, "that you poured the poison for your first husband?"[21] Following the overdetermined trajectory of the story, taking the only truly acceptable action, Morriset provided the closure that she had inappropriately sidestepped; this time she took her own life. Daguerre felt, first, a sense of deliverance, and then pity. He believed that she had at last rendered justice.

In both of these stories *l'empoisonneuse* is effectively recuperated; the moral and social order is restored through final acts of self-policing by criminal women. But such reassuring outcomes could neither assuage the anxieties that produced stories of poisoning nor account for their powerful appeal. I want to argue that these stories were symptomatic of deeper worries about women in contemporary life that gave sensational criminal narratives their cultural resonance, making these stories more important, perhaps more revealing, and definitely more "real" than the truth itself. Yes, men in the *fin de siècle* who lived with considerable domestic conflict did, in fact, visit doctors to determine whether their stomach upsets were provoked by their wives' attempts to poison them, checked for symptoms, and alerted their friends to their suspicions. But, more importantly, a much larger group could identify with the metaphoric suggestion of domestic treason, if not the literal fact, because of pervasive concerns that French society was being betrayed from within by women who seemed to be at war with the time-honoured traditions of both private and public life; women like Mme Weiss who had fatefully tried to evade her marital obligations, or like Marie Morisset who had escaped the judgment of public institutions. In effect, the trope of "domestic treason" that drove the plot of stories of poisoning had become the best vehicle for conveying pervasive worries about women who transgressed conventional gender identities and secured their goals at the expense of men and traditional (male) authority.

The poison story and the anxieties it represented were recapitulated in the criminal cases of women like Melanie Lerondeau, accused of poisoning her husband, who was convicted, even in the absence of significant physical evidence, on the basis of her alleged "character", her reputation as an "unnatural woman", a woman deemed capable of the domestic treachery of a poisoning. The depositions and transcripts in the Lerondeau case make it clear that Melanie Lerondeau was, according to the judgment of her neighbours, dangerously perverse. She inverted accepted roles and became the aggressor in the face of her husband's passivity; she refused ordinary domestic responsibilities; and she openly expressed her sexual frustrations, publicly shaming her husband. This behaviour was sufficient to cause the entire neighbourhood to believe in Melanie's latent criminality, permitting them to fill in the gaps in the story of an alleged crime so as to *prove* a poisoning. For example, witnesses stated that because Lerondeau asked for milk instead of wine to ease his stomach pains, they *knew* that he had been poisoned, while most witnesses connected Lerondeau's taking his dinner in cafés to the likelihood, if not the probability, that his wife would poison him.

These perceptions were seconded in the courtroom in the prosecutor's questioning that confirmed Melanie Lerondeau as an unnatural woman:

Q: Your household became a hell for him.
A: I loved him very much, even too much.
Q: You insulted him; you hit him.
A: Never.
Q: You threw stones to chase him away.
A: Oh!—
Q: You sent him at midnight to the barn.
A: That is a falsehood.
Q: He was very poorly clothed.
A: That I agree with. I did not maintain his clothes well enough.
Q: He was forced to eat here and there.
A: Because he worked here and there in the countryside . . .
Q: You said: "Ce c—-là, it is more than three months since he has touched me."
A: No. That is an invention of neighbours—
Q: Your hatred seemed to grow . . . Your husband feared you, feared that he would be poisoned.
A: I cannot believe that—
Q: You were violent and out of control [on the morning of the death].
A: That's true, I agree. I am a little quick-tempered, I shout—
Q: Everyone in your district accused you of killing him.
A: From jealousy . . . In small villages, those who succeed a bit are envied.[22]

It took the jury only ten minutes to bring in a conviction.[23]

Cases such as Melanie Lerondeau's typically turned on the indictment's description of the character of the defendant, which served as the filter that selected relevant details and excluded others.[24] Having identified her character, the prosecutor's case fell into a recognizable pattern. Criminologists, in fact, wrote extensively about criminal women in terms of their essential traits, defining a cast of familiar criminal "types" who reiterated enduring assumptions about women.[25] By the end of the century, a fairly consistent portrait of the potentially criminal woman was readily available. If, in her character, she

211

embodied stereotypical characteristics of femaleness – that is, she was weak, deceitful, perverse, even cruel – her behaviour was described in terms of specifically late nineteenth-century understandings of a deviant woman: she was likely to be sharp-tongued, insufficiently deferential, and publicly critical of her husband; she might invert appropriate female behaviour by refusing domestic responsibilities or by engaging in questionable sexual behaviour; she was prone to slip into excess, unable to contain or control the emotions generated by her reproductive system; or, she might be moved by a much discussed, particularly vicious, particularly female vengeance. Able to account for both motive and method, these formulaic descriptions appeared over and over again in professional writing, in the popularized versions of crime in newspapers and novels, and in the documents of judicial investigations and the courtroom interchanges of criminal cases.

The cultural credibility of the notion of domestic treason in the *fin de siècle* derived from its implicit reference to new areas of cultural tension prompted by a new kind of female disorder: the growth of an organized movement for women's rights, seeking to overturn the customary practices and legal privileges that had guaranteed male authority in the home and in the state. In effect, it was the figure of the feminist that made the crime of domestic treason so culturally resonant. By the closing decades of the nineteenth century, the feminist had joined earlier versions of disorderly women as a being, both real and imagined, whose image condensed an array of anxieties about a changing social and political world. Although feminism was not a mass movement in France, contemporaries saw it as an "irresistible wave", a force "assailing governments like a mounting tide".[26] In the words of one commentator: "In the public world, woman establishes her headquarters everywhere."[27] A series of laws in the 1880s and 1890s had begun to dismantle women's legal disabilities in civic life,[28] while feminists' efforts to reform the infamous Article 213 of the Civil Code – the clause guaranteeing the marital authority of a husband in marriage – exposed the paradox of a republican ideology that both asserted democratic principles and at the same time based its claim to legitimacy on a model of social organization constituted by hierarchically organized "normal" families that secured, above all, men's rights and women's dependence.[29]

It is usual for historians to describe the position of women in French society during this period in terms of their legal disabilities and second-class citizenship. It seems equally accurate, however, and perhaps more revealing to see these decades as a time when men correctly perceived that they were losing many of the traditional prerogatives that had defined their superior status, validated their authority and secured their masculinity. While several important issues remained contested, such as the right to initiate paternity suits, the right to marry the named party in a divorce-for-adultery case, divorce by mutual consent, and political rights, it is clear that established customs were being dismantled. The glue that had maintained a fairly stable equilibrium between the sexes for nearly a century had become loosened.

In this context, contemporary observers began to speak of the feminist and the criminal woman in precisely the same terms. Writing about women's recourse to extra-legal justice, Alexander Dumas *fils* consolidated this connection in an 1880 pamphlet with the provocative title, "Women Who Kill and Women Who Vote".[30] Critics increasingly complained that seduced and abandoned women were rarely the inexperienced victims created by the popular press, and began to characterize women's crimes of abortion and infanticide, not as desperate moves to conceal dishonour, but as the product of "*une terreur égoiste*", a cowardice that drove women to experience forbidden pleasures without bearing the consequences.[31] The kind of sympathy that had led to acquittals for female murderers had begun to lose its currency; women, like Marie Morriset in the story "Le Poison", seemed literally to be getting away with murder. One columnist observed, for example, that the "child-like" and "fragile" defendant who stood before the court was, in fact, "calculating" and "forceful", manipulating an acquittal from jurors who inadvertently became "ultra-feminists".[32] He imagined the post-courtroom scene: "She will leave the Cour d'assises, her face uplifted, . . . to hold forth in the evening at some meeting of the League for the Rights of Women where she will superbly retell her feelings as a person who has rendered justice, who has redressed wrongs."[33] Merging the unpunished *femme criminelle* and the feminist, he described what appeared to be a new "despotism of women".[34]

This vision of the world turned upside-down, of women on top, emerged as well in criminal cases that turned on the possibility that women might be capable of tricking their accusers.[35] Among the most historically persistent characteristics used to identify the female criminal was her alleged capacity for deception. According to one criminologist, "The deceitful habits that are innate in woman, the intellectual insensitiveness, the absence of logic, the rapid fading of their memories of the crime, all of these make the female criminal a liar to the point of absurdity."[36] Criminologists described women's propensity to lie as natural, indeed inevitable, as a matter of instinct and a natural defence through which they turned the tables on more powerful men.[37] In the cultural/political climate of the *fin de siècle*, anxieties about women's habitual lying became an especially urgent theme in contemporary discussions about reform of the law that prohibited women from initiating paternity suits.[38]

The case of Eugénie Belligand is intriguing in this regard.[39] Belligand was convicted in 1887 of aggravated assault leading to the victim's death and condemned to forced labour for life. The case is noteworthy, in fact striking, because of the unusually harsh sentence at a time when most female crime received light punishments or relatively short prison terms, and when acquittals for murder were commonplace. Belligand, a widow who had become a midwife after her husband's death, had had a six-month affair with an architect, Courty. When he decided to marry another woman, Courty broke with Belligand, a break followed by Belligand's apparent harassment of both Courty and his wife, encounters that often required police intervention. Finally,

Belligand ambushed Courty as he walked with a friend in the street, hurling a vial of vitriol at him; he died ten days later from his wounds. Belligand claimed that she had attacked Courty because he had refused to legally recognize the child that she had given birth to one month earlier.

In spite of an extraordinarily large dossier with testimony about every aspect of the relationship between Belligand and Courty, the details of the case remain murky. The prosecutor claimed that there was nothing to indicate Courty's paternity, emphasizing Belligand's loose morals and the fact that, if the baby had been carried to full term, Courty would have been absent for military service during the time when the child was conceived. He asserted that Belligand had engaged in previous attempts to extract money from Courty for alleged abuse when, in reality, she had fallen and injured herself, and suggested that she had bribed witnesses to say that they had heard Courty promise to recognize the child. The summary of the case states that "the facts prove that the widow Belligand only invented this paternity in order to bring her former lover again under her domination and to extort money from him."[40] In sum, she is depicted as immoral, manipulative, unscrupulous and, above all, deceitful in a quintessentially feminine way.

Most of the voluminous testimony collected in the dossier represents the prosecutor's efforts to guard against the possibility that Belligand might effectively deceive the court. There is considerable discussion among witnesses of the weight and colour of the baby in order to counter Belligand's claim that the birth was premature (hence, Courty was not away at the time of conception). The summary documents presented to the court report speculation that Belligand had not been pregnant at all, that the baby was not hers, but rather one she had secured in her capacity as a midwife; they include testimony that Belligand had refused a medical examination and instead asked a midwife to declare the birth of the child at the town hall. The report of the medical expert concluded, in fact, that it was highly likely that Belligand had recently given birth: her breasts were enlarged, pressure could elicit several drops of milky fluid, and the skin of her abdomen was covered with well-defined stretch marks. But in this case, the doctor's testimony was entirely discounted; it could not outweigh or overturn the prosecutor's story that gained its authority by narrating a recognizably female pattern of deception. In the midst of all of this testimony, the quantity of which attests to an enormous amount of energy brought to bear by the prosecution to tease out the truth of each individual charge, it is possible to forget that Belligand was tried for the crime of assault leading to Courty's death, and not for an attempt to perpetrate a false claim of paternity.

It is, of course, impossible to reconstruct a definitive explanation for the severity of the sentence in this case, but it does seem consistent with the material collected in the dossier to suggest that Belligand was found guilty of more than one violation; murder was made more horrible by its contemporary resonance with specific anxieties about the broader vulnerabilities of men at the hands of lying women. As concerns about high infant mortality, especially among poor, illegitimate children, intensified toward the end of the century, reformers increasingly urged a change in policy that would permit unmarried mothers to seek support for their children. In the context of heated controversy about the potential abuses that might arise from a law allowing paternity suits, cases such as Belligand's carried these preoccupations into the judicial process where conflicting opinions and their implications could be played out in quite specific terms.

In effect, then, accounts of the crimes that women committed not only worked to produce and reproduce gender definitions, but were interpreted in a particular historical context that gave them added cultural weight, in this case, at a moment of intense concern about women's right to initiate paternity suits and the dangers this posed for bourgeois men and the bourgeois family. Older, formulaic assumptions about a specific kind of female perversity (for example, the tendency to lie) thus gained contemporary resonance in the new criminological literature and in the courtroom, making available a set of meanings that could be mobilized to produce a unified, familiar and apparently conclusive story from among a mass of contradictory and ultimately ambiguous details. Eugénie Belligand was not merely another rejected, vengeful mistress; nor was she simply a typically deceitful woman. She was, rather, a figure who condensed multiple social anxieties that crossed back and forth between domestic and public realms, evoking both the prospect of domestic disorder and women's challenge to traditional authority.

In sum, women who sought redress through violent acts for their grievances against husbands and lovers seemed to be engaging in the same activity as feminists fighting to revise the law on marital authority. Unmarried mothers who physically, and sometimes violently pursued the fathers of their children seemed indistinguishable from feminists demanding the rights of women to bring paternity suits. Poor women who secured abortions merged in contemporary imagination with modern bourgeois women who resisted child-bearing for what were understood as "egoistic" reasons. Feminists urging liberalization of the divorce law appeared the alter-egos of women who poisoned their spouses in order to follow their own desires.

To this point, my examples have demonstrated the power of various images of female deviance, emphasizing both their cultural credibility and their instrumentality in the judicial process. I want to conclude, however, with some reflections on women's stories, both those of female defendants and those of feminists. The stories told by female defendants, even those entirely suppressed in the official documents, did not necessarily stand starkly apart from the kinds of interpretations circulating within the culture or produced in the penal process. Some women modelled their defence, for example, in the precise terms offered by their accusers, merging their voices with those of their interrogators in ways that produced contradictions and ambiguities that elude final resolution. This would usually require that their own narrative include an admission of being *surexcitée*, out of control (even as they described other, more mundane motives), and end with an expression of regret. Such stories incorporated, at the least, personal needs, community values, the expectations of the court, models of criminal stories readily available in popular cultural forms and, no doubt, some measure of calculation.[41]

But in other cases, many defendants *did* seek to put their version of events on the record and to evaluate their behaviour according to different criteria. These women, while familiar with the more canonical stories of jealousy and vengeance, referred specifically to the breach of an implicit domestic contract. They spoke especially of their economic vulnerability and of the apparent immunity of men who escaped their responsibilities, making it clear that they had relied on private justice because there was no other recourse. In generating their own defence while pointing to the moral guilt of their victims, they made use of specific expectations about appropriate gender roles, elevating in particular their own worth as good domestic managers, that were authorized generally by the culture and could be invoked to counter formulaic popular stories about eruptions of vengeful jealousy. These women were not feminists, nor did they present themselves in feminist terms. Rather, they quite regularly substituted explanations that drew upon contemporary understandings of domestic responsibility and family order, pushing criminal stories toward a social meaning.

While judicial procedures and practices generally expunged these alternate explanations from the official interpretations that appeared in indictments and summary documents, it is also true that prosecutors and jurors were listening again and again to the efforts of female defendants to explain the emotional and material circumstances of their lives. Most important, feminists had begun to write about women's issues and to demand women's rights in ways informed by the cultural information produced in the accounts narrated by female criminals. Such links emerged implicitly, for example, in a pamphlet by the popular feminist novelist Daniel Lesueur that was commissioned for the International Congress of Commerce and Industry for the Universal Exposition of 1900.[42] Although ostensibly a technical examination of economic competition between women and men, Lesueur opened her study with a general discussion of the most important problems that needed to be addressed in order to improve the lives of working women. She listed three critical reforms: the elimination of costly and complicated bureaucratic procedures in the application for marriage licences; modification of the civil code so that husbands' control of wives' property and earnings would not weigh so heavily on working women; and the institution of women's right to bring paternity suits. Lesueur's agenda could have been directly lifted out of the judicial depositions of women accused of violent crime. In each case she has underscored the very issues that female defendants identified as the grounds for their criminal acts against men who, in failing to marry them, in taking (and squandering) their income and property, and in abandoning the children produced in irregular liaisons, fatally compromised their economic viability and left them without legal recourse. Women's crimes became in this instance but another version of a feminist text, and feminist texts took their message from women's crimes.

216

What we have, then, are various stories about women's lives and women's behaviour circulating in different institutional and cultural settings, moving through different registers of meaning. Although courtroom hearings and popularized studies of women's crime often described a formulaic syndrome of female perversity, these accounts were revised by female defendants and appropriated by feminists seeking legal reform of women's familial and civic subordination. Without the broader contemporary discussion of women's place in French society, the stories told by criminal women might have remained entirely marginal, without cultural weight. But in a time of challenge to the traditional gender order, when the reform of marriage laws and paternity statutes were under discussion, and contemporaries had begun to discuss women's political rights, the different stories told by and about female criminals were drawn from the periphery of domestic life to the centre of public debate.

It is in the proliferation of "stories more terrifying than the truth itself" that we can recognize the disequilibrium of a shifting gender order. The most striking aspect of contemporary discussions of crime were not the fears of physical danger that they evoked but, rather, anxieties about a new and disturbing experience of cultural anarchy. It seemed increasingly evident to politicians and professional men that laws, institutions and the most basic customs of the society were being renegotiated through the somewhat haphazard processes of criminal trials. Traditional institutions appeared unable to guarantee traditional mores. According to one jurist, "one day it is the issue of the right to bring paternity suits, another day divorce . . . or the right to vengeance, the impotence of justice to rectify certain injuries, the unequal distribution of wealth – all pass before the court."[43] Those accustomed to thinking of themselves as arbiters of contemporary practices worried that the social problems signalled by well-publicized accounts of criminal activity appeared to be moving toward resolution in serendipitous ways, linked as much to the idiosyncrasies of the penal process and the volatility of popular opinion as to the dictates of law or established custom. In bringing their grievances to public attention, female criminals were simultaneously challenging male authority in the home and in the institutions that organized public life.

The rhetorical joining of intimate and political life in the phrase "domestic treason" was not casual or accidental; rather it captures the contemporary conviction that disordered women were a threat to both family and nation. Michelle Perrot has argued that "there are no 'facts of crime' as such, only a judgmental process that institutes crimes by designating as criminal both certain acts and their perpetrators. In other words, there is a discourse of crime that reveals the obsession of a society."[44] This underlining of cultural preoccupations returns us to Henri Thulié's analysis with which I began – to the "vices and violences" of women which were, for contemporaries, as implicated in the lives of individual men and women as in the vitality (or debility) of the state. Ironically it has been historians, dividing up the discipline between "political history", "social history" and more recently "women's history" who have obscured some of these connections.

217

In attending to the different meanings of criminal narratives, conventional distinctions between high and low cultural forms or between public and private life make no sense. To interpret the implications of these stories it has been necessary to explore both the complexities and banalities of daily domestic life on the one hand and the preoccupations of public life on the other. Women's decisions to resort to private justice as well as their own accounts of the expectations and desires that pushed them to violence must be understood in the context of inadequate formal (that is, public) protections or remedies. And, if we invert this perspective, moving from political realm to domesticity, we can see as well that debates about depopulation, divorce legislation and changes in the civil code were inflected throughout by the details of ordinary life that had become visible in accounts of women's crime. The female criminal was such a resonant figure, in the social imagination and in social spaces, specifically because she articulated a dense web of cultural concerns that dissolved boundaries between public and private worlds and stretched across the social distance that separated elites from the popular classes. Positioned dangerously on the cusp of cultural change, the female criminal dramatized for popular and expert audiences a range of issues that pointed not only to questions about women's nature, but to the very issues that animated the contemporary public arena. The criminal woman was identified as a problem, then, not because she was scarier or more disturbing than her male counterpart, but because she was positioned at the centre of transitions that would define the character and culture of Third Republic France.

Notes

1. J. Scott, " 'L'ouvrière! Mot impie, sordide . . .': Women workers in the discourse of French economy, 1840-1860", in *Gender and the politics of history* (New York: Columbia University Press, 1988); D. Riley, *"Am I that name?": feminism and the category of "women" in history* (Minneapolis: University of Minnesota Press, 1988).
2. In France women constituted a declining percentage of those arrested for crimes over the course of the nineteenth century, and, by the closing three decades, represented approximately 14 per cent of all defendants; this low number including arrests for infanticide and abortion, categories in which women were highly over-represented. Rates for violent crime by women were especially low: women constituted 5.7 per cent of those indicted for homicide; 6 per cent of indictments for theft with violence; 8.7 per cent of assault and battery cases; and 13.3 per cent of premeditated murders.
3. M. Poovey, *Uneven developments: the ideological work of gender in mid-Victorian England* (Chicago: University of Chicago Press, 1988), p. 12. See also: Scott, *Gender and the politics of history*; Scott, *Only paradoxes to offer: French feminists and the rights of man* (Cambridge, Mass.: Harvard University Press, 1996); and J. Walkowitz, *City of dreadful delight: narratives of sexual danger in late-Victorian London* (Chicago: University of Chicago Press, 1992).
4. For a full discussion of the cultural meanings of female criminality, see: E. Showalter, *Sexual anarchy: gender and culture at the fin de siècle* (London: Bloomsbury,

1990), and my recent study *Breaking the codes: female criminality in fin-de-siècle Paris* (Stanford: Stanford University Press, 1996).

5. H. Thulié, *La Femme: essai de sociologie physiologique* (Paris: A. Delahaye et E. Lecrosnier, 1885), p. i.

6. In 1870, Napoleon III's Second Empire ended when France was defeated by Prussia in the Franco-Prussian War. This humiliation was followed by a short-lived but bloody civil war. The radical government of the Commune, created in the war, was succeeded by the Third French Republic.

7. C. Steedman, "La Théorie qui n'en est pas une; or, why Clio doesn't care," in *Feminists revision history*, A. L. Shapiro (ed.) (New Brunswick, NJ: Rutgers University Press, 1994). See also: L. Kerber, "Separate spheres, female worlds, woman's place: the rhetoric of women's history", *The Journal of American History* **75**, 1988; L. Davidoff & C. Hall, *Family fortunes* (Chicago: University of Chicago Press, 1987); L. Davidoff, "Regarding some 'old husbands' tales': public and private in feminist history", *Worlds between: historical perspectives on gender and class* (New York: Routledge, 1995).

8. *Compte général de l'administration de la justice criminelle. Annuaire statistique*, 1900; Dr. G. Benoit, *De l'empoisonnement criminel en général* (Lyon: A. Storck, 1888).

9. R. de Clery, *Les Crimes d'empoisonnement* (Paris: Bureaux de la Vie Contemporaine, 1894), p. 5. The emphasis is mine.

10. The following account is taken from H. Robert, *Jeanne Daniloff: L'Empoisonneuse d'Ain-Fezza* (Paris: Editions Albin Michel, 1934).

11. "Les Petits Cahiers de Mme Weiss", *Archives d'anthropologie criminelle* 6, 1891, p. 422.

12. *Gazette des tribunaux*, 29 May 1891.

13. E. Dupré & R. Charpentier, "Les Empoisonneurs: étude historique, psychologique et médico-légale," *Archives d'anthropologie criminelle* 24, 1909, p. 7. See also; R. Charpentier, *Les Empoisonneuses* (Paris: G. Steinheil, 1906).

14. Dupré & Charpentier, "Les Empoisonneurs," p. 6.

15. J. Reibrach, "Le Posion", *Revue des deux mondes* **107** (3rd period), 1891, pp. 150-71.

16. *Ibid.*, p. 158.

17. *Ibid.*, p. 159.

18. *Ibid.*, p. 158.

19. *Ibid.*, p. 166.

20. *Ibid.*, p. 169.

21. *Ibid.*, p. 170.

22. *Gazette des tribunaux*, 30 June 1878.

23. Melanie Lerondeau was condemned to 20 years of forced labour.

24. Unlike the Anglo-Saxon system, the recommendation of an indictment by the preliminary investigation carried with it the assumption that the defendant was guilty until proven otherwise. The indictment was, therefore, more than a formal statement of charges. By repeating conventional beliefs and reproducing familiar scenarios, the indictment outlined the contours of a credible narrative that pointed to the guilt of the defendant.

25. For interesting discussions of nineteenth-century criminology, see R. Harris, *Murders and madness: medicine, law, and society in the fin-de-siècle* (Oxford: Oxford University Press, 1989); R. Nye, *Crime, madness and politics in modern France:*

the medical concept of national decline (Princeton: Princeton University Press, 1984).

26. P. Granotier, *L'Autorité de mari sur la personne de la femme et la doctrine féministe* (Paris: V. Giard & E. Brière, 1909), pp. 42, 45.

27. *Ibid.*, p. 45.

28. In 1880, new legislation mandated free public secondary education for girls, followed by the creation of teacher training schools for women (1881), eligibility for women on Departmental Councils of Public Education (1886), and the entry of women into positions as Inspectors of primary education (1889). In 1884, divorce was reinstituted, and the new law abandoned the legal distinction between a man's adultery and that of his wife. In 1893, women separated from their husbands but not divorced gained full civil capacity; four years later, all women, married or not, could act as witnesses in a civil court, that is, were considered to have a separate legal identity. Women won the right to open their own old-age pension accounts (1886) and savings accounts (1895). From 1895, women could be named as administrators of Charity Boards; in 1898, they gained similar rights on commercial boards and in mutual aid societies, and, two years later, on elected boards for labour arbitration. In 1900, women won the right to accede to the bar, and in 1907, equal rights over minor children.

29. Article 213 on the authority of the husband in marriage stipulated that men owed their wives protection while women, for their part, pledged obedience. Promulgated under Napoléon in 1804, the Code effectively placed married women under the tutelary supervision of their husbands: a husband had control of all his wife's assets and property, which she could not dispose of without his consent; in marriages controlled by community property (and this included the vast majority), the husband could sell off (aside from real estate) his wife's personal belongings without her agreement; a woman could not live apart from her husband or open a business without his formal approval; any money that she earned belonged to him; the husband had custody of minor children of the marriage, a right passed to his family if his widow remarried; women could not initiate paternity suits, nor did they have equal rights to prosecute their spouses for adultery. Only widows and some single adult women enjoyed slightly more control over their own lives.

30. A. Dumas *fils, Les Femmes qui tuent et les femmes qui votent* (Paris: Ch. Lévy, 1880).

31. R. Bouton, *L'Infanticide: étude morale et juridique* (Paris: Société des Editions scientifiques, 1897), p. 173; A. de Monzie, *Le Jury contemporain et les crimes passionnels* (Paris: Alcan-Lévy, 1901).

32. G. Jollivet, "Si j'étais juré," *Le Fronde*, 12 November 1901.

33. *Ibid.* In an effort to realign the popular balance of sympathy, Jollivet argued that the "moral disaster" that befell men deceived by their wives, the horrible doubt about paternity, was, in fact, considerably greater than the misery sustained by wives whose husbands had affairs.

34. *Ibid.*

35. In coding the crime of poisoning as indisputedly a feminine crime, a medical thesis in 1906 completed the composite representation of *l'empoisonneuse* by emphasizing the fact that contemporary poisons had become so subtle, so disguised, that even the medical expert could be tricked. Charpentier, *Les Empoisonneuses*, p. 13.

36. G. Ferrero, "Le Mensonge et la veracité chez la femme criminelle," *Archives d'anthropologie criminelle* 8, 1893, p. 149.

37. *Ibid.*, p. 138.
38. In French law, women could not bring paternity suits until 1912, a factor that complicated the responses of juries to the crimes of women who felt themselves without legal recourse in cases of abandonment.
39. Archives de la Ville de Paris et du Département de la Seine, D2 U8: 224 (1887).
40. *Ibid.*
41. Natalie Davis has suggested in her discussion of sixteenth-century pardon tales that women traditionally have had a problematic relation to their own violence and incorporate this ambiguous positioning into their self-presentation as perpetrators of crime. N. Z. Davis, *Fiction in the archives: pardon tales and their tellers in sixteenth-century France* (Stanford: Stanford University Press, 1987).
42. D. Lesueur, *L'Évolution féminine: ses résultats économiques* (Paris, 1905). Daniel Lesueur was the pen name of Jeanne Loiseau, Mme Henri Lapauze, who was the first woman to be awarded the Légion d'honneur for literature by the French Academy.
43. A. Guillot, *Le Jury et les moeurs* (Paris, 1885), p. 11.
44. M. Perrot, "Delinquency and the penitentiary system in nineteenth-century France," in *Deviants and the abandoned in French society: selections from the Annales*, R. Foster & O. Ranum (eds) (Baltimore: Johns Hopkins University Press, 1978), p. 219.

Chapter 11

The child's word in court: cases of sexual abuse in London, 1870–1914

Louise Jackson

Since the furore surrounding the 1987-8 sexual abuse cases in Cleveland, England,[1] a proliferation of studies has emerged focusing on the treatment of the child victim by the contemporary legal system and the manner in which children's evidence is extracted and treated.[2] Historians have been quick to point out that concern over child abuse is not a "new" phenomenon and, indeed, the period 1870-1914 has been highlighted as an era when the forces of media publicity, mass campaigning and statutory legislation were mobilized over the emotive topics of child prostitution, incest and the age of consent in England.[3] In France the issue of sexual abuse was recognized from the 1850s onwards as it attracted the attention of prominent forensic doctors and criminologists.[4] Its later "discovery" in England was the product of a coalition of interests between the social purity societies and the burgeoning child welfare movement. In July 1885 W. T. Stead, editor of the *Pall Mall Gazette*, printed the results of his own private investigation into juvenile prostitution in London in a series of articles entitled "The Maiden Tribute of Modern Babylon".[5] Stead intended to mobilize popular opinion and force Parliament to raise the age of consent to 16. It is clear that the term "juvenile prostitution" had become, by the late Victorian period, yet another euphemism - along with those of "moral outrage", "corruption" and "immorality" - to refer to what we now describe as child sexual abuse. Although not widespread, the term "sexually abused" was indeed used by a St Andrews surgeon in his 1864 translation of a German work on forensic medicine.[6] Widely voiced concerns about child molestation and sexual assault render it appropriate to deploy the terminology "sexual abuse" as a useful umbrella category within a nineteenth-century context.

This chapter examines how, between 1870 and 1914, child victims in sexual abuse cases were treated in London's courts of law. Using witness depositions prepared for the Middlesex Sessions, together with newspaper accounts of cases coming before the Police Courts, County of London Sessions and Central

Criminal Court, it focuses on the status, reception and treatment of boys' and girls' evidence in cases of rape, indecent assault and "unlawful carnal knowledge".‾ Stories of abuse were rigorously tested in relation to notions of gender, class, childhood and reputation. While boy witnesses might be challenged as thieves or blackmailers, girl witnesses were cross-examined to establish sexual innocence or precocity; any evidence of delinquency was used to discredit the prosecution case. Since girlhood was defined as a period of innocence in contrast to the sexual experience and maturity associated with adulthood, then girls who possessed sexual knowledge were deemed "unnatural" and, indeed, threatening. As Linda Gordon has shown in her discussion of incest cases investigated by child protection agencies in Boston, USA, during the same period, victims of sexual abuse were frequently portrayed as morally polluted and potentially contaminating.[8] In the courtroom the concept of "innocence" had a dual meaning since it could refer to both sexual innocence/experience and criminal innocence/guilt; in the consideration of sexual abuse cases, these two aspects were often conflated. There was an essential paradox involved in the consideration of the girl child's word as witness: if she really had been innocent before the alleged assault, she should not know enough about sex to describe what had happened to her; if she could not describe the assault with sufficient accuracy, then there was no case to answer.

Legal status of the child witness

The legal concept of exactly who was a child in need of protection shifted between 1860 and 1885, as the age of consent to sexual intercourse was raised from 10 to 12, to 13, and finally to 16 by the 1885 Criminal Law Amendment Act.[9] Such underage intercourse was triable at the Central Criminal Court (or county assizes) under the charge of "unlawful carnal knowledge" or its attempt. The legal concept of who was a child could also change if an indecent assault charge was preferred instead. The age of consent for indecent asssault (which covered all forms of molestation other than penetrative vaginal sex and was triable at Quarter Sessions) was fixed at 13 in 1880 and was only raised to 16 in 1922.[10] These inconsistencies meant that the way in which a young person was treated in court depended not only on the nature of a charge, but on how well individual judges were schooled in the law and how they chose to interpret it. Indeed there was considerable discussion among judges as to whether the idea of "consent" was applicable in an indecent assault charge since the notion of assault automatically implied an unwanted and intrusive physical act.[11]

It had been established, by the beginning of Victoria's reign, that children's evidence could be accepted in courts of law so long as they could understand the nature of an oath and could therefore be sworn in. Following Brazier's case of 1773, 12 judges agreed that the admissibility of the evidence of children under 7 "depends upon the sense and reason they entertain the danger and impiety of falsehood [*sic*], which is to be collected from their answers to questions propounded to them by the court".[12] Hence children of "tender years" who were brought into the courtroom were questioned first as to whether they knew the meaning of a lie. Six-year-old Lydia[13] was examined by magistrates preparing depositions for the Sussex Quarter Sessions in 1834 to see if she could be a court witness: "[Lydia] being asked if she knew the difference between Good and Evil replied Yes . . . Who will be angry with you if you tell a lie? God – Who abides in Hell? – the Devil".[14] Children were asked for an understanding of perjury within a traditional religious framework of knowledge about God and the Devil, good and evil. One can also imagine that such a line of enquiry was intended to frighten them into telling the truth.

There were instances where cases were adjourned at petty sessions level so that a child, as an essential witness, could be schooled in the meaning of the oath.[15] Judges were less likely to agree to adjournment at a higher level. In a case at the Monmouth Assizes in 1846, subsequently quoted as precedent, the Lord Chief Baron, presiding over a case involving the rape of a six-year-old "who was wholly unacquainted with the nature of an oath", decided that an adjournment would be detrimental to public justice since "more would probably be lost in memory than would be gained in any other way".[16] On average children had to wait only a few weeks before giving evidence at trial, since there was a fairly rapid turn-over in proceedings. The use of hearsay evidence – such as the repetition by a mother on oath of what her small child had told her – was usually refused. When children did appear in court it was held as crucial that their words should be backed up by that of other key witnesses or circumstantial (including forensic) evidence that the alleged act had taken place. The Criminal Law Amendment Act 1885 brought in new rulings regarding the admissibility of evidence in cases of unlawful carnal knowledge; defendants were allowed to appear as witnesses, and children of "tender years" were permitted to give evidence without being sworn in. The Act emphasized throughout, however, that no-one could be convicted on the unsupported evidence of a child accuser.

An examination of legislation and precedent provides only a small part of the picture. Newspaper reports and depositions reveal that the status of the child's word in the courtroom was rarely based on the relatively simple factors of age or understanding of perjury. By the 1870s the moral status of the child victim had become an important point of referral in courtroom practice and, in particular, in the process of cross-examination.

Moral status of the child witness

One Saturday evening in October 1880, Mrs R came across ten-year-old Lucy wandering in a Westminster street "almost in hysterics . . . very much frightened and crying".[17] The little girl had, it appeared, been molested by a drinking friend of her father. The 63-year-old labourer was taken into custody and, at Westminster Police Court, Lucy told her story of events. She said she lived with her father, who called her his "little house-keeper", and on the night in question was busy running errands when she found she did not have enough money for the sugar and tea that they needed. She went to the Jolly Miller, presumably his regular haunt, to search him out. Lucy's father sent her home and she left the pub, followed just after by the defendant who suggested they walk together and took her through the yard of the Horse and Groom. Lucy stated in court that:

> He said don't walk too quick. He kept kissing me & I don't know what he was doing. He was feeling half way up my clothes - under my clothes, not very far a little way above my knee. I screamed & during this time he got something out. I saw what it was - something in his own person. I had a pair of mittens on. He told me to take those off & I told him I couldn't as I had bad hands . . . I screamed again and then he let me go.[18]

The defendant claimed in court that the whole charge had been got up by Lucy's father to get him into trouble and that Lucy had been told by her father exactly what to say. He also attempted to cast aspersions on Lucy's reputation by claiming the ten-year-old had frequently been turned out of the yard at the Horse and Groom for behaving indecently with young boys, allegations which Lucy, recalled to the courtroom a few days later, subsequently denied. The case was committed for trial at the Middlesex Sessions and the defendant, found guilty of indecent assault, was sentenced to six months' imprisonment.

The historian must ask to what degree Lucy's evidence was influenced by the questions asked in court. She gave very specific details (exactly when, where, what he said, what she said) which produced a very individual and personal account, but it is also clear to any reader that court officials were asking questions which may have been suggestive: e.g. What was he doing? Was he feeling up your clothes? How far did he feel? In other depositions very similar stories are told and children's responses suggest exactly the same mode of questioning: "He put his hand up my petticoat; he touched my person",[19] "He had his hand up my clothes onto my body",[20] "I was sitting on the side and he had his hand up my clothes not above my knee",[21] "He put his hand up my clothes so far as my thigh".[22] Children who used the word "person" or "penis" in court - formal terminologies rather than childish pet names - might be questioned as to where they heard this vocabulary. The question of authenticity of voice was just as important for defence lawyers as it is for the historian since evidence of suggestability would entirely discredit the prosecution evidence. A case at the County of London Sessions was stopped when the child, in the following cross-examination, appeared to admit she had been taught her statement by an inspector from the National Society for the Prevention of Cruelty to Children (NSPCC) who had been instrumental in bringing the case to court:

Have you learnt this by heart? – Yes Sir.

Who taught you? – The Society man.

How many times was your statement read over to you? – Five times.

Did you learn it like a lesson? – Yes.[23]

The following week the NSPCC officer appeared in court defending the allegations, saying he may have read her statement over to her but had never taught it to her.[24] Child witnesses were essentially problematic. As court witnesses they were required to produce statements that conformed with established highly formulaic narrative models. As children, however, they had no prior knowledge or understanding of this legal script. The process of socialization that shaped the testimony of adult witnesses had to be replaced by hurried schooling – whether it be instruction in the meaning of an oath or rote learning – which exposed the artificiality of the legal statement.

Although the case in which Lucy was involved was quite specific – we find out about one particular little girl's life and one particular experience – it also reflected wider discourses surrounding the sexual abuse of girl children in this period. Central to the labourer's defence was the hypothesis that Lucy's word as witness was unreliable; first, that words had been put into her mouth by her father; secondly, that her moral reputation was questionable, and hence indicative of a tendency to corruption and the related evil of deception. This line of argument, which questioned the basic integrity of the girl witness, fitted into an established framework of criticism which was already well-trodden in the courts and in the pages of legal advice manuals. Lucy's story duplicates, together in the same text, the two most common stereotyped images of the sexually abused child: the crying, frightened child victim, innocent and wronged as depicted by the adult woman witness, and the conniving, deceitful and corrupt child portrayed by the man accused of indecently assaulting her.

Hugh Cunningham has drawn attention to the dominance during the period 1860–1930 of the romantic notion of children as innocents requiring protection, which had replaced an older Calvinist view of the child as essentially evil as a result of original sin.[25] The records of legal and welfare agencies, however, reflect a more complicated story. Innocence was clearly seen as open to corruption, particularly within a working-class environment that was frequently associated by social investigators with promiscuous overcrowding and lack of decency.[26] The social arrangements of the poor were seen as precluding the maintenance of childhood as a pre-lapsarian condition; although even middle-class children could be contaminated through masturbation, whose evils were spelt out in a range of medical and religious pamphlets.[27] The transformation from the "innocent" state of childhood to the "knowing" state of adulthood could be affected at any point regardless of age. If the gaining of sexual knowledge was the deciding moment, then sexual abuse itself rendered corruption complete. Indeed the NSPCC, in its annual reports, invariably reported the statistics for sexual abuse under the category "corruption of morals".[28] Only a corrupted and therefore "immoral" child had the ability and vocabulary to speak of sexual abuse. The court had to test whether the child really had been "innocent" before the alleged assault or whether, as a result of sexual precocity, she might be lying.

The attack on the integrity of the girl child's word, as experienced by Lucy, was a strong feature of a whole collection of nineteenth-century legal and medico-legal texts which discussed child sexual abuse. This attack was a two-pronged one. The first rested on the suggestion that little girls, as corrupt and wicked, invented stories of abuse to get themselves out of sticky situations or to cause trouble. The second line of attack was that these girls, like minah birds, had been taught their stories of abuse, often by their mothers, who either intended malice or blackmail, or who simply misconstrued a situation and forced their own interpretation on events. Lucy's case was unusual in that her father was accused of trumping up charges; usually mothers played a key role in court prosecutions.[29]

Medical jurist Dr Michael Ryan used the following blunt caricature, published in 1836, to explain how he believed charges of sexual abuse were formulated. The central character, the mother, takes her daughter to the doctor, suffering from some dubious-looking discharge:

> She goes to the medical man, who may unfortunately not be aware of the complaint I am speaking of and he says, "Good God! Your child has got the clap!" . . . I can assure you a multitude of persons have been hanged by such a mistake. I will tell you what takes place in such cases; the mother goes home, and says to the child, "Who is it that has been playing with you? Who has taken you on his knee lately?" The child innocently replies, "No-one, mother, nobody I declare you." The mother then says, "Oh, don't tell me such stories; I will flog you if you do." And thus the child is driven to confess what never happened in order to save herself from being chastised: at last she says "Such a one has taken me on his lap".[30]

Ryan was articulating a crude Victorian version of "false-memory syndrome". He identified the mother as responsible for creating the narrative of abuse, for trumping up charges, and for putting words into her child's mouth. This scenario was repeated and elaborated during the course of the century. The attempt of Birmingham doctor Lawson Tait to villify women in general and, in the following passage, stepmothers in particular, was the 1894 version of this narrative:

> Stepmothers give frequent examples of the same abominable attempts to punish their husbands by trumping up such charges, and in three instances mothers used even their own children as the instruments of their diabolical designs.[31]

Tait warned doctors of "the malice of persons, always women, who practically get up the cases or provoke them".[32] Some writers suggested that injuries could be purposefully created or faked on the child's body to back up false claims, for purposes of revenge and blackmail or to get a certificate of divorce.[33] The relationship of mother and child was, in the most extreme cases, portrayed as sinister and abusive. The possible textual stereotyping of the "incestuous father" was overwritten with the figure of the evil mother, abusing her position as childcarer and confidante. This effected a shift of blame away from any male assailant; it was the mother who was constructed as the figure of blame.

Tait's full vengeance, however, was unleashed on the little girl complainants themselves. He argued that complaints of abuse were generally lodged by "virulent little minxes", "chits" and "dirty little wretches" who lied and connived to produce an allegation of criminal assault.[34] The worst liars, he argued, were "children of almost the lowest class of population".[35] Levels of virtue or viciousness were related to class position; poverty and dirt created the corrupt liar. Although Tait had become an extremely controversial figure in British medicine as a result of his use of ovariotomy to treat "menstrual epileptic mania", he had a profound practical influence on police practice in Birmingham.[36] Employed by the city constabulary to examine all children who complained of indecent assault, he recommended prosecution in only 5 per cent of cases between the years 1886 and 1893.[37] French expert Dr Lacassagne appears to have shared his views, suggesting in 1889 that "many of the children were thoroughly corrupt and vicious, and were seeking to obtain money by exaggerated or false accusations".[38]

This emphasis on the girl child's unreliability as witness was opposed by a contrary viewpoint: that the truth could be gleaned from the child's own words and that it was absolutely essential to listen to what she had to say. This standpoint was articulated most clearly by the social purity and feminist movements in their attempts to mobilize the country to help the innocent child victim of the white slave trade;[39] but also by the NSPCC as it campaigned to improve conditions for the child in court from 1884 onwards. In its 1886 Annual Report the NSPCC included a "note to court reporters" asking journalists to have patience with and understanding for children giving evidence in court. The society added that: "little victims' tales do not hang together solely because the power of clear memory is worn and gone; they are soulless and stupified".[40] The NSPCC pointed out that although the child's evidence might have to be treated differently from adult evidence it was just as valid.

Cross-examination of girls

The child was required to tell her story over and over again: at a police station, a police court, before a grand jury and, finally, before a judge and jury if the case went to trial. Each time she faced cross-examination, sometimes by the magistrates or a defence solicitor but quite often by the accused himself if he were conducting his own defence.[41] In February 1889 a defendant at Hampstead Petty Sessions had to be stopped by the bench because he "adopted a brow-beating style of cross-examination toward the female witness".[42] Cross-examinations by defence lawyers could be an equally rough affair. In a case that came before the Clerkenwell Sessions, the Assistant Judge Mr Loveland-Loveland rebuked the defence for their cross-examination of a girl witness. In his summing-up speech he was reported as saying that: "He did not say counsel had acted unfairly, but his naturally stern appearance had somewhat terrorised the girl, and every one in court must have noticed how she broke down in the latter part of the evidence".[43]

The cross-examination sought to ascertain the precise details of what had happened, but the child's reliability as witness was often a key line of inquiry; she was asked whether she had a reputation for lying and was questioned about her general behaviour and character. One nine-year-old girl admitted that, "Mother has told me I am an artful & cunning child".[44] Girl witnesses were also questioned about their sexual reputation to establish whether they really were "little victims" or "little minxes". Twelve-year-old Catherine told the magistrate at Worship Street Police Court that:

> Mother has accused me of telling untruths sometimes, and she has some-times found me out in untruths. She has told me not to play with the boys . . . she might have discovered me in untruths about them more than once. I was once . . . in the service of Mrs M & I was discharged because I was not a good girl – I was once found in the young men's room – only once – I had been sent in to sweep the yard.[45]

Flora, also 12, who said she had been molested by a 73-year-old man, was questioned in 1875 about her relations with a young boy clerk: "Mrs C [daughter of the defendant] did not come down once and catch me in an indecent position with Charlie and she did not tell me off and turn me out . . . I have never allowed him to be rude with me and take liberties with me".[46]

Carolyn Conley has argued that a fundamental consideration in rape trials in Kent 1859–80 was "the perceived character of the victim versus the perceived character of the accused".[47] This consideration applied equally to adults and children. For women and girls moral reputation was gauged in terms of sexuality whether they were above or below the age of consent.[48] In August 1885 a nine-year-old errand-girl gave evidence against her employer's husband, whom she accused of raping her. Cross-examined by the defendant, she "admitted that she had been complained of for her forward manners".[49] Mr Bushby, magistrate at Worship Street Police Court, dismissed the case, saying that the charge "was one of those which might be made with the most terrible facility against men by little girls of unclean imagination".[50] Sexual precocity was evidenced in terms of behavioural history, but also in the language the child used to describe her body. The truly innocent child was supposed to have no knowledge of specific names for the genitals or their function. The ideal witness, due to the modesty associated with chastity, pointed to parts of her body when questioned. In one 1875 case a police inspector told the court:

> [The] child blushed & bent her head & said I don't like to say & I told her she must tell me as far as she could & she then said it was impudence. I said did you see where he took it from, did he take it out of his pocket & she said No. I said where from & she nodded towards prisoner & with her eyes cast towards lower part of his person she said from there.[51]

The 12-year-old who told the court "the prisoner put his hand up my clothes and felt my cunt" could not hope to get the support of the court in her allegations.[52]

The complexity of the variables involved in verdict and sentencing cannot be demonstrated through the production of statistical data. The moral and social status of the child victim was evaluated in relation to the reputation of the defendant as well as to other circumstantial and medical evidence. However, reports and depositions reveal that the issue of sexual precocity was an important factor in the cross-examination of girl children; it was used as evidence to cast aspersions on the reliability of victims' testimony but also, when other forms of evidence were incontrovertible, to lodge a plea of mitigation. The image of the young seductress or "little minx" carried substantial weight in court.

The abuse of boys

Press, lobby groups and protection agencies concentrated all their attentions on girl victims of sexual abuse.[53] From its foundation in 1884 the NSPCC, too, defined indecent assault in gender-specific terms; it always referred to indecent assault as being committed by men against young girls.[54] This must of course be related to the fact that the abuse of girls was seen to be much more common and was more likely to lead to criminal proceedings: 93 per cent of the Middlesex sample cases involved girl victims. The emphasis on girl children must also be seen as a result of the emergence of the issue of sexual abuse from the social purity societies' preoccupation with "fallen" women and young female prostitutes. Girls could be "fallen" but boys, according to Victorian sexual definitions, could not. The sexually abused girl was a special interest group; the boy was not and his future was never on the agenda. Carol Mavor has drawn on Monique Wittig's work to argue that the legal emphasis on protecting young girls resulted from an understanding of the female as *"the sex"*:

> Because, as . . . Wittig has argued, only females are "sexed", the laws only referred to those beings who were problematically sliding between the categories of girl and woman; male children were outside of "sex", a division set up both to mark women from girls and to mark females from the rest of society.[55]

The belief in childhood innocence and the need to protect it rested on the tension that one day the "little girl" would become a sexually knowing adult woman; her sexual potential was, therefore, implicit throughout.

230

However, the silence surrounding the 7 per cent of abused boys and their underrepresentation in the newspapers requires further explanation. Jeffrey Weeks has highlighted the attempt by police and judiciary to cover up the Cleveland Street male brothel scandal of 1889, which implicated several gentlemen and one peer in a circle of prostitution involving telegraph boys, the youngest of whom was 15.[56] It was seen as undesirable to bring the attention of the public to matters that might challenge the exclusive association of sexuality with femininity and which, therefore, threatened established codes of masculine identity. One could argue, indeed, that female prostitution and rape received so much attention in the newspapers because they provided the ideal material to titillate and entertain readers through a medium of "healthy" attention-grabbing sex and violence.[57] The gendering of abuse scripts, which can be highlighted by comparing the treatment of boys' evidence to that of girls, must be related to wider gendered discourses on childhood, adolescence, delinquency and homosexuality in this period. It will be demonstrated that, although boys, like girls, were questioned about their integrity and honesty, they were not sexualized in the way that girls were.

Debates about juvenile delinquency had led to the setting up of the first reformatory schools in the 1850s to take child offenders who would, prior to that, have been sent to adult prisons. Institutional provision was soon expanded to encompass young people deemed to have wider behavioural problems or whose home environments were seen as corrupting.[58] The gendered criteria which, as Heather Shore demonstrates in Chapter 3, emerged in depictions of male and female delinquency during the 1830s, continued to shape late-Victorian concepts of delinquency. Linda Mahood and Barbara Littlewood have argued, in their study of the child-saving movement in Scotland, that, while the delinquent girl was associated with prostitution and sexual precocity, the delinquent boy was labelled as a thief.[59] Michelle Cale has similarly concluded that girls' reformatory and industrial schools in England primarily aimed to control female sexuality.[60] I would suggest that this gendered model of delinquency was applied to all children involved in the criminal justice system, whether they appeared as defendants accused of a crime or as witnesses in another case. Child witnesses, if they were to be believed, had to prove their integrity in response to cross-examination by a defence lawyer who, as I shall now demonstrate, would submit questions based on the gendered delinquency model.

Age and class, operating together with gender, were crucial issues in the evaluation of delinquency. First, it was impossible conceptually for a middle-class child to be seen as a delinquent; delinquency was associated with poverty and immoral or "bad" upbringing and hence with the lower classes. Secondly, it was a stage that was associated with puberty. For girls in general this was perceived to commence earlier than for boys, although in individual cases it must have related to bodily appearance. It has already been shown that girls as young as nine were questioned about their sexual reputation and relations with boys. It is significant that, in all cases involving boys under 13 which came before the Middlesex Sessions, the accused was convicted, and there was no attempt to imply that the victim was a blackmailer or thief. Conversely, in cases involving adolescent boys in the 14 to 16 age group, not only were defendants all either discharged or acquitted, but the boy complainants were themselves depicted as juvenile delinquents according to the male model of such "delinquency".

Robert, aged 14, had been selling matches outside the Drury Lane Theatre at midnight in December 1870, when, he alleged, a gentleman, Mr H, asked him to show him to the dark arches below the Adelphi Theatre. He claimed the gentleman then used obscene language and molested him.[61] The arches were commonly associated with both male and female prostitutes as well as being the haunt of down-and-outs. In this particular case it was indicated that boys frequently took gentlemen to the arches and attempted to exort money from them by making allegations for purposes of blackmail. Another youth, Henry, who had been selling newspapers at the time told the court: "I guessed it was some indecency as he was going to the Dark Arches".[62] In responding to a detailed cross-examination, Robert ended up admitting that he had suspected something: "I had expected to receive some half pence for going down to the arches for rubbing his privates up and down. I thought he would give me some money without doing it."[63] The boy's life history was recited in court: how he had been in the workhouse from time to time, had had sporadic schooling, and now worked late at night on the streets selling matches. The intent behind the cross-examination seems to have been to portray Robert as a deviant youth, trying to blackmail gentlemen.

Other cases involving male adolescents follow a similar pattern. In August 1870 a well-educated gentleman of independent means was brought before magistrates at Marlborough Street Police Court accused of indecently assaulting a 15-year-old printer's boy at his Pall Mall residence. The boy, Philip, claimed Mr T had invited him in for a glass of wine, committed the assault, and then given him money not to tell. According to *The Times* Mr T was aghast at his apprehension, exclaiming, "Good God, do you intend to take me on the boy's statement?" and admitting he had merely sent him on a paid errand: "The prisoner, in defence, attributed the boy's statement to the fact that he refused to give him more money."[64] The case was committed to the Central Criminal Court for trial where Mr T was acquitted.

In January 1880 *The Times* carried a report of a similar case, starkly contrasting the class and respectability of defendant and accuser. Mr S, a barrister's clerk, was charged with indecently assaulting Albert, "a youth from a common-lodging-house in Clerkenwell". An impressive list of top barristers came forward to give Mr S what the judge referred to as "the very highest character he had ever heard in a court of justice". The jury at once returned a verdict of not guilty and extended their sympathy to Mr S in his time of distress.[65] The integrity of the adolescent boy witness could be repudiated if he could be shown to be a thief or blackmailer of low social status, aiming to make money out of an allegation of indecent assault. Adolescent boys were not treated as sexual subjects; neither was their sexual precocity played upon in cross-examination.

While "the delinquent" was associated with working-class youth, a corresponding middle-class model – "the adolescent" – was delineated from the 1880s within a plethora of medical, psychological and literary works. John Neubauer has argued that the preoccupation, in art and literature of the time, with adolescence and its attendant physical and mental state reflected a general crisis of identity within *fin de siècle* culture and society.[66] Sexual possibility was a brooding "adolescent" concern. However, while the figure of "the adolescent", male as well as female, was clearly eroticized, this eroticism was based on narcissism and self-absorption. The "adolescent" boy was delineated, not as a sexual actor who negotiated relations with other individuals, but as isolated and introverted in his sensuality. Like Dorian Gray, in his role as Basil Hallwood's muse, the beautiful "adolescent" boy was to be marvelled at but not touched.[67] In terms of the male gaze, he was neither object nor independent actor but alter-ego.

It is also important to discuss, briefly, the construction of another figure of the 1890s – the "homosexual" – in relation to issues of age, development and same-sex abuse. It has been argued that the homosexual was constructed, in both specialist medical texts and in the popular press, as being an older, middle- or upper-class man who had an exclusive desire for adolescent boys;[68] these boys, in turn, were presented as consorting with "gents" for money, gifts and other favours rather than possessing any particular homosexual preference. Jeffrey Weeks has shown how the boys who were involved in the Cleveland Street Affair of 1889 were constructed as "the victims of the unnatural lusts of full-grown men".[69] In 1895 it was Oscar Wilde and Alfred Taylor who were prosecuted for their sexual preferences, not the working-class youths with whom they consorted. Alfred Wood and Charles Parker might have been seen as gold-diggers accumulating a collection of silver cigarette cases, but their own sexualities were not at issue. The *Evening News* announced on the day of Oscar Wilde's conviction:

> We venture to hope that the conviction of Wilde for these abominable vices, which were the natural outcome of his diseased intellectual constitution, will be a salutary warning to the unhealthy boys who posed as sharers of his culture.[70]

One of the key phrases here is the inference that they "posed as sharers", that they were not of the same "constitution", either social or sexual as Oscar Wilde, and that they merely pretended to be so for other purposes. While Wilde, the full-blown homosexual, was "diseased", the boys involved were merely "unhealthy" through secondary contamination, and clearly required protection from such "dangerous" individuals. While the middle-class homosexual might develop platonic friendships with boys of equal rank and eulogize the beauty of the golden-haired adolescent, it was the working-class "rough" to whom he invariably turned for physical encounters.[71] Yet Alan Sinfield has found, through his use of memoirs and oral histories from the turn of this century, that these working boys did not identify themselves as "queer". Homosexuality was, in working-class communities throughout Britain, associated with the effete middle-class "public school-type".[72] It was vital that young boys should not be sexualized in relation to discourses on same-sex desire. To do so would threaten the basis of prevalent knowledges of "normal healthy" masculinity. The dearth of information on boy victims of abuse stems from the same origins as the desire to cover up information about same-sex practices in public schools. Oscar Wilde was a suitable figure on which to pin homosexuality because he was unusual and eccentric in so many ways; he could be easily set up as "other" in relation to the "average" Englishman.

Conclusion

The rape of the innocent was treated as the grossest outrage, but courts had to ensure the child really was innocent; it was of the utmost importance to ascertain the child's moral status. Both boys and girls were asked about their capacity to tell the truth, questioned about the language they used, and had aspersions cast on their motivations in making the claims they did. The credibility of children of "tender years" could be undermined by claiming that their stories of abuse were the fictive creations of adult parties, whether mothers or NSPCC inspectors. Attempts were made to imply that older witnesses had a delinquent reputation. However, the way in which delinquency was gendered produced a different emphasis in the way boy and girl children were treated as court witnesses. The moral reputation of girl witnesses was judged in terms of sexual innocence or precocity; sexual knowledge, as corrupting and contaminating, could transform the child into a "little minx" who could not be trusted to tell the truth. In cases involving adolescent boys, however, the figure of the thieving delinquent was the most immediate point of reference; the issue of sexual precocity was avoided.

Notes

1. B. Campbell, *Unofficial secrets: child sexual abuse, the Cleveland case* (London: Virago Press, 1988).
2. J. Morgan & L. Zedner, *Child victims: crime, impact and criminal justice* (Oxford: Clarendon Press, 1993). G. Goodman & B. Bottoms, *Child victims, child witnesses: understanding and improving testimony* (New York: Guildford Press, 1993). J. Plotnikoff & R. Woolfson, *Prosecuting child abuse: an evaluation of the government's speedy progress policy* (London: Blackstone Press, 1995).
3. For the emergence of the child welfare movement in England, see G. Behlmer, *Child abuse and moral reform in England 1870-1908* (Palo Alto, California: Stanford University Press, 1982) and H. Ferguson, "Cleveland in history: the abused child and child protection, 1880-1914", in *In the name of the child: health and*

welfare 1880-1940, R. Cooter (ed.) (London: Routledge, 1992), pp. 146-99. For social purity campaigns to raise the age of consent, see E. Bristow, *Vice and vigilance: purity movements in Britain since 1700* (Dublin: Gill & Macmillan, 1977). For feminist campaigns relating to sexual abuse, see L. Bland, *Banishing the beast: English feminism and sexual morality 1885-1914* (London: Penguin, 1995) and S. Jeffreys, *The spinster and her enemies: feminism and sexuality 1880-1930* (London: Pandora, 1985).

4. J. M. Donovan, "Combatting the sexual abuse of children in France 1825-1913", *Criminal Justice History* **15**, 1994, pp. 59-95.

5. J. Walkowitz, *City of dreadful delight: narratives of sexual danger in late Victorian London* (London: Virago, 1992); D. Gorham, "The 'maiden tribute of modern Babylon' re-examined: child prostitution and the idea of childhood in late-Victorian England", *Victorian Studies* **21**, 1978, pp. 353-79.

6. J. L. Caspar, *A handbook of the practice of forensic medicine based upon personal experience*, translated from the 3rd edn by G. W. Balfour (London: New Sydenham Society, 1864), p. 318.

7. This chapter focuses on cases coming before the Middlesex Sessions, for which all depositions survive and are now kept at the Greater London Record Office (GLRO). All indecent assault depositions were examined for the years 1870, 1875, 1880, 1885, 1890, 1895, 1900, 1905 and 1910. Seventy-six per cent of these involved children (persons under the age of 16), forming a sample of 205 child sexual abuse depositions. The conviction rate for this sample was 66 per cent, somewhat higher than that for the indecent assault cases involving adult victims (47 per cent).

8. L. Gordon, *Heroes of their own lives: the politics and history of family violence* (London: Virago, 1989), p. 216.

9. Offences Against the Person Act 1861, 24 & 25 Vict. C. 100; Offences Against the Person Act 1875, 38 & 39 Vict. C. 94; Criminal Law Amendment Act 1885, 48 & 49 Vict. C. 69.

10. Assault of Young Persons Act 1880, 43 & 44 Vict. C. 45; Criminal Law Amendment Act 1922, 12 & 13 Geo. 5 C. 56.

11. See, for example, PRO H045/9907/B20738A, letter of Chief Magistrate Sir John Bridge to the Home Office.

12. Quoted in T. R. & J. B. Beck, *Elements of medical jurisprudence*, 6th edn (London: Longman, 1838), p. 97. Brazier was convicted, at the York Assizes, of the rape of a seven-year-old girl who had given evidence but was not sworn. The 12 law lords argued that a child might be sworn if she possessed "sufficient knowledge of the nature and consequences of an oath" (see *ibid.*). Before this judgement the evidence of infants of "tender years" (under seven) had been deemed admissible whether they understood the oath or not; see W. Blackstone, vol. 4 of *Commentaries on the laws of England*, 5th edn (Oxford: Clarendon Press, 1773), p. 214.

13. All names of defendants, victims and other witnesses have been changed to ensure anonymity.

14. Sussex Quarter Sessions Eastern Division, 16 May 1834, QR/E/822, East Sussex Record Office.

15. *Hampstead and Highgate Express*, 20 May 1882, p. 4, c. e.

16. F. A. Carrington & A. V. Kirwaun, vol. 2 of *Reports of cases argued and ruled at nisi prius in courts of Queen's Bench, Common Pleas & Exchequer 1843-53* (London: Sweet, 1845-55), p. 246.

17. MJ/SPE/1880/39 Deposition 18 (GLRO).

18. *Ibid.*
19. MJ/SPE/1870/14 Deposition 22 (GLRO).
20. MJ/SPE/1870/14 Deposition 36 (GLRO).
21. MJ/SPE/1870/15 Deposition 71 (GLRO).
22. MJ/SPE/9 August 1890 Deposition 10 (GLRO).
23. *The Times*, 25 August 1890, p. 4, c. e.
24. *The Times*, 2 September 1890, p. 10, c. d.
25. H. Cunningham, *Children and childhood in Western society* (London: Longman, 1995), pp. 71, 134.
26. A. Wohl, "Sex and the single room: incest among the Victorian working classes", in *The Victorian family: structures and stresses*, A. Wohl (ed.) (London: Croom Helm, 1978), pp. 197-216.
27. R. P. Neuman, "Masturbation, madness and the modern concepts of childhood and adolescence", *Journal of Social History* 8(3), 1975, pp. 1-27.
28. It should be pointed out that the bulk of NSPCC work involved cases of neglect and, to a lesser extent, physical brutality. In 1890 "cruel immoralities" formed only 4 per cent of national cases and 7 per cent of London cases coming to the attention of the NSPCC; see NSPCC, *Sixth annual report*, 1890, p. 68.
29. See, for example, MJ/SPE/1880/03 Deposition 24 (GLRO). The mother of a five-year-old girl told magistrates: "She came in about seven with some sweets. I questioned her and, in consequence of what she told me, I went in search of the prisoner."
30. M. Ryan, *A manual of medical jurisprudence compiled from the best medical and legal works* (London: Sherwood, Gilbert & Piper 1836), pp. 318-19.
31. L. Tait, "An analysis of the evidence in seventy consecutive charges made under the new criminal law amendment act", *Provincial Medical Journal* 13, 1894, pp. 226-33, p. 232.
32. *Ibid.*, p. 228.
33. W. B. Kesteven, "On the evidence of rape in infants", *Medical Times and Gazette*, 1859, p. 361.
34. Tait, "An analysis", p. 231.
35. *Ibid.*
36. J. A. Shepherd, *Lawson Tait: the rebellious surgeon 1845-1897* (Kansas: Colorado Press, 1980), p. 214.
37. Tait, "An analysis", p. 229.
38. *British Medical Journal*, 1889, p. 451.
39. Bristow, *Vice and vigilance*; Bland, *Banishing the beast*.
40. NSPCC, *Second annual report*, 1886, p. 9.
41. Defendants are referred to as "he" throughout the chapter since all those accused of child sexual abuse in the Middlesex sample were male. In a wider case study of child sexual abuse cases coming before the Central Criminal Court, Middlesex Sessions and County of London Sessions in the period 1870-1914, males formed 98 per cent of a total sample of 871 defendants. See L. Jackson, *Child sexual abuse and the law: London 1870-1914* (PhD thesis, University of Surrey, 1997).
42. *Hampstead and Highgate Express*, 2 February 1889, p. 7, c. a.
43. *Child's Guardian* 8(1), 1894, p. 7.
44. MJ/SPE/1880/18 Deposition 2 (GLRO).
45. MJ/SPE/1870/18 Deposition 9 (GLRO).
46. MJ/SPE/1875/08 Deposition 68 (GLRO).

47. C. Conley, "Rape and justice in Victorian England", *Victorian Studies* **29**, 1986, pp. 519-37.
48. See L. Zedner, *Women, crime and custody in Victorian England* (Oxford: Clarendon Press, 1991), pp. 66-7.
49. *The Times*, 11 August 1885, p. 3, c. e.
50. *Ibid.*
51. MJ/SPE/1875/17 Deposition 85 (GLRO).
52. MJ/SPE/1880/27 Deposition 34 (GLRO).
53. Bland, *Banishing the beast*; Bristow, *Vice and vigilance*; Gorham, "The maiden tribute".
54. NSPCC, *Annual reports*, 1885-1914.
55. C. Mavor, "Dream rushes: Lewis Carroll's photographs of little girls", in *The Girls' Own: cultural histories of the Anglo-American girl 1830-1915*, C. Nelson & L. Vallone (eds) (Athens: University of Georgia Press, 1994), pp. 156-93, p. 169.
56. J. Weeks, "Inverts, perverts and Mary-Annes: male prostitution and the regulation of homosexuality in England in the nineteenth and twentieth centuries", in *Up against nature: essays on history, sexuality and identity*, J. Weeks (ed.) (London: Rivers Oram Press, 1991) pp. 10-45.
57. P. Wagner, "The pornographer in the court room: trial reports about cases of sexual crimes and delinquencies as a genre of eighteenth century erotica", in *Sexuality in eighteenth-century Britain*, P. Boucé (ed.) (Manchester: Manchester University Press, 1982), pp. 120-40, p. 120.
58. M. May, "Innocence and experience: the evolution of the concept of juvenile delinquency in the mid-nineteenth century", *Victorian Studies* **17**, 1973, pp. 7-29.
59. L. Mahood & B. Littlewood, "The 'vicious girl' and the 'street-corner boy': sexuality and the gendered delinquent in the Scottish child-saving movement 1850-1940", *Journal of the History of Sexuality* **4**, 1994, pp. 549-78.
60. M. Cale, "Girls and the perception of danger in the Victorian reformatory system", *History* **78**, 1993, pp. 201-17.
61. MJ/SPE/1870/27 Deposition 44 (GLRO).
62. MJ/SPE/1870/27 Deposition 44 (GLRO).
63. *Ibid.*
64. *The Times*, 12 August 1870, p. 11, c. e.
65. *The Times*, 15 January 1880, p. 4, c. c.
66. J. Neubauer, *The fin-de-siècle culture of adolescence* (New Haven: Yale University Press, 1992).
67. O. Wilde, *The picture of Dorian Gray* (London: Ward, Lock & Co. 1891).
68. E. Cohen, *Talk on the Wilde side* (London: Routledge, 1993), p. 20.
69. Director of Public Prosecutions, quoted in Weeks, "Inverts", p. 20.
70. Quoted in Weeks, *Coming out: homosexual politics in Britain from the nineteenth century to the present* (London: Quartet, 1977), p. 20.
71. A. Sinfield, *The Wilde century: effeminacy, Oscar Wilde and the queer movement* (London: Cassell, 1994), p. 149.
72. *Ibid.*, pp. 145-7.

Chapter 12

⠒

Women's crimes, state crimes: abortion in Nazi Germany*

Gabriele Czarnowski

On 29 May 1935, just over two years after Hitler's assumption of power, the domestic servant Hedwig F.[1] and her child died in a hospital in Munich. Despite the fact that she was in the seventh or eighth month of pregnancy, two weeks earlier Munich's Hereditary Health Court had ruled that she was to be sterilized on account of schizophrenia.[2] Instead of waiting until after the birth to perform the operation, the public health officer in charge of the case not only initiated immediate compulsory sterilization but also ensured that the advanced pregnancy was "interrupted" for eugenic reasons. He based his decision on an illegal circular from the head of the Reich Medical Board to the German medical profession, made without the knowledge of the courts and the ministries. Hedwig F. haemorrhaged to death from the caesarian section undertaken to induce premature birth. Her child lived for half an hour, perhaps dying from the absence of routine natal care. For this reason, Ms. F.'s acting guardian submitted criminal charges against the participating physicians to the Munich public prosecutor's office. With the agreement of the Reich Minister of Justice the prosecutor's office halted the proceedings in January 1936.[3]

During the afternoon of 24 October 1944, in the last few months of the Second World War, the former midwife Marie B. was executed in Hamburg at the age of 77. Although her criminal record was otherwise clear, seven months earlier the Hamburg regional superior court (*Landgericht*) had sentenced Marie B. as a "dangerous habitual offender" to 12 years' penal servitude for 29 counts of "commercial abortion"[4] committed between 1935 and February 1943. She admitted to having performed abortions over a period of decades

* Translated by Marlene Schoofs

238

and estimated the total number to be around 150. Following an appeal by the public prosecutor's office, the Supreme Court changed the sentence to the death penalty. Although even the Hamburg Gauleiter was in favour of a pardon in view of the woman's advanced age, this was denied by the Reich Minister of Justice citing "authorization by the Führer", and the sentence was carried out.[5]

The fates of these two women and the child illustrate the extreme poles of the scope of National Socialist abortion policy, the former case from an early period of Nazi rule and the latter a few months before its demise. Policy spanned compulsory sterilization and infanticide by deliberate negligence on the one hand, and capital punishment for repeated abortion on the other. Hedwig F. and her child were victims of National Socialist negative eugenics that sought to promote the "eradication of the hereditarily diseased" by compulsory sterilization and abortion. Marie B. was a victim of the National Socialist battle against "criminal abortion", reaching its nadir in the Second World War with the physical elimination of abortionists.

Abortion, abortion policies and prosecution of "criminal" abortions in the Nazi era have yet to be analysed in systematic or comprehensive form. Thus far they have been treated as topics peripheral to other issues or only isolated aspects of them have been studied. Among historians, the primary approach to this area has been to discuss whether repressive abortion policies were responsible for the rise in the birth rate during the 1930s.[6] This has generated a debate as to whether Nazi population policies can be described more accurately in terms of pronatalism or antinatalism, a debate which has generally been carried out on the basis of a very narrow pool of sources. While abortion as one instrument of Nazi racism and antinatalism has been discussed,[7] virtually no work has been done on the prosecution of clandestine abortions. The failure to examine criminal records may partially account for why the executions for abortion carried out from 1942 to 1945 remain largely unknown.[8] Historians have to date either overlooked these events entirely or assumed that capital punishment was not imposed on Germans.[9] My research now suggests that the question of the primacy of pronatalism or antinatalism cannot be resolved in favour of one or the other.[10] Nazi Germany developed a comprehensive and sophisticated system of selective reproduction: it entailed the entire spectrum from prosecuting and prohibiting abortion to permitting and coercing it. On the one hand, these policies aimed to destroy the traditional subcultural structures that enabled women to a certain extent to end unwanted pregnancies even during the Nazi period. On the other hand, a complex administrative system was set up for those abortions authorized, desired, and/or compelled by the state for medical, eugenic and racial reasons.

This essay elucidates some of the previously neglected aspects of abortion in Nazi Germany. The different types of action taken by the state against the "criminal underground" are examined, with particular attention to capital punishment, and the impact of these policies on women with unwanted pregnancies. This discussion is preceded by a historical outline of penalties for abortion in Germany and a survey on abortion policies during the 12 years of Nazi rule.

Abortion as a crime in German history

Abortion, along with infanticide, numbered among the classic "female" crimes. The German Penal Code of 1871 prescribed punishment both for women who took measures against themselves and for those who had their foetuses killed in the womb or aborted by third parties, as well as for these third parties. Attempts were punishable whether or not they were successful, as was the procurement of abortion instruments or abortifacients. Crime statistics for the first half of the twentieth century thus show abortion as one of the few crimes for which women constituted the majority of persons convicted. Women composed roughly two-thirds of the total. In addition to those who either were pregnant or thought they were, these figures included female family members, work associates or neighbours who had assisted them as well as professional female abortionists. The considerably lower number of men were convicted primarily for aiding and abetting, but in some cases for performing simple or commercial abortion.

The first secular legislation in Germany was found in the Imperial Law Code of Charles V (*Peinliche Gerichtsordnung*) of 1532 and provided the death penalty for aborting "a living child".[11] The death penalty for this offence was eliminated in the German states in the course of the eighteenth century and the penalty progressively lessened. Parallel to this lessening of the penalty, however, there was an extension to the temporal limits for the act of abortion. They increasingly came to include the early stages of pregnancy, even well before the child in the womb begins to move, which had long been considered a definitive sign of "a living child". This evolved against a background of changing developments in embryology and in conjunction with the transition in deliveries by midwives to those by obstetricians, usually male, who were increasingly engaged in overseeing and restricting midwifery.

The abortion law (§218 of the Penal Code of 1871, which became binding for all the German states when the Reich was formed) provided for penal servitude for the pregnant woman as the standard penalty in the case of abortion, or imprisonment for a minimum of six months under mitigating circumstances. It was not until the reform of 1926 that the pregnant woman's act was reclassified from a felony to a misdemeanour. Penal servitude was replaced by imprisonment and the minimum sentence reduced to a term of a few days or a modest fine.[12] In contrast, commercial abortion - as an act performed for money - remained subject to penal servitude after 1926, as did operations performed without the consent of the pregnant woman. In 1927 the Reich Supreme Court allowed pregnancy terminations on medical grounds in emergency cases which the Reichstag had failed to legalize a year before. This was the state of prohibition and permission regarding abortion when the National Socialist Party entered government in January 1933.

Chronology of Nazi abortion policies

The Nazi state was ruled not by justice but by injustice though functioning in many respects in accordance with a legal system. As a racial state, it did not recognize general human rights, but rather special rights (*Sonderrechte*) based on eugenic, medical and "racial" classifications. The extent to which this was true for abortion policies can be seen in the systematic change in placement of the abortion article in the draft of a National Socialist People's Penal Code of 1937. Abortion was no longer located in the section on "crimes and offences against life" as it was in the Penal Code of 1871, but appeared under the heading "assault on race and genetic heritage" in the section on "protection of national vitality" (*Schutz der Volkskraft*). National Socialist abortion policies represented an unremitting subversion of the prohibition on abortion by urging or coercing abortion for "hereditarily diseased" women and those of "alien races" (*fremdes Volkstum*), while simultaneously restricting, prosecuting and increasing the penalties for abortion on women of the preferred "race" with "valuable" or "flawless hereditary material".

As its first measure to restrict voluntary abortions, in May 1933 the new government prohibited newspaper advertisements of abortifacients and of abortion services which had been a widespread practice in the Weimar period.[13] The ban of advertisements of abortion services was designed to rob the teams of medical abortionists and midwives of their clients, particularly women coming to the large cities, and thus to put a stop to their business. Advertisements in medical and pharmaceutical journals were exempt. In July 1933 the cabinet passed the Law for the Prevention of Hereditarily Diseased Progeny as the basis for compulsory eugenic sterilizations.[14] Because it omitted pregnancy terminations, the head of the Reich Medical Board, Dr Gerhard Wagner, in a confidential memorandum to physicians, called for this "loophole in the law" to be closed and for eugenic terminations to be performed "until all hereditarily diseased persons have been sterilized".[15] He assured physicians impunity with the backing of Hitler and without informing the judiciary. Consent on the part of the women was considered irrelevant, and there was no time limit after which the operation could not be performed.

This deliberate violation of the law, together with the first abortion rulings by the Hereditary Health Courts, led to the Sterilization Law being changed in 1935 to combine both anti- and pronatalist agendas.[16] On the one hand, pregnancy terminations on racial hygienic grounds were legalized up to sixth months of pregnancy if the woman was also compulsorily sterilized. The two operations were to be combined as far as possible, and the law stated that the woman was to consent to the abortion. It remains an open question in how far the physicians in public health offices and hospitals actually respected women's wishes regarding their pregnancies after this change in the law. Surviving files document both that compulsory abortions were performed and that compulsory sterilizations were delayed until after delivery. And on the other hand, pregnancy terminations on medical grounds were permissible for the first time in law rather than by a legal ruling, as in 1927. In return for his concession on women's consent to eugenic abortions, Dr Wagner was given official authority by the state to organize the process for therapeutic abortions.

The introduction of abortion on medical grounds into the German penal code, however, was anything other than a liberalization of pregnancy terminations. For women and doctors the legalization of abortion on medical grounds brought universally instituted restrictive bureaucratic procedures. The Nazi reform required a specific new and arduous process of assessment. Whereas in Weimar Germany women had to consult two doctors, but these could be of their choice, who decided independently whether a termination was justified on medical grounds, by 1935 a Reich-wide system of assessment centres for therapeutic pregnancy terminations and sterilizations was set up under the auspices of the Reich Medical Board. Women no longer had a free choice of doctors when seeking a termination of pregnancy, and the operation had to take place in a hospital. In contrast to Weimar Germany, the Nazi process removed abortions from the private doctor-patient relationship, disempowered general practitioners and family doctors in favour of clinicians and restricted the determination of grounds to purely scientific indications.[17] The number of abortions performed on grounds of health declined dramatically in the Nazi period. In 1932, the last year of the Weimar Republic, as many as 34,612 cases were reported but only 1,949 were reported for 1936. In the time between October 1935 and December 1940 (a little over five years), only 9,701 abortions on medical grounds were deemed justified by the assessment centres; but 4,072 applications by family doctors to perform terminations were turned down. At least 62 women among those whose requests had been rejected died.[18] In contrast, the number of terminations on eugenic grounds combined with compulsory sterilizations is estimated at 30,000 for the period from 1934 to 1945; the number of deaths is unknown.[19] Hedwig F. was one of the victims.

The third significant item regarding abortion in the Sterilization Law of 1935 was the introduction of mandatory registration by name at the public health offices of pregnancy termination, miscarriage and premature birth. This comprehensive documentation programme was the first attempt to establish a detailed overview of the extent of premature births. It also facilitated tracing clandestine abortions by fostering co-operation between public health officers and criminal investigation departments. The police, too, developed innovative methods to combat widespread abortion. In 1936 Himmler as chief of the police founded the Reich Headquarters for Combating Homosexuality and Abortion within the Prussian (later the Reich) Department of Criminal Investigation.[20] The Reich Headquarters sent specialized Gestapo teams to assist the local criminal police and set up a central index of commercial abortionists compiled from the reports of the local police authorities and public pro-secutors' offices. By 1939/40 this index already contained 8,000 names.[21] The considerable rise in criminal charges for abortion between 1936/37 and 1939, the start of the Second World War, can be traced in large part to these intensified efforts to illuminate the "criminal subculture".

The subversion of §218 on racial lines began with the deliberations by the courts in abortion cases involving Jewish women. Thus, for example, the court of lay assessors (*Schöffengericht*) in Lüneburg acquitted a Jewish domestic worker of attempted abortion in 1938.[22] In contrast, the jury court (*Schwurgericht*)[23] in Hanover did convict two Jewish women of abortion the year after – but for the following reasons:

Entirely free and unrestricted authorization of abortion for Jewish persons living in Germany cannot be permitted, regardless of how undesirable such progeny may be from the *völkisch* standpoint . . . German women in whom the will for children has not been sufficiently strengthened despite all educational efforts would all too easily find their way to . . . Jewish abortionists.[24]

As early as 1937 the draft of the National Socialist People's Penal Code (which was never enacted) also proposed legalised abortion following illegal sexual relations between Jewish and non-Jewish Germans, the so-called racial defilement legislation (*Rassenschande*).[25] Judges from a Nürnberg court, how-ever, followed the 1936 decision of the Supreme Court that declared abortion as "not justified by the attempt to prevent the procreation of a person of mixed race".[26] This early Supreme Court ruling shows how quickly and pro-foundly the logic of the 1935 "Nürnberg Race Laws"[27] had entered into judicial considerations on penalties for abortion, even when that logic was still being rejected. Six months after the start of the Second World War the question of abortion for Jewish women was raised again, this time by Wagner's successor, Conti, the new head of the Department of Health at the Reich Ministry of the Interior, at an interministerial meeting at the Reich Ministry of Justice. Conti also called for capital punishment for commercial abortionists. At this meeting the Justice Ministry representative, Roland Freisler, still considered the intro-duction of capital punishment to be "going too far", whereas two years later he promoted it. Regarding the "question of pregnancy termination for Jewish women at their own initiative", Conti and Freisler decided to postpone a decision "until the outcome of the Jewish problem in the *Altreich* can be more clearly anticipated".[28] In September 1940, without the knowledge of the Reich Ministry of Justice, Conti issued a secret decree to the public health offices and medical councils. Citing "special authorization", it permitted abortion and sterilization on "racial" grounds, following rape, on the grounds of "hereditary disease on the part of the progenitor" and other "cases not addressed by the law in which . . . pregnancy termination seems advisable".[29] These cases were judged by the same body that was responsible for killing disabled and Jewish children in special hospitals, namely the so-called Reich Committee for Scientific Registration of Serious Hereditary and Inherent Diseases.[30] Subsequent decrees pointed out that prostitutes and Polish women ought to be targets of this ruling, too. Parallel to this, a police decree dictated that "moral crimes and abortions among Poles" not be prosecuted if Germans were not involved.

The main abortion article 218 of the penal code was not changed until 1943. Its "reform" entailed both a dramatic increase in the severity of the penalty and an abrogation of this very penalty, depending on who had performed the operation and on which pregnant woman. On the one hand, penal servitude was re-introduced as the standard punishment for abortionists and even used for the aborting woman "in particularly serious instances". For multiple abortions on German women, the death penalty was instituted on account of "repeated injury to the vitality of the German people". On the other hand, article 218 was "not to be applied to offences against persons who are not of German ethnicity and citizenship".[31] Thus Polish and Czech women and those assisting them in occupied Poland and Czechoslovakia were not prosecuted in German courts, as long as their influence did not extend to any "ethnic German" women. And this provision also treated with impunity Germans who performed abortions on foreign women. For it was around this time that Conti initiated mass abortions on Polish and Russian forced labourers within the Reich. Starting in mid-1943, the decisions regarding these high numbers of "racially" stipulated abortions were made by the same bodies responsible for placing as many restrictions as possible on abortions on medical grounds for German women, namely the assessment centres for pregnancy terminations.[32]

These terminations on female forced labourers were also subject to selection. If pregnant Polish women and girls were "of good race" (*gutrassisch*) according to medical opinion, they had to undergo a "race examination" by a so-called fitness assessor from the SS Race and Settlement Office (*Rasse- und Siedlungshauptamt-SS*). He decided whether the termination was to be permitted or prohibited in accordance with the same procedure used for the "Germanization" of the Polish population in those parts of occupied Poland that in 1939 were integrated into the German Reich.[33] The same was true for women from the Soviet Union if they claimed to be pregnant by a German or "Germanic" man. If the "race examination" found a "desired addition to the population", the abortion was forbidden and the baby taken from the mother after a while in order to turn it into a proper "German child". With or without a "race examination", abortions were performed on the majority of these women, generally with coerced consent. Many forced labourers who had managed to avoid having an abortion by keeping their pregnancy secret, however, could no longer save their children. Thousands of "foreign national" (*fremdvölkisch*) infants were separated from their mothers shortly after birth and kept in unsuitable places such as garages, stalls or huts. Almost all died from malnutrition and neglect.[34]

The extent of clandestine abortions

Although the number of therapeutic abortions performed within confidential physician-patient relationships during the Weimar Republic was very high compared to that of the National Socialist period, it still represented only a fraction of all pregnancy terminations. As Cornelie Usborne has shown, it was more common for abortions to be performed outside the official medical establishment than within it.[35] Most of these abortions occurred in communities widely condoning these practices and remained therefore largely undetected. They were generally carried out with care and to the satisfaction of the women concerned.[36] Marie B., the midwife executed in Hamburg, would be a typical example in this regard. She had been active for decades, apparently no deaths or disabilities had resulted during this time, and she was not apprehended by the police or the courts. It is not known why she fell into the hands of the police in 1943. Although the majority of abortions were not performed by physicians, many women consulted doctors or midwives if they haemorrhaged after an abortion or natural miscarriage. This was the starting point for the mandatory registration initiated in 1935. It had two aims: first, to combat abortions within the sphere of private doctor-patient relations but more especially to combat clandestine abortions by commercial abortionists; and secondly, the establishment of new Reich Statistics of Miscarriages aimed for an overview of the extent of those "premature births" above and beyond the tightly restricted abortions on medical grounds, and eugenic terminations desired by the state. What form did this mandatory registration take? What consequences did it have? Every miscarriage, every perinatal death, every premature birth up to the eighth month of pregnancy and every pregnancy termination on medical grounds had to be reported within three days by the attending midwife or physician to the appropriate public health office on a form standardized throughout the Reich: the woman's name, address, number of children and marital status; the age, size and sex of the foetus, where the expulsion took place, the cause and information pertaining to possible illegal conduct.[37] From these very intimate details regarding women's bodies public health officers had to pass on the following data: number of pregnancy terminations on medical grounds, number of miscarriages, number of premature births, those with febrile complications. The Reich Statistics of Miscarriages did not compile figures for eugenic pregnancy terminations. Thus the principle of eugenic selection operated even within statistics.

Medical statisticians praised the new quality of the data from this gigantic operation as a masterpiece of German organization. They were no longer dependent on estimates based on extrapolating figures from health insurance, medical institutions and childbed fever, or on miscarriage statistics from individual municipalities, but could use the individual cases registered to generate statistics of an unprecedented reliability. In the first three years the public health agencies reported around 200,000 cases per year.[38] Physicians and the police agreed that by far the largest share of the 200,000 miscarriages registered annually were in fact abortions. Estimates here centred around 90 per cent; but estimates differed regarding the number of miscarriages that remained unregistered. Whereas the number of criminal abortions in the Weimar Republic was thought to be between 400,000 and one million per year,[39] the number of undetected cases during the Nazi period was estimated between 120,000 and 600,000 each year.[40] In view of these figures, many then lamented the general lack of success in combating abortion. Nevertheless, mandatory registration did reveal many cases which otherwise would not have become known.

As to how effective those "mandatory registrations" were in leading to prosecutions for criminal abortions, events in Hamburg show that the number of cases registered outstripped the resources and personnel available to investigate them: in this city, not nearly all those women reported could actually be interrogated and examined. At any event, the investigations by the public health office in Hamburg were discontinued at the start of the war,[41] though the police, in Hamburg as elsewhere, continued to investigate cases on the basis of registration data. In Nürnberg, for example, extant trial reports show that the criminal investigation department was pursuing in 1941 the miscarriages registered in 1938.[42] In the city of Düsseldorf, 110 abortionists (male and female) were convicted of 688 counts of abortion from January 1937 to April 1941 on the basis of miscarriages registered. Those convicted included eight physicians, seven midwives and seven health practitioners.[43]

In view of the strict monitoring, far more women turned to self-help procedures during the Third Reich than during the more liberal Weimar Republic. Articles in professional medical journals were in agreement that a change in abortion methods took place. A study based on the registration forms in Hamburg stated that "of the demonstrated criminal miscarriages, self-performed abortions have increased in number whereas commercial abortions and those performed by others have undergone a decline".[44] A similar finding was reported by a public health physician from Dortmund, an industrial city in the Ruhr district.[45] A gynaecologist generalized beyond his home district of Kiel that "knowledge required for self-performed abortions has increased and plays a significant role today". What most surprised him was the "skill" which the women displayed in light of how difficult "we gynaecologists" know it is "to hit the cervix" (!). The women's knowledge, he continued, was usually obtained "from acquaintances who have done it before".[46] It can not necessarily be concluded that this "self-help" was in fact more dangerous and led to a greater number of injuries and deaths. As another gynaecologist from Kiel noted, "One comes across cases of severe blood poisoning to a conspicuously infrequent degree." And he added the conjecture "that they are going about it – at least in our area – under more sterile conditions than they used to".[47]

Despite all efforts on the part of public health officials, police and the judicial system, it was difficult to prove in retrospect that a "criminal" abortion had taken place, especially if the operation had been carried out with care, whether self-performed or otherwise. Public officers of health, gynaecologists and police surgeons were in agreement that "there is no sure sign which distinguishes the criminal from the spontaneous abortion"; and "not all terminations accompanied by a fever are criminal, and by no means all criminal terminations are accompanied by a fever".[48] Not least because of the above, family doctors were increasingly criticized for not performing their mandatory registration duties to a sufficient extent and with sufficient care. Both the results of their examinations and their knowledge of the women and their family situations could be utilized to better effect in identifying criminal abortions. In the light of this background information it is revealing that family doctors constituted the overwhelming majority of all physicians convicted of abortion between 1937 and 1939 (although physicians were a minority of all people convicted).[49]

Criminal prosecution of abortion

In addition to the laws and decrees addressing the "crime of abortion" as such, there were also general laws and police practices that had an impact on both aborting women and abortionists among common criminals. This legislation manifested the characteristic dichotomy with respect to prosecuting abortion. The first such law concerning abortionists was the November 1933 Law against Dangerous Habitual Offenders and concerning Measures for Security and Correction.[50] It prescribed stricter penalties for "dangerous habitual offenders" that could extend penalties to as much as five years of penal servitude for misdemeanours and fifteen for felonies such as commercial abortion. For professional abortionists, the "measures of security and correction" could mean suspension or prohibition of their licence to practise their regular profession, but could also entail preventive detention or commitment to a psychiatric institution. Preventive detention usually meant an indefinite period of imprisonment, although with a review every three years. Competing with these penalties handed down by the courts were those imposed by the police – "protective custody" (*Schutzhaft*) in lieu of the court-imposed penalty, before the latter began, during or even after its expiration. This meant being sent to a concentration camp for an indefinite period of time.[51] Parallel with these harsher penalties, various amnesties created an opposing current: the results of the proceedings by the prosecutor did not lead to trial in cases when the expected prison term did not exceed a certain duration. Those profiting from this were a substantial number of women who had induced their own abortion or had undergone one performed by somebody else. Women's accomplices also went unpunished under these rulings. But increasingly harsh penalties were handed down to abortionists, especially when the court suspected commercial grounds. It was not until the Second World War that the Reich Ministry of Justice exerted considerable influence on judges and the Supreme Court in an attempt to exact harsher penalties for simple abortions as well.

By the mid- to late 1930s, middle-aged and elderly midwives already comprised the majority of medical professionals convicted by the German courts for "commercial abortion". These data were compiled in an internal study carried out by the Reich Office of Statistics and commissioned by the Reich Ministry of the Interior.[52] The study showed a total of 880 medical professionals, of whom 528 were men and 352 women. Of these, 604 were convicted for having performed an abortion on others. Although male physicians (240) comprised the majority of all medical professionals convicted for abortion-related offences, they were convicted less often for commercial abortion. Ninety-five midwives were convicted on this ground as compared to 84 physicians (78 male, 6 female) and 74 health practitioners or nature therapists (67 male, 7 female). Women practitioners also received longer sentences. The "proportionally higher participation by (convicted, G.C.) female medical professionals in commercial abortion"[53] led to the consequence that the terms they served were often longer, and that almost half (48 per cent) of the women convicted for having performed abortions on others were sentenced to penal servitude, compared to a good third (38 per cent) of the men. The courts, however, ordered "security and correction measures" for twice as many men as women practitioners (89 men to 41 women, or 69 per cent to 31 per cent). Suspension of the licence to practise for up to five years in general after having served the terms was by far the most common (121, or 92.5 per cent), compared to 6 cases, or 5 per cent, of preventive detention and 3, or 2.5 per cent, of commitment to a psychiatric institution. Judicial practice did not only discriminate against women but also against non-doctors: whereas 73 per cent of all doctors convicted for commercial abortion were sentenced to penal servitude, among non-doctors the proportion was as high as 84 per cent (see Table 12.1).

Two years after the beginning of the Second World War an amendment to the penal code allowed "habitual offenders" to be sentenced to death[54] – a provision which was indeed applied concerning abortion. On 31 March 1942 at a conference for public prosecutors at the Reich Ministry of Justice, Freisler declared: ". . . we have a case in Oldenburg where an utterly criminal woman was constantly committing abortions and has been sentenced to death via the decree on habitual offenders. The decision has already been made that the execution take place."[55] The 42-year-old crane operator Hans F., too, was executed as a "dangerous habitual offender" for three non-commercial abortions performed in 1936 and 1943. In 1932 he had been sentenced to four years' penal servitude for between 110 and 120 counts of "commercial abortion". He had also served ten terms in the course of his life for theft and possession of offensive weapons.[56] According to National Socialist criminology regarding offenders, previously convicted or long-time abortionists were considered "incorrigible", and "predisposed" or "compulsive offenders".[57] From this perspective, their activities were considered particularly detrimental to "German national vitality" during wartime and could only be expiated and halted by the death penalty.

Table 12.1 Criminal abortions by medical professionals in the German Reich, 1937–39

Profession[1]	Doctors			Midwives	Health practitioners			Nursing professions[2]			Others[3]			Total		
	m	w	m+w	w	m	w	m+w	m	w	m+w	m	w	m+w	m	w	m+w
Number tried	240	13	253	189	129	10	139	47	123	170	112	17	129	528	352	880
of these:																
acquitted			58	18			6			18			18	79	39	118
convicted																
§218 II	99	2	101	65	44	1	45	14	13	27	37	4	41	194	85	279
§218 IV	78	6	84	95	67	7	74	19	27	46	23	3	26	187	138	325
Penalties																
prison	113	5	118	82	52	5	57	20	15	35	36	4	40	221	112	333
penal servitude	58	3	61	77	57	3	60	13	24	37	26	2	28	146	109	255
correct. measures	41	2	43	34	40	2	42	3	3	6	5	–	5	89	41	130
Age[4]																
21–49	142	7	149	57	73	6	79	28	25	53	48	5	53	291	100	391
50 and older	35	1	36	103	38	2	40	5	15	20	12	2	14	90	123	213

This table shows the total numbers of all medical personnel tried for abortion. The breakdown of the various categories of practitioners focuses on those who performed abortions on a third party, rather than on women who underwent abortions. It ignores a number of practitioners considered less relevant, such as medical students. This explains why the individual figures do not necessarily add up to the correct total.

1 M: men; w: women; m+w: men and women
2 Nursing professions: nurses, masseurs, masseuses; 83 of the nurses were convicted for having undergone an abortion
3 Others: chemists, druggists, retailers of hygiene articles; most of them were convicted for aiding and abetting abortions on others (§§218 II, IV)
4 Age of those convicted for having performed abortions on a pregnant women
§218 II: simple abortion on a pregnant women
§218 IV: commercial abortion

Table 12.2 Death sentences presently known from German courts in "Greater Germany" for abortion

Nationality	Habitual offender of the law		Criminal decree on Poles and Jews		§218 n.v.		Total
	Women	Men	Women	Men	Women	Men	
Polish	-	-	7	2	-	-	9
German	4	4	-	-	1	-	9
Austrian	3	1	-	-	2	-	6
French	-	-	-	-	1	-	1
Total	7	5	7	2	4	-	25

§218 n.v.: §218 new version: Decree on the protection of marriage, family and motherhood

In the same year – 1941 – the Criminal Decree on Jews and Poles introduced special legal rulings on the criminal prosecution of the population in incorporated Poland. This decree was exceptional in allowing unrestrictedly severe penalties, including capital punishment. "Anti-German convictions" sufficed to incur such penalties.[58] Ludwika W., a 74-year-old married fortune-teller was executed on 5 March 1943 in Inowroclaw, a town in the newly established Nazi administrative district of Wartheland in occupied Poland. She had apparently been consulted for much of her life by women seeking abortions. The Hohensalza special court (*Sondergericht*) sentenced her to death for performing abortions on four "ethnic German" (*volksdeutsch*) women at their request. The police and judiciary did not pursue proceedings for abortions which she was found to have performed on Polish women, although their statements were used against her.[59] The 67-year-old married Zofia M. was guillotined in Königsberg on 10 August 1944 for having complied with the urgent requests of a German (*reichsdeutsch*) nanny who was pregnant by her employer. As the defendant stated to the police, she had learned her skills from a doctor in Warsaw and had performed abortions since the end of the First World War.[60]

Decrees on punishing "war crimes" enabled German judges to become legal murderers in the later years of the war: the civil penal jurisdiction in Nazi Germany passed a total of approximately 16,000 death sentences, 15,000 between 1940 and 1945; more than three-quarters of these were carried out. In comparison, fascist Italy re-introduced capital punishment in 1931, but passed only 156 death sentences and carried out only 88 of them.[61] Against this background, the number of death sentences for abortion seems to be relatively low – but these sentences were nevertheless crimes on the part of the judiciary and the government. Up to this point my research has yielded 25 death sentences for abortion in the so-called "Greater German Reich" during the period 1942 to 1944 (see Table 12.2).[62] Twelve of the defendants, seven women and five men, one of them a doctor from Vienna, were sentenced to death as "dangerous habitual offenders". In nine other cases, the death sentences were based on the "Criminal Ordinance on Jews and Poles". These were passed on seven women and two men from the western parts of occupied Poland which had been incorporated into the German Reich. Four death sentences passed on female abortionists were based on the 1943 version of article 218. The national distribution of the eighteen women and seven men was as follows: nine Poles, nine Germans, six Austrians, and a French woman from Alsace. Four of the women were midwives, one a daughter of a midwife, and one had begun but not finished her education as a midwife. One abortionist was a former nurse, one had worked at a physician's practice before marriage. Two of the men were physicians. It is no coincidence that these two individuals convicted were a "Jew" and a "half-Jew". Jewish physicians were pursued especially tenaciously for abortions – even though they could not be incriminated as much as expected – and they were also given comparatively harsher penalties than non-Jewish physicians.

Nineteen of the condemned individuals were executed, fourteen women and five men. As for the others, we know the following. Three of the death sentences passed on Polish citizens were commuted to eight, seven and five years of "harsh penal servitude". But the reprieves probably did not save the defendants' lives. A 72-year-old Jewish doctor from Sosnowiec was handed over to the Gestapo when they demanded him "for evacuation" and it seems very probable that he did not survive.[63] The third large-scale deportation of Jews from Sosnowiec was taking place at this time.[64] And two abortionists from Poznan, a midwife and a midwife's daughter, were handed over to the police following their reprieves and sent to the concentration camp at Auschwitz. Their subsequent fates are not known. Nor do we know what happened to a young Polish man or the French woman. Extant files do not refer to executions, but it is not clear what happened to them otherwise. A death sentence from the Nürnberg special court on a baker's wife in November 1944 was not carried out, and after the Nazi period commuted to a prison sentence of one year and three months.[65]

Other abortionists were not killed directly by order of the courts but instead died during imprisonment, particularly in occupied Poland in the so-called "severe penal camps", or they were handed over to the police for "extermination by labour" as the Reich Minister of Justice and Himmler had arranged in 1942.[66] Of the 58 women who had been convicted of abortion in 1937 and 1940–44 and who were inmates of the Polish Women's Prison in Fordon on the Weichsel River, 2 died during their imprisonment, 27 were handed over to the Gestapo during or after their terms, and according to the files 13 died at Auschwitz shortly after the respective "transfers".[67] Germans suffered this fate as well, such as the labourer Johanna P. from Munich who for one case of attempted abortion was sentenced (in 1934) as a "dangerous habitual offender" to a year of penal servitude to be followed by preventive detention because she already had a few convictions for abortion. She died a few months after "admission" to Auschwitz in 1943.[68]

These casualties of the later war years, which included an astonishingly high number of middle-aged and elderly women, among them many midwives, represent the culmination, both symbolic and actual, of the political and legal persecution under National Socialism of "criminal" abortions, i.e. those not authorized by the state.

Conclusion

During the National Socialist era in Germany, the conception of abortion as a crime was deeply embedded in the Nazi racial policies, and cannot be understood except in this light. On the one hand, "criminal abortion" was prosecuted as an "attack on race and genetic heritage" and this "crime" was selectively punished, to the extreme of death sentences and executions for abortions on "healthy German" women who were expected by the state to carry every viable conception to term. On the other hand and according to the same logic of "protecting" the "race and genetic heritage", numerous forms of intimidation and coercion were exercised on women to abort if their pregnancies were classified as "undesirable" for eugenic, racial and "ethnic political" (*volkstumspolitisch*) reasons, to the extreme of mass abortions on Polish and Russian forced labourers.

The legality of pregnancy terminations on medical, eugenic and subsequently racial political grounds was encoded for the first time in Germany under National Socialism. But if abortion was permitted, it was utterly without regard for the agency of women; rather, it was placed exclusively in the service of "higher" aims and was subject to external decision-making powers. If the wishes of the pregnant woman matched the rulings of the medical, state or party functionaries authorizing an abortion, it was generally pure coincidence. A decision for or against abortion was based on medical findings, professional judgment, hereditary assessment or the results of the "racial examination", but it never meant respect for the pregnant woman.

National Socialism dissolved the traditional matrix of abortion, criminality and (the female) gender. On the one hand, it sought to destroy the clandestine and private forms of the "old" criminal abortion culture by the most draconian means; and on the other, it decriminalized terminations of pregnancy by establishing certain grounds. But because these terminations of pregnancy were ordered irrespective of the wishes of pregnant women and were carried out against their will, abortion ceased to be a "female" crime and became a crime of the state against women.

The research for this chapter was made possible by the financial support of the Deutsche Forschungsgemeinschaft, Bonn and the Förderprogramm Frauenforschung of the Berlin Senate.

Notes

1. The name of Hedwig F. and all names of defendants and plaintiffs in this article are pseudonyms. The collections of the federal archive departments, *Bundesarchiv* (BA), cited here have in the meantime been largely moved to the BA Berlin-Lichterfelde.

2. In Nazi Germany approximately 300 Hereditary Health Courts affiliated with the general court system ruled on sterilizations, based on the Law for Prevention of Hereditarily Diseased Offspring, 14 July 1933. Compulsory sterilizations could be ordered if the court found one of the following grounds: congenital feeblemindedness, schizophrenia, epilepsy, manic depression, Huntington's chorea, congenital blindness or deafness, severe physical deformities or severe alcoholism. From 1934 to 1945 approximately 200,000 men and 200,000 women were sterilized. Cf. G. Bock, *Zwangssterilisation im Nationalsozialismus* (Opladen: Westdeutscher Verlag, 1986).

3. Bundesarchiv Abteilungen Potsdam, 30.01 RMJ/10161, f. 215-218, 10162, f. 104.

4. Up to 1943, the abortion article §218 of the German Penal Code (StGB) made a distinction between simple and commercial abortion. The latter was punished with penal servitude as an act performed for money, i.e. for business reasons; on the other hand, non-commercial abortion was punished with imprisonment.

5. Bundesarchiv-Zwischenarchiv Dahlwitz-Hoppegarten (BA-ZA D-H), 30.01 RMJ *Geschäftsstellen* IV g^2 4790/44.

6. T. Mason, "Women in Nazi Germany, 1925-1940: family, welfare and work", *History Workshop* **1**, 1976, pp. 74-113, 102f.

7. See especially the study of Gisela Bock, *Zwangssterilisation*, pp. 440ff.

8. An exception is the overview article by H. P. David, J. Fleischhacker, C. Höhn, "Abortion and eugenics in Nazi Germany", *Population and Development Review* **14**, 1988, pp. 81-112, which mentions three death sentences, one of which had been handed down in Germany and two in Austria during its incorporation into the German Reich.

9. See Bock, *Zwangssterilisation*, p. 163. On pp. 160f., Bock cites figures indicating that there were fewer convictions for the Nazi period of 1933-42 (39,902) than for the Weimar years 1922-32 (47,487). These figures do not, however, prove that National Socialists were less ardent in prosecuting abortion, because they handed out much more severe penalties.

10. This ambivalence is also emphasized by A. Grossmann in *Reforming sex: the German movement for birth control and abortion reform, 1920-1955* (New York: Oxford University Press, 1995), pp. 149ff.

11. For this paragraph, see G. Jerouschek, *Lebensschutz und Lebensbeginn: Kulturgeschichte des Abtreibungsverbots* (Stuttgart: Ferdinand Enke, 1988); B. Duden, "Die 'Geheimnisse' der Schwangeren und das Öffentlichkeitsinteresse der Medizin", *Journal für Geschichte* **1**, 1989, pp. 48-55; E. Fischer-Homberger, *Medizin vor Gericht* (Darmstadt: Luchterhand, 1988).

12. C. Usborne, *The politics of the body in Weimar Germany: women's reproductive rights and duties* (London: Macmillan, 1992), pp. 173f. Cf. also the English translation of the 1871 abortion law and the amendment of 1926 in Appendix I of Usborne, pp. 214f.

13. C. Usborne, "Wise women, wise men and abortion in the Weimar Republic", in *Gender relations in German history*, L. Abrams & E. Harvey (eds) (London: UCL

Press, 1996), pp. 143-75. J. Woycke, *Birth control in Germany 1872-1933* (London: Routledge, 1988), pp. 91f., 95.

14. Bock, *Zwangssterilisation*, pp. 80ff.

15. Bundesarchiv Koblenz (BAK), R 43 II/720.

16. *Reichsgesetzblatt* I 1935, pp. 773, 1053.

17. Reichsärztekammer (ed.), *Richtlinien für Schwangerschaftsunterbrechung und Unfruchtbarmachung aus gesundheitlichen Gründen* (München: Lehmanns, 1936).

18. C. Lauterwein, "Die Todesfälle in Großdeutschland nach Ablehnung einer beantragten Schwangerschaftsunterbrechung aus gesundheitlichen Gründen vom 1.10.1935 bis 31.12.1940", *Zentralblatt für Gynäkologie* 67, 1943, pp. 761-84.

19. Bock, *Zwangssterilisation*, pp. 388, 380, estimates that about 4,500 women died by forced sterilization altogether.

20. C. Schoppmann, *Nationalsozialistische Sexualpolitik und weibliche Homosexualität* (Pfaffenweiler: Centaurus, 1991), pp. 186ff.

21. G. Grau (ed.), *Homosexualität in der NS-Zeit. Dokumente einer Diskriminierung und Verfolgung* (Frankfurt a.M.: Fischer, 1993), pp. 154f.

22. *Informationsdienst der Reichsleitung des Rassenpolitischen Amtes der* NSDAP, BAK, NSD, 17/2-1938.

23. A *Schwurgericht* had five jurors and three judges, whereas the *Schöffengericht* had two lay assessors and one judge.

24. The sentence was published in *Deutsche Justiz* 101, 1939, pp. 572f.

25. BAK, R 22/855.

26. Staatsarchiv Nürnberg (StA N), *Staatsanwaltschaft bei dem Landgericht Nürnberg-Fürth*, Pr. Nr. 570.

27. The Nürnberg Laws of 15 September 1935 comprised the *Reichsbürgergesetz* which defined who was a Jew, and the *Blutschutzgesetz* which prohibited marriage and sex between Jews and non-Jews.

28. BAK, R 18/3806.

29. Institut für Zeitgeschichte München, MA - 1159.

30. Cf. E. Klee, *"Euthanasie" im NS-Staat. Die Vernichtung "unwerten Lebens"* (Frankfurt am Main: Fischer, 1985), pp. 294ff.

31. *Reichsgesetzblatt* I 1943, pp. 169-71.

32. Rundschreiben vom 11.3.1943, *Informationsdienst des Hauptamtes für Volksgesundheit*, BAK, NSD, 28/7-1943.

33. M. Hamann, "Erwünscht und unerwünscht. Die rassenpsychologische Selektion der Ausländer", *Beiträge zur nationalsozialistischen Gesundheits- und Sozialpolitik* 3, 1986, pp. 143-80; Robert L. Koehl, RKFDV: *German resettlement and population policy 1939-1945* (Cambridge, Mass.: Harvard University Press, 1957).

34. On this holocaust of infants for Niedersachsen, see R. Reiter, *Tötungsstätten für ausländische Kinder im Zweiten Weltkrieg* (Hanover: Hahnsche Buchhandlung, 1992).

35. C. Usborne, "Wise women", pp. 143-75; C. Usborne, "'Abortion for sale': the competition between quacks and doctors in Weimar Germany", in *Illness and healing alternatives in western Europe*, M. Gijswijt-Hofstra, H. Marland, H. de Waardt (eds) (London: Routledge, 1997), pp. 183-204.

36. Usborne, *The politics of the body*, p. 186.

37. Some of these registration forms are located for example in the Brandenburgisches Landeshauptarchiv Potsdam, Pr. Br. Rep. 45 D, Luckau 185.

38. E. Meier & H. Schulz, "Die neue Reichsstatistik der Fehlgeburten: Ergebnisse für die Jahre 1936 bis 1938", *Reichs-Gesundheitsblatt* **15**, 1940, pp. 349-57. On former abortion statistic methods, see S. Gross Solomon, "The Soviet legalization of abortion in German medical discourse: a study of the uses of cross-cultural scientific relations", *Social Studies of Science* **22**, 1992, pp. 455-85.

39. Usborne, *The Politics of the body*, p. 186.

40. E. Philipp, "Der heutige Stand der Bekämpfung der Fehlgeburt", *Zentralblatt für Gynäkologie* **64**, 1940, pp. 225-55, p. 242; Meisinger, "Die Bekämpfung der Abtreibung als politische Aufgabe", *Deutsche Zeitschrift für die gesamte gerichtliche Medizin* **32**, 1939/40, pp. 226-44.

41. H. Franz, "Zur Statistik des Abortes in Hamburg", *Der öffentliche Gesundheitsdienst (ÖGD)* **6**, 1940/41, Teilausgabe A, pp. 205-8, p. 208.

42. StA N, *Staatsanwaltschaft bei dem Landgericht Nürnberg-Fürth* Abg. 1984-85 Pr. Nr. 1447, 1475, 1489, 1499.

43. BAK, R 18/3806.

44. Franz, "Statistik", pp. 207f.

45. Med.-Rat Dr. Wollenweber, "Das Gesundheitsamt im Kampfe gegen den Geburtenrückgang", *ÖGD* **5**, 1939/40, Teilausgabe A, pp. 447-61, 455.

46. Philipp, "Der heutige Stand", pp. 245f.

47. Walter Schäfer, "Ausgewählte Kapitel der für den Amtsarzt wichtigen Frauenkrankheiten", in *ÖGD* (A) **5**, 1939/40, pp. 365-7, p. 367.

48. Philipp, "Der heutige Stand", p. 247.

49. *Abtreibungskriminalität* f. 227, see footnote 52.

50. *Reichsgesetzblatt* I 1933, pp. 995ff.

51. Cf. a general discussion of this area in L. Gruchmann, *Justiz im Dritten Reich 1933-1940* (München: Oldenbourg, 1988).

52. "Criminal abortions by health practitioners in the German Reich from 1937 to 1939" (*Die Abtreibungskriminalität der Heilpersonen im Deutschen Reich in den Jahren 1937 bis 1939*), BAK, R 22/1157.

53. BAK, R22/1157, f. 229v.

54. *Reichsgesetzblatt* I 1941, p. 549.

55. H. Boberach (ed.), *Richterbriefe: Dokumente zur Beeinflussung der deutschen Rechtsprechung 1942-1944* (Boppard: Harald Boldt, 1975), p. 440.

56. BA-ZA D-H, 30.01 *RMJ*, *Geschäftsstellen* IV g⁵ 1841/44.

57. D. Dölling, "Kriminologie im 'Dritten Reich'" in R. Dreier & W. Sellert (eds) *Recht und Justiz im "Dritten Reich"* (Frankfurt: Suhrkamp, 1989), pp. 194-225.

58. *Reichsgesetzblatt* I 1941, p. 759. Cf. D. Majer, *"Fremdvölkische" im Dritten Reich* (Boppard: Harald Boldt, 1981), pp. 606ff.

59. Archiwum Panstwowe (AP) Bydgoszcz, *Sondergericht Hohensalza* 891.

60. AP Warszawa, *Sondergericht Zichenau* 562.

61. Bundesminister der Justiz (ed.) *Im Namen des Deutschen Volkes: Justiz und Nationalsozialismus* (Köln: Wissenschaft und Politik, 1988), p. 206.

62. Since submitting this chapter I have found a further 15 cases involving death sentences. All cases will be discussed in detail in my forthcoming study *Abortion in Nazi Germany*.

63. AP Katowice, *Sondergericht Kattowitz* 1263.

64. *The black book of Polish Jewry* (Frankfurt: Syndikat, 1995), p. 158 (reprint of J. Apenszlak (ed.), *Black book* (New York: American Federation for Polish Jews, 1943)).

65. StA N, *Anklagebehörde bei dem Sondergericht Nürnberg* Nr. 2694.

66. H. Grabitz, "In vorauseilendem Gehorsam . . . Die Hamburger Justiz im 'Führerstaat'. Normative Grundlagen und politisch-administrative Tendenzen", in *"Für Führer, Volk und Vaterland . . .": Hamburger Justiz im Nationalsozialismus*, Justizbehörde Hamburg (ed.) (Hamburg: Ergebnisse-Verlag, 1992), pp. 21–73, p. 71.

67. AP Bydgoszcz, *Wiezienie Fordon*, Prisoners' files collection.

68. Staatsarchiv München, *Staatsanwaltschaften* Nr. 15696.

Chapter 13

♨

Gender norms in the Sicilian Mafia, 1945–86

Valeria Pizzini-Gambetta

Introduction

The aim of this essay is to analyse the meaning of gender norms that have operated within the Sicilian Mafia since the end of the Second World War. The Mafia is a criminal association renowned for being "full of male chauvinists".[1] In fact, it is an all-male group and no woman has ever been admitted into it.[2] In spite of their exclusion women have featured in norms upheld by this criminal group.

I argue that the exclusion of women and their symbolic status can be explained mostly by the use of violence by the Mafia and the establishment of the reputation necessary for the industry of protection to prosper. Gender norms have mostly supported these two essential tools of Mafia trade. Nevertheless an exclusively functional explanation of gender norms does not suffice to account for Mafia members' behaviour as it appears in court and in statements made by state witnesses. In order to make sense of this I focus on the Sicilian Cosa Nostra organization. First of all I give a methodological account of my sources, followed by illustration of the markers of Cosa Nostra identity. Then I argue how and why women have been excluded and illustrate their place in the Cosa Nostra code of behaviour. Subsequently I explain this gender issue in relation to the management of reputation. Finally, I conclude with a tentative explanation of how gender norms became part of Mafia members' beliefs.

One central area for analysis is the place of women in conversation and gossip within the Mafia. Mafia members refer to women in official talk, but they have hardly ever featured in small talk.[3] However, there has been neither shortage of gossip within the Mafia, nor lack of opportunities for such gossip. In the period under discussion in this paper members spent most of their time in the exclusive company of other men: celebration as well as everyday socialization happened among men only. Furthermore, the vagaries of their trade involved long periods during which *mafiosi* (Mafia members) shared close quarters and plenty of anxiety. They spent most of their time either in gaol, or in hiding during gang warfare. In these conditions small talk happens easily, and in exclusively male company women are usually one of the hottest topics of conversation.

However, according to insiders, *mafiosi* preferred to entertain themselves talking about the Mafia rather than discussing women. Transcripts of taped conversations confirm this. Furthermore, in their letters from prison, *mafiosi* tended to confine themselves to discussing their judicial trials. This contrasts with ordinary male prisoners, who wrote about women and prospects of future riches, as well as focusing on their trials.[4] These more diverse concerns accord with the interests of *macho* groups and Sicilian men in general. According to the Sicilian writer Vitaliano Brancati, Sicilian men believe that: "Talking about women gives more pleasure than women themselves."[5]

Contrary to *macho* mystique Mafia members generally seemed ill at ease in the presence of women. For example, during the 1970s in Palermo two prominent members could not hide their embarrassment when visited by an ordinary criminal from Milan. He was in the company of two shapely female professional dancers: "The two bosses", reported judge Giovanni Falcone, "glanced at them sneakily although with interest. They never looked them straight in their eyes".[6]

It would be wrong to explain this purely in terms of Sicilian backwardness or awe of beauty. Members of the American Mafia were more accustomed to "loose" women than Sicilian *mafiosi* were. Nevertheless they were equally uncomfortable in the presence of women. In 1984 Anthony "Duck Tony" Corallo - boss of the Lucchese family in New York - told a friend during a taped telephone conversation: "F—king guys . . . his wife comes to him . . . sends words to my cousin. And, ya know, sending a woman around us, *we don't feel right, we don't need her*".[7]

I would like to suggest that this surprising shyness with women stemmed from the fact that specific gender norms were crucial to distinguish the Sicilian Mafia from other criminal societies, and to assess the reputation of both the individual members and the organization.

Methodology

The word "Mafia" has often been misused to refer to Sicilian organized crime in general or as a synonym for collusive power; however, here I use it in a more specific way. It refers to a particular criminal organization called Cosa Nostra, based mostly in Western Sicily and known as the Mafia since the late 1940s. It is not to be confused with the American Cosa Nostra which, although bearing a similar name, is an independent criminal organization.

During the last 15 years a great deal of new information on the Sicilian Mafia has come to light, most of it from the so called Palermo maxi trial. This trial was held in court in 1986 to judge more than 700 alleged Mafia members.[8] It was based on the confessions of several insiders who turned state witnesses under a recently enforced Italian witness protection programme.

My sources are lengthy confessions by several of those who turned state witnesses between 1984 and 1993. Their lives within the Mafia span from 1946 to 1992. Tommaso Buscetta became a member in 1946, Antonino Calderone in 1962, Gaspare Mutolo in 1973, Salvatore Contorno in 1975, likewise Francesco Marino Mannoia and Vincenzo Marsala, Vincenzo Calcara in 1980, and Leonardo Messina in 1982. They belonged to different Mafia "families", both in urbanized areas and the countryside, and occupied different positions in the Mafia hierarchy. Thus this sample of Mafia members represents a diversity of regions, Mafia positions, and periods.

Their revelations allow a better understanding of source material previously collected. Witnesses against the Mafia, in fact, are not a recent phenomenon. Police officers were inundated by anonymous letters accusing people of being members and informants were in large supply. However, they hardly ever confirmed their statements in court. Now the information supplied by anonymous letters and informants can be matched with the recent confessions by Mafia members highlighting important aspects of the history of the Mafia.

Gender norms will not be addressed in theory, but rather described as they emerged from fragments of Mafia members' daily lives in Sicily since the end of the Second World War to the early 1990s. To do so we cannot trust blindly the words of *mafiosi* who turned state witnesses. They can hardly resist the temptation of accusing their enemies of having breached long-established rules[9] that may indeed have lapsed by the time the accusation was made. Although we cannot use the statements to assess soundly when a rule was established, we can still read through them to assess that a rule was actually upheld.

Ellikson[10] has shown that to trust "aspirational statements" is methodologically flawed even when the sources are ordinary people, let alone trusting them coming from thugs. According to Ellikson in order to assess the practical significance of a rule it is not even enough for it to be stated nor for it to be breached. Rather it is necessary to look at patterns of ordinary behaviour and at the application of sanctions. In other words, any assessment of a norm should take into account the daily life within the group upholding the norm itself. This is obviously difficult for historians, even more so when the topic is a secret society.[11] However, statements made by *pentiti* - the name under which *mafiosi* who turned state witnesses are known - and conversations taped by law enforcement agencies often yield fragments of daily life.[12] A great deal of the conversation among *mafiosi*, moreover, is about correct procedure and behaviour: that is, it is about acting according to the rules.

Cosa Nostra

Thanks to the information made available by state witnesses the mistaken belief that the Mafia represented a criminal behaviour in Sicilian culture has been overcome. The norms regulating such behaviour – honour, *omertà* (the vow of maintaining silence), friendship and reciprocity – had been explained as a set of cultural norms.[13] It is clear now that the Mafia was instead an organization[14] made of individual units called "families".[15] Each family ruled on a territory and was hierarchically structured. It was headed by a *rappresentante* (boss), whose aides were a *vice rappresentante* (underboss), and a *consigliere* (advisor). The underlings were called *soldati* (soldiers) and organized in groups each placed at the orders of a *capo decina* (head of a group of ten men).

What is still unclear, however, is when and how Cosa Nostra actually developed.[16] Evidence for the period before the Second World War remains fragmented. The confession of Melchiorre Allegra, a doctor from a village near Trapani, is one of the very few accounts about the Mafia given by insiders before the Second World War. He joined the "family" of the Palermo district of Pagliarelli in 1916 and confessed his membership in 1937.[17] Allegra's testimony will be considered as evidence for a plausible continuity and evolution of norms.

Apart from Allegra's testimony other evidence hints at several different sects since the second half of the nineteenth century and it refers consistently to Cosa Nostra only since the late 1940s. Nevertheless the evidence is sufficient to claim that several structured organizations have existed since the nineteenth century. Most of them were probably established as mutual help associations. They had an internal hierarchy and upheld a set of norms.[18] One of these fraternities, called Cosa Nostra at least since the late 1940s, has been more successful than others and still exists today. Its main focus shifted over time from protecting its own members, i.e. mutual help, to selling private protection. According to Diego Gambetta[19] each Mafia family today can be considered as a firm selling private protection. Cosa Nostra is the cartel that controls the market for private protection in Sicily. While the families remain independent, they recognize each other if they enrol their members through the same initiation ritual and share the same sign of recognition.

The history of the term "Mafia" is bound together with another term very important for this paper: "men of honour". The word "Mafia" is not necessarily helpful for understanding the continuity of the organization in Palermo. In fact, it stemmed from outsiders who used it to refer to a secret society they could not otherwise identify.[20] The word "Mafia" was used for the first time in 1865 in a report concerned with the underworld and the sources of political unrest in Palermo, prepared by the Prefect of that city for the Minister of the Interior. What was then called *Maffia* was a constellation of sects that might have had occasional contact with one another. They certainly did not share a common name or membership. Members of the secret society later to be known as Cosa Nostra have addressed each other as "men of honour" at least since the nineteenth century.

"Men of honour" were the thugs portrayed in *Li mafiusi di la Vicaria di Palermo*, a play written in 1862 by Giuseppe Rizzotto and allegedly based on first-hand information given by Iachinu Funciazza, inmate in the Ucciardone prison in Palermo. Funciazza was a member of a secret criminal organization.[21] Many have looked to the play for the origin and spread of the name Mafia.[22] It portrays life within the Ucciardone prison and the criminal authority that ruled it. The name of the latter, however, is *Camorra*, the old Italian word for organized crime. The name of the members of the Camorra is *omini d'onuri* (men of honour). In 1916 Melchiorre Allegra was admitted to a secret society "whose members were called men of honour".[23] The sect, he was told, was known as the Mafia; however, that word was never used and members addressed each other as "men of honour".

Tommaso Buscetta, member of the Mafia family of Porta Nuova in Palermo since 1946, declared that the name Mafia was a literary invention; the organization was named Cosa Nostra and its members called themselves "men of honour".[24] In 1987 Antonino Calderone, a member of the Mafia family in Catania, emphasized that those who underwent the initiation ritual were called "men of honour".[25] The ritual can be traced back to 1876.[26] Although minor variations have occurred, the ritual that is performed today is much the same as that uncovered between 1870 and 1880.[27]

Ever since the initiation ritual and the title of "man of honour" have remained the most treasured items of members' identity. Therefore, we can trace back at least to the same period the two main pre-conditions of membership: to be a man and to have honour. I shall consider in what follows the first of these terms; whereas the second will be the object of the section about the "professional code".

Exclusion of women

As far as I know no woman has ever undergone the initiation ritual, certainly no one since the Second World War. Mafia members are adamant about this and judicial files support this view.[28] This does not mean that women did not perform a role in support of the Mafia - a task they shared with many non-Mafia men in Sicily. Such support roles are however peripheral to the argument of this paper so will not be further discussed here.

Discrimination against women is the obvious starting point to analyse gender norms within the Mafia. Mafia members have explained this discrimination with *ad hoc* arguments similar to those given in other domains to justify the exclusion of women. They referred to women's inability to keep secrets or their being too emotional to be reliable *mafiosi*. These are inadequate arguments: not all women are too talkative or emotional, nor do all men bear silently with a "stiff upper lip". A better argument is needed to explain why women are still not admitted into Cosa Nostra.

Cosa Nostra has remained an isolated stronghold of exclusive maleness today. Even among other criminal societies in the south of Italy it is an exception. The presence of women is not a recent phenomenon in the Neapolitan Camorra and the 'Ndrangheta in Calabria.[29] The units of those organizations

were based on kinship ties and, as kin, women were involved in the functioning of the crime units. When men were killed or went to gaol their female
relatives could step in to keep the unit going.[30] Cosa Nostra, instead, tried to
prevent the overlapping of kinship ties and Mafia families. Often members of
the same natural family were refused admission or, when initiated, belonged
to different Mafia families.[31] Separation between kinship and the organization
excluded women from the Sicilian Mafia: the role they might accidentally
acquire through kinship ties would not be sanctioned.

Discrimination against women is hardly surprising in the Mafia at the turn
of the century. No profession allowed women into its ranks, and clubs and
associations were mostly segregated by gender.[32] However, the fact that Cosa
Nostra remains an enclave of discrimination requires an explanation. Traditional behaviour could hardly explain the discrimination against women in this
instance.[33] Cosa Nostra has proved its willingness to change in several other
fields regardless of its "heritage".[34] An alternative theory refers to the construction of masculinity. According to this interpretation the initiation ritual would
mark the passage from childhood to manhood of which membership of the
Mafia would be the representation *par excellence*.[35] This theory is fascinating.
However, it shows a superficial knowledge of initiation rituals. Rites of passage usually happen around puberty if not earlier.[36] Mafia members undergo
the ritual much later. The median age at initiation of the *pentiti* who are my
sources is 27 years. Moreover, rites of passage are staged to stress gender
differences and members of the opposite sex are aware that a ritual is being
performed, and may take part in it either in person or symbolically.[37] This is
certainly not the case in the initiation ritual into Cosa Nostra, performed
exclusively for men and by men. Femininity takes no part in it and it is not a
concern of the "men of honour" during the initiation ceremony.

Initiation rituals can be either rites of passage or rites of admission. La
Fontaine has pointed out that a rite of admission differs from a rite of passage,
since only the former gives access to a structured social unit.[38] The initiation
ritual into the Mafia is a rite of admission and not a rite of passage. It marks the
boundaries between Cosa Nostra and other criminal societies. To avoid confusion with ordinary criminals is of great concern to Mafia members. As Antonino
Calderone pointed out: "It is important to distinguish the real *mafiosi*, that is,
those who belong to Cosa Nostra, from the others."[39] This concern sometimes
emerged from the ritual oath proclaimed by novices. "This society is not the
Camorra nor the 'Ndrangheta" were the first words dictated to Salvatore
Migliorino, a member from Naples, during his initiation ritual.[40]

A more practical explanation for the lasting discrimination against women
in the Mafia can be found by looking at Cosa Nostra as the industry of private
protection. In this trade a reputation of toughness is extremely important. It
prevents violence from being actually performed, thus saving the resources of
Mafia members.[41] This might have discouraged the admission of women into
Cosa Nostra's ranks in the past and might still prevent them from becoming
members. In order to commit crimes, women need to overcome their reputation

of being non-violent and appear to be more aggressive than men.[42] Therefore a credible threat put by a woman needs a clear display of violence. From this point of view the admission of women would be a cost rather than a benefit for Mafia families.

It could be argued that external incentives to change might help to overcome women's handicap in the Mafia trade. In ordinary industries continuing discrimination against some categories of people has become extremely costly in the last few years since politically incorrect behaviour by firms' executives has been punished by customers boycotting their products. On the other hand, concurring with public opinion has been highly rewarded.[43] The pressure of egalitarian movements was among the factors that forced institutions such as English university colleges and the Army in many countries to open their ranks, often grudgingly, to women. Cosa Nostra, obviously, has never been under this kind of pressure and has not had any incentive to admit women as members. Moreover, women are not campaigning for equal rights within the Mafia. Rather they are gaining strength by participating in recently developed popular movements in Sicily that employ strategies of non-violent resistance to the Mafia. Women then have been little use as members of the Mafia but remain in great demand as shrines of Mafia members' reputations. This role is outlined and protected by the Cosa Nostra code of honour.

The professional code

It wasn't simply because of their Mediterranean culture that honour among *mafiosi* was important.[44] According to Alexis de Tocqueville, "every time men come together to form a particular society, a conception of honour is immediately established among them, that is to say, a collection of opinions peculiar to themselves about what should be praised or blamed".[45] Tocqueville does not give a definition of honour although he captures the ubiquitous presence of that concept and its relative content according to different reference groups. To have the right to be accorded "honour" is to be treated as an individual having a certain worth. This right is recognized by a reference group, can be acquired and lost, can be the object of a claim, and it is certified by the code of behaviour of the group itself.[46]

The object of honour among Mafia members is the reputation needed to supply credible protection.[47] The performance of the initiation ritual makes a Mafia family a proper reference group. Rites of admission usually give access to intangible assets like knowledge and bonding.[48] In the Mafia it also gives access to a more specific intangible asset: the collective reputation as reliable protectors that can be improved or harmed by members' behaviour. Therefore, during the initiation ritual the novice is told the golden rules of Cosa Nostra, the professional code that prevents their collective reputation being damaged. The *mafioso* code of behaviour can be explained by the organization's involvement in the protection industry.[49] This explanation is consistent with the fact that criminal or underground groups who happen to deal in protection developed similar, although not identical, codes of behaviour, no matter whether they lived in Palermo, Kobe (Japan), South Philadelphia, East London or elsewhere.

Codes of honour, then, are not given. Psychologists and game theorists have shown that norms can be established afresh through repeated interaction and that they lock in as arbitrary conventions.[50] They arise within groups according to mutual expectations and the group's ability to enforce the rules.[51] Such an ability is frequently displayed by the Mafia. According to state witnesses most of the murders perpetrated by Mafia members were to punish their peers who had breached rules of conduct. Norms about women were not excluded from harsh sanctions, and it is these specific norms that are considered next.

The rules listed in Appendix A are taken from rituals performed in Catania since at least 1962.[52] We have no entire decalogue for other provinces. Nevertheless statements from Palermo and other provinces indicate that these rules were widely practised. Mafia families, though, were independent authorities within their territories and it is not correct to assume that they shared an identical set of norms by default. In fact variations were not uncommon. The norms listed in Appendix B include those which were mentioned incidentally in statements by *pentiti*. These norms regulate behaviour in three domains: safety and secrecy; testing Mafia members' qualities as protectors; and enhancing their reputation.

Most rules about women emerged only after the Second World War. It does not necessarily mean that they were not practised before but there is no evidence for it. Basic norms about secrecy and self-help hint at a possible development, or definition, of those norms. Women became a feature of these general norms in this process. We could see it as a sort of cumulative course of learning and adjusting to circumstances. We cannot be sure that these rules have not changed since the foundation of the secret society. This is partly due to the different quality of the sources and to the uncertainty about Cosa Nostra itself. From the little information made available at the time, organizations discovered in the nineteenth century gave priority to secrecy, self-help, loyalty and mutual recognition.[53] These are basic needs for any secret society.

Secrecy, an obvious need of the society, was tight, and relatives of Mafia members regardless of gender were considered outsiders. It is not uncommon to encounter the following sentence in statements by *pentiti*: "We let him go since there was his wife; there were also other women, therefore we had to look for a private place to settle the argument."[54] The presence or sudden arrival of women usually froze conversations to guarantee secrecy and safety because women were assumed not to keep silence: their loyalty to the organization was not trusted.[55] Who would be loyal to a group of which she was not a member? Women were seen as more likely to be loyal to their natural family than to the Mafia unit. On the other hand, the convention of keeping relatives ignorant about Cosa Nostra was a protective device. It spared them the risk of coming under suspicion of leaking information about the Mafia families: the less one knew the less one could tell.[56]

Paradoxically, however, the same prejudice that engendered the rule caused it to be breached as well. Mafia members relied so much on women's alleged loyalty to their natural family that they admitted they always told female kin their whereabouts. In case something went wrong they trusted that their women would pursue their *vendetta* (revenge) and go to the police.[57] However, this seldom happened and we must conclude that there was plenty of wishful thinking on the side of *mafiosi*.

When Melchiorre Allegra was made a member in 1916 a few more rules happened to be mentioned. Murder was allowed but only if authorized by bosses. Theft, however, was forbidden.[58] In 1916, then, rules were no longer strictly functional to general needs of secret societies. They also banned or controlled criminal activities. There was no sign yet of rules about women. However, Allegra was a medical doctor, belonged to the middle class, was educated and practised an honourable profession. Probably he did not need instructions about how not to look like a thug. From his testimony his behaviour towards women conformed to the standards of his class at the time.

It was Tommaso Buscetta who mentioned norms about women for the first time in 1984. This evidence is among the most controversial and, at least in this respect, should be considered with great caution. He pushed more than anybody else the image of the "good old mafioso", and the protection of the "weak" is an obvious rhetorical device to pursue that end. However, at least on one rule we can trust him because he was sanctioned for breaching it. He claimed that his first crime had been: *"fare le corna a mia moglie"* (to be unfaithful to my wife).[59] Later on he confessed to killing several men. According to Buscetta these killings were the dispensing of his kind of justice: they were not crimes.[60] Killing, in fact, was a crime for Cosa Nostra only if not authorized by bosses. On the other hand, to lead a loose life was a crime in itself. Buscetta's membership was frozen in 1972 because of his weakness for women. Many Mafia members have suffered a similar fate. As a Sicilian saying reads: *"Per li fimmini e lu vinu, l'omu perde lu giudiziu"* (For women and wine, a man makes himself a swine).

Norms often rule on weakness of will[61] and the norm about not coveting other members' women was no exception. It has been explained as a by-product of the fundamental norm about self-help. Members were under a strong obligation to hide their peers in need of help, and temptations could arise in members' homes.[62] Group solidarity ran serious risks in those situations and this rule was taken very seriously.[63] It caused great anxiety among members since it was strongly enforced and sanctioned.[64] In at least one case it was among the reasons for the *mafioso* to turn state witness.[65]

Buscetta also mentions the rule against protecting prostitutes which is possibly the only one about women that has been enforced over the longer term, since the nineteenth century. According to Antonino Cutrera, a senior police officer at the turn of the century, *ricottari* (pimps) occupied the lowest level of the underworld in Palermo. They were usually young men between 18 and 30: hardly any pimp became old in that trade. They were either killed or convicted, or they retired upon marriage. Only after retirement were some of them enrolled as *mafiosi*.[66] The norm against pimping has never been relaxed,[67] rather it has been strengthened over time. Having a reputation for protecting prostitutes has prevented obvious candidates become members of Cosa Nostra.[68] Those who hoped to become members of the Mafia knew well that a reputation as a pimp would affect their careers.[69] The rule against pimping was seen by members as a *limen* (threshold) between "men of honour" and other criminals. Antonino Calderone claims – and he is not the only one – that men of honour are those who do not protect prostitutes.[70] According to Calderone a *mafioso* was not permitted to engage in every kind of business. Smuggling, fencing, theft, burglary, and obviously legal business were permitted,[71] but pimping, petty extortion, and loansharking were improper for a man of honour. Calderone explained the rule as "a matter of principle . . . Others were involved in prostitution . . . ordinary criminals".[72] Accordingly, *mafiosi* stigmatized other criminal organizations:

> The Calabrians – and the Neapolitans as well – allowed prostitution. When brothels were legal most of them made a living around those places. Sicilians never did. . . . we despise those who exploit prostitutes . . . For this reason we have always judged Calabrians inferior. Let alone Neapolitans, they did not even deserve our trust.[73]

Mafiosi's rejection of prostitution rested on the principle that women were not commodities. Closely linked to this was the idea that women deserved distinctive treatment: this was dealt with by the rule about proper behaviour. A Mafia member's reputation and his behaviour were tightly linked. He could lose his honour as much at the hands of women as at those of his male kin, his friends, and by his own actions.[74] To avoid boastfulness, to be a faithful husband, to keep one's word and repay one's debts proved a man of honour's propriety.

To have an ordered sexual life was strongly required among *mafiosi*. As in spy stories, a mistress could be a vessel of the enemy.[75] For this reason *mafiosi* were discouraged from behaving as womanizers and encouraged to settle with a woman: "a wife even if she knows that her husband is a criminal [. . .] is prepared to accept any hardship for the sake of a faithful and loving man".[76]

For obvious reasons the evidence for this statement is obscure. We can hardly pretend to know the part that such feelings as love, fear, self-deception or indifference played in the silence women kept about their men's business. There is only one published interview with the wife of a Sicilian Mafia member.[77] Felicia Bartolotta Impastato married a *mafioso* and her life turned into a nightmare when one of her sons became a left-wing campaigner against the Mafia in the 1970s. Torn between contradictory loyalties, Felicia Bartolotta kept silent until her son was eventually killed in 1978 after her husband died in a car accident. Felicia Bartolotta knew too well that her husband was a *mafioso* and that he was neither faithful nor loving. In her youth she was convinced by the local Mafia boss to forgive her husband and come back to him after she caught him with another woman. Nevertheless she never reported him to the police. She, as many other women, was under the illusion that the Mafia her husband belonged to was not all bad.

The integrity of marriage was at the core of the rule prescribing proper behaviour toward women. This has been explained as the desire to conform to middle-class moral standards.[78] This explanation does not however take into account that *mafiosi* with common-law partners were both accepted by their peers and promoted in the organization without reference to their irregular cohabitation. This behaviour is hardly compatible with traditional middle-class morality. Moreover *mafiosi* decided to conform selectively and pragmatically. They conformed in ways related to the needs of their trade, inducing trust and establishing a reputation of reliability. A steady marriage and proper behaviour toward women were excellent ways to prove one's trustworthiness: they were not values in and of themselves.

Marriage can be considered as a contract *par excellence*. Marriage meant a commitment for life in Italy, where divorce was not allowed before 1976. To cheat on a wife showed an inability to endure difficulties in order to keep one's word. "We were always very careful with our image," claimed Gaspare Mutolo in 1993, "because, if I scold, try to kill or force a boy to marry a woman because he was her boyfriend, I must be the best in the neighbourhood - where the *mafioso* is esteemed both by men and women - I must be a model".[79] A credible *mafioso* could not play around with his reputation and respect.

Steady marriages were also used to measure the status of Mafia families. Keeping mistresses attracted reproach. "In the family of Pippo Calo", the same source claims, "two or three people had lovers (it was called 'the family of street-sweepers' 'cause they had no morals)."[80] And again, "We did not think much of the family of Trapani," claims Gaspare Mutolo, "nor of Catania. They are different from the Palermo families. Some men of honour have [tarnished] origins . . . Others kept a mistress . . . For this reason we never thought much of those districts."[81]

Since behavioural norms affected the reputation of Mafia members they were extremely sensitive about them. It was best to avoid the topic of women in conversation altogether. If women were mentioned by *pentiti* as a topic of gossip, which was rare, it was either to criticize a fellow member[82] or to locate the cause of long-lasting rivalry among members. For example, when two prominent members were imprisoned together they had to be put in separate cells because they had come to hate each other. This was because one of them had referred in public to the other's punishment - his rank had been lowered - after his arrest in the company of a woman who was not his wife. Consequently, the latter's rage had to be restrained by the prompt intervention of fellow in-mates.[83] This episode was not a unique case. Contrary to obvious expectations, in this case no woman was the direct cause of rivalry between men: it was the rule regarding appropriate male behaviour that was the issue.

Generally, women were trouble and the whole topic was loaded with normative demands. To talk about them meant either to expose one's misconduct or weakness, or to cause offence to other members. Because of this there was a norm, silently enforced, not to bring up the subject in order to avoid trouble among fellow members. This rule deprived women of neutral status and promoted among *mafiosi* a sense of unease and embarrassment in their presence.

Reputation management

Rules about avoiding killing women and avenging wrongs done to them were drawn along the lines of reputation management. The prohibition against killing women applied only to relatives of Mafia members. In at least one case the breach of this rule was given as one of the reasons why a member turned state witness.[84] Female relatives were not to be victimized during gang warfare.[85] This rule marked the subtle distinction between Mafia wars and family feuds that has been apparent at least since the late 1940s. The latter involved natural families and women were not spared.[86] Mafia wars instead reflected the effort to keep Mafia units and kin separate. Wars broke out when disputes among Cosa Nostra members could not be settled by other means. They were strictly a matter for insiders.

Very few female relatives of *mafiosi* have been killed during gang warfare. In 1946 Antonia Greco, mother of Michele Greco, former head of the Commission,[87] became one of the very few women killed deliberately during gang warfare. Since then there have been at least two major Mafia wars in Palermo and its surroundings. Apparently no woman suffered any violence in the war of 1958 to 1963. In the war of 1978 to 1983 only six women died out of hundreds of casualties.[88] Their deaths apparently happened accidentally. Recently a few women have become targets of intimidation against *pentiti*. This does not necessarily mean that there has been a significant change of the norm. By seeking police protection *pentiti* forfeited the protection of the organization and as a result their female relatives lost their immunity. Besides, there is strong evidence that efforts were made to spare women even if they were in the company of male targets.[89]

The application of the rule, however, reached beyond what the "aspirational statement" claims. There is also evidence that *mafiosi* spared women *per se* even when they were caught committing crimes prohibited by Cosa Nostra. Kidnapping, for instance, was banned by the Mafia in Sicily during the 1970s and this rule was enforced rigorously. When a kidnap happened *mafiosi* searched all over Sicily to find the culprits. They duly found them. On one occasion, in 1977, among the kidnappers was a woman who should have been executed along with her male accomplices. But Gaetano Badalamenti, at the time head of the Commission, ruled to spare her. Since her crime had to be atoned her husband was killed instead, although he had not taken part in the kidnapping.[90] This punishment reflects the concept of personal liability applied within the Mafia. Each *mafioso* was responsible for the action of his own relatives and friends because they were considered his own property.

More convincing evidence about this rule, however, can be found in the way it was breached. Mafia members, in fact, killed women, both relatives of theirs and not, and did so to an extent we will never be able to assess. This happened either because they were asking too many questions about someone missing, or because they had been unfaithful. These executions could not easily be recognized as Mafia murders. Very conveniently a robbery was staged, or a shoot-out among drug dealers.[91] But why was camouflage necessary? After all, no rule had been breached: "No rule ever existed according to which Cosa Nostra prohibits the killing of women," Antonino Calderone sternly claimed.[92]

The principle of protecting women was excellent advertising for Cosa Nostra and this could hardly be consistent with the open execution of women. The foundation myth of the Sicilian Mafia is rooted in the adventures of the *Beati Paoli*, a fictional brotherhood that, according to tradition, protected the weak from injustice and violence in Palermo in the eighteenth century.[93] The *Beati Paoli* were actually mentioned during the initiation ritual in the Mafia. Several *pentiti* declared they had read the book, a considerable achievement considering that they were often barely literate.[94] This popular novel, along with the adventures of King Arthur's knights, made most of vernacular culture in western Sicily. According to this culture women were those to fight for. They could never kill or be killed unless they betrayed their own nature.

However, in order to protect secrecy and their personal honour among their peers, sometimes *mafiosi* had to execute women. Camouflage allowed them to manage their reputation according to different audiences. Insiders would understand the reasons for those murders but outsiders would not be able to attribute them to Cosa Nostra.

The outsiders instead were given ostentatious displays of protecting women. In the mid-1970s, for instance, a woman tourist had her handbag snatched in Palermo. Mafia families searched for the culprit, and found it was a petty criminal. Contrary to the usual habit of secretly disposing of the bodies of men they executed, the killers left this thief's corpse in Palermo city centre with a note written in poor Italian: "This is the bastard that hurt the tourist. This is how rats of his sort end up in Palermo".[95] Naturally the message was not signed but was later explained by a *pentito*.

Conclusion

Reputation had to be maintained as much within the neighbourhood as within the Mafia. Reputation, though, was an elusive asset and could not be assessed *per se*. Therefore it was attached to more visible items that became symbols of it.[96] Women were important for testing both reputation for toughness and reliability. To have one's women respected meant strength whereas to respect them and be faithful to one's own wife meant reliability. Symbols cannot be randomly chosen since their meaning must be able to be shared by those who need to assess the elusive good. In other words symbols are conventions and have to be rooted in local beliefs. For example, a colourful display of bird feathers on one's head would not quite do in Sicily as a display of reputation. On the contrary, the way in which women are treated and respected would.[97]

An exclusively cynical interpretation of the rules about women, however, does no justice to the problem.[98] It does not help us to understand why Mafia members are caught boasting among themselves about having helped women. As one of them claimed: "To protect a woman is always a fact to be proud of among Mafia members."[99] Neither does it help us to understand why *mafiosi* referred to behaviour towards women to enhance their own reputation and to challenge that of their rival. Jon Elster has pointed out that norms not grounded in belief fail to have the "grip on the mind" necessary to their enforcement.[100] The ambiguity around the concept of reputation is probably part of the belief formation process among members of Cosa Nostra.

A peculiar episode can help to illustrate this point. The *Beati Paoli* was quoted in court in 1993 during a heated exchange between Salvatore Riina, the supreme head of the Sicilian Mafia, and an accuser of his, Gaspare Mutolo. Riina raised the topic when he called Mutolo by the name of the police informant in the novel. Mutolo retaliated promptly, inviting Riina not to mention the *Beati Paoli* since he had betrayed the most important values the novel taught them, that is to protect the weak and not to kill women. The *Beati Paoli*, as any "gospel", is open to interpretation. What this episode should teach us is that both members of the Mafia aimed at the other's respective tender spots according to their own beliefs.

When Gaspare Mutolo and Salvatore Riina challenged each other on the *Beati Paoli*, they were not playing to the general public. They were challenging each other on their own terms. Behaviour as such reflects shared beliefs among members of Cosa Nostra. Belief formation, in this case, is the by-product of the inability of the mind to recognize the distinction between internal and external audiences for a member's reputation. Many members came to believe, so to speak, "their own press".

Appendix A

Mafioso professional code as proclaimed during the initiation ritual in Catania in 1962

1. Members must offer refuge to each other.
2. Members must not covet each other's women.
3. Members should never report a crime to the police.
4. Members must not steal from each other.
5. Members must not protect prostitution.
6. Members must avoid disputes among themselves.
7. Members must never pass any information about Cosa Nostra to outsiders.

8. Members must always behave properly.
9. Members must never introduce themselves directly to other members.
10. Members should be executed by other members only on reasonable grounds.
11. Members must remain forever loyal to their Cosa Nostra family.

Appendix B

Practical rules for *mafiosi* concerning women
1. Do not inform women about La Cosa Nostra activities.
2. Do not covet another member's women.
3. Be faithful to your wife.
4. Treat women with respect.
5. Do not protect prostitution.
6. Avoid talking about women.
7. Demand respect for your women.
8. Avoid killing a woman.
9. Avenge wrongs done to a woman.

Notes

1. N. Gage, *Mafia! Inside story of the Mafia in America and in Britain* (London: Talmy, 1973), p. 95.
2. G. Falcone & G. Fiume, "La mafia tra criminalità e cultura", *Meridiana* **5**, 1989, pp. 199-209.
3. The distinction between official talk and small talk can be elusive. Mafia members in fact claim they never gossip, since spying and secrecy are essential to their trade. Therefore everything they say is seen as a relevant statement and given official status. However, most knowledge is passed on privately and concerns personal matters that would qualify as gossip in different circles. See D. Gambetta, "Godfather's gossip", *Archives Européenne de Sociologie* **35**(2), 1994, pp. 199-223.
4. A. Grimaldi, *Mery per sempre. L'amore, la donna, il sesso, raccontato dai giovani detenuti del Malaspina di Palermo* (Palermo: La Luna, 1987).
5. Quoted in E. Biagi, *Il boss è solo* (Milano: Mondadori, 1986).
6. G. Falcone & M. Padovani, *Cose di Cosa Nostra* (Milano: Rizzoli, 1991), p. 78 (my translation).
7. Taped conversation cited in J. Goode, *Wiretap: listening in on the American Mafia* (New York: Simon & Schuster, 1988), p. 65 (my italics).
8. Tribunale di Palermo, Camera Penale, "Sentenza ordinanza della Corte d'Assise di Palermo contro Abbate Giovanni + 703", Palermo, 8 November 1985, Cambridge University Library.
9. Italian historians challenged this view, showing that trials were often the result of gang warfare. In these trials the losers would accuse the sometimes younger and more aggressive winners of having betrayed established rules. Today's losers were

invariably yesterday's winners and the tradition was re-invented over and over again. See D. Novacco, *Mafia di ieri, mafia di oggi* (Milano: Feltrinelli, 1972); P. Pezzino, "Per una critica dell'onore mafioso", in *Onore e storia nelle società mediterranee*, G. Fiume (ed.) (Palermo: La Luna, 1989); S. Lupo & R. Mangiameli, "Mafia di ieri, mafia di oggi", *Meridiana* **7-8**, 1990, pp. 17-45.

10. R. C. Ellikson, *Order without law: how neighbors settle disputes* (Cambridge, Mass.: Harvard University Press, 1991).

11. N. Passas (ed.), *Organized crime* (Aldershot: Dartmouth, 1995).

12. Excellent examples of this are among the transcripts of taped conversations published in Goode, *Wiretap*, and M. Haller, *Life under Bruno: the economics of an organized crime family* (Philadelphia: Pennsylvania Crime Commission, 1991).

13. The literature about the Mafia code as a set of cultural norms is huge and dates back to the late nineteenth century. Among the many see G. Pitré, *Usi, costumi, credenze e pregiudizi del popolo siciliano* (Palermo: Libreria Pedone Lauriel, 1889); H. Hess, *Mafia and mafiosi: the structure of power* (Lexington, Mass.: Lexington Books, 1973); A. Blok, *The Mafia of a Sicilian village* (Oxford: Basil Blackwell, 1974); J. Schneider & P. Schneider, *Culture and political economy in western Sicily* (New York: Academic Press, 1976); L. M. Lombardi Satriani, "Sulla cultura mafiosa e gli immediati dintorni", *Quaderni del Mezzogiorno e delle Isole* **14**, 1977; P. Arlacchi, *La Mafia imprenditrice* (Bologna: Il Mulino, 1983); R. Catanzaro, *Il delitto come impresa* (Padova: Liviana, 1988); C. Duggan, *Fascism and the Mafia* (New Haven: Yale University Press, 1989).

14. See the findings of P. Pezzino, *Una certa reciprocità di favori* (Milano: Franco Angeli, 1990); D. Gambetta, *The Sicilian Mafia: the business of private protection* (Cambridge, Mass.: Harvard University Press, 1993); S. Lupo, *Storia della mafia* (Roma: Donzelli, 1993).

15. "Family" is the acknowledged name of a Mafia unit. No one became a member of the Mafia as a single organization since membership was and still is strictly defined as belonging to a "family" and being subject and loyal to that family only.

16. See V. Pizzini, "La storia della mafia tra realtà e congetture", *Studi Storici* **35**(2), 1994, pp. 435-46.

17. The previously misplaced file on Allegra was unearthed by a journalist and published in a Sicilian daily newspaper, *L'Ora*, between 22 and 25 January 1962 (henceforth cited as "Allegra" followed by the date of the issue). A copy of the original document held among the documents collected by the Parliamentary Commission on the Sicilian Mafia between 1963 and 1975 is not available to scholars.

18. F. Lestingi, "L'Associazione della Fratellanza nella provincia di Girgenti", *Archivio di Psichiatria e Antropologia Criminale* **5**, 1884; G. Alongi, *La maffia* (Palermo: Sellerio, 1977, reprint of the original issue of 1886); A. Cutrera, *La Mafia e i mafiosi: origini e manifestazioni* (Palermo: Reber, 1990 reprint of the original edition of 1900).

19. Gambetta, *The Sicilian Mafia*.

20. For a subtle analysis of the meaning of the word and how it has become a brand name for Sicilian organized crime, see Gambetta, *The Sicilian Mafia*, pp. 127-55.

21. G. G. Lo Schiavo, *100 anni di Mafia* (Roma: Bianco Editore, 1964).

22. D. Novacco, "Considerazioni sulla fortuna del termine Mafia", *Belfagor* **14**, 1959, pp. 206-14; C. Lo Monaco, "A proposito della etimologia di Mafia e mafioso", *Lingua Nostra* **51**, 1990, pp. 1-8; Gambetta, *The Sicilian Mafia*, p. 136.

23. Allegra, *L'Ora*, 22 January 1962.
24. Transcripts of statements by Tommaso Buscetta, 1984, i, pp. 4-5, 3 vols, Cambridge University Library.
25. P. Arlacchi, *Gli uomini del disonore. La biografia di Antonino Calderone* (Milan: Mondadori 1992), pp. 3-4.
26. D. Gambetta, *The Sicilian Mafia*, Appendix II.
27. Cutrera, *La Mafia e i mafiosi*, p. 121; Lestingi, "L'Associazone della Fratellanza"; P. Pezzino, *Una certa reciprocità di favori: Mafia e modernizzazione violenta nella Sicilia postunitaria* (Milano: Franco Angeli, 1990), p. 211.
28. G. Fiume, "Ci sono donne nella Mafia?", *Meridiana* **7-8**, 1990, pp. 293-302.
29. V. Ciconte, *'Ndrangheta dall'Unità ad oggi* (Roma-Bari: Laterza, 1992).
30. Arlacchi, *La Mafia imprenditrice*; Ministero dell'Interno, "Rapporto annuale sul fenomeno della criminalità organizzata per il 1992", pp. 163, 182, Biblioteca della camera dei Deputati, Rome.
31. D. Gambetta, *The Sicilian Mafia*, p. 269.
32. It was only in 1919 that the Italian Parliament passed a law to enable women to practise any profession and to hold jobs as civil servants (L. 1176/1919).
33. P. Arlacchi tried to explain it as a remnant of traditional behaviour in "La condizione della donna in due tipi di società mediterranea tradizionale", *Quaderni del Circolo Semiologico Siciliano*, **26-7**, 1987.
34. Falcone & Padovani, *Cose di Cosa Nostra*, p. 23; Lupo, *Storia della Mafia*.
35. G. Casarrubea & P. Blandano, *L'educazione mafiosa* (Palermo: Sellerio, 1991), p. 103; R. Siebert, *Le donne. La Mafia* (Milano: Il Saggiatore, 1994), pp. 26ff.
36. D. D. Gilmore, *Manhood in the making: cultural concepts of masculinity* (New Haven: Yale University Press, 1990).
37. J. La Fontaine, *Initiation* (Manchester: Manchester University Press, 1986), pp. 117, 125.
38. La Fontaine, *Initiation*, p. 15.
39. Arlacchi, *Antonino Calderone*, p. 4.
40. "Seduta 12 novembre 1993. Audizione del collaboratore di giustizia Salvatore Migliorino", p. 3109, transcripts of statements by Salvatore Migliorino given to the Parliamentary Antimafia Commission, 1993, Biblioteca della camera dei Deputati, Rome. For an explanation of the Mafia members' concern to distinguish themselves from ordinary thugs, see Gambetta, *The Sicilian Mafia*, pp. 100ff.
41. Gambetta, *The Sicilian Mafia*, pp. 34ff.
42. A. Campbell, *Out of control: men, women and aggression* (London: Pandora, 1993), p. 98.
43. "Why bosses like it", *Economist*, 11 March 1995.
44. The concept of honour in the Mediterranean is extremely controversial and still unclear. See J. Davies, *People of the Mediterranean* (London: Routledge & Kegan Paul, 1978); D. D. Gilmore (ed.), *Honor and shame and the unity of the Mediterranean* (Washington: American Anthropological Association, 1987); Fiume, *Onore e storia nelle società mediterranee*. According to F. H. Stewart, *Honor* (Chicago: University of Chicago Press, 1994), honour is as widespread in Northern Europe as it is in the Mediterranean region.
45. A. de Tocqueville, *Democracy in America*, J. P. Mayer (ed.) (New York: Harper & Row, 1969), p. 620.
46. Stewart, *Honor*.
47. Gambetta, *The Sicilian Mafia*, pp. 45-6.

48. G. Simmel, *Sociologia* (Milano: Edizioni di Comunità, 1989).
49. For a theoretical explanation, see Gambetta, *The Sicilian Mafia*, pp. 118ff; Haller, *Life under Bruno* gives a contextual account of norms related to the protection industry in an American town.
50. On norms and repeated interaction, see C. Bicchieri, "Norms of Cooperation", *Ethics* **100**, 1994, pp. 839-911, and Bicchieri, *Rationality and coordination* (Cambridge: Cambridge University Press, 1993). On arbitrary interactions, see J. Mackey, "Ending footbinding and infibulation: a convention account", *American Sociological Review*, **61**, 1996, pp. 999-1017.
51. J. Coleman, *Foundation of social theory* (Cambridge Mass.: Bleknap Harvard, 1990), p. 242.
52. Transcripts of statements by Antonino Calderone, 1988, iii, pp. 734-8, 4 vols, Cambridge University Library; Arlacchi, *Antonino Calderone*, p. 56.
53. Alongi, *La Maffia*; Cutrera, *La mafia e i mafiosi*; Lestingi, *L'Associazione della Fratellanza*.
54. "Seduta del 9 febbraio 1993. Audizione del collaboratore di giustizia Gaspare Mutolo", transcripts of statements by Gaspare Mutolo given to the Parliamentary Antimafia Commission, 1993, Biblioteca della camera dei Deputati, Rome, p. 1233.
55. Calderone transcripts, p. 170.
56. *Ibid.*, pp. 165-6.
57. Arlacchi, *Antonino Calderone*, p. 171.
58. Allegra, *L'Ora*, 22 January 1962.
59. E. Biagi, *Il boss è solo* (Milano: Mondadori, 1986), p. 12.
60. P. Arlacchi, *Addio, Cosa Nostra: la vita di Tommaso Buscetta* (Milano: Rizzoli 1994), p. 6.
61. J. Elster, *The cement of society* (Cambridge: Cambridge University Press, 1989).
62. Arlacchi, *Antonino Calderone*, p. 56.
63. In many armies, for instance, officers' affairs with their peers' wives are officially punished.
64. Tribunale di Palermo, "Verbale di testimonianza della teste Beneddetta Bono", in "Procedimento penale contro Abbate Giovanni + 703", 1985, pp. 41, 58, in author's private possession.
65. M. Bettini, *Pentito: una storia di mafia* (Torino: Bollati Boringhieri, 1994), based on the life and statements of Vincenzo Calcara, pp. 131-44.
66. A. Cutrera, *La malavita di Palermo* (Palermo: Forni, 1900), p. 48.
67. Detectives and judges in the Palermo judicial district confirm that the Mafia has never been involved in prostitution: Camera dei Deputati, Commissione Parlamentare di Inchiesta sul fenomeno della Mafia, *Materiali allegati alla relazione finale*, leg. v-vii, vii, I, p. 660.
68. P. Arlacchi, *Gli uomini del disonore*, p. 5.
69. Tribunale di Palermo, Anselmo + 64, *Rapporto Honoratti*, p. 304, in author's private posession.
70. Arlacchi, *Antonino Calderone*, p. 5.
71. Although the prohibition of theft is stated in general, in Palermo it is applied only to other members' or customers' property.
72. Arlacchi, *Antonino Calderone*, p. 144 (my translation). The protection of prostitution is practised by other rings of organized criminals such as the Chinese Triad societies: see Che Yhu Kong Vin, *Triads: an economic analysis of organised crime* (PhD dissertation, University of Exeter, 1996). The American Mafia also

has a reputation for protecting prostitution, but the evidence is disputed. The MacClellan Report claimed that the American Cosa Nostra was involved in every lucrative criminal activity, including prostitution: Camera dei Deputati, Commissione Parlamentare di Inchiesta sul fenomeno della Mafia, *Materiali allegati alla relazione finale*, leg. vii, vol. IV, subvol. XIV, book I. A close examination of Mafia files by Mark Haller does not confirm that claim: Haller, *Life under Bruno*, p. 6; M. Haller, "Illegal enterprises: a theoretical and historical explanation", *Criminology*, **28**(2), 1991, pp. 207-35.

73. *Ibid.*, p. 141 (my translation).
74. Obligations to keep one's word, to repay debts, and not to compromise oneself in adventures whose results were too uncertain were of prime importance in regulating *mafioso* reputation.
75. Gambetta, *The Sicilian Mafia*, p. 121.
76. Mutolo transcripts, p. 1238.
77. F. Bartolotta Impastato, *La Mafia in casa mia* (Palermo: La Luna, 1986). More accessible seem to be the wives of American Mafia members: J. F. O'Brien & A. Kurins, *Boss of Bosses. The fall of the Godfather: the FBI and Paul Castellano* (London: Simon & Schuster, 1991); J. H. Davis, *Mafia dynasty: the rise and fall of the Gambino family of organized crime* (London: Coronet, 1993).
78. R. Catanzaro, *Il delitto come impresa* (Padova: Liviana, 1988); Siebert, *Le donne. La Mafia*.
79. Mutolo transcripts, p. 1239.
80. *Ibid.*, p. 1238.
81. *Ibid.*, p. 1245.
82. The only time a member is said to have indulged in talk about women and gambling was when Tommaso Buscetta spoke about Alfredo Bono, a member and prominent drug dealer. In so doing, Buscetta stressed the relationship between a tarnished spirit and a tarnishing trade (Buscetta transcripts, iii, p. 80).
83. Transcripts of statements by Francesco Marino Mannoia, 1990, pp. 28, 88, in author's private possession.
84. Mutolo transcripts, p. 1224.
85. This norm is clearly stated by Antonino Calderone, Tommaso Buscetta, Totuccio Contorno and Francesco Marino Mannoia.
86. For the illustration of several feuds where women were victims, see S. Wilson, *Feuding conflict and banditry in nineteenth-century Corsica* (Cambridge: Cambridge University Press, 1988).
87. The Commission is the acknowledged authority to settle disputes among families and between members and their *rappresentante*. There is evidence of a commission-like body being active at the turn of the century: Ministero dell'Interno, *Rapporto del Questore di Palermo Sangiorgi al Procuratore del Re, 8 novembre 1898*, Fondo ministero dell'interno, Divisione generale della pubblica sicurezza., b.1, f.1, Archivio Centrale dello Stato. It vanished afterwards. A commission was established in 1957 and dismantled in 1963. The commission mentioned by most *pentiti* was established in 1973.
88. G. Chinnici & U. Santino, *La violenza programmata* (Milano: Franco Angeli, 1989).
89. Felicia Buscetta, Tommaso's daughter, was spared by the men who killed her husband and two male friends of his who happened to be in the *pizzeria* where the massacre was perpetrated. The killers turned to the woman and said: "You don't, you don't [die]. We don't kill women" (*La Stampa*, 13 February 1986).

90. Mutolo transcripts, pp. 1224-5; Calderone transcripts, ii, pp. 492-3.
91. Mannoia transcripts, pp. 332-46.
92. Arlacchi, *Antonino Calderone*, p. 170 (my translation).
93. William Galt (Luigi Natoli) published the adventures of the *Beati Paoli* in 238 episodes in the local newspaper *Il Giornale di Sicilia* between 1909 and 1910.
94. Antonino Calderone very proudly stated that he had read those books; see Arlacchi, *Antonino Calderone*, p. 56.
95. Mannoia transcripts, pp. 107-8.
96. D. Gambetta, "Inscrutable markets", *Rationality and Society* 6(3), pp. 353-68.
97. For a subtle analysis of the symbolic power of women in Sicily, see M. Giovannini, "Woman: a dominant symbol within the cultural system of a Sicilian town", *Man*, 3, 1981.
98. Siebert, *Le donne. La Mafia*, is among those who believe the Mafia was exclusively cynical and exploited themes from popular culture to pursue its goals.
99. Calderone transcripts, ii, pp. 492-3; see also Mutolo transcripts, p. 1225.
100. Elster, *The cement of society*.

Index

277